CONNECTING SPHERES

Connecting Spheres

Women in the Western World, 1500 to the Present

EDITED BY

MARILYN J. BOXER

San Diego
State University

JEAN H. QUATAERT

State University
of New York, Binghamton

FOREWORD BY

JOAN W. SCOTT

Institute for Advanced Study,
Princeton

New York Oxford
OXFORD UNIVERSITY PRESS
1987

Oxford University Press

Oxford   New York   Toronto
Delhi   Bombay   Calcutta   Madras   Karachi
Petaling Jaya   Singapore   Hong Kong   Tokyo
Nairobi   Dar es Salaam   Cape Town
Melbourne   Auckland

and associated companies in
Beirut   Berlin   Ibadan   Nicosia

Copyright © 1987 by Oxford University Press, Inc.

Published by Oxford University Press, Inc.,
200 Madison Avenue, New York, New York 10016

Library of Congress Cataloging-in-Publication Data
Connecting spheres.
Bibliography: p.   Includes index.
1. Women—History—Cross-cultural studies.   2. Women—History—United States.
3. Women—History—Europe.
4. Feminism—History—Cross-cultural studies.
I. Boxer, Marilyn J. II. Quataert, Jean H.
HQ1150.C66   1987   305.4   86-17949
ISBN 0-19-504123-2   ISBN 0-19-504133-X (pbk.)

2 4 6 8 10 9 7 5 3 1

Printed in the United States of America

To our spiritual mother
SIMONE DE BEAUVOIR
1908–1986

PREFACE

About twenty years ago, a new phase began in the history of the human search for knowledge. From ancient days, Hebrew, Greek, and other philosophers questioned the nature of the universe and of human existence. Medievalists debated the relations of divinity and humanity, of the sacred and profane. Thinkers of the Enlightenment sought to expose the laws of nature and civilization. But never did the great minds of the Western world subject to sustained scrutiny the nature and condition of the female sex.

In the last two decades, scholars of America, Europe, and Asia, led by academic women in the United States, have undertaken a systematic examination of the history of women—their social roles and relationships, their perspectives, and their behavior. As scholars and as women who have benefited from the mid-twentieth century rebirth of the feminist movement, we are privileged and proud to be a part of this enterprise, which is termed ''women's studies.'' Beginning in the mid-1960s with a few courses scattered from Seattle to New Orleans to Chicago to New York, and with two women's studies programs founded in 1970 at San Diego State University and Cornell University, women's studies has grown to encompass some 450 programs and tens of thousands of courses. The history of women has played a special part in this huge undertaking, for it offers a passkey to understanding both past and present. No discipline has been more receptive to the new feminist scholarship than history and few colleges or universities in the United States today remain without at least one course in women's history.

The next step is to see that no history course be without material on women. For this purpose, the history of women must be integrated into the main themes of Western civilization. The connections between the so-called separate spheres of women and men must be traced and their mutual dependency revealed. Broken links between women's lives in different places must also be connected and bridges built between the sexes and the peoples of the many continents. Our task is to make a beginning; our book is concerned with connecting spheres.

As co-authors and co-editors, we began our joint work over a decade ago in a search for the comparative history of women in the European socialist and feminist movements that we had researched in separate national contexts. We continued to collaborate on women's work in the home industries of France and Germany. From the latter, especially, we discovered how thick and how rich were the interconnections between women's work in the privacy of their homes and the public and political arenas where decisions affecting family and workshop were made. We conceived this book as an essay in making explicit connections between the so-called private and public lives of women and men. It is a book that puts women *into* history.

We want to thank the many persons who have contributed to our work. We include all those who have studied and written in women's history and women's studies—our own students at San Diego State University and the University of Houston–Clear Lake who have stimulated us and cheered us on; our co-workers and colleagues across the United States and in Western Europe, on whose work we have built our own. Numerous individuals have contributed their time and insight in reviewing parts of the book, including Reva Greenburg, Sarah Hanley, Steven Hause, Linda Holler, Kathleen Jones, Claire Moses, and Karen Offen, as well as Joan Scott, who generously read it all in an earlier and longer version. We also thank our astute and supportive editor, Nancy Lane.

One of the pleasures amid the pains of authorship has been working with our contributors, whose excellent case studies illustrate the work being done on the frontiers of knowledge in women's history. We have also enjoyed the benefits of working with Janet Hamann and Debbie Wilson, of San Diego State University, who painstakingly persevered through manuscript preparation in the spirit of mutual aid and offered many helpful suggestions. Cartographer Barbara Aguado assisted with the figures and maps, and Debbie Wilson deserves credit for the index. Finally we express our gratitude to Claire, Larry, and Brian Boxer and Don and Eliot Quataert, for their years of support for our struggles to combine in our lives the spheres of family and work.

San Diego   M.J.B.
Houston   J.H.Q.
April 1986

CONTRIBUTORS

Marilyn J. Boxer is Professor of Women's Studies and Dean of the College of Arts and Letters at San Diego State University. Co-author and editor with Jean Quataert of *Socialist Women: European Socialist Feminism in the Nineteenth and Early Twentieth Centuries* (1978), she has published articles on French women's history and on women's studies in numerous journals including *French Historical Studies,* the *Journal of Social History, Signs: A Journal of Women in Society and Culture,* and *Women's Studies International Forum.*

Lyndel Butler has previously assisted with translations of *Reigen* by Arthur Schnitzler and the correspondence of Einstein with Queen Elizabeth of Belgium. She currently teaches German at Bellaire High School in Houston.

Barbara Franzoi is Associate Professor of History at the College of Saint Elizabeth, where she teaches European history, international studies, and women's history. She is the author of *At the Very Least She Pays the Rent: Women and German Industrialization, 1871–1914* (1985). Professor Franzoi is currently involved with initiatives for international education in the state of New Jersey. The teaching module: "Impact of Economic Change on Women in Developing Countries," *Global Interdependence: Case Studies for the Social Sciences* will be published by the Woodrow Wilson National Fellowship Foundation, Princeton.

Donna Gabaccia is Assistant Professor at Mercy College, Dobbs Ferry, New York, where she teaches women's, social, and immigration history. She has written several scholarly articles on kinship, family, and women's work among southern Italians. Her book *From Sicily to Elizabeth Street* appeared in 1984. She is currently preparing for publication a manuscript entitled *Red Towns and Their Migrants: A Case Study of Western Sicilians on Two Continents.*

Sandra M. Gilbert, Professor of English at Princeton University, is co-author with Susan Gubar of *The Madwoman in the Attic* (1979); co-editor with Gubar of *A Norton Anthology of Literature by British and American Women* (1985); and author of a book of poems, *Emily's Bread* (1985). She is working with Gubar on a sequel to *Madwoman,* to be entitled *No Man's Land: The Place of the Woman Writer in the Twentieth Century,* from which "Soldier's Heart" is drawn.

Sarah Hanley is Professor of History at The University of Iowa. She is the author of *The Lit de Justice of the Kings of France: Constitutional Ideology in Legend, Ritual, and Discourse* (1983) and numerous articles on ideology and politics.

Maryanne Cline Horowitz is Associate Professor of History at Occidental College. Her current research focuses on the Renaissance and Reformation debate on women and on the circle of friends of Michel de Montaigne. Her articles have appeared in *Journal of the History of Ideas, Journal of the History of Philosophy, Harvard Theological Review, The Sixteenth Century Journal,* and *Studies in the Renaissance* and other journals.

Olwen Hufton is Professor of History at the University of Reading and author of *The Poor* *of Eighteenth-Century France* (1974); *Europe: Privilege and Protest* (1981); and many articles and books including the forthcoming *Women in Early Modern Europe.*

Sibylle Meyer studied sociology in Berlin and is affiliated with the Institut für Zukunftsstudien und Technologiebewertung in West Berlin. She has written numerous articles on housework and with Eva Schulze co-authored a book on women's experiences in Berlin during the post-war reconstruction of West Germany.

Karen Offen is an independent scholar affiliated with the Center for Research on Women at Stanford University. She is a co-editor of *Victorian Women: A Documentary Account of Women's Lives in Nineteenth-Century England, France, and the United States* (1981), and of *Women, the Family, and Freedom: The Debate in Documents, 1750–1950* (2 vols., 1983), both published by Stanford University Press. She is completing a book on *The Woman Question in Third Republic France, 1870–1914*, and is working on a sequel, *The Politics of Motherhood in France, 1920–1945*. Her most recent work focuses on the comparative history of feminism.

Barbara Corrado Pope is Director of Women's Studies at the University of Oregon. She has a Ph.D. in history from Columbia University and has written a number of articles on women and on religion in nineteenth-century France.

Jean H. Quataert is Professor of History and Director of Women's Studies at the State University of New York at Binghamton. She is the author of *Reluctant Feminists in German Social Democracy, 1885–1917* (1979) and co-author and editor with Marilyn Boxer of *Socialist Women: Studies in European Socialist Feminism in the Nineteenth and Early Twentieth Centuries* (1978). Her new research reevaluates aspects of European industrialization from the perspective of the rural household and the domestic and extra-domestic work of women and men.

Joan Scott is Professor in the School of Social Science at the Institute for Advanced Study (Princeton, New Jersey).

Richard Stites is Associate Professor of Russian History at Georgetown University. He has written *The Women's Liberation Movement in Russia* (1978) and *Revolutionary Dreams: Utopia and Experiment in the Russian Revolution* (forthcoming), and has co-edited with Alexander Bogdanov *Red Star: The First Bolshevik Utopia* (1984) and *Bolshevik Culture: Experiment and Order in the Russian Revolution* (1985).

Frank Tallett is Lecturer in European History at the University of Reading. His major interests lie in the fields of religious and military history in the period between 1500 and 1800.

Maria-Barbara Watson-Franke is Professor of Women's Studies at San Diego State University. An anthropologist by training, she has carried out field work in South America and in Europe. Her published work has focused on culture change and female education among the Guajiro from Venezuela, the life history in anthropological research, and the process of interpretation in anthropology. Her research also includes work on women in West and East Germany.

Luise White has a Ph.D. from Cambridge University and wrote her doctoral dissertation on "The History of Prostitution in Nairobi, Kenya." She currently teaches African history at Rice University.

Merry E. Wiesner is Assistant Professor of History at the University of Wisconsin–Milwaukee. She is the author of *Working Women in Renaissance Germany, Women in the Sixteenth Century: A Bibliography*, and articles on various aspects of urban social history during the early modern period.

CONTENTS

FOREWORD

In the fall of 1984, I arrived in Paris on my way to a conference at UNESCO on the history of women. At the airport an officious customs officer asked the usual question about the nature of my business in France, and then queried me on the topic of the conference I was attending. When I replied "the history of women," he responded mockingly, "Do women have a history, Professor? And what might it be?" I was taken aback not only by his hostility, but by the difficulty of answering such questions. Of course women had a history, but one so rich and unmined that no single phrase or story-line could capture it. The women's history movement of the last fifteen years has revealed the complexity and diversity of women's experience as well as the historically relative meaning of the term "woman" itself. Thus, the only way to know women's history, I thought, was to study it in all its variety. But to the customs man I only said something placating about how much I hoped to learn at the conference. I suspect that he did not believe there was anything new to learn because his view of women was fundamentally ahistorical. For him, women were probably defined by their bodies; they were objects of male desire or agents of reproduction, performing timeless, "natural" functions that do not figure in textbook histories. From this perspective the term "women's history" was an oxymoron, ridiculous, easy to ridicule.

The encounter with the official presented me with the very outlook women's history sets out to refute. In opposition to the idea of timelessness, women's history insists that women's experience is shaped in time. Even the most "natural" of functions, sexuality and childbirth, have been practiced differently in different epochs. Against the idea that the essential qualities of femininity never change, women's history offers a vast array of female types and extensive evidence about how ideals of femininity have changed. If the results of all this research have not yet reached French bureaucrats, they have been acknowledged in the academy and they are being incorporated into the history curriculum. *Connecting Spheres: Women in the Western World,* in fact, represents just such an acknowledgement and incorporation of themes long neglected.

Connecting Spheres illustrates the accomplishments of women's history in many ways. In its interesting format—a series of overviews and a group of individual articles—the book preserves the mode of inquiry from which this field has been fashioned. New information and insights have been steadily accumulated through careful study of specific subjects, making larger, more general syntheses possible. The title asserts that women are historical beings: they are affected by monumental developments such as demographic transitions and political revolutions and they are active participants in the movements and events of their times. *Connecting*

Spheres shows that women consistently mattered in social, economic, and political terms; that women's history is not limited to the narrow course of feminist political movements in the modern period. The book offers a complex history, a patchwork quilt of colorful themes rather than a neat linear narrative. There are many characters here—queens and serving maids, factory workers and housewives, nuns and prostitutes, suffragists and antisuffragists, socialists and fascists—whose stories differ. Indeed, these stories must be told separately for their contexts, causes, and effects are different. There is no Woman in Western history; there are only women who cannot be reduced to singular character traits, behaviors, or outlooks.

Neither can women's lives be explained by one cause. *Connecting Spheres* requires us to look at many factors in order to explain the experiences of women. Thus, Sarah Hanley argues that statebuilding led to the promulgation of laws that gave parents greater control over their children's marriage choices in early modern France. In the process, errant daughters were more severely treated than sons. In the modern period, Donna Gabaccia points to the influence of Italian unification on economic developments that deprived peasant women of productive roles. In some periods, religious teachings were incorporated not only into church policy, but into education as well; scientific discoveries created new possibilities for women and reproduced prevailing beliefs about them. Technological breakthroughs have sometimes improved, sometimes worsened the conditions of wage-earning women. And ideas about separate male and female spheres—of work and domesticity, public and private—which now seem the source of women's subordination, were once used to justify demands for improvements in women's status.

If causality is complex, so is the notion of women's experience. In all ages there have been normative definitions of masculinity and femininity, but such received wisdom has had differing impacts on the different lives of women. Differences of social class often made it impossible for women in the same era to identify with one another: the world of hardworking peasant mothers, who nursed their own babies as well as the babies of the rich, was not the same world as that inhabited by noble women, who bore the children others cared for. The necessity to earn wages differed fundamentally from the desire to find fulfillment in work: hence, a nineteenth-century middle-class doctor had little in common with a lower-class factory girl. Religious differences have sometimes separated women of the same class; thus in late nineteenth-century France, Catholic middle-class women tended to conservative politics within the orbit of the Church, while their Protestant counterparts became leaders of major reform movements. There has been no eternal essence to "womanhood" that provided a common denominator for women's experience past or present. Women have always had to interpret their womanhood within the contexts and parameters of their lives.

Those parameters could be terribly confining, as disobedient daughters imprisoned in convents could testify; they could be confusing, as the doctors' debates on the role of women's organs in the reproductive process reveals; they could be flexible, as evidenced by the initial events of the Russian Revolution. But parameters alone—the pressures of economic conditions, the teachings of religious authorities, the legal strictures about marriage and citizenship—have never set the limits on human imagination and behavior. As always, the possibility for change—

the very core of historical interest—resides in the variety of individual and collective behavior.

Connecting Spheres puts women into history where they belong—at each turning point and major development; in processes of change large and small; as objects of debate and active participants in events—in short, everywhere. After reading this book one can no longer ask if women had a history. For the answer is clearly yes. As a unified group we cannot say women had a singular, identifiable history. We can say, however, that they have always been part of history, experiencing its impacts and contributing to its movement. That statement seems so self-evident after reading this book that one wonders how scholars could have thought the contrary. Inevitably, we are left to ponder questions about the writing of history itself: How did it happen that women became invisible as historical subjects? How was it possible to overlook their participation for so long?

Joan W. Scott
Institute for Advanced Study

CONNECTING SPHERES

INTRODUCTION

Restoring Women to History

This is a book about women's history. But women, like men and children, live inextricably linked with other human beings. They are influenced not only by the unique experiences that befall every person but also by the inherited ideas and institutions they share with others of their generation. Whatever their differences of race, class, religion, sexual preference, language, and culture, they participate from birth until death in an ongoing tale of human action, reaction, perception, and interpretation. They inevitably belong to a social culture that we define as "civilization." To understand themselves and their world, they often seek knowledge about the past—of their family and of their collective ancestry. For most Americans of the late twentieth century, this means tracing human culture back across the ages of Western civilization to times past that, but for the work of historians, would have been lost. In some cases it is too late; we cannot all find our family tree, for the records of our forebears—especially if they were poor or persecuted—may have disappeared. So we study history and identify with the collective experience of our nation, of our people, however defined. But if we are looking for the history of women we have a special problem, for few female individuals appear in most accounts of the past. Yet common sense tells us women have always been part of the social fabric. Women's work, after all, was never done, and behind all great men, we have been told, stood women who nurtured and inspired them.

To help us find the story of these women we must begin by considering how history itself has been composed. The story of Western civilization stretches back beyond recorded time to the myths and legends told by ancient seers. Passed from generation to generation by storytellers, such tales form the basis of the earliest written narratives, the epic poems, the liturgies and dramas as well as songs which collectively constitute an important part of what we today call ancient *history*. Although in later times we have narrowed our definition of history from its original meaning of "a relation of incidents" to include only those "professedly true," to the "facts," the Greek word *historia* is the source as well for our word "story," a narrative of fictitious events. And, if asked to distinguish "history" from "story," most of us today would fall back on the common contrast between fact and fiction. History is a chronicle of facts.

Which facts? Obviously no history book, even one drawing on the largest computerized information banks, could contain all the facts, every experience of every person who ever existed anywhere. This would not be possible in Western civilization, or, say, American history even if—another impossibility—all such things were known. What we know as history is thus limited to those experiences and events that were deemed important enough to be remembered—and recorded for later and wider recollection. History is essentially what has been included in history books, the collective work of generations of writers who were chosen for that purpose by virtue of special knowledge, training, or position. Out of the vast, almost infinite, universe of human experience, they, the educated men who wrote the history books (and most historians have been men), created by their selection of events not just a story, but history. History, therefore, comprises selected experience, elevated into significant events by virtue of inclusion in historical narratives. And these choices were made according to the values and purposes of the historians.

History traditionally has been written to recount and to record important *public* events. Most of its conventional themes deal with wars and revolutions, outbreaks of violence, and contests of might for prizes of territory, political power and public place. In the many dramatic struggles for hegemony recorded by historians, from the city-states of ancient Greece to the nation-states of modern Europe, Africa, and Asia, most of the contenders have been men. Except for a few women born to the throne like Queen Elizabeth I, or called to martyrdom like Joan of Arc, most women took no part in military and political contests, or in other public events that were deemed worthy of incorporation in the annals of history. Nor, except for soldiers and servants, did most ordinary men. Traditional history was the platform of political elites; civilization the creation of civic leaders.

The story of common men enters the tale from time to time, if only implicitly: the invaders who terrorized early medieval Europe, the sailors whose muscle-power propelled the great explorers' ships, were, one assumes, men; but we know nothing of their lives except that they were there, on hand to obey and to work. The labor of ordinary men entered history only after a major philosophical reevaluation took place concerning the worth of work. And so, in the twentieth century, economic and labor history were born. But this was one hundred years after the "Declaration of the Rights of Man" had established the claim of ordinary men to political participation and the English political economists had exposed the labor theory of value. The definition of work, moreover, remained confined by limited notions about the sphere of production; much of women's work (unpaid and for family use) continued to be invisible to economic theorists and labor historians. Furthermore, it was the struggle of workingmen to live, organize, and fight for *political* power that became part of the broadened public record. The inclusion of these themes did not challenge the dominant understanding of historical significance: the focus remained on men (privileged and now the nonprivileged) struggling for power in the *public* arena.

The women who lived in the past continued to be absent from history. Despite an occasional allusion to an exceptional woman, a woman "worthy" because she nurtured, inspired, or, in rare cases, substituted for man, "her story" was not written. The history of women as a social group must of necessity focus on private and personal, not public and political, events. It therefore challenges the inherited assumption that historically significant events are publicly recognized events only. Most women through most of history have been excluded from arenas of public power, relegated to women's quarters and women's work, denied the apprenticeships and education requisite to autonomous existence. Defined primarily by relationships with men—fathers, husbands, sons, and lovers—women passed their lives subsumed within families. There were exceptions. When the family order constituted the public order and their families belonged to the leading circles, then some women gained power, privilege, and responsibility generally deemed incongruent with their "nature" as weak, dependent beings.[1] But even in these cases, their exploits were rarely preserved. Quite simply, women did not appear in the official accounts of male-dominated institutions or the formal records of political and economic associations that served as sources for the writing of history. Few men wrote biographies of women; few women had the leisure and education to produce autobiographies.

The omission of women from history books, then, can be explained without recourse to a conspiracy theory of history. Men never sat in council and decided to keep women down by eliminating their lives from the chronicles of history. Besides, Helen of Troy, Joan of Arc, Lucrezia Borgia, Charlotte Corday, and a few others who played important roles in men's stories won recognition. When women did something men considered important—inspired or defeated a powerful army, poisoned or fatally stabbed an eminent leader—their deeds were duly noted. Otherwise, they were relegated to the realm of daily routine, to the domestic functions prescribed for them by priests and philosophers, physicians and politicians, patriarchs of all callings who followed Aristotle, Aquinas, and, more recently, Freud, in defining women as imperfect men. Many of the great leaders of Western thought did trouble themselves to explain the nature of women's inferiority, locating the limits of women's possibilities for achievement in some weakness of spirit, mind, or body. When the ancient philosopher Protagoras and the Sophists declared that "man is the measure of all things," and Aristotle stated that "the female state [is] a deformity [which, however,] occurs in the ordinary course of nature," for purposes of reproduction of the species; and when Aquinas, over a millenium later, echoed the Greeks with his assertion that "woman is defective and misbegotten," they took the biological male as the model for human being. Scholars of all eras have followed suit and used terms, categories of analysis, and definitions that denigrate women, when they do not altogether ignore them. Even recently, in turning attention from heroes and headline events to obscure and ordinary occurrences, the habit remains strong, as witnessed by this statement in a review of Fernand Braudel's widely acclaimed work, *The Structures of Everyday Life:*

> While *Homo medievalis* was the prey of wolves, unidentified bacilli and viruses, he had, nevertheless, the permanent task of providing food and shelter for his family.

This example shows the use of sex-biased, though supposedly "objective" or "neutral," terms. Women as well as men fell victim to disease, and women perhaps even more than men shouldered the responsibility for feeding their families. No question, however, that "the family" belonged to "him"; the traditional family in Western cultures was a patriarchal, male-dominated and -defined institution and should be labeled as such. While women labored alongside men in fields and shops they won little recognition for their crucial work in production, or even in reproduction. They might "manufacture societ[ies]"; but "women's work," however essential to survival, was hardly the stuff of history.[2]

Partly because women's status has been subsumed under that of the men who were their masters and guardians, traditional interpretations of historical events were easily cast in universal terms and the long sweep of history was structured about turning points of limited significance for the female sex. Athenian "democracy" seems a less worthy ancestor of our own when we learn that its "rule by the people" excluded most men and all women (who lived secluded in women's quarters, if not as slaves or concubines). The twelfth-century "reform" of Catholicism in the Cluny movement appears less progressive from the viewpoint of nuns and managers of female monasteries who thereby lost their autonomy and gained male overseers. The Renaissance brought not "rebirth," but regress for some feudal noblewomen, those few of their sex who enjoyed power and influence in church and state as long as their families constituted the public order.[3] The "Great" Revolution of 1789 in France granted neither liberty nor equality to women; and in the interests of fraternity, Napoleon's lauded Code of Laws subjected women henceforth to discriminatory standards in marriage, sexual behavior, and education. Another major "democratic" upheaval of the late eighteenth century, the American Revolution, ushered in a long-sustained era of "common men," whose gains seem less progressive from the perspective of those women who lost legal rights and professional opportunities. Where colonial women could enjoy property rights and engage in business ventures or medical practices, their nineteenth-century descendants faced exclusion through new laws and professional organizations. Milestones of advancement for men may mark gravestones of opportunity for women.

Viewed from the perspective of women, history requires other signposts. A historian of the thirtieth century, dividing a total human history into chapters, books, and courses, might well deemphasize the "Renaissance" of the fifteenth century and the "Revolutions" of the eighteenth. Searching the record for "world-historical'' events to serve as markers and turning points, this scholar might pause at the dawn of (what we call) the modern age, to acknowledge the import of the Enlightenment thinkers who saw that human intervention could liberate humanity from arbitrary rule and human invention could increase mastery over nature. But she or he might stop to erect a monument only in 1844 or 1877 or 1936 or 1967— choices based, as always, on values, and here selected for their significance in the struggle for freedom from the biological necessity of recurring childbirth that was imposed throughout earlier ages on half of humanity.

What have these dates to do with Western civilization? The dates are hall-marks in the conquest of reproductive freedom for women. The vulcanization of rubber in 1844 made possible the mass production decades later of safe, effective artificial contraception; the widely publicized trial of Annie Besant and Charles Bradlaugh in London in 1877 for distribution of a birth control pamphlet brought knowledge of new possibilities to the minds of millions; the legalization of traffic in contraceptive devices and literature, in the United States in 1936 and in France in 1967, after decades of criminal prosecution, offered release from unwanted pregnancy and hope for self-determination to vast numbers of human beings.[4] Isolated because of their sex, segregated into schools with curricula designed for ''ladies,'' hired for jobs paying less than subsistence wages, deprived of rights to compete for many others by ''protective'' laws, biology was in fact destiny for women, all because of the ''special needs'' of the female organism, and the su-perior interest of the ''race'' (species) in their reproductive capacity. Freed from biological constraints, however, women can ''leave off spending their lives in universal house-service,'' and more easily become ''world-servants'' rather than ''house-servants,'' more ''human,'' less ''female,'' and more free to participate in the work which the pioneer American feminist Charlotte Perkins Gilman (1860– 1935) believed defines the *human* species.[5]

With the political, ideological, and technological changes of the late eigh-teenth and the nineteenth centuries came a new sense of human agency that slowly allowed some women to achieve what we today call reproductive freedom. A new era in human history thus dawned, but the forces of the past had long-lived con-sequences for the future. For without a history of women, which provides the basis for understanding the temporal and cross-cultural variations in women's lives, historians, philosophers, poets, and scientists still too often spoke abstractly of women's so-called ''nature,'' and, on the basis of inherited ideas or personal preferences, prescribed what women ''ought'' to be. Because of misleading no-tions of the ''eternal feminine'' or ''natural woman,'' many discussions of women were (and are) *ahistorical,* ignoring differences in the female experience by era, as well as by class, race, culture, religion, marital status, and other attributes, both ascribed and achieved, that profoundly affect human beings. As the German existentialist philosopher Dilthey pointed out in the nineteenth century, ''What [wo]man is, only [her] history tells.'' In our own time Simone de Beauvoir has written, ''One is not born, but becomes, a woman.''

There is a second source of distortion related to the absence of women's his-tory. This is the tendency to view women only relative to men. To be sure, women have served men as nurturers, as mothers, wives, nurses, and teachers. Having seen women primarily in these roles, men tend to think of women in these terms—or, again abstractly, as the inspiration for their own actions and achievements, as the muses and "fair ladies" of writers and warriors. Modern men are defined by occupations—"what does he do?" ask most typical parents about the prospective boyfriends of their daughters. "Who is she?" ask the parents of sons. Women today continue to be identified first and foremost by relationship to men—whose wife, daughter, mother, lover is she?

But this perspective leads us to ignore or to diminish women's own experiences and the real importance of their multiple contributions to social life. It obscures the other roles women play and the work that they do. More importantly, it suggests that change is impossible. Feminism, for example, seems less radical and more "natural" when the long tradition of female protest is known. Simone de Beauvoir, Betty Friedan, and Gloria Steinem are daughters of Mary Wollstonecraft, Flora Tristan, and Lucy Stone. Women's work in paid employment strikes many people even today as a new departure, because of misinformation about the economic contributions of women in the past. The importance of women's work to the premodern family economy is reflected in the eighteenth-century observation that "none but a fool will take a wife whose bread must be earned solely by his labour and who will contribute nothing towards it herself." False ideas about women necessarily lead to incorrect views of history and sometimes to fallacious assumptions about the "nature" of womanhood. Would the founder of psychoanalysis, Sigmund Freud (1856–1939), whose essays on femininity have exercised extraordinary influence on twentieth-century concepts of womanhood, have asked his infamous question, "What do women want?" if he had studied women's history?

While ideas, attitudes, and customs about women's nature and roles are passed on from generation to generation and serve to narrow options, all such notions are reinforced by, and, in turn, influence social structures. Institutions of law, government, business, and education reflect both age-old biases against women and the economic, educational, legal, and political liabilities long attached to female status. For example, laws that have denied women equal rights in voting, jury service, control of property, credit, choice of domicile, and so forth stem from the English common law, transplanted to the United States, according to which women upon marriage entered an institution where "the husband and wife are one and that one is the husband."

The present-day near-monopoly of power by men in government, business, and education also reflects old attitudes about women's weaknesses. In the nineteenth century, when traditional religious doctrine began to lose its force, "scientific" explanations were invented to justify the inherited interpretations of public life that excluded women's contributions. Doctors replaced priests in enforcing sanctions that restricted women's roles. Where the church had for centuries prescribed limited roles for women in religion, politics, and other social activities on grounds of women's moral weakness—the hereditary "curse of Eve"—now the medical profession utilized biological evidence of women's smaller brains, more sensitive nerves, and periodic procreative "illnesses," to the same purpose. As women's confidants, physicians gained access to intimate knowledge that they used to support a double standard in family and society. For example, they advised women that marriage was "the best of all purgatives to chase away their bad moods," and counseled men that "a modest woman seldom desires any sexual gratification for herself. She submits to her husband but principally to please him. . . . Love of home, children, and domestic duties are the only passions [women] feel."[6]

To break through chains of custom and law requires more than the lonely voice of reason. History is filled with men and women who pointed out biases that impinged on women's lives. Speaking in the fourteenth century, Chaucer's Wife of Bath opined that "there is no libel on women that the clergy will not paint." Aware of the power of holding the pen, she confronted androcentricity (male-centeredness):

> By God, if women had but written stories
> Like those the clergy keep in oratories,
> More had been written of man's wickedness
> Than all the sons of Adam could redress.

With Christine de Pisan's book, *The City of Women* (1404), the voices of real women began a rebuttal of the early misogynist (expressing hatred toward women) literature. Discovering through self-analysis and observation of other women that the evils attributed to her sex existed in male minds rather than in female nature, she also declared that "the books that so sayeth, women made them not." If contempt for women remained "public and unashamed" for several centuries more, henceforth at least it was countered by an equally long and vehement defense. Mary Astell, an Englishwoman of the late seventeenth century, "despaired of learning anything about women from books, 'because the writers, being men, envious of the good works of women haven't recounted their great deeds.' "[7]

Almost two hundred years of "modern" feminism—often dated from Mary Wollstonecraft's *A Vindication of the Rights of Woman* (1792)—parallels demographic, economic, political, and ideological changes that have fundamentally altered the condition of women of various classes, races, and nations. Yet the old ideas persist; they appear, disappear, and reappear in new guises. Whatever the "true" nature of sex differences, they will never, as John Stuart Mill (and Harriet Taylor) pointed out in the 1860s, be known as long as old ideas preclude consideration of other possibilities.[8] Prerequisite to change is new knowledge and awakened consciousness. What the Wife of Bath and Christine de Pisan knew must become common wisdom. The potential exists today, thanks to the women's liberation movement of the mid-twentieth century and its academic wing, women's studies.

Founded in the late 1960s, women's studies began in response to demands by students, faculty, and community women to learn the "truth" about women. Foremost in the minds of these modern daughters of Christine de Pisan and Mary Astell was the need to find their heritage, to rediscover the past, to find women in history. The first women's studies courses, often taught by volunteer instructors to students seeking to learn regardless of university "credit," were typically history courses. Through the development of women's studies, this new feminism became "a major structure for thinking about our world." Women's studies, that is, provided a new perspective from which to view, to organize, to evaluate, and to reinterpret knowledge. Stoutly resisted by some disciplines, woman-oriented scholarship was more readily accepted by others, including some branches of history. Perhaps because it developed contemporaneously with the "new social" history, women's history at last won wide support for the opinions of the Wife of Bath and Pisan—that women's experiences differed distinctly from men's perception of them.

Women's history is not, however, altogether new. While the "history of women's history" is of recent origin, there have always been some historians who wrote about notorious women, often stressing their character and moral influence. Joan of Arc, Elizabeth I, and Marie de Medici did not lack biographers. Studies of witchcraft demonstrated that not all women have been content to sweep the family hearth with their brooms. However, as an inquiry into the lives of women of less than aristocratic origin or dramatically atypical behavior, women's history is closely related to movements for reform in female status and it parallels the quest for personal freedom in Western civilization. The "scientific," or systematic, study of women's history began in the early nineteenth-century debate on the evolution of women's rights of inheritance and the relationship of the family to the state. Social critics of both liberal and conservative bent recognized that the status of women, as of men, depended on the juridical and political status of the family in the social order. The immediate concern of conservatives was not "the rights of women," but revision of the laws governing inheritance, so as to strengthen the power of patriarchal families. For liberals, it was often the "rehabilitation of the flesh" from Christian connotations of sin. But in examining the role of women and the "social relationship of the sexes," these "social scientists" adopted a method with important implications for understanding women's history. Their studies of the status of women revealed the social and relational, as distinct from the biological or "natural" attributes of sex.

This was history *about* women. Women's history written also *for* women appeared in the early twentieth century when several economic historians—English and American women—produced pioneer works on the extent and contributions of female labor force participation and its implications. In this era also a lone female voice, Mary R. Beard, reviewed the political history of women's condition and protested as false and mischievous assertions of universal female subjugation. Until rediscovered in the 1970s, however, these works could do little for good or ill, for they were out of print and included on few lists of required or essential readings in academic history courses.[9] But 1970 brought to the forefront of Western consciousness a formidable challenge to the idealized separation of spheres along gender lines that most historians had accepted and reinforced in their work. Thousands of women—especially university students and faculty, journalists and government employees, all well-placed to gain public attention—began to recognize the false ground of the dichotomy and to insist that "the personal *is* political." That summer, *Time* magazine even published a cover story on "sexual politics." No longer would "political" and "public" be synonymous terms, both separate from and opposed to "personal" and "private." No longer could historians and other scholars ignore women's lives. In the same way that great interest in economic history followed closely periods of economic depression and labor unrest, that new programs in minority and ethnic group history emerged in the wake of racial conflict and civil rights movements, so a veritable avalanche of new studies on women filled the pages of journals and blanketed the shelves of bookstores in the decade after the "rebirth" of feminism. For the first time, courses on women in history—designed largely *for* as well as *about* women—appeared in college curricula.

While women in society continue, as they always have, to *make* history, they are determined today that their contributions will be recognized and *recorded.* Increasingly, feminists can ground their actions in theories drawn from the new scholarship in women's studies, often supported by knowledge learned in works on women's history. Scholars have compensated for the absence of women in conventional courses by rediscovery of the long tradition of feminism, reading works showing *Women, Resistance and Revolution* (1974), though *Hidden from History* (1973), and told to *Suffer and Be Still* (1972); now *Becoming Visible* (1977) and seeking *A Widening Sphere* (1977)—all titles of books on women in European history. After numerous works demonstrated women's contributions to male-defined history, historians of women moved on to a less "compensatory" approach, publishing *Women, Work and Family* (1978), *Fit Work for Women* (1979), and *A Heritage of Her Own* (1979), books that emphasize the value of women's experience apart from the politics and purposes of men. Historians of the nineteenth century, especially, have proposed the idea of "women's culture," meaning "the separate values, experiences, institutions, relationships, rituals, and consciousness that nineteenth-century women developed out of their separation from the male domain of public life and their restriction to the private sphere." *Ladies of the Leisure Class,* a recent example, draws on materials and insights from anthropology, psychology, and literature to show French bourgeois women as agents in maintenance of a premodern world view that validated their domestic and religious roles.[10]

Influenced by the new social historians, many of whom (men and women) chose women as subjects for investigation, historians of women spent a decade in retrieving the data necessary for new woman-centered works that are sensitive to the realities of women's lives. An innovative emphasis by social historians on systematic analysis of quantifiable data happily coincided with the recognition by feminist scholars of the role of earlier generations of social scientists in the "social construction of the second sex." Early in the development of women's studies, psychologist Naomi Weisstein exposed descriptions of women's "nature" by male psychologists as prescriptions reflecting men's desires, while psychologists Sandra Bem and Daryl Bem and political scientist Jo Freeman demonstrated the power of social processes to shape definitions of femininity, which serve to control female behavior.[11] This conjuncture led, not without some problems, to a fruitful union of the methodologies, sources, and theories in the new social history with the questions raised by the new women's history. The net result has been a lively debate over such issues as the impact of industrialization on women's work, family roles, and social power; the links between modes of production, the design of social space, and concepts of womanhood; and the nature of relationships among women within the subculture of women's purported separate sphere, including their collective action for economic as well as political and social goals. In short, considerable information about women has been uncovered, recorded, and analyzed. To borrow the construct of Joan Scott, "her-story" has been fashioned as has the social history of women—but as yet, only in part, for women's history needs to be integrated back into, and in turn, to restructure, political history.[12] The writing of a complete human "history," to replace the truncated "story," waits upon this task.

The progress of writing women's history can be divided into three overlapping phases. First came the task of *dismantling:* exposing assumptions, interpretations, and practices that led to the omission or distortion of women's presence in the past. Next followed the work of *discovery:* searching sources old and new for the data needed to add women's experiences to the corpus of materials that comprise the written record of history. This research "discovered," for example, a wide variety of women's movements that were part and parcel of the European political scene in the late nineteenth century and women's charitable activities that were used to launch a critique of male dominance and power. It also "uncovered" neglected feminist writers, established the centrality of the "argument about women" in Western thought, and traced the importance and influence of women's networks for family survival during periods of revolutionary upheaval and economic transformation. Furthermore, the popularity enjoyed and prestige won by the new social history and its practitioners motivated inquiry on such related topics as demographic patterns, family structures and functions, sexual attitudes and behaviors— all of which influenced and, in turn, were affected by women's lives. Through recognizing sex and gender as central categories of analysis, scholars in the new field created a history that paralleled and often intersected more traditional work. They challenged all historians to rethink old truths and to raise new questions in ways that included women's experiences and perceptions.

At this stage, the growing and sustained acceptance of the importance of women as both subjects of and agents in the historical process has produced a torrent of publications. Without slackening, it has moved women's history into a third phase: *reconstruction,* or integration of the new knowledge about women and female perspectives into the more traditional political and economic narrative. The "re-vision" of history from the perspective of women has produced a "double vision"—the seeing of two images—that now calls for integration.[13] As a step in this complex process of writing human history, this book connects women's lives to the major economic, social, intellectual, and political developments in the Western world during the last five centuries. It "re-views" the major events and ideas of half a millenium of Western history from the perspective of women's contributions and experiences. Beginning in the finite, earth-centered, male-defined world of Ptolemy, our narrative ends in a universe of ever-expanding horizons where both women and men move into space and face the discovery of new worlds, new life-forms, other galaxies—or, alternatively, of collapse through war and nuclear devastation.

The focus on women adds richness to the content of this chronicle. It also alters the perspective and, by emphasizing women in their own right, exposes the misconceptions through which their personal lives and collective values were denigrated or ignored by power elites and by historians. Less arithmetic than geometric, the effect of the change is to reshape our understanding of the relationship between individual and society in both the past and the present. It shows us that our social system rests on assumptions that contradict important values in society and it calls for a new perspective.

We begin each section with an overview chapter that presents a broad-ranging analysis of the main forces shaping and being shaped by women's experiences. The first deals with the early modern era, 1500–1750; the second concerns the "age of revolution"; and the third covers much of the twentieth century, 1890 to the present. We follow each overview with case studies that develop important themes of the period. They are designed to demonstrate the workings of women's history: to show the kinds of questions raised, the types of evidence used, the methods of analysis employed, the variety of concepts derived. As you will see, these case studies offer a dramatic illustration of what is missing in traditional histories. You will find that old interpretations take on new meaning when a new category of analysis—gender—is added to the historical perspective.

We open this new history by exploring important themes in the early modern period. Part I deals with religious reformation and political centralization. It reveals that both processes invoked ideas and created structures pregnant with meaning for women. For example, the consolidation of political power in centralized states both drew on the patriarchal family as a model and strengthened its authority. Absolute monarchies promulgated laws that enhanced the patriarch's power. However, the breakup of religious hierarchy fostered the spread of education and favored the growth of an individualism that began to undermine familial influence. These changes also reinforced an increasing differentiation of men's and women's roles that was based in a growing market economy. So problematic was the role of women in a changing but still male-defined society that even the scientists of the early modern period found difficulty reconciling their discoveries and their prejudices. Especially for women, the changes created contradictions between social ideals and social reality that gave birth to female protest.

The human story continues in an era of political upheaval and economic transformation. Part II focuses on change and continuity as a result of the "dual revolution"—the political revolution that restructured the state and redefined the political roles of subjects, and the industrial revolution that changed traditional methods and locations for the production of goods and the provision of services. When seen from the perspective of women, the change is less dramatic and perhaps less progressive than commonly portrayed. Excluded from citizenship and defined by their family and household roles, women struggled throughout the nineteenth century to appropriate for themselves freedoms promised by the loosening of inherited values and traditions. Counterposed against economic and demographic shifts that prepared the ground for new roles for women (as indeed for men) was a newly developing ideology of domesticity that sought to channel narrowly the female option. As men followed the dictates of production and increasingly found work separate from home and family, women discovered new means to reconcile gainful employment and domestic duties. Industrial homework, originally used by all members of the family to supplement agricultural income, became finally the preserve of women. The middle-class ideal of the wife without profession, the leisured lady free to embellish herself and her home, lay beyond the grasp of most rural and urban families. And even the lady of apparent leisure often worked hard to maintain her carefully controlled, and hardly carefree, domesticity. Our studies of a cross section of female experiences show that most women were concerned primarily with women's multiple responsibilities, and not with women's rights.

Finally the flow of women's history brings us into the present century. Part III treats the more familiar era of welfare states and developing countries, and of peoples connected by markets and media to others they may never know in all parts of the world. It brings us head on into conflict over women's roles founded in traditional views of women's nature, on the one hand, and the imperatives of both a new social organization and a new egalitarian ethos, on the other. When, after decades of struggle, for example, victorious revolutionaries in Russia sought to transform personal as well as political, spiritual as well as economic life, they begot massive resistance rather than promised revision in social relations. The circumstances of change, amid deprivation, destruction, and death, perhaps doomed all efforts at radical reconstruction. While war and revolution released women from traditional constraints and encouraged them to enter nontraditional roles, their new-found opportunities were contingent and short-lived. Changes came only as makeshift responses to the imperatives of economic, political, and diplomatic decisions. Yet, sometimes changes have unplanned effects and transform the consciousness of those forced into new roles. For some women today, altered self-awareness both reflects new roles and portends deep-seated readjustments in the social fabric. The history of the last five hundred years, however, suggests that this process will require a major reorientation in social values.

For more than half a millenium one idea has loomed large in the West—that people themselves, as well as their historians, came to regard as a central ingredient of liberal democratic society: the notion of the individual. Individualism has been identified by historians and philosophers of the modern Western world as one of its most important principles and as a universal goal. It was once popular to organize the history of Western civilization itself around the growing acceptance of the idea of individualism. Individual liberty and freedom for self-fulfillment were deemed essential to the progress of humanity. Personal happiness and social welfare demanded that individual sovereignty be limited only by social necessity. In art as in politics, unfettered individual liberty became the touchstone of an ideal, virtuous society. From Michelangelo's *David* to Beethoven's *Eroica Symphony* and Shelley's *Prometheus Unbound,* the Western world has celebrated the image of the rebellious individual who defied both natural and social constraints to test the limits of human potential. At its romantic extreme, human genius was released from all moral and social obligation. This glorification of individualism belonged to the story of (mostly male) elites.

Many people in Western societies today continue to take pride in individualism, considering personal dignity and self-determination as distinctive and supreme virtues of the free world. They may even pose individual self-expression as a universal ideal. This stands in stark contrast to societies, past or contemporary, that subordinate the rights of the individual to the needs of the state. But what happens to this ideal when history is revised to include women? To be a realistic goal for all, individual liberty requires changing the very fabric of society, a position that many are not willing to accept. One fearful response to the emergence of autonomous, self-defining women has been, "Who takes care of the children?" Another has been the feminist demand for shared parental responsibility. Still another is a nostalgic urge to turn the clock back.

While most people gradually have accustomed themselves to material changes, to automobiles and airplanes, to radios and television sets, to canned foods, frozen foods, and "fast foods," they have been less ready to accept concurrent changes in personal roles and social relationships, especially the "liberation of women." Thus the "subtle revolution" of women's increasing labor force participation and distance from family authority, which resulted from reorganization in structures and methods of work, and was accelerated by war, revolution, and rising material expectations, is at times misunderstood. It may even fuel attacks on nontraditional women. Seen by some as willful rejection of responsibility toward family, women's changing work patterns more often reflect their need to continue making the traditional female contributions to the family under changed circumstances. It may, however, also express women's responsiveness to the ethos of a society that treasures individual liberty as a precious value, and defines it as a kind of self-fulfillment free of social ties. This perspective ignores not only the role of women in the family and the benefits of family to men, but also the very real interdependence of all people. And it neglects the underlying social supports without which individuals could not achieve their goals. Moreover, it obscures the social basis for the survival of the individual and for the formation of individual psychological identity. This integral relationship between the individual and the social is highlighted by our reassessment of the historical experience of women.

We see our task today as that of creating a new social environment that facilitates the development of *individual* identity along with *group* responsibility—for both women and men of all diverse cultures and lifestyles. As historians, we participate intimately in this endeavor by relating a story of human experience that reveals the limits of unrestrained individualism and stresses the significance of social ties. The new history and the future world that include women alongside and equal to men must reconnect the many aspects of human existence heretofore divided into separate spheres and labeled as "men's world" (of individual achievement) and "women's place" (of social support).

The influence of history on our lives extends far beyond the knowledge we accumulate of the experiences of our forebears. For history, like all moral tales, has a power beyond cognition; it has a "mythic power to link our lives with larger forces." [14] Every generation constructs its own understanding of the past in order to connect the individual lives of its members with a collective identity. Through serendipity, sexual politics, or "the cunning of history," the body of knowledge created by feminist scholars of the last fifteen years is at hand today to aid in the task of revival. This new history, like the old, will reflect the values and purposes of the historians who write it. It is the hope of the authors that this book, by restoring women to history, will also restore history not only to women, but to all who seek to improve human understanding by transcending the separation of the personal from the political, of man from woman, of individual from group, of past from present.

NOTES

1. Joan Kelly-Gadol, "The Social Relations of the Sexes: Methodological Implications of Women's History," *Signs* 1, no. 4 (Summer 1976): 809–823.

2. *The Ladies Wreath* (1852) cited by Mary P. Ryan, "Femininity and Capitalism in Antebellum America,"in Zillah P. Eisenstein, ed., *Capitalist Patriarchy and the Case for Socialist Feminism* (New York, 1979), p. 166.

3. Joan Kelly-Gadol, "Did Women Have a Renaissance?" in Renate Bridenthal and Claudia Koonz, eds., *Becoming Visible: Women in European History* (Boston, 1977), pp. 137–164.

4. On 1844 and 1877 see Norman E. Himes, *Medical History of Contraception* (New York, 1970), pp. 187, 243–245; on 1877, also J. A. and Olive Banks, *Feminism and Family Planning in Victorian England* (New York, 1964), pp. 90–91. On 1936, see discussion of United States v. One Package of Japanese Pessaries in David M. Kennedy, *Birth Control in America: The Career of Margaret Sanger* (New Haven, 1970), pp. 248–257. On 1967, when the Neuwrith Law authorized the sale of contraceptives in France, see Shari Steiner, *The Female Factor: A Report on Women in Western Europe* (New York, 1977), p. 137.

5. Charlotte Perkins Gilman, *The Home: Its Work and Influence* (Urbana, IL, 1972, orig. 1903), p. 317; *Women and Economics: The Economic Factor between Men and Women as a Factor in Social Evolution* (New York, 1966, orig. 1898), p. 269; and "Our Androcentric Culture," in Gilman, *The Forerunner* I, no. 1 (1909): 24.

6. Angus McLaren, "Doctor in the House: Medicine and Private Morality in France, 1800–1850," *Feminist Studies* 2, no. 2/3 (1975): 45; William Acton, *The Functions and Disorders of the Reproductive Organs,* 8th American ed. (Philadelphia, 1894, orig. 1857) in Erna Olafson Hellerstein, Leslie Parker Hume, and Karen M. Offen, eds., *Victorian Women: A Documentary Account of Women's Lives in Nineteenth-Century England, France, and the United States* (Stanford, 1981), p. 178.

7. In Joan Kelly, "Early Feminist Theory and the *Querelle des Femmes,* 1400–1789," *Signs* 8, no. 1 (Autumn 1982): 14, 20.

8. John Stuart Mill, *The Subjection of Women,* in Alice S. Rossi, ed., *John Stuart Mill and Harriet Taylor Mill, Essays on Sex Equality* (Chicago, 1970), p. 148.

9. Alice Clark, *Working Life of Women in the Seventeenth Century* (New York, 1919); Ivy Pinchbeck, *Women Workers and the Industrial Revolution: 1750–1850* (New York, 1969, orig. 1930); Edith Abbott, *Women in Industry* (New York, 1913); Mary R. Beard, *Women As Force in History* (New York, 1946).

10. Sheila Rowbotham, *Women, Resistance and Revolution* (New York, 1974) and *Hidden from History* (New York, 1974); Martha Vicinus, ed., *Suffer and Be Still: Women in the Victorian Age* (Bloomington, IN, 1973); Bridenthal and Koonz, *Becoming Visible;* Martha Vicinus, ed., *A Widening Sphere: Changing Roles of Victorian Women* (Bloomington, IN, 1978); Nancy Cott and Elizabeth H. Pleck, eds., *A Heritage of Her Own: Toward a New Social History of American Women* (New York, 1979); Louise A. Tilly and Joan W. Scott, *Women, Work, and Family* (New York, 1978); Sandra Burman, ed., *Fit Work*

for Women (New York, 1979); Cynthia M. Patterson, "New Directions in the Political History of Women: A Case Study of the National Woman's Party's Campaign for the Equal Rights Amendment, 1920–1927," *Women's Studies International Forum* 5, no. 6 (Fall 1982): 586. Patterson and others now use the social history of that "women's culture" in new approaches to women's political history; Bonnie G. Smith, *Ladies of the Leisure Class: The Bourgeoises of Northern France in the Nineteenth Century* (Princeton, 1981).

11. Naomi Weisstein, "Psychology Constructs the Female, or the Fantasy Life of the Male Psychologist," in Michele Hoffnung Garskof, ed., *Roles Women Play: Readings toward Women's Liberation* (Belmont, CA, 1971), pp. 68–83; Sandra L. Bem and Daryl J. Bem, "Training the Woman to Know Her Place: The Power of a Nonconscious Ideology," *ibid.*, pp. 84–96; Jo Freeman, "The Social Construction of the Second Sex," *ibid.*, pp. 123–141.

12. Joan Wallach Scott, "Survey Articles: Women in History II: The Modern Period," *Past and Present* 101 (November 1983): 154.

13. Kelly, "Social Relations," p. 811; Joan Kelly, "The Doubled Vision of Feminist Theory: A Postscript to the 'Women and Power' Conference," *Feminist Studies* 5, no. 1 (Spring 1979): 216–227.

14. Katherine Kish Sklar, "The Uses of History," lecture at American Writers Congress (New York, October 1981).

I

WOMEN IN THE AGE OF RELIGIOUS UPHEAVAL AND POLITICAL CENTRALIZATION

Overview, 1500–1750

There is nothing magical about the year 1500, the date we chose to start our story. It begins the century of the religious Reformation, a period of upheaval and crisis out of which emerged Europe's political shape, but the events of the sixteenth century had been long in the making. The *Respublica Christiana*—the medieval Latin Christian world of one God, one Church, one Empire—was already being transformed. In the prior century, the church had not been able to assert a unifying influence and was fragmenting along geographic lines. The Gallican (French) church claimed administrative independence from the Holy See in Rome and, in disputes over authority, Catholic bishops often allied with their territorial princes or kings against the centralizing efforts of the papal court.

New cultural values that drew their inspiration from Classical Greece and Rome had emerged in the urban, more secular environment of the Italian city-states. A new norm of civic activism and political commitment was put forth over and above the Christian ideal of contemplative monastic living. Because of their concern with immediate circumstances and this world, its proponents were known as "humanists." Conscious of a deep gulf separating them from the medievalists, they spoke of the need for a "renaissance," or rebirth. This rebirth would be guided by a study of the rhetoric, poetry, grammar, history, as well as the moral philosophy, of classical antiquity. It signified becoming reconnected to the classical world. These ideals did not replace Christian values, however; in fact, what is meant by the Western tradition as opposed to the Eastern (Oriental) or Middle Eastern traditions, is the blending of ancient classical ideas and notions with Judeo-Christian values and beliefs in the geographic area of Europe and later of America as well. Humanism could be reconciled with religious beliefs and it exerted indeed a powerful influence on the theology and philosophy of medieval scholars (scholasticism). Particularly in northern Europe, humanists (known as Christian humanists) at the turn of the sixteenth century concentrated their critical faculties on examining the scriptures. ''We must affirm nothing of God but what the scriptures tell us about Him,'' was their first principle. They also stressed education, primarily for the purposes of deepening piety and encouraging more meaningful participation in religious life. This new emphasis on education as a means to virtue had great significance for women. Early in the development of Renaissance humanism, leading scholars wrote treatises on the education of women.

The religious Reformation was part of a wide series of events that was shaping the course of European history. Tensions over this refashioning of religious norms affected the evolution of the more secular realms of politics, community, and family life in ways that had far-reaching consequences for women. The substitution of Protestant contractual for Catholic sacramental marriage in the long run established a new legal basis for the equality of women. As a profound crisis of authority, the Reformation eventually recast the character of European politics, thought, society, and religion. Much of the Germanies, also Switzerland, Scandinavia, and Britain, permanently renounced the authority of the pope, and for a century good parts of France (the Huguenot areas) were in the reform camp as well. The motives for conversion were not simple; they represented a complex mix of sincere religious convictions and more mundane calculations of political and financial gains. Since salvation was at stake (and in dispute), it was a time of real intolerance, on which leaders capitalized to achieve concrete political advantages.

As reform ideas spread through towns, communities, and countries, religion and politics became intertwined. The nearly one-and-a-half centuries following Luther's call for debate at the palace church in Wittenberg in 1517 involved a series of civil wars (in France and later in England) and international wars (played out in central Europe). In the course of these conflicts Catholicism, too, became revitalized. After doctrinal clarification at its Council of Trent (1545–1563), the church launched its own, Catholic reformation. The spreading social and political ferment brought important, long-term changes. It accelerated the process of state formation, the broad origins of which went back to earlier efforts of kings and princes, the so-called new monarchs, to establish their authority against the counterclaims of nobles and towns to their own inviolable ''privileges and liberties.'' For many European subjects, political instability reinforced the case for centralized authority. The revision of boundaries among major institutions of society—family, church, and government—necessarily affected female roles. As society became increasingly complex and the private realm more clearly differentiated from the public, did women gain or lose status? How did women respond to the new religious ideas? Why did the patriarchal family become a symbol of dynastic authority? How did the increasing separation of domestic and civic spheres influence the relationships between the sexes?

So far, we have discussed the broad political consequences that issued from the Reformation crisis. Paralleling the process of state-building were economic changes (''the commercial revolution'') that affected the fortunes of the European states as they worked to increase their power and prestige over and against their neighbors. The discovery of America and the new sea routes to the East had widened trade and commerce and stimulated economic growth and production beyond that controlled by the guilds, those urban corporations that had been responsible for most marketable goods manufactured in the medieval world. New markets and increased demand also changed the nature of production in the household and of family life. In the preindustrial world, most people lived and subsisted only because they belonged to a family, or to the household of a family, whose members worked together to produce the food, clothing, and other goods essential to life. The economic changes of the early modern period brought new opportunities for commercial gain to those fortunate enough to produce beyond subsistence needs. Accumulation of a marketable surplus affected family wealth and status, relationships between masters and servants, parents and children, and also husbands and wives. Among the many factors in family life altered by economic development were the age at marriage, the number of children, the relative status of single and married women, and the place of residence selected by people as they sought strategies to survive and prosper. As women were affected by all these changes, they also played important roles in shaping the outcome. How did female labor in both urban and rural settings contribute to the economic development of early modern Europe? How did women respond to the new conditions? In what ways did the extension of commercial capitalism reinforce the tendency of the new state to consolidate decision making under men's auspices?

In the wake of the Reformation, along with political and economic change, came intellectual ferment so intense and so extensive as to be termed a revolution: a scientific revolution. To appreciate the significance of the new ways of thought, we must define the word ''science'' broadly as knowledge—knowledge obtained by systematic study, by observation and classification of natural phenomena, by experimentation for the purpose of discovering general truths. A few women took part, inspired by the scientific methods and philosophical propositions that were beginning to undermine the old intellectual order. Conscious of themselves as a social group, they proposed extending education to women and restructuring domestic authority in order to improve the position of the female sex. These women writers were the descendants of a line of thinkers stretching back to the fifteenth century that today we would term ''feminist.'' If we look for the factors that account for the presence of debate on ''the woman question'' in one period of history and its relative neglect in another era, we will find, in this case, the emergence of new ideas that challenged ancient and hoary views about women. The rise of science put Aristotelian concepts of woman's physiology and role in reproduction to the test—and, before the bar of reason, they faltered.

In the previous pages we have summarized briefly several lines of European development in the centuries we are investigating in Part I. We take a similar approach in the Overviews to Parts II and III. Without doing injustice to the complexity of events, we want you to be familiar with the broad themes of modern history before we turn to the changing roles of women. Since our purpose is to integrate women's experiences into the overall pattern of historical development in the West, we have raised general questions concerning the forces that have influenced most directly women's lives. These questions are designed to help you read more critically the ensuing narrative and case studies.

Confronting Traditions: The Origins of the "Argument about Women"

The waning of the old feudal order in Europe was signaled by the growing importance of a new class of educated people. The group was urban and a product of the social mobility that commerce as well as new bureaucratic and university careers had introduced into the more static world of feudal Europe. Beginning in the mid-fifteenth century, its members served the new monarchs in their efforts to transform themselves from chief feudal lords (the first among equals) into sovereign rulers. It is the women of this group that primarily interest us. As daughters of humanists, of business and clergymen, they benefited as individuals from the spread of learning, which still was limited to a tiny proportion of the population. In reading the venerable authors of the past, however, these educated women could not escape the prejudicial and hostile views about the inferiority of the female sex that were a part of secular as well as religious texts. Their response was to propose alternative ways to assess woman's condition, and they initiated what became a tradition of "feminist" theorizing in Western thought.

Their earliest spokeswoman was Christine de Pisan (1364–1430?), whom we have already met in the Introduction. Their ranks included the Venetian poet Lucrezia Marinella (1571–1653), the British playwright Aphra Behn (1640–1689), and women from whom we shall have occasion to hear more fully later on, such as Jane Sharp (fl. 1671), Elizabeth Cellier (fl. 1680), and Mary Astell (1668–1731). What lay at the heart of their protest was the conviction that women were full human beings, not creatures restricted by nature or feminine biology. And their remedy was to open to women the fruits of their culture, the education in "arms and letters" as it was conceived at the time; women's true capabilities then would become manifest. Marinella wrote, "I wish that these [detractors of women] would make this experiment: that they raise a boy and a girl of the same age, and both of sound mind and body, in letters and arms. They would see in a short time how the girl would be more perfectly instructed than the boy and would soon surpass him."[1]

This conclusion contradicted the assertions of women's inferiority that had been passed down from ancient classical author to Christian writer in Western history to that date. Christine de Pisan has left a remarkable testimony of her own struggle when confronting the authority of these learned men. It was, she wrote, "too much [to hold], that so many famous men . . . should have lied, and in so many places, for I could scarcely find a volume [of moral philosophy], whoever its author, without . . . some chapters or sections blaming [women]."[2] Traditions represent accumulated wisdom based on shared perceptions and beliefs that become part of each generation's intellectual convictions. As Pisan recognized, there was a long tradition of misogynist thinking in the Western world, but it was man-made, not indicative of the natural state of affairs. And she and the other early feminists began to turn the historical record around in order to acquire a heritage to be proud of. They set out to capture the exploits of great ladies—the "women worthies"—and to "discourse on the excellence of women."

These exceptional individuals initiated an intellectual defense of women that continued and gained credence during the famous four-hundred-year-long "Querelle des femmes" (argument over the nature of women). The time of Christine de Pisan, the Renaissance, was a period of intellectual ferment, empirical inquiry, and experimentation, but all that creative energy did not alter the general negative assessment of women's capabilities or the normative belief that women's proper place was ensconced in domestic life, subject to the authority of fathers, husbands, or other men. Two reasons account for the perpetuation of these ancient beliefs at a time of otherwise significant transformation of values. First, these beliefs offered a persuasive and comprehensive justification for common biblical assertions about women. Second, they supported the philosophically conservative bias of most scholars. The inherited notions about women were an integral part of the structure of the dominant Christian philosophy of the Renaissance—scholasticism. To replace its method and argument by an alternative system of thought implied severing all ties to contemporary philosophical usage. Renaissance scholars, too, relied on previous authority in developing their arguments. The great Renaissance astronomer Galileo in the *Dialogue Concerning the Two Chief World Systems—Ptolemaic and Copernican* (1632) captures well the force of tradition when he has Simplicio, a confused peripatetic (a devotée of Aristotle), protest "Who would there be to settle our controversies if Aristotle were to be deposed? What other author should we follow in the schools, the academies, the universities? What philosopher has written the whole of natural philosophy, so well arranged. . . . Ought we to desert that structure under which so many travelers have recuperated?"[3] Especially in a time of religious, political, and economic upheaval, continuity in the hierarchy of relations between the sexes would be reassuring.

Aristotle's system of thought rested on the principle of duality, in which one element was superior to another, and this position was incorporated by the scholastics into their own Christian edifice. The male principle in nature was associated with activity and perfection, while the female was conceived of as passive and deprived. The duality male/female was paralleled by the dualities active/passive, form/matter, and perfection/imperfection. In using this notion of male/female, we can observe how through time the classical and Christian views were merged to produce the belief system that was characteristic of the West. Aristotle had argued that nature always sought to create the most perfect thing, which was the most completely formed. Such a creature, he claimed, was the male. Neither Aristotle nor his influential thirteenth-century scholastic follower

Thomas Aquinas meant that females contradicted the intentions of nature. Both sexes were necessary to procreate the species. In explaining the purpose of female being, Aquinas synthesized his understanding of Aristotle with the account of the creation of woman in Genesis (1:26–7, 2:22–3):

> With reference to nature in the species as a whole, the female is not something manqué, but is according to the plan of nature, and is directed to the work of procreation.[4]

By the time of the Renaissance some doctors had turned against Aristotelian thought and argued that women were equally perfect (though lesser) beings (Chapter 4). This progressive-sounding position did not translate into advocacy of greater equality for women, but it helped solve one potentially bothersome problem—to understand the successes of queens or the influence of strong wives. Renaissance doctors posited two intermediary types between the perfect woman (born from the dominant female semen in the left-hand side of the uterus) and the perfect man (resulting from the dominant male semen in the right side of the uterus): effeminate males and viragoes (strong, manlike women). Thus, the dramatic exploits and achievements of queens, abbesses, and heroines were credited to physiological "abnormalities," an explanation that obviated examination of the circumstances under which women could develop their potentials more fully.

From their understanding of physiology, scholars were quick to generalize about woman's psychology, and here the learned medical voices blended in well with venerable theological beliefs. Prey to a hysterical animal within her (the uterus), woman could not control her emotions, nor discipline her sexual impulses, nor act in any consistent fashion according to reason. This justified her relegation to home and hearth and exclusion from participation in public affairs. Clergymen reached the same conclusion, though partly for different reasons. In the accounts of man's superiority over woman in the theological tracts of the medieval world, her passivity and imperfections were attributed to the malediction laid on woman at the Fall and to her uncleanliness during menstruation, a concept adapted by Christians from Judaic law. Eve's betrayal and the monthly "curse" were used to justify many of the restrictions placed on women's earthly participation in the life of the church. This was notwithstanding the basic Christian tenet that while woman was the inferior of man by nature, she was his equal by grace. There would be no difference in status of the sexes in heaven; they shared the same spiritual destiny. In the present world, however, women were enjoined to cover their heads in church and to wear their hair long as signs of submission. Not formed in the image of God, they were excluded from the priesthood, and because Eve's words had bewitched Adam, they were barred from preaching or speaking in church. Above all, they were subject to their husbands in marriage. Although marriage itself was considered an imperfect state, it was a necessary evil for weaker mortals unable to achieve the celibate ideal embodied in the priesthood. Church, custom, and law placed wives squarely under husbands' authority. Both classical and Judeo-Christian teachings and common proverbs praised Patient Griselda, the chaste, submissive wife in medieval literature.

These widespread beliefs represented a formidable obstacle to women assuming authoritative public roles in social and political life. But such norms, or ideological notions, are insufficient to explain fully women's status and historic experiences. As we will see in the course of this chapter, these misogynist views played a decisive role in shaping women's experiences in certain contexts, while in others they were less influential. The reality of women's lives defies the universality of norms. History demonstrates numerous contexts within which women exercised considerable authority, responsibility, and decision-making power that belied the image of them as weaker vessels. In these cases, the material conditions of women's lives overrode the values and norms that sought to channel life along certain ideal paths.

In the early medieval world, women of rank played an active part in public life as suited their central role in the management of family property. Many of the economic documents of the day—the sales contracts, letters of exchange, leases, and donations—identified men by their mother's name. Because of her extensive managerial functions of overseeing the serfs, paying and collecting rents, producing and exchanging goods, an upper-class woman was a well-known personage in the local community and her name alone was sufficient to identify her children. Family lineage counted more than gender. Often, women's behavior was governed by practical and informal arrangements not codified in judicial statute. Women did whatever was needed to ensure the continuity of the family estate, particularly when warrior-husbands departed for military ventures, crusades, or pilgrimages. With the demise of the Roman Empire, central rule had broken down and public authority was being exercised by powerful families. There was an overlapping of jurisdictions and the early medieval world made no clear distinction between the public realm and the private sphere. To the extent, then, that women were part of the governing nobility, they exhibited considerable authority over a range of public activities. For a long time, well into the early modern period in fact, politics remained dynastic and family ties were essential to the exercise of political power. This meant that some women who were members of powerful aristocratic families continued to play significant roles in dynastic conflicts among states as well as in political struggles over the centralizing efforts of the new monarchs within the states of Europe. On the same model, some women in religious orders, usually women of aristocratic heritage, exercised important administrative powers.

The Reformation

Defying stereotypes, women in good measure also were instrumental in spreading the ideas of the religious Reformation to the communities, towns, and provinces of Europe after 1517. In their roles as spouses and mothers they were often the ones to bring the early reform ideas to the families of Europe's aristocracy and to those of the common people in urban centers as well. The British theologian Richard Hooker (1553?–1600) typically explained the prominence of women in reform movements by reference to their ''nature,'' to the ''eagerness of their affection,'' not to their intelligence or ability to make conscious choices. Similarly,

Catholic polemicists used notions about women's immature and frail "nature" to discredit Protestantism.

The important role played by women in the sixteenth-century Reformation should not surprise us, for they had been equally significant in supporting earlier heresies that challenged the established order and at times the gender hierarchy, too. Many medieval anticlerical movements that extolled the virtues of lay men praised lay women as well. For example, the fourteenth-century followers of John Wycliffe in England, known as Lollards, encouraged women to read the Bible and recite the Scriptures at their meetings; evidence suggests that women might even have preached on occasion. Wealthy women of aristocratic families who were allied together in the southern French province of Carcassonne were the vanguard of the Albigensian heresy in the twelfth and thirteenth centuries. Albigensians professed a radical dualism of good and evil and held that Satan, the principle of evil, was an independent deity, not a fallen angel of God. The adherents were ascetics, who withdrew from the evil world around them to free their spirits. When St. Dominic, who later founded the Dominican Order, converted the area back to orthodox Latin Christendom, he took great pains to win over these influential noblewomen.[5] Since the message of the Reformation, like that of the earlier religious movements, meant a loosening of hierarchies, it had a particular appeal to women. By stressing the individual's personal relationship with God and his or her own responsibility for behavior, it affirmed the ability of each to find truth by reading the original Scriptures. Thus, it offered a greater role for lay participation by women, as well as men, than was possible in Roman Catholicism.

The way was paved by the movement of Christian humanism in France, England, and the Low Countries at the end of the fifteenth century. Religious reformers utilized the new learning to deepen and strengthen individual piety; they hoped gradually and peacefully to reform the church from within. Two of the outstanding humanists, the Dutchman Desiderius Erasmus (1466–1536) and the Englishman Sir Thomas More (1478–1535), both acknowledged the importance of bringing religious education to women. Erasmus summed up their belief in his treatise on Christian marriage:

> The distaff and spindle are in truth the tools of all women and suitable for avoiding idleness. . . . It would be better if [people] taught [their daughters] to study, for study busies the whole soul. . . . It is not only a weapon against idleness, but also a means of impressing the best precepts upon a girl's mind and of leading her to virtue.[6]

More ironically grounded his advocacy of improved education for women in the old prejudices.

> If the female soil be in its nature stubborn, and more productive of weeds than fruit, it ought, in my opinion, to be more diligently cultivated with learning and good instruction. I do not see why learning . . . may not equally agree with both sexes.[7]

Influenced by these Renaissance humanists in the northern states of Europe, significant educational opportunities opened up for women of the aristocracy, many of whom later patronized the new learning in their own courts and lands. The humanist movement helps account for the group of remarkably talented and renowned female rulers and educators of the sixteenth century, which includes Queen Elizabeth I (1558–1603), Lady Jane Grey (1537–1554), and Catherine Parr (1512–1548) in England as well as Marguerite of Angoulême, Queen of Navarre (1492–1549) and Jeanne d'Albret (1528–1572) in France. Encouraged and often educated by the humanists, women began to participate in the discussions over church reforms, to debate the Scriptures, and to speculate on theological problems.

Translation of Luther's ideas reached France by 1519 and struck a receptive chord among the educated French noblewomen. Many, like Marguerite of Navarre, never officially converted to Protestantism but nevertheless turned their provinces into asylums for religious fugitives in the decades of turmoil to come. Marguerite even sheltered the Protestant reformer, John Calvin (1509–1564). The elder sister of Francis I, the King of France at the time of Luther's revolt, she was excluded from succession to the throne by the Salic law (introduced into France between the fourteenth and fifteenth centuries). Marguerite was a devotée of the new learning, a true Lady of the Renaissance who, it is said, read Dante in Italian, quite probably Plato in Greek, and Luther in broken German. She was a writer and poet of considerable merit in her own right; her most important work is the *Heptameron*, modeled on Boccaccio's *Decameron*, which presents the tales of travelers whose lives express virtue and honor and contrast with the debauched and depraved ways of clerics and monks. One charming (and protofeminist) story relates the adventure of a boatwoman who cleverly avoids rape by two Franciscan friars and delivers them quaking into the hands of villagers, who are delighted to catch the hypocritical clergy. Many of her verses, such as "The Primacy of Scripture" or "Justification by Faith," expressed in poetic form basic tenets of Protestantism. Through the printing press, her writings, as those of Christine de Pisan, were made available to well-born urban women in France who were encouraged to read and study according to the ideal of the humanists. The future Queen Elizabeth I translated one of her poems, "A Godly Meditation of the Soul."

At the French court, under the auspices of Anne de Beaujeu (1441–1522), a whole generation of ladies-in-waiting, the daughters of many of the leading noble families, had been educated according to humanist principles. These noblewomen, tied together by bonds of blood and marriage and by their earlier association as young girls at court, were active in the French Reform movement. In the 1520s they sponsored the educational and religious reforms associated with the evangelical movement led by Lefevre d'Etaples; it stressed meditation, prayer, and a life guided by reading the Gospel. For their own daughters' educations, they often chose tutors of reformed leanings and even specified the curriculum.

The first generation of French Protestant women were the daughters, granddaughters, and close associates of these educated aristocrats. This group of Protestant (Huguenot) activists emerged around mid-century and openly advocated Calvinism and the French Reformed church that John Calvin was guiding from

Geneva. All of these Huguenot women were strong-minded, independent persons, and a disproportionate number of them were widows. They found in Calvinism a way to enhance their participation in the religious and political events of the day. Thus, they carved out more meaningful roles in society than was otherwise possible. They converted friends and kin, protected pastors and educators, and gave money and advice to their male associates. In the lands that had gone Huguenot, they helped reform the system of law, levy new taxes, reorganize economic life, and they debated the question of the proper structure of the Reformed church. Even after the decline of the Huguenot cause, its women continued to be active in founding schools and establishing poor relief.

But what about the common women who lived in cities? What accounted for their conversion? At the heart of urban lay religious life, supporting both religious and secular causes, stood confraternities, associations that also fostered new urban solidarities. Organized around craft guilds, they sponsored banquets and celebrations, held plays and festivities, and arranged for processions on their saints' days and masses to honor the souls of their dead members, friends, and relatives. In Lyons and other important cities, these were men's experiences; women were less likely than men to be members of the confraternity. However, even before the Reformation, as a result of the emphasis on the new learning, urban women who had access to vernacular devotional literature joined reading groups and began to discuss and debate theological issues. The churchmen were not at all sympathetic to such activity. "Why they are half theologians," complained a Franciscan priest vigorously. "They own Bibles the way they own love stories and romances. They get carried away by questions on transubstantiation [the doctrine that in the Sacrament bread and wine become the actual body and blood of Christ] and they go 'running around from . . . one [female] religious house to another, seeking advice . . .' "[8]

The Protestant movement affirmed the right of women to read the Scriptures in the vernacular. It offered women who previously had not found much room for expressing their religious beliefs a new and clearly welcomed option: that of joining with the men of their families to talk seriously about religious matters. Even at church, men and women could raise their voices together in song and share religious expression. The women who became Protestants in Lyons were not the most learned women of the city but precisely those who found in religion a rewarding outlet for their new educational interests. They belonged mostly to middle-class families of artisans, merchants, and members of the professions; their ranks included a disproportionate number of widows with employment of their own in dressmaking, midwifery, and innkeeping. The new opportunities for intellectual and spiritual growth that conversion to Protestantism implied complemented an independence that some middle-class urban women, like the aristocratic Huguenot women, already had obtained.

After a half century of civil wars, France remained a Catholic nation; in other parts of northern and central Europe, the Reformation was institutionalized by official decree and maintained by resort to armed leagues. Claiming the right of *ius reformandi* (the power to reform), many dynastic states and Imperial cities opted for Lutheranism, introducing Lutheran bishops, doctrines, and forms of worship, encouraging clerical marriages, secularizing (nationalizing) church property within their borders, and closing the convents. Luther himself had called upon the princes and urban magistrates to oversee religious reform, and the strong arm of authority seemed all the more crucial in light of massive peasant rebellions and the Anabaptist challenge that rejected authorities of both church and state and threatened to turn the Reformation into social revolution. In 1555, a compromise was reached between Lutherans and Catholics that established the principle of one religion for each territory—*cuius regio eius religio.* If a ruler decided in favor of Lutheranism, then his subjects were to be Lutheran. Christianity was assuming the character of political ideology.

Through decades of armed religious conflict and massive emigration of refugee families, the Reformation had an immediate impact on the lives of women of all classes. One important and positive result was the stimulus it provided to educate girls so that they could read the Bible and other devotional literature. In the Saxon city of Zwickau, as in other areas, the city council set up a girls' school as early as 1525. Since it was designed primarily to instill correct moral virtues rather than to stimulate intellectual development, the new educational program did not appreciably improve women's position in society. Furthermore, by introducing a new moral sensibility, the reform movement affected ambivalently, if not negatively, two vocations that had been important for women in the pre-Reformation era: that of nun and that of prostitute. The nunneries were closed down wherever the Reformation triumphed. The nuns "did not go willingly," however; they were among those who resisted reform most tenaciously. In a society that elevated spirituality to the highest level, a religious vocation for women offered opportunities unequalled in the profane world. Indeed, by dedicating a daughter to the church, a family could hope not only for reward from God but also for special respect from neighbors and local officials. For example, in the early 1600s, Benedetta Carlini, a young woman from a mountain village in Italy, was pledged to the church by her father in gratitude for God's having spared her and her mother through a difficult birth. From early childhood Benedetta won privileges beyond her sex. When she began to have visions and fall into trances during which God and Jesus visited her, she achieved a kind of power and fame that could bring profit to her entire village. According to historian Judith Brown, Benedetta's claims were later rejected by church authorities who imprisoned her for the rest of her life (some thirty-five years), because they feared the power of "holy women" to influence the rest of society. In Benedetta's case, after one investigation by local religious leaders confirmed her claims to be a true visionary, emissaries of the pope undertook a second investigation and judged her guilty of fraud—a very serious offense in a society torn by religious conflict. The church, believing "all novelty is dangerous and all unusual events are suspect," punished impostors severely. The case against Benedetta rested on testimony by her cellmate that during some of the nun's trances she had initiated lesbian sexual acts. Henceforth, this talented woman who, as abbess, had supervised the convent and its staff, administered extensive agricultural properties, and overseen the production and marketing of silk, was deprived of all activity, forbidden to speak, and perhaps even made to eat on the floor.[9]

Convents had provided women uncommon opportunities and a place of refuge away from male supervision. Therefore, in Catholic areas they continued to be important and to perform essential social functions. Sarah Hanley demonstrates (Chapter 1) that when conflict over family authority broke out, the convents often were used by families as "official detention centers" for errant female members. In some cases they also solved financial problems for families unable or unwilling to provide dowries sufficient to assure their daughters appropriate marriages. Admission to a convent cost only a fraction of the price of a dowry. Throughout the early modern period the nuns also provided much-needed public service, as the study by Olwen Hufton and Frank Tallett (Chapter 3) reveals. They offered educational and vocational training to youths, oversaw children while mothers worked, and ministered to the sick in hospitals.

Since Protestant reformers celebrated marriage over the Catholic ideal of celibacy, family living became one of the bases of respectability in post-Reformation society. Therefore, with equal vigor, although less successfully, reformers attacked the widespread and public presence of prostitutes, just as they railed against clerical concubinages and other forms of behavior that contemporary norms considered to be sexually immoral. Brothels had been a regular part of late medieval society, usually regulated by city officials. In England, licensed brothels survived until the reign of Henry VIII (1509–1547); there, they had come under the jurisdiction of the bishop of Winchester and the women were known as "Winchester geese." They signified a moral attitude that was willing to make concessions to human nature. Since in many occupations, marriage was only possible after completion of extended study or apprenticeship training, the population in urban centers typically consisted of large numbers of young, single men. In some places servants and other economically dependent men were even legally prohibited from marrying. Prostitution was considered economically preferable to indigent marriages.

Under the imprint of a new moral sensibility, the reformers now sought to banish prostitutes and to confine sex solely to marriage. City fathers, first under Protestantism and later reformed Catholicism, developed novel institutional mechanisms to oversee and control the moral behavior of the populace. For example, in Calvin's Geneva, the infamous consistory, composed of twelve male elders and the city's eight or ten pastors, met weekly to punish moral transgressions; in Zwickau, city councillors appointed a panel of clergy and councillors to sit as a marital court. The Zwickau panel often sought advice from the Lutheran consistory in Wittenberg. At the outset, in treating sexual offenders, the Genevan consistory made minimal distinctions according to gender. Calvin envisioned ideal relations between the sexes as "differentiated equality," allowing for neither "male tyranny" nor "female autonomy," but requiring instead reciprocal cooperation under male leadership. In practice, this meant that males were held as responsible for their sexual behavior as were females. Of 320 city inhabitants banished for marital troubles between 1564 and 1569, 56 percent were men. But by the early seventeenth century, the double standard had returned to Geneva; men, who were merely "sowing wild oats," received reduced punishment, whereas unchaste and adulterous women were "whipped through the streets and banished." Heightened moral concerns, in the long run, also brought a growing preoccupation with girls' virginity and wives' chastity.[10]

The early Puritan reformers and moralists sought to confine sexuality to marriage, treating premarital and extramarital intercourse as sex crimes—fornication and adultery. They also refused to dissociate sex from procreation. On the ground that it violated God's intentions and denied women the saving grace of bearing children for Christ, they opposed contemporary folk notions about contraception. By the mid-seventeenth century, as we will see shortly, birth control practices spread among the men and women of some well-off European families who were ignoring these norms. But the power of prescription can be seen in the low rates of illegitimacy characteristic of the early modern period, despite the prevalence of relatively late marriages and considerable celibacy. The fate of women who bore bastards—and they were usually servants or wage laborers vulnerable to coercion by masters or seduction by lovers who promised to wed—varied considerably. In parts of Germany, they were sometimes fully integrated into family life with undiminished inheritance rights for their children. More commonly, however, they faced the denial of employment and shelter, social ostracism, and public humiliation. In France, unwed mothers, called *fille-mères* (girl-mothers), were required to file a "declaration of pregnancy" stating, often in great detail, the circumstances under which they had become pregnant. Often they gave birth in hospitals run by religious or other charitable institutions; these were unhealthy places dreaded by most people as symbols of poverty and of death. In some places, public officials subjected unwed mothers to considerable pressure to reveal the names of the fathers of their illegitimate children; in colonial America, unwed women who had refused to cooperate earlier might be prevailed upon to speak the truth while suffering labor pains. Such responses also must be seen in light of the importance of the family economy: few individuals of either sex could survive outside a mutually supportive cooperative group.

The Reformation did not markedly transform women's place in society, and the reformers had never intended to do so. To be sure, they called on men and women to read the Bible and participate in religious ceremonies together. But Bible-reading reinforced the Pauline view of woman as weak-minded and sinful. When such practice took a more radical turn in the direction of lay prophesy, as occurred in some Reform churches southwest of Paris, or in the coming together of women to discuss "unchristian pieces" as was recorded in Zwickau, reformers—Lutheran and Calvin alike—pulled back in horror. The radical or Anabaptist brand of reform generally offered women a more active role in religious life than did Lutheranism, even allowing them to preach. "Admonished to Christian righteousness" by more conservative Protestants, Anabaptists were charged with holding that "marriage and whoredom are one and the same thing." The women were even accused of having "dared to deny their husbands' marital rights." During an interrogation one woman explained that "she was wed to Christ and must therefore be chaste, for which she cited the saying, that no one can serve two masters."[11]

The response of the magisterial Reformers was unequivocal. The equality of the Gospel was not to overturn the inequalities of social rank or the hierarchies of the sexual order. As the Frenchman Pierre Viret explained it in 1560, appealing to the old polarities again, the Protestant elect were equal as Christians and believers—as man and woman, master and servant, free and serf. Further, while the Reformation thus failed to elevate women's status, it deprived them of the emotionally sustaining presence of female imagery, of saints and protectors who long had played a significant role at crucial points in their life cycles. The Reformers rejected the special powers of the saints and downplayed, for example, Saints Margaret and Ann, who had been faithful and succoring companions for women in childbirth and in widowhood. With the rejection of Mary as well as the saints, nuns, and abbesses, God the Father was more firmly in place.

Political Centralization and Witchcraft

Partly because of the unanticipated enthusiasm that the challenge to authority had unleashed, the magisterial Reformation consciously sought to enhance the powers of secular officials. Challenged by Anabaptists, with their greater emphasis on women's religious roles, and by peasant rebellions, Luther became more conservative, qualifying his notion of the priesthood of all believers and upgrading the responsibilities of the established male clergy. Calvinism represented a form of theocracy in which the clergy governed the public realm. The dominant political conflict of the age concerned delimiting contested lines of public authority, although often it was couched in religious terms. In France, the Huguenots, typically southern French aristocrats, saw in Calvinism a way to counteract the centralizing tendencies of the Catholic Valois dynasty. Similarly, in central Europe, princes used Lutheranism to challenge the authority of the Catholic Austrian Emperor. Henceforth, new institutions of bureaucratic control and new offices in the courts of law would ensure that the faithful lived a good, orderly life in God's new political realm.

The novel uses of religion to strengthen the political legitimacy of Europe's regimes help to explain the timing of the great witch hunts and the thousands of organized trials and executions of suspected witches that took place in the sixteenth and seventeenth centuries in Europe. During these two centuries witchcraft was a capital crime throughout most of Europe. Witchcraft trials are of central importance in European history, not only for what they say specifically about women's social position and vulnerability (since more often than not it was women who were executed as witches), but also for the light they shed on the socioeconomic and political changes transforming early modern life. Historians once believed that there were two major outbreaks of witchcraft trials in Europe, the mass executions in fourteenth-century France and Italy and those in the early modern era. But recent research has shown conclusively that this picture was based on forgeries; in fact, there were comparatively few trials in the fourteenth century. It was in the half century before 1500 that the number of trials increased in France, southwest Germany, and Switzerland, foreshadowing the great outbreaks of the sixteenth and seventeenth centuries. This discovery has altered the interpretation of Europe's witch hunts.[12]

The persecution and trial of witches were widespread phenomena in urban and rural areas of both Catholic and Protestant lands. They concentrated, however, in border areas in which the lines of legitimate authority were in question. After nearly a half-century of neglect, witch trials began to multiply in the 1560s and sentiment rose to panic proportions by the end of the century. There were mass trials in central Europe, as well as in France, England, Switzerland, and elsewhere. The end of the century saw further geographical extension into the Rhineland between France and the Germanies and the Basque lands between France and Spain. Events reached fever pitch during the decade of the 1620s; the trials continued throughout the century. Sweden experienced them for the first time in 1669 and 1676 and the last major outbreaks occurred in Salem, Massachusetts, in 1692 and in Paisley, Scotland, in 1697. The final legal execution of a witch apparently occurred in Switzerland as late as 1782.

Who were Europe's witches? Those accused were predominantly women. In Scotland, southwest Germany, and Switzerland, around four-fifths of the accused witches were women. England recorded even higher proportions. In France, the appeal cases that reached the Parlement of Paris indicate that significant numbers of "cunning men" or male magical healers were accused of malice. Overall, however, men were a distinct minority, for the most part located in areas where witchcraft was confused with heresy. The association of "witch" with "woman" predated these mass-organized witch hunts. It harked back to Aristotle's notions of female imperfection and the Judeo-Christian association of woman with evil and sin. "The reason is easie" said James VI of Scotland (r. 1603–1625) in discussing why women were more inclined to witchcraft than men. "[F]or as that sexe is frailer then men is, so is it easier to be intrapped in these grosse snares of the Devill, as was well proved to be true, by the Serpents deceiving of Eve at the beginning, which makes him the homelier with that sex ever since."[13] Notions about witches, devils, sorcery, orgy, and the evil-eye had long been part of popular beliefs in European and in other societies as well. Yet, such ideas must be distinguished from witch hunting, which was unique to Europe and was directed and organized by governmental elites for political purposes.

Witches, then, were typically female, and all females were potential witches; but they were not randomly selected. In England and Salem, Massachusetts, they were often old and poor, certainly less well off than those who accused them; and they were nearly always in a fairly close relationship to the accuser, usually a neighbor or relative, who could be either male or female. In Scotland, they were women with a "ready, sharp, and angry tongue"; quarrelsome women who were married and in their mid-life and came from the bottom rungs of the peasantry. In Germany, large numbers of widows were burned as witches. The accused frequently had a local reputation as a potential evil-doer and was often charged with having made a covenant with the devil. Some women quite readily accepted the label for the power and enhanced status it might give them in the local community. As the Scot Agnes Finnie declared menacingly at her trial, "If I be a witch, you or yours shall have better cause to call me so." In other cases confessions were won by torture.

Despite regional variations, the typical European witch was not a young, immature woman but rather an adult, quite often a single or widowed and eccentric female who defied the boundaries of acceptable behavior for her sex and might, without other support, become a financial burden to the community. The new ideas of Protestantism as well as Reformed Catholicism required, furthermore, that women assume personal responsibility for their own salvation. In this new context witchcraft was an activity defined by law as criminal, for which the woman herself, not her husband or guardian, was responsible. On one level, pursuit of witches in the local community represented a particularly violent reaction by men and other women against this view of woman as an independent adult. But witch-hunting served additional functions, particularly in areas recently converted to Protestantism. Calvinists believed that God was just and punished those who sinned with hardships; misfortunes, which were ever-present under subsistence conditions of poor nutrition, high mortality, pests, and plagues, were not God's tests of fidelity and strength but were clear indications of sin and of God's just punishment for transgression. Under these conditions, belief in witchcraft was a welcome an-swer to death and disease. Psychologically, it shifted the blame from the afflicted people onto others like destitute old women who were socially more vulnerable.

The multiple and useful functions served by witch hunts and trials testify to the variety of intellectual and social changes that were slowly transforming early modern Europe. The most common motive throughout Europe as a whole was political—the trials were used to strengthen the authority of post-Reformation rul-ers and to confirm the legitimacy of the new regimes. The trials were not sponta-neous but organized from above. They aided secular authorities in taking over jurisdictions that previously had been the preserve of the ecclesiastical courts. These magistrates passed statutes against witchcraft that included new, legal defi-nitions of sexual and religious offenses, among them bestiality, adultery, and blas-phemy. They instituted new mechanisms of social control, including sessions and courts created to handle the charges, countercharges, and appeals, and also to supervise the social and moral behavior of the territory's subjects. But witch-hunting remained important only as long as Christianity served as a legitimizing political ideology. In time, as European society became increasingly secular, it lost its cohesive force and function and large-scale organized witch hunts disap-peared from the scene of history.

Political Centralization and the Early Modern Family

The presence of witch trials in the various states of Europe, which increased the level of misogyny in society, also served to strengthen weak lines of central au-thority. Everywhere in post-Reformation Europe, the task of princes and kings was to amass more effective powers in the new state bureaucracies—by levying taxes, stimulating trade, and expanding political offices and public jurisdictions, including regulation of individual behavior. For example, in the first half of the seventeenth century Cardinal Richelieu, advisor to Louis XIII and chief architect of the emerging system of French absolutism, opposed the nobility's recourse to dueling, thus striking a serious blow at aristocratic privilege. By upholding only the king's justice in the realm, he undercut the earlier rights of nobles to take the law into their hands. Similarly, in the next century, central government began to limit ecclesiastical power by curtailing the autonomy of religious orders. State-building in this instance impinged on one of the few areas of autonomy open to women outside the family.

In this critical process of state-building, kings and princes began to rely on a new analogy that entwined the authority of the state with that of the family. Kings ruled their realm as fathers ruled their roost. The idea that "a man's house is his castle" dates from this period. The legal subjection of wives to husbands and of children to parents reinforced, so the early modern political theorists assumed, the obedience of each subject to the growing claims of the centralizing state. Neither the authority of kings nor that of fathers was contractual; it was part of the natural order, akin to the power of God to command obedience from Christians. The analogy was persuasive because it mirrored actual changes in family structure and power, which the Reformation crisis had reinforced.

The Reformation reorganized the moral basis of the family and strengthened the father's position over wife, children, and servants. To be sure, in permitting priests to marry and extolling the married life above the celibate ideal, it challenged the traditional medieval hostility to sexuality and particularly the deep-seated prejudices associated with the female body. Furthermore, since marriage was no longer a sacrament but a civil transaction, reformers countenanced divorce; by the Ordinances of Wittenberg (1553) and those of Geneva (1561) adultery and desertion were recognized as legitimate grounds for divorce although, in practice, divorce was virtually as difficult to obtain under Protestantism as it was under Catholicism. In eighteenth-century Geneva, for example, the city averaged only one divorce per year. Between 1670 and 1799, in all of England only 131 divorces were granted, usually to peers who wanted second wives to give them sons.

In important ways, the family had become a pivotal institution in reformed conceptions (and after the Council of Trent for Catholics, also); and it was given many important religious functions to fulfill. Its members were expected to spend evenings together reading and discussing the Bible and other devotional literature. Protestants were also enjoined to say prayers at meals. These family-centered rituals offered new roles to women and some, as pastors' wives, enjoyed new public duties, supporting their husbands' efforts but also engaging separately in charitable and educational endeavors in local communities. But it was the master of the house who was given ultimate authority. Paul had proclaimed, "Wives, submit yourself unto your own husbands, as unto the Lord. Children, obey your parents in the Lord." A Bible published in England in 1537 went further. It added to the patristic admonition the counsel that, if faced with a rebellious wife, a husband "endeavoureth to beat the fear of God into her head, . . . that thereby she may be compelled to learn her duty and do it."[14] Protestant interpretation of the Bible made such strictures a part of daily life.

Legal changes were reinforcing these patterns of family authority. Since the introduction of Roman Law into many of the provinces of Europe in the thirteenth century, the father of a family—as long as he had made no testament to the contrary—was the sole master of the family patrimony, free to dispose of it as he liked. Powerful aristocratic families used this law to establish primogeniture—to pass their lands to one son only in order to preserve intact the foundation of their wealth. This practice left other sons to seek careers in military or ecclesiastical ranks and daughters to be given dowries, often very generous awards intended as compensation for their renunciation of claims to the family lands. Dowry settlement also served as a form of insurance for the landed classes, helping to guarantee a daughter's survival so that if by chance all male heirs died, the estate could pass through her line to her sons. Such an option was especially important at a time when "demographic accidents" often left aristocrats without male heirs. Particularly after the sixteenth century in France and elsewhere, new laws were passed and judgments rendered that placed property even more firmly under the control of the men of families. They severely curtailed the ability of married women to act in their own or their children's interests, to control their wealth, or choose their domicile. In England, for example, a law of 1540 empowered husbands, who were already vested with control of their wives' estates, to extend their rights by long leases well beyond their own lifetime, and to retain the rents from the land. Husbands enjoyed also the means to prevent their wives from escaping tutelage to live an independent life. In a ruling of 1663, a court decided that "if a woman who can have no goods of her own to live on, will depart from her husband against his will and will not submit herself unto him, let her live on charity, or starve in the name of God; for in such case the law says her evil demeanor brought it upon her, and her death ought to be imputed to her own wilfulness."[15] In France, if a woman received a separation, her dowry was returned to her; if the husband could prove adultery by his wife, however, he kept the dowry, used its fruits, and merely paid her "board" in a convent. Often, therefore, men who knew their wives were about to seek a separation accused them of adultery and tried to fabricate a case.

The early modern family was not the institution that we think of today, although by the seventeenth century the salient characteristics of our "modern" family could be glimpsed in the households of Europe's educated and professional middle classes. In the early modern world, the very term "family" was vague; the German language had no word for the grouping of parents and children that we think of as family. In France, family meant lineage, a line, a dynasty—that is, a set of kinfolk who did not necessarily live together in one residence. It also referred, however, to persons living under one roof, which included parents and children but also apprentices, servants, and friends. Furthermore, there was no notion of privacy; people often lived together in one room, worked, ate, and slept there, and parents, servants, and children regularly went to sleep in the same room. Equally important was the absence of love and emotional intimacy as the basis of marriage. In fact, for a long time the church had condemned love as a motive for marriage, because it was seen to interfere with the love of God. For members of the aristocracy, a marriage represented specific social and economic calculations—it solidified an important alliance, enhanced the economic position of the group, or served political ends. Individual choice played a minimal role and family strategy overrode personal desire. Sarah Hanley (Chapter 1) pursues this theme further by analyzing a conflict in France between church and state over the conditions of marriage, which ultimately enhanced the power of the family. Lawyers and jurists set out to strengthen their own family alliances and transform the well-born family into a more effective political force. They did so by creating a body of civil law on marriage that favored patriarchal power. Women were the losers; the new legal context favored paternal rights over those of mothers and children.

The Reformation and concurrent growth of commercial capitalism unleashed new sentiments that in the course of time turned the early modern family into its modern counterpart. The changes began first among the well-born, predominantly in the urban, literate, business, and professional communities, but also among some of Europe's landed aristocrats. Their experiences gradually became normative (that is, the ideal patterning of family living) for the rest of society. The transformation in family structures and roles had important consequences for women, as we will see in more detail in Parts II and III of this book. But in our period, three major changes affected the early modern family in the well-off classes—the ''discovery of childhood,'' the legitimization of love in marriage, and the beginning of the use of birth control practices within marriage.

By placing responsibility for salvation on the individual, the Reformation opened up new possibilities in parent/child relationships. Childhood was defined by Catholic moralists and pedagogues as God's innocent age, ''to which we must all return . . . the age when hatred is unknown, when nothing can cause distress; the golden age of human life, the age which defies Hell, the age when life is easy and death holds no terrors. . . .''[16] Puritans held more to the idea of ''original sin,'' but the conclusion for both groups of reformers and educators was clear: children needed to be segregated from adult (corrupt) society, carefully supervised, molded, and strengthened so that later as adults they would be strong enough to withstand the temptations of the devil and evil ways. Thus began a campaign to separate children from servants, and, for the sake of ''decency,'' boys from girls; to expurgate the historic texts deemed inappropriate for children's minds; and to develop toys and games suitable for young people. With this ''discovery'' of childhood as a separate stage of life would come the social ''invention'' of motherhood, the definition of the woman as primarily responsible for the care and nurturance of children. Manuals written for confessors after the Council of Trent began to stress parents' duties to their children. Between 1578 and 1687, catechisms were revised to place increasing stress on love between parents and children. Similarly, love between husband and wife was admitted into the marriage sanctuary, first by the Puritans who were insistent that love was a prime duty, and later, in the eighteenth century, by members of the elite in France. Sex within marriage was seen to strengthen the conjugal bond.

It was in this period, too, for reasons debated by historians, that some men and women began to undertake conscious control of family size. The fact that in France and England after the mid-seventeenth century, the fertility rate of the upper classes fell below that of the lower—despite the better nutrition and earlier marriages of the former—suggests the appearance of new attitudes. Perhaps couples realized the financial drain of numerous progeny on the family economy that, among the upper classes, no longer was dependent on the offsprings' labor. Perhaps parents, admonished more than before to assure the wellbeing of individual children, recognized that economic resources stretched further for fewer people. Primarily by means of *coitus interruptus,* termed by indignant clergy and "populationists" the "new Onans," some couples began to place their material welfare above religious stricture. The poorer classes, however, continued to beget many offspring, though infant mortality, through natural causes, neglect, and infanticide, claimed fifty percent or more. If more survived than the family could feed or profitably put to work, excess children either died of malnutrition or left at an early age to live as servants or apprentices with another family.

Whatever the motive, birth control was of real benefit to women, who were burdened in former times with perpetual pregnancies. Alice Thornton, a seventeenth-century Englishwoman who, unlike the vast majority of all women before recent times, was able to write her autobiography, has left us a graphic portrayal of the significance of childbearing in a woman's life. Daughter of a high-ranking public official, Thornton married at the age of 24, stoically bore nine children (seven fewer than her sister) in eleven years and watched six of them die. She was continuously sick or suffering from pregnancy until she was widowed. Faced with an indebted estate and advised to marry an illiterate man "of indifferent parts or honesty," rather than struggle to administer it herself, she declined. Her countrywoman and contemporary, Jane Constable Josselin, married at 20 years to a country clergyman of comfortable estate, gave birth to ten children in 21 years, of whom five survived their parents. She also suffered three miscarriages. Since she weaned her infants between twelve and nineteen months, she was "with child" or nursing one almost continuously for more than two decades.[17] While Jane Josselin lived to be 82, such intensive childbearing would have consumed the entire adult life of a woman of average life expectancy—about 37 years in the seventeenth century. No wonder that the letters and diaries of Europe's well-off women increasingly contained references to their desire and endeavors to limit pregnancies. Let us stress that these efforts affected only a very small proportion of Europe's families in the early modern period, so small that family limitation did not yet show up in the aggregate demographic statistics of the European states.

Women's Work in the Peasant Household

For a majority of the common people in Europe, the family still functioned as it had earlier: as the basic economic unit of society. In preindustrial times individuals survived only as a part of a family economy to which everyone contributed labor. As Olwen Hufton shows, a few women might live in "spinster clusters" (convents and the like), pooling resources and skills, but most people of both sexes depended for food, clothing, and shelter on a household. Work typically was organized in the setting of the family—to be more exact, in the household— for household members included servants and apprentices along with husbands, wives, children, kinfolk, and friends.

It was once accepted without question that the preindustrial peasant household was a large, extended family embracing multiple generations that ensured stability and deference to age and gender hierarchies. It was only with the industrial revolution and urbanization in the nineteenth century, so the argument ran, that the lower-class family became "nuclear," composed solely of father, mother, and children. This interpretation, however, has been relegated in large measure to myth. Marriage, baptismal, and funeral records and early census data show that households of peasants, laborers, and poor people in reality were small, consisting of four to six persons on average throughout much of western Europe in preindustrial times. Multigenerational living was not typical. Yet, given the prevalence of servants in the past, a majority of the total population lived in much larger households than the average size. For example, in Kent, England, in 1676 the small households of tradesmen, laborers, and the poor accounted for a majority of dwellings but only one-third of the population. Two-thirds of the population lived in more complex households of better-off yeomen and gentry. The higher the social status of the head of household, the greater the numbers under his roof. Furthermore, counting persons does not tell anything about relationships among family members and peer groups or about their ties to kin outside the place of residence. Finally, the once prevailing simplistic image of family evolution from extended to nuclear has been shattered by other evidence. It is only with improved longevity in the nineteenth and twentieth centuries that demographic conditions have become more favorable to the existence of multigenerational families. Multigenerational living has become relatively more prevalent in industrial societies.[18] These debates aside, it is incontrovertible that the labor of each member of the peasant household was indispensable for the survival of the whole; and the birth of too many children or the death of either spouse put intolerable strain on the family economy.

The vast majority of people in the early modern period were peasants, tilling the land or caring for livestock and eking out a bare subsistence, producing essential foodstuffs, clothing, a roof to cover their heads, and securing fuel. In western Europe, peasants were free as to their persons, although the land they tilled was encumbered with rents, dues, and labor services—vestiges of the older feudal system. In eastern Europe, popularly demarcated by the Elbe River that ran through Prussia, and Russia, most peasants were serfs, obliged to provide labor services to the lord. They could neither work outside the lord's estate nor marry without his consent. Early modern society was divided into estates or orders, legal categories that assigned rights and obligations. A person's legal status was determined at birth. Peasants were the largest social group—well over 85 percent of the total population of most countries of Europe—and had the fewest rights. The social historian Pierre Goubert captures well the rhythm of rural life in France.

> Inside France there was a small annual movement of servant-girls, apprentices, and once more adventurers from country to town, the migrations of some tens of thousands of beggars, and a small number of soldiers. . . . [Most] people remained bound to the land, plot, hut, cottage, or *quartier* [neighborhood] where they grew up. Old France is characterized not by unrest, social mobility, and popular migration, but by sedentariness. Except for the perennial adventurers, people only became mobile when driven by necessity, which usually meant destitution.[19]

Women's productive work was extensive in this preindustrial world. In the countryside they might be seen caring for dairy animals and poultry, planting and tending the garden, and on occasion even hoeing and threshing, the latter two tasks generally regarded as men's work. They procured, processed, preserved, and prepared the family's food and took action—sometimes direct action through riot—if bad harvests, inflated prices or other forces threatened their subsistence. The first responsibility of married women was to feed household members. For the most part, they produced goods for the family's immediate use rather than for exchange—although it was typically women who marketed eggs, vegetables, and other surplus foodstuffs and brought into the peasant economy the little cash it had. Women regularly made butter, cheese, and bread and brewed beer as well. After food production their most urgent duty was garmentmaking, manufacturing items of clothing for the entire household. They spun yarn and wove coarse cloth for linens as well as clothing, made soap, washed, bleached, and dyed fabric, gathered feathers to make pillows, and managed their small enterprise and its family labor force. Work in the households of the more wealthy peasants, those who had property, was typically sex- as well as age-specific. There was men's work and there was women's work, adult work and children's work; but only together could the household economy manage to survive.

Women, the Guilds, and the Urban Economy

In urban settings, women also produced many of the goods that the family used on a daily basis. In addition, as wives and daughters of guildsmen, they participated in the processes of goods manufacture and they often supervised the work of apprentices and journeymen, too. Much of the daily organizing and running of the shops fell to them. So time-consuming and disruptive to their daily routine was the care of infants that they regularly employed wet nurses. Wet-nursing was common practice from the sixteenth through the nineteenth centuries; gradually, with urbanization, a separate occupation—called in France, *meneur*, the intermediary—emerged to facilitate the exchange of infants and arrange that urban babies be sent out to the countryside to peasant women who also had recently given birth. At earlier times, the practice of turning their infants over to nursemaids was largely confined to upper-class women who wanted to free themselves for court life and aristocratic entertainment. Now the growth of the urban middle classes created a new market for women of meager means but with a "full breast of milk." The rural bourgeoisie also often placed their children with wet nurses. By the mid-nineteenth century, the commerce in infants had increased so much that a wet-nursing "business" and a government bureau, handling tens of thousands of exchanges, developed in France. The social and economic reasons for this great demand will be discussed in Part II.

In the early modern period, religious views on the purposes of marriage also played a role in the promotion of wet-nursing. As long as sexual attraction and physical love were not primary motives for marriage, and sexual intercourse served (ideally at least) only the purpose of procreation, the sanction against sex during lactation could be maintained. Since it was commonly-accepted medical wisdom that sexual arousal of a nursing mother ruined her milk, and that pregnancy dried her breasts, intercourse was frowned on until the suckling was weaned, usually a period of one or two years. As the sexual bond between marital partners loomed larger among the ideal purposes of marriage, a conflict arose between the needs of parents and infants. According to the historian Lawrence Stone, "moral theologians, with their concern for holy matrimony and the avoidance of 'unnatural practices' and of adultery, were forced to choose between advising the resumption of sexual relations with a nursing mother, thus endangering the life of the child; or forbidding it, thus risking adultery by the sex-starved husband. When in doubt, they tended to prefer the former." Wet nurses were the natural beneficiaries of this shift in sentiment. Wet-nursing continued to be condemned by the fledgling medical community (it was feared the child would imbibe the mental and moral characteristics of the nurse, and mothers were warned particularly against employing red-headed nurses), but it flourished because it met crucial economic and emotional needs. Yet death rates among infants put out to nurse were extremely high: 90 percent among foundlings in Rouen in the late eighteenth century, compared to 38.1 percent of the merely indigent. Nursed by their mothers, only 18.7 percent perished. Wet-nursing thus helps account for the extremely high infant mortality rate in urban centers in the early modern period.

The evolving market economy that was stimulating large-scale production for export while boosting the wet-nursing business, placed barriers on women's chances to be independent entrepreneurs or artisans. Increasing reliance on private property, and the growing use of cash and credit disadvantaged women, who were losing legal control over money and property. Capitalist advances meant a shift in the nature and character of women's work. At one time, in the heyday of the medieval commune and guild production, women had been admitted as master craftsmen. Not all guilds did so, apparently, but thirteenth-century Paris had eighty mixed craft guilds of men and women and fifteen female-dominated guilds for such trades as dressmaking, gold thread, yarn, and silk manufacture. Central European guild statutes mentioned female participants in the thirteenth century. A policy of admitting women to a variety of nonagricultural occupations was compatible with a society that needed to use fully the productive capacities of all of its members. But increasingly, as commercial capitalism expanded, merchant-capitalists had sufficient funds to stimulate production outside of and in competition with the guilds. Guilds responded by restricting their own membership and removing women from independent artisanship. Merry Wiesner (Chapter 2) provides in rich detail an example of this process and of other changes affecting women in the urban economy between 1500 and 1650.

By the seventeenth century, in urban centers of Europe it had become more and more difficult for women to work as artisans in their own right. Furthermore, men tended to monopolize the lucrative urban export industries. For example, when watchmaking became a successful export craft in Geneva, guild statutes changed and prohibited masters from teaching the skills to any woman, including their own wives and daughters. Silk manufacturing in Lyons was arranged as "free labor," that is, outside guild monopoly, and until 1561 access to the occupation had been unrestricted. At that time, however, the market began to look uncertain and about "158 merchants and masters engaged in various kinds of silkmaking met before a notary to set up 'good order' among them, prevent 'ruin,' and 'obviate disturbance, debates, and disputes.' " They limited the number of male apprentices to two per master and eliminated women apprentices altogether. Even in spinning, that female art par excellence, men began to replace women as masters. In Rouen, in the late eighteenth century, a new government policy of fiscalization—the selling of patents by the crown—replaced the traditional practice that permitted women to transfer guild membership to their children and thus to maintain control of the industry. Increasingly, women heads of shops gave way to better-financed men.[20]

If women lost out as independent producers they nonetheless continued to facilitate day-to-day economic exchanges in the cities. The local market was filled with licensed stands run by women. In Nuremberg, for example, they sold citrus fruits which came from southern Italy, spices from the Orient, and salted fish from Scandinavia.[21] Clearly, the local urban economy still relied heavily on women.

Protoindustrialization and Women's Work

Similarly, rural home or cottage manufacture for export rested on women's labor contributions. In the sixteenth and seventeenth centuries in western and central Europe, manufacture of goods for distant markets mushroomed in the countryside when urban guilds no longer could meet the demand for their products. Extending beyond the urban setting described by Wiesner (Chapter 2), this was *rural* manufacture or "protoindustry," as it is now called. This activity was based on hand technology and it predated both mechanization and factory production. That the work took place outside the jurisdiction of the guilds was a distinct advantage to women because, as we have just seen, guilds increasingly curtailed female labor.

In the countryside extending from Flanders, Normandy, the Rhineland, and Bavaria to the Saxon-Bohemian borderland, Silesia, and the Zurich uplands, a wide range of products such as yarn, cloth, nails, and scythes, as well as pins, pots, and clogs came to be made in rural households. Production was organized by commercial capitalists who provided the workers with the raw materials and undertook to sell the finished goods, but the manufacturing itself was dispersed over thousands of workers' homes (cottage industry). In this household setting men and women made their livelihood combining industrial and agricultural activities. In the course of time the income from cottage production became not just supplemental but essential to the survival of the rural homestead.

The spread of industry in the countryside drew the households into a distinct sociocultural world. New social rules came to influence inheritance patterns, fertility rates, and family formation as well as gender work roles. Prior to the appearance of rural industry, a peasant with several sons customarily left his lands to only one and the others remained single or sought their livelihood elsewhere. But listen to the calculations of a villager recorded in 1792 in the Zurich uplands after the advent of weaving and spinning in the area.

I [might] have three or four sons, and [now] each will get some meadowland, at
least one cow, a small amount of arable land, etc. This should yield some good
things to help see the household through and working the small plot would leave
enough time to provide the rest from industrial wages. It is enough even if one
has but a small corner to set up a spinning rod and loom and space for a little
garden to grow vegetables.[22]

In this way, rural industry altered the rules by which families were formed and
helped to fragment landholding. As owners of small cottages, sons and daughters
of peasants and former day or migrant laborers could marry and start their own
families. In areas of protoindustry, the incidence of marriage was high and couples married earlier than was true among the peasantries. Populations became
exceptionally dense. In addition, in this rural household setting, men and women
shared productive tasks and, in contrast to the peasant family economy, work
patterns broke the bonds of gender role divisions.

At the present stage of research into protoindustrial work it is difficult to generalize about the extent of job sharing among men and women in cottage industry.
The French plateau of Normandy—the pays de Caux—offers one example. There
spinning and weaving were introduced into the countryside in the early eighteenth
century. The growth of cottage textile work initially did not signify a major change
in the sexual or seasonal division of labor, at least when seen from the perspective
of an individual's primary occupation. It did, however, open up new supplemen-
tary employment opportunities for villagers. Men and women worked the fields
during the harvest time, and women went into spinning yarn and men into weaving cloth during the rest of the year. Traditionally in the region, spinning had been
considered women's work and weaving men's work and sex-typing of tasks continued through most of the eighteenth century. The sex division of labor loosened
at the end of the century because of the growing demand for weavers, which male
labor could not meet because of the continuing demand in agriculture, crafts, and
merchant trades. At that point, women went into weaving as well as agricultural
day labor (which also began to require more hands), and the former two male
occupations became sexually integrated.[23]

By contrast, evidence from the Rhineland and the Saxon Oberlausitz reveals a
relative absence of division of labor by sex in protoindustrial households engaged
in weaving. In central Europe, it is clear that the fusing of industrial activities and
subsistence farming within a single residence forced its members to forego tradition and seek out flexible social alternatives. Within the weaving household, jobs
tended to be fluid and exchangeable and not gender- or age-specific. At times,
adult male weavers engaged in so-called "children's work," winding the bobbins
(spools for yarn) along with young children present in the household; at other
times, they commissioned an adult neighbor. Wives might prepare the warp but
so would husbands, and often husband and wife wove on one piece alternately.
The means of production for these family operations were contributed by both
partners as part of their marriage agreement. Alarmed middle-class commentators
traveling in protoindustrial areas of the Rhineland described a world that in their
eyes was topsy-turvy. Men were seen "cooking, cleaning, and sweeping" when

their wives were busy meeting work orders.[24] These industrial households were integrated into the market economy and from the start worked for cash. Cash income was increased when both partners wove and family members probably thought of time as money. To save time, they readily helped one another out by sharing the nonpaid labor tasks as well. Shared work in weaving stands in contrast to agriculture, where complexity led to a gender-based division of labor.

Professionalization and Women's Work

Protoindustry flourished outside guild control and the states of Europe had not yet begun to regulate the world of work as they would later by restricting child and female labor, by establishing a maximum work day, or by determining minimum health and safety standards. In the absence of regulation, women could assume productive roles equal to those of men. It was when work was publicly controlled—whether by specifying the various steps in apprenticeship training or by requiring secondary and university education for professional opportunities—that women were placed at a distinct disadvantage.

An examination of changes affecting the job of midwife is illustrative. This important female occupation was transformed in the early modern period because of new professional standards that were increasingly attached to medicine. Professionalization was achieved at the price of first, bypassing, and later, outlawing women, who once had been centrally involved in the healing process. The desire of physicians, surgeons, and apothecaries to monopolize the new science of medicine coincided with the objective of government officials to oversee the study of medicine so as to check witchcraft. In London as early as the time of Henry VIII for example, anyone discovered practicing medicine without proper training or licensing might be declared a witch. Because of the long-standing beliefs in women's irrationality and inferiority, the schools of medicine and anatomy were closed to them.

The disadvantages of not obtaining the latest scientific knowledge were recognized by several mid-seventeenth century Englishwomen, who tried to extend training to midwives. Jane Sharp, for one, wrote a manual entitled *Complete Midwife's Companion; or, The Art of Midwifery Improved* (1671), in which she translated and made available to English readers many new practices and ideas from France, Holland, and Italy; these she combined with her own considerable experience of forty years. Sharp defended the long-standing practice of midwifery by women and admitted only one deficiency. Women were having trouble obtaining "Knowledge of Things as Men may, who are bred up in Universities . . . where Anatomy Lectures being frequently read, the situation of the Parts of both Men and Women, and other things of great Consequence are often made plain to them."[25] Her book was designed to rectify the shortcoming. In 1687, as a preliminary step to making scientific training available to women, Elizabeth Cellier petitioned the king to form a midwives' "corporation," to be run by the "most able and matron-like woman among them." Her goal remained unrealized and by the end of the century the trend was irreversible: male midwives and later doctors of obstetrics took over the services needed at birth and the birthing chair gave way to the delivery table. Already in the seventeenth century, people were enamored with science and were impressed with the doctors' aura, training, and technical vocabulary. Wealthy families showed distinct preference for educated male midwives; they cost more and conferred status on the families that could afford them. Doctors took advantage of their monopoly over learning. Hugh Chamberlain, for example, in his midwife's manual pointed out that "it [cannot] be so great a discredit to a Midwife . . . to have a Woman or Child saved by a Man's assistance, as to suffer either to die under her own hand." But it took several more centuries at least for the benefits of science to outweigh completely those of tradition. In hospitals, women attended by doctors died of infection more frequently than those served by midwives. Only in the mid-nineteenth century did the Austrian physician Ignaz Semmelweis diagnose the causes of puerperal fever and require doctors, who also treated the ill, to wash their hands in chlorinated lime before each pelvic examination and birth of a child.

The Scientific Revolution and Renewed "Arguments about Women"

The "Argument about Women" became an important subject of public debate in the seventeenth century. As Maryanne Horowitz shows (Chapter 4), debates among embryologists about women's formative role in conception were part of the scientific revolution. Accurate understanding of female biology, however, was long delayed by the tenacity of inherited ideas. Ironically, at the very time when new microscopic studies began to reveal women's equally active contribution to the embryological process, male medical practitioners were taking control of its conclusion, childbirth. Nonetheless, like Jane Sharp and Elizabeth Cellier, who tried to use medical science to benefit women, a group of well-born Englishwomen in the mid-seventeenth century turned the age's commitment to reason and critical thinking to their own advantage. In the process, they carried the pro-woman tradition one step further. Their ranks included the Quaker Margaret Fell Fox (1614–1702), the philosophers Anne Conway and Margaret Cavendish, the Duchess of Newcastle (1623–1673), and Mary Astell, the "first self-avowed sustained feminist polemicist in English."

These activists and scholars differed from the earlier "feminist" writers and thinkers. They thought of women as a group and thus were less inclined to hail the exploits of exceptional individuals. Through their own work, they sought to demonstrate the intellectual potential of the female sex as a whole. They adopted for much of their intellectual ammunition the ideas and methods of the great French philosopher and mathematician, René Descartes (1596–1650). Often called the father of modern philosophy because he freed philosophical thought from the confines of medieval scholasticism, Descartes's method rested on doubt and rejection of all accepted ideas and opinions. His first rule was never to accept anything as true which was not clearly and distinctly seen to be so. His followers were known as Cartesians.

Mary Astell, a devoted Cartesian who was deeply religious as well, began her inquiry by doubting all knowledge except that of a perfect God. Like Descartes, she then established human existence by unfolding each step that demonstrated God's plan on earth. Using reason and rational argument, she "proved" how custom and inherited prejudice interfered with women's chances to employ and develop their God-given rational capabilities. Astell recognized that women were in a terrible bind. They were kept ignorant and their ignorance was used to dismiss efforts to improve their training. Her fundamental insight has been the foundation of recurring waves of feminism: the nature and behavior of the female sex are not something "natural" but products of conditioning and environment. Women's defects, Astell felt, grew out of faulty early education, which subsequently exercised a powerful influence over the course of their lives. To reverse this situation she developed a rigorous program of study that owed its inspiration to Descartes and to the epistemology of the influential British philosopher of liberalism, John Locke (1632–1704). Unlike most of her predecessors who had addressed the question of educational reform for women, she did not prescribe a series of books for women to read but emphasized method—how to think critically and how, in the search for truth, to move from the simple and sure to the complex and problematic. She called for a secular religious vocation through higher education for spinsters, women like herself who chose not to marry.

The "Argument about Women" also took on new significance in France and became a cultural metaphor for advocacy of social as well as political change. The cause of women henceforth was often linked with movement for fundamental reordering of society. In France, in the early seventeenth century, a new nobility had been created by the monarch, who sold public offices that were passed on as family property to the next generation. These men and women were called the *noblesse de robe* (nobility of the office, literally, of dress) and their presence in French upper society was regarded with hostility by the older titular nobility, the *noblesse d'épée* (nobility of the sword). While the new nobility was resented by the old, special criticism was directed at the social gatherings of men—and women— of unequal position in salons in Paris and other urban centers in the first half of the century. Salons were organized, run, and directed by women related to the new nobility who set the standards of proper behavior, values, and manners for aristocratic society, and brought together writers and their patrons and other members of the elite. As the old and new elites met in the salons, many people brought into question, through example as well as discussion, the proper stratification of French society. The controversy often centered on the public role that women had assumed in overseeing salon life, for women were the real light of the salon. A highly successful Parisian gathering of the mid-eighteenth century was orchestrated by Madame de Boufflers "with her brisk manner, at once jaunty and imposing, her epigrams, the originality of her judgments, her authority on conduct, and the talent of her taste. She threw open her house to pleasure, earnestness, novelty, letters. . . ."[26] Those who accepted this role for women also favored a more open society—ennoblements for wealth, intermarriage among the two elites, and a more flexible social hierarchy.

In the debate of the day, these advocates of change are known in history as the Moderns. In contrast, the opponents of women's roles in salon life (known as the Ancients or Traditionalists) sought to restrict the entry of wealthy upstarts into the social elite and to keep it small and homogeneous. In seventeenth-century France, The Moderns included a variety of women and men: Marie Gournay, François Poulain de la Barre, Michel de Pure, Jocquette Guillaume. They took it as their task both to defend the women of the salons and to argue vigorously against other aspects of custom, tradition, and religious authority. They advocated a whole new foundation for marriage which they labeled, in its present form an ''institution of slavery,'' claiming for well-born women as for aristocratic men a choice of whether or not to marry and a chance for those wed for political or social reasons to find affection and meaningful companionship outside of marriage. In some cases, they chose as a model England, where ladies termed ''bluestockings'' had emerged as cultural leaders, praising the apparent greater freedom of movement and of marriage enjoyed by English women—and men. The ''companionate marriage'' among Puritan business classes seemed to promise greater happiness. In any case it served fewer economic and political purposes than the alliances of earlier ages.

The Traditionalists who opposed women's public roles sometimes shunned salon life altogether; they preferred all-male literary gatherings. Their ranks included several abbés, doctors at the Sorbonne, and lawyers, as well as the well-known philosopher and advocate of aristocratic reform, François Fénelon. Fénelon's views, particularly his treatise on education entitled *The Education of Girls* (1687), illustrate well the underlying motives of these men. He constructed an educational program that would not promote aristocratic women's participation in salon life. It purposely failed to include the requisite social and intellectual tools needed to run a salon. Thus, Fénelon excluded humanistic study because of its orientation toward the civic life and public leadership roles, which he considered inappropriate for women. But he also bypassed much literature—comedies, novels, books on the art of proper conversation, classical mythology, and poetry. The ideas in these works would turn girls' attention away from their important domestic functions. ''All is lost,'' he warned, ''if your daughter becomes infatuated with *bel esprit* and disgusted with domestic cares.''[27]

Fénelon did not stop with his objection to women's prominence in the urban salons and at the French court at Versailles. Embedded in his protest was deep concern with the successes of monarchical absolutism and centralization in France and the fact that the nobility spent its days in endless pursuit of luxury, prestige, and empty power at the Bourbon court. Fénelon saw proper education for girls as a means to regenerate the titular aristocracy and keep it pure. He planned to revitalize the old nobility's domestic and agricultural life in the provinces by turning the aristocratic girl into a competent wife and mother who could oversee the family estate and manage family life. Girls were to learn bookkeeping, the demands of agricultural labor, the local customs and laws of their lands, as well as the more standard domestic arts of sewing, cooking, and supervising servants.

In France, then, the ''Argument about Women'' emerged as a key issue of controversy because the social structure was being strained by economic changes, the spread of wealth to merchants and professional people, and their subsequent legal ennoblement. The debate harks back to the old *Querelle* over women's roles that Christine de Pisan had launched in the fifteenth century. That it reemerged so centrally in seventeenth-century France reveals how alterations in the social structure created an intellectual climate in which social and sexual relationships needed to be redefined.

Political Liberalism and the Status of Women

A similar reassessment of the foundation of political authority took place across the Channel. Between 1640 and 1660, England had experienced a disastrous civil war over the question of the king's rights as against the prerogatives of the people's representative, Parliament. We have already seen how the efforts by Europe's kings and princes to centralize authority elicited considerable political dissatisfaction that helped to shape the Reformation crisis. This conflict accounted, too, for the *Fronde* in France (a mid-seventeenth-century aristocratic uprising after the death of Louis XIII), for Fénelon's backward-looking critique, and for the English civil war. The war itself and the Restoration that followed in England generated heated discussion over the basis of legitimate authority, in the course of which the liberal political theory of natural rights was formulated. This theory became the ideological basis for the later American and French Revolutions. Curiously, the royalists and the parliamentarians argued the issue partly by analogy with the marriage bond. In time, the arguments developed around the example of marriage were elevated to independent principles and became the basis of the liberal position on marriage and female equality.

Contractual thinking had become widely popular in British political thought, so that both royalists and parliamentarians spoke in contractual terms. Royalists believed they had found the ideal defense of kingly authority in drawing an analogy with the marriage contract. Marriage, they said, was a contract that created an unequal relationship between the two consenting parties. Both the man and the woman freely entered into marriage but God had established the husband's rule over his wife, and consent, once given, was irrevocable. As the royalist Dudley Digges developed it, drawing on scripture and a reading of family behavior, "There is a contract between Husband and Wife, the violation of which on the man's part doth not bereave him of his dominion over the woman." Similarly, once men freely had joined together to form a monarchy, royal authority was as fixed as that of husbands and there was no right of rebellion.

Parliamentarians were forced to debate the royalist conception of marriage in making their case. Initially, they took advantage of the right of divorce, which we have seen was recognized by both Luther and Calvin in specific cases. If God had provided the remedy of separation in establishing marriage, so, too, he must have provided the remedy of resistance in creating government. But it was John Locke who advanced the liberal argument by abandoning scripture altogether in favor of natural law theory. As Locke stated it, if all beings were free and equal in the state of nature, then when they agreed to marry they were free to set whatever terms to their relationship they wished as long as they met the needs of child care, which Locke posited as the only natural requirement of marriage. Conjugal society, he believed, was created by "a voluntary Compact between Man and Woman"; marriage, thus, did not mean consenting to pre-existing rules and rights. Couples who agreed to marry could set some of the terms of their relationship. "Community of Goods and the Power over them, mutual Assistance, and Maintenance, and other things belonging to Conjugal Society might be varied and regulated by that Contract, which unites Man and Woman in that Society, as far as may be consistent with Procreation and the bringing up of Children. . . ."[28] Locke went even further and argued that the contract could be terminated. The concept of natural rights introduced the novel proposition of limited authority into Western thought.

As we have seen, the seventeenth century was an innovative period. The scientific discoveries and philosophical propositions of great thinkers like John Locke and René Descartes, as well as those of the physicist and mathematician Sir Isaac Newton and the scientist and essayist Francis Bacon, transformed the understanding of the physical and human world. The age saw significant advances in scientific methods of inquiry, in the development of new theories of knowledge, and in the emergence of the school of natural law. These developments added up to an intellectual revolution that challenged the inherited world view of Aristotle, the classical writers, and the scholastics, and constructed a new one in its place. It was left to the next century, the Age of Enlightenment, to popularize these theories and apply them to human society.

For the position of women at the threshold of the industrial age, however, the legacy of the seventeenth-century intellectual revolution was ambiguous. The philosophy of natural rights—the proposition that all men (and women) are free and equal in the state of nature—was potentially liberating. To be sure, it took time to extend these rights to women, but in England, France, and America, where political liberalism triumphed, women had a ready-made argument for equality. They also could appeal to the Lockean view of marriage in expanding the rights of the married woman. As we will see in Parts II and III, however, it would be difficult for women to appropriate this liberal version of individual autonomy in light of what was increasingly seen as their proper role in society—as mothers, responsible for the home and for safeguarding family and collective values. Women were regarded primarily as social beings, not as individuals. Indeed, the realm of individual action could only exist in the presence of a realm of social support offered largely by women (and male servants). In addition, the two realms—the individual and the social—were recast by political liberalism, which distinguished between the worlds of civic and family life to a much greater extent than was true in early modern political theory. The liberal notions rested on the idea of two separate spheres: the public and the private. In the course of time, each sex would be assigned, ideally, to a different sphere. Locke had rejected the older belief that the family was analogous to civil society and that the basis of authority in one realm was, by extension, the same in the other. Locke knew clearly what was meant by political power—that of a magistrate over a subject—and it was different from the father's authority over his children, or the husband's over his wife. A political ruler was not the same as a father in the family or a captain of a ship. The family was a private institution in liberal political thinking, preceding civil society. It was a haven and the state had no right to intrude into its affairs. In addition, the new definition of citizen that political liberalism advanced worked to women's disadvantage (and also to lower-class men's) because ownership of property became the foundation of political participation in the liberal state. Birth, status, dynastic or family ties and privileges—all important in previous eras—no longer automatically conferred political rights. As Locke wrote in the *Second Treatise of Government*, property alone was the basis of the exercise of citizenship. Government was the creation not of all people in an area but of all landowners, who banded together to protect their property. "Man's" natural rights were to life, liberty, and property—and women were excluded from ownership of property and, thus, from participation in the new state constructed on the basis of citizenship.

These theoretical formulations of *political liberalism* constituted a new context for women's efforts to become part of the political community in the West, which we will develop in the overview section of Part II. We will also see the wide-ranging social transformations that accompanied its corollary, *economic liberalism*. The workings of history are never simple. While philosophers debated the nature of human existence, the structure of their ideal state, and the "natural" role of women, economic forces set in motion by commercial capitalism began to erode the bases of traditional society, including hierarchies of age, class, and sex. Ultimately, massive disjunctures between the old and new, the ideal and the real, led from an "age of reason" to an "age of revolution." While many women, and their daughters and granddaughters as well, continued to spend their lives doing traditional "women's work," others faced new possibilities and new vulnerabilities.

NOTES

1. In Joan Kelly, "Early Feminist Theory and the *Querelle des Femmes,* 1400–1789," *Signs* 8, no. 1 (1982): 21.

2. *Ibid.,* p. 13.

3. In Ian Maclean, *The Renaissance Notion of Woman: A Study in the Fortunes of Scholasticism and Medical Science in European Intellectual Life* (Cambridge, 1980), p. 92.

4. *Ibid.,* pp. 8, 9.

5. Nancy L. Roelker, "The Appeal of Calvinism to French Noblewomen in the Sixteenth Century, *Journal of Interdisciplinary History* 11, no. 4 (Spring 1972): 404.

6. In J. O'Faolain and L. Martines, eds., *Not in God's Image: Women in History from the Greeks to the Victorians* (New York, 1973), p. 182.

7. For More, see Lawrence Stone, *The Family, Sex and Marriage in England 1500–1800,* abr. ed. (New York, 1979), p. 142.

8. Natalie Z. Davis, "City Women and Religious Change," in her *Society and Culture in Early Modern France* (Stanford, 1975), pp. 65–95.

9. Judith C. Brown, *Immodest Acts: The Life of a Lesbian Nun in Renaissance Italy* (New York, 1986).

10. E. William Monter, "Women in Calvinist Geneva (1550–1800)," *Signs* 6, no. 2 (1980): 191–193; Susan C. Karant-Nunn, "Continuity and Change: Some Effects of the Reformation on the Women of Zwickau," *Sixteenth Century Journal* XII, no. 2 (1982): 21–26; and Mary Elizabeth Perry, "Deviant Insiders: Legalized Prostitutes and a Con-

sciousness of Women in Early Modern Seville,'' *Comparative Studies in Society and History* 27, no. 1 (January 1985): 138–158.

11. In Karant-Nunn, ''Continuity and Change,'' p. 39.

12. The following discussion of witchcraft draws heavily on the innovative study by Christina Larner, *Enemies of God: The Witch-hunt in Scotland* (London, 1981).

13. Alfred Soman, ''The Parlement of Paris and the Great Witch Hunt (1565–1640),'' *Sixteenth Century Journal* IX, no. 2 (1978): 31–44. For James VI, Larner, *Enemies of God*, p. 93.

14. Jean-Louis Flandrin, *Families in Former Times: Kinship, Household, and Sexuality* (Cambridge, 1979), p. 118; also Stone, *The Family, Sex and Marriage*, p. 138.

15. ''Modern Reports of Select Cases Adjudged in the Court,'' in O'Faolain and Martines, *Not in God's Image*, p. 232.

16. Philippe Ariès, *Centuries of Childhood: A Social History of Family Life*, tr. by Robert Baldick (New York, 1962), p. 110.

17. ''From the Autobiography of Mrs. Alice Thorton,'' in Joan Goulianos, ed., *By a Woman Writt* (Baltimore, 1974), pp. 30–53; Alan Macfarlane, *The Family Life of Ralph Josselin* (New York, 1970), pp. 81–91; 199–204.

18. On the evolution of the family, see John R. Gillis, *For Better, For Worse: British Marriages, 1600 to the Present* (New York, 1985) and Michael Mitterauer and Reinhard Sieder, *The European Family: Patriarchy to Partnership from the Middle Ages to the Present*, tr. by Karla Oosterveen and Manfred Hörzinger (Chicago, 1982).

19. Pierre Goubert, *The Ancien Régime: French Society, 1600–1750*, tr. by Steve Cox (New York, 1973), p. 43.

20. Monter, ''Women in Calvinist Geneva,'' p. 203; Natalie Z. Davis, ''Women in the Crafts in Sixteenth-Century Lyon,'' *Feminist Studies* 8, no. 1 (Spring 1982): 68; Daryl M. Hafter, ''Power vs. Privilege: A Case Study of the Spinners' Guild in Eighteenth Century Rouen,'' paper presented to the Social Science History Association (Bloomington, IN, November 1982).

21. Merry E. Wiesner, ''Paltry Peddlers or Essential Merchants? Women in the Distributive Trades in Early Modern Nuremberg,'' *Sixteenth Century Journal* XII, no. 2 (1981): 3–13.

22. Rudolf Braun, *Industrialisierung und Volksleben* [Industrialization and Everyday Life] (Erlenbach-Zürich, 1960), pp. 60–61.

23. Gay Gullickson, ''The Sexual Division of Labor in Cottage Industry and Agriculture in the Pays de Caux: Auffay, 1750–1850, *French Historical Studies* 12, no. 2 (Fall, 1981): 177–199.

24. Douglas R. Holmes and Jean H. Quataert, ''An Approach to Modern Labor: Worker Peasantries in Historic Saxony and the Friuli Region over Three Centuries,'' *Comparative Studies in Society and History* 28, no. 2 (April 1986): 191–216; also, Jean H. Quataert, ''Combining Agrarian and Industrial Livelihoods: Rural Households in the Saxon Oberlausitz in the Nineteenth Century,'' *Journal of Family History* 10, no. 2 (Summer 1985): 145–162; Jean H. Quataert, ''The Shaping of Women's Work in Manufacturing: Guilds, Households, and the State in Central Europe, 1648–1870,'' *American Historical Review* 90, no. 5 (December 1985): 1122–1148.

25. Hilda L. Smith, *Reason's Disciples: Seventeenth Century English Feminists* (Urbana, IL, 1982), pp. 97–98; Alice Clark, *Working Life of Women in the Seventeenth Century* (New York, 1968), p. 274; Moira Ferguson, ed., *First Feminists: British Women Writers 1578–1799* (Bloomington, IN, 1985).

26. Edmond and Jules Goncourt, *The Woman of the Eighteenth Century* (New York, 1927), p. 43.

27. For the debate in France, we have used primarily Carolyn C. Lougee, *Le Paradis des Femmes: Women, Salons, and Social Stratification in Seventeenth-Century France* (Princeton, 1976).

28. Mary Lyndon Shanley, "Marriage Contract and Social Contract in Seventeenth-Century English Political Thought," *Western Political Quarterly* 32, no. 1 (March 1979): 80.

1

Family and State in Early Modern France: The Marriage Pact

Sarah Hanley

In the early modern period, the interests of the family and the state intersected in the public arena, where the family played an important political role. Through marriage alliances, inheritance practices, and patronage, family members exercised decisive power and influence in public life. Because these power networks were built through family alliances, parents increasingly demanded the right to determine marriage decisions of their offspring. The marriage act, however, was subject to the jurisdiction of the ecclesiastical courts of the Catholic church, which maintained that at least nominal consent of the couple was necessary for a valid marriage. A serious conflict arose when the family practiced coercion and the church held fast to the ecclesiastical principle of consent. As Sarah Hanley shows in this innovative study of early modern France, the balance in the struggle was tipped by the process of centralization, or state-building, that expanded secular jurisdiction over marriage arrangements. As members of potentially powerful families, jurists strengthened their own family networks by rewriting the laws governing marriage; in this case, family priorities coincided with those of the monarchical state. But the family is not an undifferentiated unit, and the laws promulgated between 1556 and 1639 effectively enhanced the power of men over the women and children in the family. Hanley offers five court cases, what she calls ''dreadful family dramas,'' which graphically reveal the sex-specific consequences that these legal changes wrought for women's lives. To be sure, while family patriarchs did not always move against female cohorts, they certainly had the legal power to do so. When women began to mobilize for women's rights several centuries later, these inequalities in marriage laws were among the earliest targets for elimination. Hanley bases this study on changes in the marriage laws and on court cases heard before the Parlement of Paris, the supreme court in France, where cases could be appealed from the ecclesiastical courts of the Catholic church. Her work illustrates the impact of political centralization on the personal lives of women.

In the history of Western civilization one institution has been transformed beyond recognition—the family. The social structure and function of the modern family (nineteenth through the twentieth centuries) bears little resemblance to that of its early modern counterpart (sixteenth through the eighteenth centuries), and the difference between the two types of units reflects varied stages in the development of the state. In the West, modern states are characterized politically by the separation of public (state) and private (individual) interests, and economically by sustained industrial growth, which supports large populations. Citizenship in a state underwrites the life chances of individuals by guaranteeing basic social services (education, social security, welfare, etc.); therefore, citizens collectively maintain the state bureaucracy over time. To the contrary, early modern monarchies were characterized politically by intertwined private–public (family–state) relations, and economically by subsistence economies which could support only small populations. Membership in a family provided the only means of human survival through networks of influence (marriage alliances, inheritance practices, patronage, and apprentice systems); consequently, relatives planned strategies to perpetuate, or reproduce, family lines across generations. The most pressing business of early modern times was the maintenance and extension of family networks, which were agencies of both social reproduction and economic production; and the negotiation of proper marriage alliances, critical to that endeavor, depended on effective parental authority. This essay traces the alliance of patriarchs and politicians for the express purpose of controlling the formation of marriage in France between 1556 and 1789.

In very early times, prior to the year 1000, the marriage act involved a secular legal contract negotiated by parents with little concern for the personal consent of either bride or groom. From around the year 1000, however, marriage gradually shifted from its secular base to one religious and ecclesiastical in orientation. Marriage became subject to the law of the Catholic church (canon law) and problems regulating it were judged in ecclesiastical (church) courts. During this shift from secular to ecclesiastical realms, the nature of the marriage contract also changed. Whereas the earlier secular legal contract was coercive, that is, it did not consider the consent of the couple, the new ecclesiastical marriage act, subject to canon law, came to require at least nominal consent. This change of tenor from coercion to consent reflected general concern over mounting cases of marriage litigation in ecclesiastical courts. Besieged with requests for annulments and separations, many of them brought on behalf of women, troubled canon lawyers sought remedies. Around the year 1140 the lawyer Gratian (in his *Decretum*) posed the thorny question, "May a daughter be given in marriage against her will?" and answered in the negative based on the opinion that "A father's oath [in the contract] cannot compel a girl to marry one to whom she has not assented." In his argument Gratian alluded to a psychological factor in the making of a marriage. "Consent makes a marriage," he said, because of the "marital affection" involved between two people. Neither the church nor a feudal lord nor a family could supply that element of affection, so there could be no proper marriage when consent was absent. Gratian's argument was innovative, because it undermined the traditional teachings of the Old Testament [*Deuteronomy* 22:16], the early church fathers, popes, and other received sources. By introducing the notion of individual consent or choice into canon law, Gratian's rubric challenged parental authority: nominally, at least, children might refuse the commands of parents in contracting marriage. In the wake of that challenge, a contest developed between two institutions for control over the connubial fate of children—the church (as the guarantor of choice) and the family (as the agent of coercion).

Between the twelfth and fifteenth centuries the contestants effected an uneasy balance of power: the church supported the precept of consent in marriage, but the family, eminent in its own domain, often ignored the directive. Over the next two centuries, however, this balance of power was disrupted, and the scales tipped heavily to the side of parental authority. During the sixteenth, seventeenth, and eighteenth centuries family power overwhelmed church influence in marriage arrangements. How did the power of families to control marriages advance dramatically at the expense of church authority? The story is best told by reference to early modern France, where family and state closed ranks against women, children, and church between 1556 and 1789.

In early modern times, state-building required the support of a political–professional elite that was loyal to the monarch and capable of staffing administrative and judicial offices in the kingdom. That elite emerged in France during the sixteenth and seventeenth centuries from the ranks of the bourgeois gentlemen who were trained in the famous law schools. Participating in the peculiar French system of venality (sale of office), these legists purchased royal offices from the monarchy and then legalized the hereditary transmission of offices (as family property) to the next generation. The partnership proved mutually agreeable: through the sale of offices king and state obtained financial assistance and professional service; through the acquisition of hereditary rights, office-holders augmented family fortunes and prestige. This welding of public and private interests gave rise to a new *noblesse de robe* (nobility of the robe, named for their judicial gowns), which thenceforth vied for status with the old *noblesse d'épée* (nobility of the sword, named for their military garb). Following the tradition of French legal humanism, these learned and patriotic legists of the *noblesse de robe* guarded French public (i.e., constitutional) law and French private (i.e., civil) law against the encroachment of church prerogatives and canon law. Practicing as judges and councillors in the Parlement of Paris (a supreme court), they applied the law to specific cases, amended it on occasion, and shaped the law over time to suit their own priorities. Since the consolidation of familial networks headed the priority list, the question of parental authority loomed large. The political bargain struck between family and state placed the ultimate power over the formation of marriage in the hands of the family.

The terms of the bargain reflected the sociopolitical and sexual ideology propagated by leading jurists. In the 1550s Jean de Coras complained about the problem of clandestine marriage (made secretly without parental consent). He labeled those unions as "polluted conjunctions" that disturbed the public good. Supposedly based on individual free choice and mutual affection, they really were products of reckless human passion. Since such liaisons were against divine law, natural law, and human reason, French laws should be enacted to prevent them. In the 1580s Pierre Ayrault sounded the same note. He emphasized the separation of political and religious authority. God had divided his empire with Caesar, so popes had no right to interfere with public affairs in France. In fact, the "Sorbonnists" (canon lawyers and theologians at the University of Paris) were predators who allowed the church to steal children from mothers and fathers and ruin families in the process. The monarchical state should make its own laws to maintain families and disallow church interference. Others abhorred clandestine marriages that were conducted by Huguenot (Protestant) ministers. They viewed French law as the vehicle for assuring the public character of marriage in a time beset by religious strife. In the 1600s the jurists Barnabé Brisson, Jérôme Bignon, Pierre Séguier, and others followed suit. They too denied church cognizance over secular matters and placed marriage contracts under French civil jurisdiction. At stake here was the success or failure of state-building, which depended in some measure on the ability of the new *noblesse de robe* to form powerful family networks through marriage alliances.

At the international Council of Trent, the French delegates challenged church authority during the debates over marriage regulations. The French bishops repeatedly demanded that the church authorize parental control of marriage, but the other church prelates stood fast and denied that a valid marriage required parental consent. The church regulations governing marriage were quite minimal: first, they required the publication of banns announcing a marriage (in order to discover impediments, such as bigamy, incest, or *rapt* [abduction]); second, they required the presence of two witnesses (in order to prove the ritual took place). Actually the crux of the dispute between church and state lay in the definition of a clandestine marriage. For the church prelates the term "clandestine" signified a union that was invalid because it lacked requisite publicity (banns and witnesses); for the French legists the term signified a union that was invalid because it denied natural and legal propriety (parental consent). When the French delegates failed to reform marriage law at the Council of Trent, the legists at home picked up the standard in the courts.

To effect French hegemony over marriage law, the legists in the Parlement of Paris initiated a legislative reform movement that lasted for a century. Straightaway they promulgated laws against clandestine marriage; then they secured legal jurisdiction over disputed cases. At the outset, the discourse extolled the familial rights of mothers and fathers vis-à-vis children. The arguments of Coras and Ayrault raised philosophical and biblical standards of filial piety to sway opinion. Recounting the sighs, tears, and lamentations of parents who were perversely deceived by ingrates, they held that divine and natural law obliged children to honor mothers and fathers and that French law should follow suit. Evidently their colleagues agreed. In 1556 the Parlement of Paris registered a civil statute that overruled canon law. First, the statute decreed that persons who married without parental consent could be deprived of family support and disinherited. Second, it lengthened the age of minority (requiring parental consent) from 20 to 30 years for males, from 17 to 25 years for females. At the same time the Parlement registered a companion statute that forbade women to hide a pregnancy or to deliver a newborn baby secretly. Following this extraordinary statute women were required to declare a pregnancy officially and to birth a child before witnesses. Those who failed to do so and delivered a dead child, or said they delivered a dead child, would be charged with the crime of murder and punished by death as an example to others. That was not the end of it. In 1578 the Parlement registered the Ordinance of Blois which made the publication of marriage banns stricter, demanded the presence of four witnesses instead of two, and required the officiating priest to have proof of the ages of the couple and the consent of their parents. Even more draconian, the ordinance decreed that persons who married without parental approval (and their accomplices) would be charged with the crime of *rapt de violence* (forced abduction) or *rapt de séduction* (willing elopement), and worse, it declared the crime of *rapt* a capital offense punishable by death. Clearly, the new laws supported parental authority, not individual choice.

Toward the end of the century, the tone of this discourse struck a new note as the legists turned to strengthen paternal rights. The seventeenth-century shift of emphasis from parental authority to paternal power accompanied the move from legal theory to judicial practice. Whereas the earlier generations had promulgated the new marriage laws in the Parlement of Paris, the later ones actually prosecuted cases of *rapt* brought to the Parlements. Determined to punish transgressors, legists such as Bignon and Séguier invoked severe Roman law notions of paternal power *(paterfamilias)*, which strengthened the legal position of fathers at the expense of minors and women. According to Bignon and cohorts, families should be headed by authoritarian male figures who commanded obedience from children and wives. Since paternal authority proceeded directly from God, children and women (including widows and unmarried daughters) owed obedience to fathers and husbands. Disturbed by the rising number of *rapt* cases on the dockets, the later generation of legists closed remaining loopholes. In 1629 the Parlement of Paris registered the Code Michaud, which again expanded the definition of a minor (who must attain parental consent) to include widows age 25 and under, and decreed that priests could perform marriages only for known members of the parish who produced proof of parental consent. Finally, in 1639 the Parlement registered a decree that summarized all these provisions of 1556, 1578, and 1629, and added still others. This statute required parental consent (on pain of disinheritance) regardless of the age of the parties, making majority age irrelevant. Thus members of the older generation for their entire lifetimes could control members of the younger generation even into their middle age. In addition to promulgating legislation against clandestine marriage, the Parlement of Paris subjected marriage law to state jurisdiction.

Once the monarchical state created its own body of civil law on marriage, a clash between the state and church authority arose. Who had jurisdiction over these cases, the Parlements or the ecclesiastical courts? In fact, the judges in the Parlement of Paris steadily assumed jurisdictional supremacy through an appeal procedure, which allowed disputed decisions from ecclesiastical courts to be appealed in the Parlement of Paris. As the decades wore on the Parlements encroached at every opportunity. Marriage was a civil contract, not a religious one, the legists argued, because it involved transfers of family property (lands, valuables, offices) that were subject to the jurisdiction of Parlements. Furthermore, trials for the capital crime of *rapt* belonged in Parlements, because the crime in French law entailed the death penalty, which ecclesiastical courts could not impose. Although the Parlements rarely invoked the death penalty for cases of *rapt,* preferring to levy fines, the ingenious inclusion of capital punishment automatically placed such cases in their bailiwick. Indeed, the crime of *rapt* came to be regarded as a kind of treason against family and state. In the early seventeenth century the supremacy of Parlements over church courts was sealed when the French clergy finally acquiesced to the change of venue. In a decree of 1634, the Parlement of Paris directly assumed judicial competence over marriage arrangements, and the French Assembly of the Clergy, when polled by the king, concurred. All along the French prelates, caught between two masters, played a waiting game. Many of them belonged to the same families as the legists and shared in common family strategies and patriotic sentiments.

French laws governing the formation of marriage had come to reflect the sociopolitical and sexual ideology of the *noblesse de robe* and its supporters. Clandestine marriage was outlawed and punished. A binding marriage required public notice and parental, that is, paternal consent; nonconformists (regardless of age) could be excised from the family unit and disinherited, which jeopardized chances for survival; and they could be prosecuted in the Parlement for the crime of *rapt.* Furthermore, the concealment of a pregnancy or the delivery of a child in secret was enough to convict a woman of murder if that child were born dead. Illicit sexual conjunction was a risky business.

Set in this patriarchal context, a series of dreadful family dramas were played and replayed on the public stages of Parlements. Armed with the law, some parents singlemindedly tracked down errant children involved in clandestine marriages and sued them in the courts; others brazenly manipulated the laws to release children from earlier marriages when better opportunities appeared; some fought clandestine marriages for so many decades that their children had no lives left to live; and still others brought family secrets out of coffers 150 years later to the ruin of innocent descendants. The court cases tell the human tale.

Case Study 1

In 1587 Pierre Houlbronne (age 17) left Boulogne-sur-mer (with parental permission) and sought employment in Paris at the *Palais de Justice* (law courts). In Paris the same year he met a widow, Elisabeth Pallier, and moved into her house. The two cohabited for eight years and children were born from the union. When Pierre decided to leave Elisabeth in 1595, she filed a complaint with the ecclesiastical judge, who imprisoned Pierre pending investigation. In the hearing Elisabeth testified that they had been married secretly by a Huguenot minister (Pierre's preference) and that the children had been baptized in the Catholic church (her preference). Although Pierre could not deny cohabitation or paternity, he testified there had been no valid marriage. Since there were good reasons to presume that a marriage existed between the two, the ecclesiastical judge ordered them to regularize the union. Pierre acquiesced and was released from prison. They signed a marriage contract before two notaries and solemnized the marriage in the Church of Saint Jacques.

But Pierre's parents, Valleran Houlbronne and Jeanne Deschamps, challenged the marriage. They appealed the decision of the ecclesiastical judge to the Parlement of Paris and charged Elisabeth with *rapt de séduction* and *rapt de violence*. The alleged marriage was invalid, they argued, on two counts: first, in 1587 Pierre had been seduced by Elisabeth while a minor (17 years old) and still subject to his parents; second, in 1595 Pierre had been forced by Elisabeth and the ecclesiastical judge to solemnize a marriage while still a minor (25 years old) and through extortion, the threat of continued imprisonment. Pierre corroborated the charges: he was forced to marry Elisabeth in 1595 or remain in prison; he could not have assented freely to a marriage at any time because he was a minor and lacked parental consent. Elisabeth countered the charges. She insisted that Pierre had freely assented to cohabitation from 1587 and to solemnize the marriage in 1595. She also noted that Pierre had lived on her assets in the early years and suggested that the Houlbronne parents wished to dissolve the marriage to arrange a better match for Pierre with a Marie Michel. Elisabeth stated in no uncertain terms that "What God hath joined together, no man can put asunder." The Parlement of Paris overruled the church verdict and found for the parents. The court declared the Houlbronne-Pallier marriage null and void, ordered Pierre to pay Elisabeth a sum of money, and allowed both parties to contract future marriages. Pierre married Marie Michel two years later. For Elisabeth and the church her marriage was valid because it followed long cohabitation freely chosen, the birth of children, and a belated public church wedding. For the Houlbronne family and the legists that marriage was invalid because it lacked parental consent. The Houlbronnes manipulated the law to make a better match for Pierre at the expense of Elisabeth Pallier and the Houlbronne-Pallier children (now legally illegitimate).

Case Study 2

In 1619 César Brochard (already a lawyer in Parlement) and Susanne Guy (a woman of lower social status) eloped and married without parental approval. César's father, Jean Brochard (a royal councillor), sued his son to invalidate the marriage. The Parlement of Paris ruled for the father and judged the alleged marriage null and void. The court found César guilty of evading parental authority, ordered him to beg parental forgiveness for such impropriety, and required him to enter the monastery of Saint Victor and remain there until released by parental declaration. The court declared Susanne guilty of *rapt (de séduction)*, forced her to renounce the marriage before the Brochard parents and four witnesses and to beg pardon from the king for the crime, and banished her from Paris for a decade. Jean Brochard had asserted parental rights over individual choice and won. He sued his own son in court to prevent a marriage not suited to family priorities, and he made use of a monastery as a short-term detention center for the errant son. The real victim, however, was Susanne, exiled for ten years from her own home and lacking marriage prospects.

Case Study 3

In 1636 Marc de Brion and Louise Gaudart (both 18 years old) married with the consent of the Gaudart family. Charles de Brion (seigneur de Hautefontaine), father of Marc, promptly sued Jacques Gaudart, father of Louise, for *rapt (de sé-*

duction). The Gaudart family aided and abetted Marc's seduction, he argued, by condoning the courtship and the marriage. As a result, Marc's reckless passion for Louise interfered with his university studies and threatened his future career. The Parlement of Paris found for Marc's father, Brion. The court declared Louise's father, Gaudart, guilty of *rapt* (of Marc) and ordered him to pay Brion 46,000 livres (damages). The court found Marc guilty of acting without parental consent, fined him 24,000 livres (to pay for the bread of prisoners), and confined him to the monastery of Saint Victor until released by his parents. The Brions no doubt had better marriage prospects in mind for Marc; the Gaudarts would find few good prospects for Louise in the aftermath of such scandal and with a depleted dowry.

Case Study 4

In 1647 the Duke of Attichy sued his daughter following her announced intention to live independently. She had spent several miserable years in a convent, left without taking solemn vows, and refused to return. In secular life she rejected all marriage plans and wished to live on her own inheritance (perhaps bequeathed by her mother or a relative). The Parlement of Paris ruled for the father: although unwed daughters could not be forced to marry or to enter convents, they were obliged by divine law, natural law, and French law to obey the will of fathers. Tied to paternal households in this manner, unwed daughters could never achieve independence regardless of age, disposition, or financial condition. They remained subject to paternal power until death did them part.

Case Study 5

In 1732 Louis-Henri de Saulx de Tavannes (marquis de Mirabel) and Ferdinande-Henriette-Gabrielle de Brun, who had known each other for years, wished to marry. Ferdinande's parents, Agathange-Ferdinand de Brun (marquis de Roches) and the marquise de Roches, who could not abide each other, fought a mortal battle over her future: the mother favored a union with Louis and encouraged the courtship; the father opposed the union and arranged a marriage with someone else. In May of 1732 after much plotting, Louis helped Ferdinande (accompanied by four servants) to flee from the family château. Apparently they did not plan to marry secretly but intended to install Ferdinande in a convent, where she could attempt to resist the impending marriage free of paternal pressure. Ferdinande tried to gain admission to three convents but was turned away because there was no one (i.e., parents, relatives) to vouch for her. The convents no doubt thought that the entourage looked suspicious and feared legal liability as accomplices. Caught in this limbo and short of funds, the desperate couple was tracked down by Ferdinande's father, the marquis de Roches, who filed a complaint of *rapt (de séduction)* against Louis (and the servants) and obtained a royal order *(lettre de cachet)* to retrieve Ferdinande. The marquis de Roches ordered his daughter to enter a convent in Metz; then he transferred her to Paris, first to the Convent of Saint Elisabeth, then to the dreaded Convent of Saint Pélagie. Although Louis and Ferdinande formally begged pardon of the marquis for their precipitous action, he turned to the law.

Consumed by fury at Ferdinande's presumed "betrayal," the marquis de Roches accused his daughter of "odious treason," refused to see her, and severed financial support. Supportive to the end, the marquise de Roches visited her daughter at Saint Elisabeth's, took her word that no clandestine marriage had been contracted, treated her with loving kindness, and supported her financially. When the marquis transferred Ferdinande to the Convent of Saint Pélagie, the marquise rented an apartment for both of them at the Convent of Les Dames de la Croix.

Doubly enraged by this mother-daughter solidarity, the marquis refused to see either of them and drew the sword of paternal power. He obtained a royal order that separated mother and daughter, forced the marquise back into the paternal household, and transferred Ferdinande into the austere Convent of La Madeleine, which housed "sexually promiscuous" women under severe rule. For the first four years there she was forbidden to speak to anyone or to write letters to her mother. Ferdinande remained virtually imprisoned in convents for fourteen years, ten of them at La Madeleine, where she eventually took simple (not final) vows and served as superior of the house. Whereas monasteries served families as short-term detention centers for errant sons, convents provided long-term prisons for errant daughters.

In the meantime, Louis went to court. In 1738, a couple of years after Ferdinande was incarcerated in La Madeleine, the court convicted Louis of *rapt* and sentenced him to death. Since women could not bear witness in the Burgundy court without a husband's consent, the marquise de Roches could not testify for Louis, even though she separated from her husband in the same year. Given the severe sentence, Louis fled from France and lived in exile for eight years. Crushed by the legal weight of paternal power, the three (Louis, Ferdinande, and the marquise) must have welcomed the death of the marquis in 1746. Mercifully freed from paternal authority, Ferdinande left the convent for secular life, while Louis returned to France and obtained a pardon. But the terrible story does not end there. Just when rejoicing might have been in order, Louis died in 1747 and the marquise died in 1748. At this point Ferdinande, quite alone in the world, suffered a further blow upon finding herself disinherited by her beloved mother. Astonished and bewildered by the terms of the testament, Ferdinande brought suit in court against the next of kin. Apparently the aged marquise, bereft of her only child and separated from her husband, fell prey to the avarice of relatives. For years Charles-Paul Bureau de la Rivière (count de Montal) and Marie-Anne de Monsaulnin (countess de Montal) played upon the emotions of the lonely old woman. Ferdinande deserved disinheritance, they convinced her, because the daughter had lied to her mother when she denied having contracted a clandestine marriage with Louis in 1732. Ferdinande had already been disinherited by her spiteful father (she received only a *légitime,* a small portion of his estate); now she had to spend another decade fighting a brutal battle for survival, which depended upon her right to the maternal inheritance. Before this case was settled, the principal parties, young and old, had wasted their lives away. The marquis' display of paternal power shows how complete the subjection of children (especially females) and women in the family could be if taken to extremes under the laws governing the formation of marriage in the old regime.

In early modern France the eminent *noblesse de robe* controlled the formation of marriage and policed childbearing in concert with the state. The legal reforms promulgated by this family-state coalition subjected the interests of children and women to a patriarchal and familial *raison d'état* that promoted state-building. The human effects of this tenacious marriage pact seem clear: when paternal consent became the touchstone of a valid marriage, patriarchs and politicians triumphed over children, women, and church. Looking back from his vantage point in the mid-nineteenth century, Alexis de Tocqueville discussed the ascendance of paternal power over the formation of marriage and lamented the unnatural juxtaposition of human passion and legal statute, which placed such a heavy burden on the young. Yet for all his acuity in judging the old regime, de Tocqueville failed to grasp an essential point. The human effects of the marriage pact cannot be assessed without resort to the gender component. In any analysis of marriage formation within familial networks, women must be considered independently of men. One must perforce recast the question and ask: What were the effects of the marriage pact on women? At first glance the obvious can be stated. In early modern times, the less privileged groups in society in terms of access to status, wealth, and power were young people and women. On second glance, however, a corollary appears that is not so obvious. Across the board, the effects of the marriage pact were gender-specific. As young male members of families aged in this society, they usually had the opportunity to assume power over family resources; whereas females tended to remain less privileged whatever their age and often permanently so.

There is no doubt as to the public nature of the marriage pact. The peculiar rituals of pardon exacted from young people and the parental use of detention centers highlight the quasi-public nature of the family—a familial state within a political state, where family rules, written into law, were enforced. Some monasteries and convents served as official detention centers for errant members of families just as the Châtelet supplied an official prison for criminal subjects of the state. Yet in the case of males, detention was short-time; whereas in the case of females, detention could be quite long-term. Despite the fact that the French marriage pact legally undermined the church's principle of consent, many convents ignored the conflict of interest and gave institutional support to the new laws by helping to enforce family regulations. In this peculiar system, which required such support for the marriage pact to work, women policed women, sometimes in a moderate manner, other times with frightening severity. For the women forcibly held in these institutions, the sentences must have seemed, and often were, interminable. Young men like César Brochard and Marc de Brion could not remain long in the monastery of Saint Victor, because the patriarchal system required that they fulfill public offices and guard family interests in generational turn. But the young women fared less well. Once placed in a convent for contracting a clandestine marriage, it was not easy to return to secular life. Susanne Guy was actually forced into exile for a decade, and Ferdinande de Brun remained in the especially penitential austere environment of the Convent of La Madeleine for fourteen years with incarceration lifted only on the death of her father. Others shared similar fates.

To make matters worse, the same system attempted to regulate childbearing in order to prevent abortion and infanticide, obvious byproducts of clandestine marriage, too. Gradually the professional midwives, a licensed corporate group, policed the actions of pregnant women, in particular those without husbands. Thus clandestine childbearing fell under the same rubric, as midwives became the official witnesses for live and dead births, women policing women in the service of family-state priorities.

In the wake of the patriarchal marriage pact, access to paths of social mobility were also restricted for women. In the female ranks widows (even young widows) enjoyed considerable room to maneuver before the family-state marriage pact was forged. It was not uncommon for widows, especially those who ran small businesses, to marry young men, as Elisabeth Pallier wed Pierre Houlbronne, and facilitate their rise in the world. Whereas earlier church law regulating marriage protected widows like Elisabeth, following the marriage pact in 1556 Pierre could live off of Elisabeth's assets long enough to get a start in life, then abandon wife and children with near impunity, and finally fashion a better marriage opportunity for himself. Likewise, before the pact Susanne Guy and Louise Gaudart could bring decent dowries to unions and contract upwardly mobile marriages to young men like César Brochard and Marc de Brion. But after the pact outlawing clandestine marriages, young women caught in this vise were ruined morally, often confined to convents, left with dowries severely depleted by fines, and denied future marriage prospects.

Finally, the marriage pact, combined with the statute forbidding concealment of pregnancy or secret birthing, fashioned a world for women wherein human passion, illicitly indulged in terms of these social mores, spelled social, economic, and emotional ruin. To be sure, the young as a whole bore the brunt of the costs of state-building, but women in particular paid the highest price for contracting clandestine marriages in early modern France. The slow process of reversing such inequities began during the violent revolution in 1789, when militant women took their grievances to the streets, but it took another century of strife before the reversal took hold.

SUGGESTIONS FOR FURTHER READING

Davis, Natalie Zemon. *The Return of Martin Guerre*. Cambridge, 1983.

Donzelot, Jacques. *The Policing of Families*. New York, 1979.

Duby, Georges. *Medieval Marriage*. Cambridge, 1979.

Forster, Robert, and Orest Ranum, eds. *Family and Society: Selections from the Annales*. Baltimore, 1976.

Goody, Jack. *The Development of Family and Marriage in Europe*. Cambridge, 1983.

Hanley, Sarah. *The Lit de Justice of the Kings of France: Constitutional Ideology in Legend, Ritual, and Discourse*. Princeton, 1983.

Herlihy, David. *Women in Medieval Society*. Houston, 1971.

Rabb, Theodore K., and Robert I. Rotberg, eds. *The Family in History: Interdisciplinary Essays*. New York, 1975.

Rosenberg, Charles E., ed. *The Family in History*. Philadelphia, 1975.

Wheaton, Robert and Tamara K. Hareven, eds. *Family and Sexuality in French History*. Philadelphia, 1980.

2

Women's Work in the Changing City Economy, 1500–1650

Merry E. Wiesner

It was once a commonplace notion that in earlier times a woman lived a life "free of economic worries." She cared for the house and children, wove, knit, and embroidered a little. Change came, so the argument ran, with the "progress" of industrial and commercial development that, by tearing asunder home and workshop, forced her out of her sheltered existence. Nothing could be further from the truth, as Merry Wiesner's description of women's work in the city economy between 1500 and 1650 reveals. The study rests on archival materials for southern German cities, which include municipal ordinances, wills, tax records, concessions to run market stalls, and petitions by widows to town councils. For those with an artistic bent, the single-leaf woodcuts from the period would offer an excellent supplement. These cumulative sources document how involved women were in goods production, in retail trade, and in domestic and medical services. The chapter makes a number of innovative points. First, Wiesner broadens the standard definition of work by looking beyond the labor officially organized by guild statutes, which increasingly excluded women's participation. She describes the daily routine of the artisan's wife, who fed the apprentices, sewed for them, and kept records. So essential was this contribution that guilds insisted every master-craftsman be married. Second, she shows that the commercial changes, or "the advent of capitalism," opened up new jobs for women in urban home industries, particularly in cloth production, while closing them in others. Finally, Wiesner raises the important issue of how women's work was perceived by urban magistrates and male workers. She demonstrates a subtle but significant shift in attitudes toward women's work. Whereas once a husband and wife who typically shared tasks in municipal employ would both be referred to as officials, by the end of the period, they customarily would be described as the "official and his wife" even if she continued her official functions. As Wiesner concludes, the character of women's work was not just a function of economic factors.

The period from 1500 to 1650 is one of major economic change in Europe, change usually described as "the commercial revolution" or "the advent of capitalism." In the Middle Ages production of goods went on in towns and cities for local use.

Other than a few luxury items such as spices and silk, goods were rarely shipped further than a few miles. In the cities, production of most items was carried out by craft guilds, which regulated the price and quality of manufactured items and limited the amount each workshop could make. Workshops were small, usually including no more than the master craftsman and his wife and children, one or two journeymen, and one or two apprentices.

Very gradually, however, these highly localized city economies became part of an international trading network. Merchants and bankers began to buy manufactured goods to be shipped long distances and engaged workshops to produce articles for the international market. They resented the limitations imposed by the guilds and often hired rural households to produce for them, particularly in the making of cloth and clothing. In some cities the guilds were not very strong, and so urban households as well as rural ones became part of the domestic industrial system.

The impact of these changes on the economy, on politics, on social classes, and on work itself has been analyzed and argued over for decades, and the rise of capitalism viewed as both a positive and negative development. Almost all of these discussions have focused on men, however, often without realizing it. The merchant-capitalists were men, most of the guild masters were men, as were most of the journeymen. Did the commercial revolution also affect women? Indeed, it did profoundly, changing the kinds of work opportunities available to women and ultimately transforming the functions of the family as well, as women, men, and children began to receive individual wages for their work, rather than producing goods as a family. But were economic factors the sole determinants of women's work choices?

In order to explore how women's lives were affected by the changing city economy, we will first look at the employment opportunities available to them in the traditional guild system, the system that prevailed in most parts of western Europe in 1500. Then we can examine the women's role in the new, capitalist cottage industries. We must also consider occupations that were not greatly affected by the development of capitalism, such as domestic service, hospital work, and retail sales, for these employed a great many women. I will be taking most of my examples from the cities of southern Germany, for these cities, which had well-organized guilds, provided great opportunities for merchant-investors, and had a wide range of service occupations available for women. They are also cities that have extensive records for the early modern period, which is important because it is much more difficult to find information about working women than about working men.

With the exception of a few female guilds in Cologne, Basel, Paris, and several other French cities, the guilds were male organizations, and their structure followed the male life cycle. A boy became an apprentice at about age ten to thirteen, and learned the craft for a set number of years, beginning with very simple tasks and working up to more complicated ones. When the master-craftsman for whom he worked felt he had mastered the skills needed, the boy received his apprenticeship papers and became a journeyman, working in the shops of several different masters for several years. When he had perfected his skills, he could apply to a guild in a town to become a master-craftsman. If the guild members determined there was enough demand for their product to allow another shop, they let the young man make his masterpiece; if this was judged worthy of acceptance, he paid a fee and could open his own workshop and take on apprentices and journeymen. The boys and young men who were apprentices and journeymen generally lived with the master-craftsman and his family, often in a house attached to the workshop.

Girls and women fit into the guild system in a much more informal way. In the high middle ages (the twelfth and thirteenth centuries) girls had been taken on as apprentices in some craft guilds, especially those which required delicate work and great manual dexterity, but by the late Middle Ages (fourteenth and fifteenth centuries) they no longer were formally accepted as apprentices. Generally there was not any specific prohibition against female apprentices, but references to them simply disappear from the records.

This did not mean, however, that there were no longer any women working in guild shops. The daughters of a master-craftsman could learn their father's trade alongside his journeymen and apprentices. Some master-craftsmen went so far as to adopt a number of young women so that they could have more workers in their shops. Master-craftsmen also hired women as maids and pieceworkers to do simple tasks like polishing, packing, and cleaning.

The most important woman in any shop was the master's wife. The guilds recognized how important she was, for they required that every master-craftsman be married. She had to feed and clothe not only her own family but also the apprentices, journeymen and any domestic servants that lived in. She also worked in the shop and often sold the products her husband had made, either from the shop or from a stand at the city marketplace. She was often responsible for keeping records and collecting debts and for purchasing raw materials. If her husband was away, she ran the shop in his absence, directing the journeymen and apprentices.

Because the master-craftsman's wife was familiar with everything involved in running the shop, she was generally allowed to continue the shop after her husband died. Masters' widows in many towns ran breweries, printing presses, bakeries, brickyards, and other shops for years after the death of their husbands. Workshops run by widows often made up as much as ten to fifteen percent in some crafts. City governments were willing to let widows continue in business, for this meant the family would be self-supporting and not need public financial assistance. Widows paid all guild fees, but they could not take part in the leadership of any guild, for they were women and had not made a masterpiece themselves. If a journeyman married a widow, he was usually charged a much lower fee to enter the guild, which made widows very attractive marriage partners. Marrying a widow also provided the journeyman with a fully equipped shop, and a wife who was experienced in production and sales, which made her even more attractive.

Thus there were girls and women working in many capacities in guild shops, but their ability to do so was not officially recognized or discussed in guild ordinances, except for that of masters' widows. Girls did not go through a formal apprenticeship, so their work in the guilds depended on their relationship to a guild master, not on their own level of training. A woman's work in the guilds changed when her status changed from daughter to wife to widow and followed the female life cycle. Because these changes—marriage, the death of a spouse, remarriage, the birth of children who needed care—happened at different points in each woman's life, women generally did not develop a strong sense of kinship with other women of their age group. Women frequently switched occupations on remarriage, carrying their skills at buying and selling with them and learning to make a new product; this kept them from developing a strong sense of occupational identity as well, unlike male craftsmen who stayed in one guild their whole lives.

Specific restrictions on women's work in the guilds began in the fifteenth century in southern Germany, with the first limitations those on widows' rights. The time a widow was allowed to keep operating a shop after her husband's death was limited, often to as little as three months. Frequently she could not hire any new apprentices or journeymen, or even keep the ones she had. In some cases, she was able to keep working only if she had a son who could inherit the shop. Tax records indicate that widows usually had the poorest households in the city, for with no apprentices or journeymen, they could not produce enough to escape poverty.

Along with restrictions on widows' work, other limitations of women's work in the guilds began in the sixteenth century. Under the pressure of commercial capitalism, guilds saw their markets shrinking and one response was to limit women's productive roles in goods manufacture. Masters were no longer allowed to hire female maids and pieceworkers, and even the number of their own daughters that they could employ in a shop was limited. Women were not taught new processes of production in crafts like brewing, bleaching, and dyeing, or allowed to use new tools or machinery, such as frames for knitting stockings or ribbon looms, so they could not work as fast or as efficiently as men.

Because women's participation in guild shops was not guaranteed by guild regulations and ordinances, and because widows had no political voice in running the guilds, women as a group were not able to protect their right to work. Individual women, especially widows, often requested that they be allowed to work despite the restrictions, appealing to the city council or other municipal authorities by stressing their poverty, old age, or number of dependent children and praising the mercy and "Christian charity" of the authorities. These requests were often successful, for city authorities felt it was "always better for someone to work than to receive public charity"; they never allowed women as a group to continue working, however, but limited the permission to the woman making the request. Thus authorities increasingly came to view women's work as a substitute for charity, and were suspicious of women who were too successful or were not needy enough.

As the opportunities for women in the guilds decreased, those in the new domestic industries increased, particularly in cloth production. Early modern techniques of cloth production necessitated at least twenty carders and spinners per weaver, so that cloth centers like Augsburg, Ulm, or Strasbourg could keep many urban and rural women employed. The women picked up their raw wool to be carded or carded wool to be spun from a cloth merchant, and were carefully checked when they brought it back to make sure they had not substituted inferior wool or wet the yarn to make it heavier, for they were paid by the weight of the yarn. So many women turned to spinning to supplement agricultural income, augment their husband's meager wages, or support themselves if they were not married (which is why in English an old unmarried woman is called a "spinster"), that wages were kept low. Spinners could rarely support a family on their wages, and in some cases could not even support themselves. Nevertheless, spinning was seen as an essential part of being a woman. Women were expected to keep spinning when they were in jail, in the hospital, or had even lost a hand or foot.

No other occupation became quite as identified with women as spinning, but women worked in many other types of domestic production. In cities where weavers were hired by capitalist investors, women as well as men wove, although in cities where weavers were a strong independent craft, guild women were forbidden to weave or allowed to weave only coarse cloth for dishtowels and veils. Sewing and seamstressing were seen as proper female occupations, and wealthy women established small endowments to teach poor girls to become seamstresses. Along with cloth and clothing, women also made cheap, simple items such as brushes, combs, candles, soap, thimbles, brooms, needles and pins, wooden bowls and spoons. Such products required little training and no expensive raw materials, and could be sold locally or traded long distances. They had never been regulated by guilds and were free for anyone to make; men working in their spare time after their first job was over for the day, and women working as much as their family responsibilities permitted. Because these small items were not highly profitable and could be made by a woman working alone, the women making them were not seen as a threat to anyone's economic well-being or social status.

Despite their low wages and low social status, women involved in domestic industry were viewed somewhat suspiciously if they were not married or did not live in a male-headed household. This suspicion of masterless persons, both female and male, was evident throughout Europe during the early modern period. As more people worked for wages in their own homes or as day laborers in a shop, they were no longer part of a household headed by an older, male master-craftsman, as young people had been earlier when they were primarily maids, apprentices, and journeymen. Though their wages were low and their ability to support themselves precarious, they did have more freedom now to move from place to place, to congregate with others of their own age, to discuss religion and politics, to compare employers and experiences—all of which city and state authorities viewed with great alarm. Governments began to pass harsher laws against vagrancy and begging and ordered young people, especially women, to live in households that were headed by an older male relative or employer. Such laws were never very effective, however, because the number of young women was simply too great, and, as the Augsburg spinners commented, they were not so dumb as to work as spin-maids for the weavers when they could earn three times as much spinning on their own.

Even though they were unsuccessful, these attempts to force young women into male-headed households point out that the kind of work women did at any particular point was not dependent on economic factors alone. As the economy changed, authorities feared a breakdown in public order and tried to force people back into patriarchal households. This fear combined with religious ideas that marriage was the "natural" vocation for women—for all women in Protestant areas and for most women in Catholic areas—and with popular and scholarly notions about women's weaker nature and proper subservient role. All of these together meant an increase in hostility toward unmarried women, a hostility which may have played a role in the upsurge of witchcraft accusations and trials (see Overview, Part I).

In terms of women's work, this suspicion of unmarried women led authorities to view their work always as temporary, just a stop-gap until the woman could attain her "natural," married state. This helped to keep women's wages low, which was also justified as a way of getting women back into male-headed households. It may have actually had the opposite effect, for women's low wages meant they were more attractive as wage- or pieceworkers than men, and their living independently meant the merchant-investor did not have to worry about feeding or clothing them.

It is tempting to look at this ever-increasing employment in the new capitalist industries as a victory for working women, for it was not dependent on their marital status or relationship to a master-craftsman. If we look at what this actually meant for women, however, we find a somewhat bleaker picture. In 1500, many women had been essential parts of household workshops, their status recognized by the community, with some authority over journeymen and apprentices as well as maids and children. By 1650, masters' wives and widows could no longer have an active role in production. The women who worked received lower wages than did men for similar work and had no supervisory authority. Their wages were so low they often had to work twelve to sixteen hours a day to support themselves and take whatever work was available, particularly if they had a family to support. Freedom to live and work independently also meant freedom to starve. The economic need for cheap labor and the values of public order and the patriarchal household all worked together to keep women's wages low, whether the woman was an independent spinner, a widowed pinmaker with a family to support, or half a married couple who wove for a merchant-investor.

So far we have been looking at one area of the economy—production—in which there were great changes during the early modern period. When we turn to other occupations in which there were a large number of women working, we find less dramatic changes. If we want an accurate picture of the entire spectrum of women's work, however, we must also look at these other occupations.

Domestic service was perhaps the largest employer of women throughout the period. It was a stage in life for many women, until they had reached the age of marriage and had earned a small dowry. A girl might leave her own home when she was as young as seven or eight to become a servant, sometimes in the home of a relative, but more likely in the household of a complete stranger. She might find employment in her own town, or travel to a nearby city where households were larger and employed more servants. Because most Europeans married quite late, often waiting until they were 25 or 30, her career as a servant might be as long as twenty years before marriage.

Service was also a lifelong occupation for many women, who worked their way up in a large urban household from scullery maid to children's maid to chambermaid or cook, or more likely remained with a family as its single servant their whole lives. Employers often left things to their servants and maids when they drew up their wills, with comments such as "for her forty years of devoted service and care for my children." Servants were rarely paid more than room and board, so these gifts from employers were a welcome treat, as inventories taken at the death of maids indicate they usually owned no more than the clothes in which they were buried.

A young girl looking for her first position often depended on her older siblings or relatives to find one for her, or she might simply go house-to-house. In some parts of Europe there were hiring fairs at one or two specific times a year, where employers and servants could come together to find each other. Some cities in Germany also had licensed employment agents to whom a girl or boy could go to find what positions were available. These employment agents were generally older women, the wives or widows of craftsmen or city officials who possessed a good knowledge of the households in their neighborhood. They were paid both by the servant and by the employer and were expected to follow certain rules—not take gifts or bribes, or house any servants themselves or store their trunks, which might contain stolen goods.

The increasing suspicion of masterless persons in early modern Europe led to various laws regulating the conduct of maids and servants. They were not to change positions more than once a year or stay in a public inn between posts. They were not to speak out against any employer or leave a position unless they could prove an employer had mistreated them. They were not to wear fancy clothing or demand wages along with their room and board. These laws appear quite strict, but their effectiveness is doubtful, for they were repeated year after year in many cities, which is a good indication they were consistently being broken.

Despite problems people had with servants, domestic service was viewed as the most acceptable occupation for a young woman. She lived with her employer, who was responsible for her behavior and activities. Cities also legislated the conduct of employers; they were not to treat servants too harshly, but were to be sure they acted "decently, modestly, and industriously," and did not behave in a "disobedient, contrary, untrue or otherwise inappropriate manner." The advantages of service for a young woman were the security it offered, the training in running a household, and the opportunity to meet other young people, particularly if she worked in a large urban household. As opportunities for women in other occupations decreased, those in domestic service remained the same or increased as larger household staffs became more fashionable and maids were used for production-related tasks such as spinning. Despite the disadvantages, such as the lack of independence and low salary, a greater share of the women who worked outside their own homes were domestic servants in 1650 than in 1500.

Along with domestic service there were a number of other service occupations that provided employment for women throughout the period. Many of these were viewed as extensions of a woman's functions and tasks in the home—cleaning, cooking, caring for children and old people, nursing the sick. They often required no training beyond what a girl learned from her mother, and were generally poorly paid and had low status. Despite this, because a woman could work or not work as her financial situation or family responsibilities changed, they remained practical employment options for women who had no specialized skills.

Medical institutions such as hospitals, pest-houses, infirmaries, and orphanages employed women in a variety of ways. The day-to-day operations of many hospitals were handled by a hospital-mistress or keeper, who was responsible for the physical needs of the hospital and patients. She handled all purchases and payments, oversaw the kitchen, led the patients in prayer, and also examined patients when they were admitted and on a regular basis.

This diagnostic function might surprise us, as hospital keepers had no medical training, but hospitals in early modern cities were very different than modern hospitals. They were not refuges for people with contagious diseases, who were sent to small infirmaries or pest-houses outside the city walls. The hospitals themselves were for the infirm elderly, people with chronic, noncontagious diseases, poor expectant mothers, the handicapped, people recovering from injuries, foundling children, and mentally retarded or psychologically disturbed children or adults. It was important that those with contagious diseases be kept out of the hospitals so that the disease did not spread to those already weakened by injury or old age. Because the hospital keeper oversaw all patient admissions, it was her responsibility to prevent those with typhus, typhoid, leprosy, cholera, bubonic plague, or similar diseases from being admitted.

The hospital keeper was assisted by other women hired as cooks, nurses, laundresses, and children's maids, and men hired as shepherds, nurses, and servants. Very large hospitals also had a male hospital keeper. During the early modern period many cities combined smaller hospitals into one large hospital so that the city council would have more control over the hospital's policies and administration. They also secularized many institutions, taking them over from the church. Every employee, from the hospital keeper down to the goosegirls and shepherds, had to swear an oath of loyalty and promise to perform his or her job ''faithfully and truly.''

Women also cared for those with contagious diseases in the small pest-houses and infirmaries. Most of these institutions were opened only when an epidemic moved through the area and closed again when the disease had passed. Very little could be done for such patients except to keep them clean and fed. Physicians would rarely enter a pest-house, for they were afraid of catching the disease, though this was perhaps a blessing in disguise, for their only treatment of such illnesses was to bleed the patients, which only made them weaker.

In addition to their work in medical institutions women also worked independently as medical practitioners and as midwives, although growing professionalism increasingly pushed women out of practicing medicine. This professionalism also affected other service occupations. Older women traditionally ran small primary schools in their own homes, teaching young children to read; but during the sixteenth century they were forbidden to teach boys, for now this was only to be done by the official city schoolmaster. (This was an economic issue as well, for the schoolmaster was paid per pupil, and so lost money when female teachers "stole" pupils away from him.) During the medieval period couples had often shared positions as minor city officials, such as toll collectors, grain inspectors, and gatekeepers, with both husband and wife taking the oath and receiving a joint salary. Gradually the women's names disappeared from the records, as these minor city officials tried to emulate the higher officials, like notaries, lawyers, and judges. These higher positions all required university or professional training, and so were closed to women; gradually the lower positions were closed to them as well, even though no special training was required. In fact, the wife of a gatekeeper or toll collector kept on sharing her husband's work, but she was no longer considered an official in her own right.

Women had also been appraisers, for most cities required an inventory and appraisal of all property and goods whenever someone died or property was being divided. They appraised the value of everything from houses and fields to dishtowels and spoons, often writing up the list themselves. Thus these women were literate and knew the market value of every kind of household item. During the sixteenth century, however, cities began to require specific legal language in inventories, which was difficult for women who could not receive formal legal education. Appraisers gradually became city officials which meant women were excluded.

We might expect that the growth of merchant capitalism would have a great impact on women's work in sales, but this was not the case. Almost all long-distance merchants and traders in the Middle Ages had been men, and the merchant-capitalists who invested in production for the international market were also men. Carrying out long-distance trade required financial resources that were unavailable to most women, as well as freedom to travel that was limited for women both by family responsibilities and by the lack of places for female travelers to stay. Unaccompanied female travelers were often suspected of being prostitutes or thieves and some cities specifically forbade inns to take them in.

Though women were not active participants in the rise of international commerce, they continued to dominate retail sales in every city. The city marketplace, the economic as well as geographic center of most cities, was filled with women. They sold fruits and vegetables that had been grown locally; mushrooms, berries, and herbs they had gathered in the woods surrounding the city, oranges and spices brought into the city by long-distance merchants. Farmers' wives sold eggs, milk, butter, and cheese; fishermen's wives fresh and salted fish; hunters' wives game and fowl. Female brandy makers had their stands, as did sauerkraut makers, sausage makers, and pretzel bakers. Poor women sold simple wooden implements, cookies, candles, and soap, for which they had received permission from the city council, to keep them from needing public charity. Pawnbrokers sold used clothing and household articles, and female money-changers exchanged travelers' money for that which was accepted in the city. Because there was no way to preserve food easily, women had to shop every day, and the marketplace was where they met their neighbors, exchanged information, and talked over recent events.

Every city had laws that regulated what went on at the marketplace, but, unlike the guild regulations, these did not differentiate between women and men. Everyone who sold at the market was ordered to use correct weights and measures and to sell things at an appropriate price. No one was to sell stolen goods, booty received from soldiers, or merchandise that came into the city from areas suffering from the plague or other epidemics. City inspectors dumped out milk that had been mixed with chalk water, confiscated bread found to be "too coarse and rough," or ordered "stinking dead goose-bellies" taken out of the city whether the seller was a woman or a man. Husbands and wives often shared an occupation in food production, like butchering or baking, and both could be hauled into court and fined if something was wrong with their products or sales techniques. These occupations were organized into guilds, which unlike manufacturing guilds did not feel pressure from capitalist investors; food production remained local and small-scale, and masters' wives, widows, and daughters continued to be active workers in these shops.

In addition to selling at the marketplace, women also ran small retail establishments throughout the city. They made beer, mead, and hard cider, and ran taverns to dispense their beverages. They operated small inns and sleeping-houses for poor people who could not pay to stay in the more expensive larger inns. They pickled and smoked meat, washed innards and prepared tripe, working in their own kitchens and selling from the market or directly from their home. Women also sold food and other items house-to-house, carrying baskets and trays, though city governments tried to limit or prohibit this because it allowed questionable merchandise to be sold more easily.

Women continued to play an important role in retail sales throughout the early modern period. There was little opposition to them for economic or status reasons because these were not high-paying, high-status occupations. During the late sixteenth century, however, the increasing suspicion of masterless persons and unmarried women did lead several cities to try to limit retail sales to widows and married women. "Young female persons who could easily do some other kind of work, like being a maid," were ordered to quit selling but the law was difficult to enforce. Whether it was enforced or not, though, it does point out again the mistrust of young unmarried women working independently.

In conclusion, we have discovered that women's work was affected by concerns about status, worries about public order and propriety, and ideas about women's nature and proper role. Economic and ideological factors together combined to determine which occupations would be closed, remain open, or offer increased employment to women. Occupations that required formal education, large initial capital, or extensive traveling were closed to women, either by explicit prohibition, legal restrictions, custom, or the impossibility of combining such occupations with family responsibilities. Women worked at jobs that required few tools, short training or none at all, and limited supervisory duties—jobs that were poorly paid and could be done part-time. They changed occupations much more frequently than men and moved in and out of the labor force as their individual and family needs changed. Because women often fitted their work around the life-cycle of their families, moving in and out of jobs as children were born and grew up or as their husbands died and they remarried, they had to take whatever low-skilled, low-paying jobs were available. In fact, because women worked in the kinds of occupations they did, even major economic changes may not have made much of a difference in their actual experience. The working conditions of a spinner did not change very much when the cloth industry changed from guild control to capitalist. We must always be careful of assuming that change affected women in the same way it affected men.

Despite the increasing restrictions in many occupations and the low status and low pay of most jobs open to them, women continued to work. They were much less likely than men to worry about issues of status. Supporting themselves and their families was their primary concern, and they were willing to use any arguments necessary to be allowed to continue working. Unfortunately for the long run, the arguments that were successful stressed the stop-gap, temporary, emergency nature of their work, they they should be *allowed* to work because of the authorities' pity and charity, rather than that they had a *right* to work. Such arguments were successful in the short run, for these women continued to work, but were ultimately harmful as they devalued women's work, thus contributing to the idea that "women's work" was always less important than "men's work." We should not judge these early modern women too harshly, however, for the question for them was one of survival.

Note: Most of the material in this article comes from unprinted manuscripts found in the city archives of Nuremberg, Stuttgart, Strasbourg, Augsburg, Munich, Frankfurt, and Memmingen, the Bavarian state archives in Nuremberg and the Wuerttemberg state archives in Stuttgart. The exact references may be found in my book, listed in the suggested readings below. The translations are my own.

SUGGESTIONS FOR FURTHER READING

Brown, Judith. "A Woman's Place Was in the Home: Women's Work in Renaissance Tuscany." In Margaret W. Ferguson, Maureen Quilligan and Nancy J. Vickers, eds., *Rewriting the Renaissance: The Discourses of Sexual Difference in Early Modern Europe.* Chicago, 1986.

Davis, Natalie Zemon. "Women in the Crafts in Sixteenth-Century Lyon." *Feminist Studies* 8 (Spring 1982): 46–80.

Eccles, Audrey. *Obstetrics and Gynecology in Tudor and Stuart England.* Kent, OH, 1982.

Fairchilds, Cissie. *Servants and their Masters in Old Regime France.* Baltimore, 1984.

Hanawalt, Barbara, ed. *Women and Work in Pre-Industrial Europe.* Bloomington, IN, 1986.

Jacobsen, Grethe. "Women's Work and Women's Role: Ideology and Reality in Danish Urban Society, 1300–1550." *Scandinavian Economic History Review* 31, no. 1 (1983): 2–20.

Prior, Mary. "Women and the Urban Economy: Oxford 1500–1800." In *Women in English Society.* London, 1985.

Wiesner, Merry E. "Paltry Peddlers or Essential Merchants: Women in the Distributive Trades in Early Modern Nuremberg." *Sixteenth Century Journal* XII, no. 2 (1981): 3–13.

———— *Working Women in Renaissance Germany.* New Brunswick, NJ, 1986.

Willen, Diane. "Guildswomen in the City of York, 1560–1700." *The Historian* 46, no. 2 (February 1984): 204–218.

3

Communities of Women, the Religious Life, and Public Service in Eighteenth-Century France

Olwen Hufton and Frank Tallett

In the early modern period, it was extremely difficult for women to survive outside the household. As Merry Wiesner shows (Chapter 2), there was growing hostility to ''masterless persons.'' Hufton and Tallett look at a group of women who neither married nor lived with their families but who survived by pooling resources and skills and forming what was in essence a substitute family, what Olwen Hufton has called aptly a ''spinster cluster.'' The nun in Catholic countries has been the subject of little secular historical research. As this chapter demonstrates, investigation of the work of nuns and sisters successfully combines a number of important themes. One concerns the organization of social and educational services in the early modern period. Nuns and sisters provided most of the social services in the past; they staffed the hospitals for the sick, ran charitable institutions providing shelter for the needy, worked in orphanages, and sought to rehabilitate ''fallen women.'' Whatever the degree of female literacy at the end of the ancien régime, it was due to the teaching of the women's orders. Second, the Counter-Reformation, with its practical orientation, gave rise to numerous new orders, congregations, and associations for females. As Hufton and Tallett note, women became ''the executive arm of the social policy of the Counter-Reformation in spite of the (church) hierarchy, which concerned itself largely with controlling their activities.'' The older contemplative orders, to which wealthy women paid dowries for the privilege of joining, were on the decline, replaced by a whole range of new, socially oriented congregations. By providing social services, these orders created ''challenging careers'' for women outside marriage, at a time when alternative opportunities for fulfillment were few and far between. And this is the third theme stressed by Hufton and Tallett. The nun, protected by her habit, faced numerous hardships and challenges. ''Such an adventurous and dangerous life was simply not open to a woman on any other terms.''

We have three conflicting versions of the nun in traditional French society. One is the particular legacy of the Enlightenment, perhaps best encapsulated in Diderot's *La Religieuse (The Nun),* and interprets the nun as the reluctant and unnatural product of parental greed, driven into a useless and possibly immoral life to prevent inroads into the family estate. She is thus cut off from the fulfillment of woman's natural role as wife and mother, and is, as Madame Roland describes, dead to the world. The second version draws upon an ancient hagiographical tradition, reinforced by the immense spiritual flowering during the Counter-Reformation with its attendant rhetoric, of the nun devoted to a life of social as well as spiritual service. This image emerged with particular clarity during the French Revolution. Faced with the abolition of monastic vows and given the possibility of leaving their communities in 1790, a majority of women demonstrated exemplary devotion to their vocation (in stark contrast to the men) and opted to remain under vows. In response to fervent popular demand many stayed at their posts as teachers, nurses, or in orphanages, establishments devoted to the elderly, the poor, or the morally aberrant. There is a third interpretation. This recognizes the nun's social commitment but devalues her services by insisting upon her ignorance and incompetence. This image is founded in the more pragmatic critique generated by doctors and educational and social theorists during the Enlightenment and perpetuated in the nineteenth century by a republican and anticlerical tradition. The doctors were cogent critics. They struggled in the course of the eighteenth century to apply new pharmacological and medical concepts to the treatment of the sick in the hospitals and encountered hostility from the nuns, who controlled funds and had a different interpretation of what was fitting (refusing to permit, for example, the dismemberment of corpses in the cause of medical analysis). Other critics stressed the limited educational content of the nun's teaching work; her emphasis, for example, on Catholic teaching and morality, rather than on useful or civic qualifications. Taken a step further, she was open to the charge of conditioning girls in particular to church dominance and perpetuating superstitious dogma and practice.

Victim, social martyr, ignorant incompetent: imagery of so contradictory a nature needs some explanation. The professional historian has generally given scant attention to the nun, a neglect all the more surprising given the profusion of research on the male clergy in the eighteenth century. This short study is intended to highlight issues which need consideration, to point to some general trends, and to suggest where further work needs to be done if we are to have an impartial assessment of the nun. An appreciation of her services is critical to an understanding of women's roles in traditional societies, and also to any attempt to highlight elements of continuity in professional organization into the contemporary period. Even in twentieth-century Britain the vocabulary of nursing, with "sisters" in starched uniforms ruled by a "matron" redolent of a mother superior, is striking, and this is not surprising given Florence Nightingale's overt emulation of the Daughters of Charity. Moreover, we might reasonably reflect upon the genesis of the lingering conviction that women with time on their hands—single women above all—should give themselves to unremunerated social or charitable work, a conviction that draws upon a deep-rooted tradition of women seeking an outlet in philanthropy and service.

We cannot be certain of the precise number of women who took religious vows in the eighteenth century. An estimate, based on a list of religious pensioners drawn up in 1817, suggests a total of approximately 80,000 regulars and *congréganistes* of both sexes in 1790—26,000 men and 55,000 women. It seems likely, however, that the estimate of 1817 is a chronic underrecording of the situation prevailing on the eve of the Revolution, and fails to take fully into account many who only took "simple" vows and were only loosely attached, or hardly attached at all, to a specific religious house. Nevertheless, the proportion of women to men (70 percent to 30 percent) indicates that more women than men sought a religious life in the eighteenth century. Less perhaps did so than a century before or a century later—by 1878 there were more than 125,000 women religious in France.

Such inadequate statistical material as we have suggests that the women who chose the religious life exercised specific options. There was no single standard nun, but a range of religious vocations, differing over the seventeenth and eighteenth centuries. At one end of the spectrum were the old religious orders, Benedictines, Augustinians, Bernardines, etc., characterized by the fact that the members, though individually committed to poverty, were corporately rich, paid considerable dowries for the privilege of entry (and hence were often aristocratic), swore solemn vows, wore religious dress, and were cloistered. They were primarily dedicated to the contemplative life, and their decline may plausibly be explained by the increasing hostility shown toward a life dedicated merely to prayer by educated elite circles, sensitive to Enlightenment criticism. Even before such criticism became manifest, however, the dynamic thrust of the female vocation was toward a religious life with a more clearly defined practical role. The Counter-Reformation, which reached its fullest flowering in France in the seventeenth century, gave rise to a spate of foundations with well-delineated social functions. The Ursulines, for example, founded in Italy in 1535 and introduced into France in the early seventeenth century with the help of Madame de Sainte Beuve, were the Church's oldest teaching order. The Filles de Notre Dame de Charité (Sisters of Our Lady of Charity), founded by Saint Jean Eudes, set themselves to rehabilitate fallen women. The Visitandines were established in 1610 by Saint François de Sales and Sainte Jeanne de Chantal, primarily to visit the sick.

These orders, a few of many, had a number of common traits. First, they sought to give practical expression to the social philosophy of the Counter-Reformation, which rearticulated the obligation of the Christian individual toward the poor and needy. Second, they owed much to the efforts of a number of extremely wealthy and pious widows who brought financial means, influence, and dedication, which provided the dynamic for establishment and expansion. Pauline teaching, which urged chastity and good works upon the widow, was reemphasized, and a series of cogent spiritual directors gave guidance to this reservoir of widow-power. These new establishments became magnets attracting a spectrum of educated and wealthy women, the daughters of nobles and financiers, as well as mobilizing others of less elevated social status for more menial services. To read Gueudré's account of the Ursulines, given the task of rearing generations of aristocratic girls in the Catholic faith, rescuing the daughters of newly converted fathers whose mothers remained attached to Protestantism, and of spreading Catholic education for girls to Canada, is to comprehend how challenging a career was offered to the nun, who, protected by her habit, faced innumerable hardships and challenges. Such an adventurous and dangerous life was simply not open to a woman on any other terms.

Yet the Ursulines, the Filles de Notre Dame de Charité, and the Visitandines were all to become monastic orders proper, with enclosure, the veil, and solemn vows, thus limiting their untrammeled powers of initiative for work in the community. The papacy and the episcopal hierarchy had a long tradition of hostility toward the uncontrolled presence of large numbers of women (and of men) circulating freely in the community, immune from control. Enclosure and a "rule" (code of discipline) resolved this dilemma. It had also some positive advantages. Institutionalization meant the perpetuation of the house, even when the individual initiative flagged, and establishment could attract funding and contribute to an *esprit de corps*. But the disadvantages were also apparent. The Visitandines, who tried to resist claustration, appreciated that they would be cut off from society. For the Ursulines, it meant restricting most of their teaching functions to boarders who had to pay for the privilege, though many of the houses used the funding from the school fees paid by the nobility to finance the teaching of selected poor girls. Above all, enclosure meant a certain loss of spontaneity, and a rule entailed ossifying in a certain mold.

The Ursulines and the Visitandines perhaps failed to escape conversion into enclosed orders because of their sheer size, which frightened the Catholic hierarchy. Indeed, it is tempting to posit that women became the executive arm of the social policy of the Counter-Reformation *in spite of* the hierarchy, which concerned itself largely with controlling their activities. Yet once enclosed, their numbers began to decline. Women looked elsewhere for a fulfilling practical life outside marriage. The trend in the seventeenth and early eighteenth centuries was toward the establishment of congregations (religious societies without permanent vows) rather than orders. Most of them were very small and their influence was circumscribed within certain localities. An exception in size, extent, and influence were the Filles de la Charité (Sisters of Charity), founded by Saint Vincent de Paul and a widow, Louise de Marillac. Vincent de Paul was insistent that he had not founded a religious order. "Your convent will be the house of the sick," he told the sisters, "your cell a hired room, your chapel the parish church, your cloister the city streets or the hospital wards, your enclosure obedience, your grill the fear of God, your veil modesty." Their function was to go into the villages and make domiciliary visits to the sick and poor, administer soup kitchens, care for the orphaned, prisoners, and wounded soldiers. In exchange for food, lodgings, care, and attention for themselves in illness and good treatment in old age, they contracted to serve in the *hôpitaux généraux* and *hôtels Dieu* (hospitals for the poor) and charitable institutions founded by ecclesiastics or municipalities. Known as *soeurs* (sisters) rather than *religieuses* (nuns), they swore only simple vows, which were renewed annually, and in the beginning had no distinctive dress. As Saint Vincent had intended, the harshness of the work attracted good village girls, rather than aristocratic women, and although dowries were later asked when the girls took their vows, they were modest enough to ensure wide entry.

The Counter-Reformation also produced confraternities of pious lay folk (of both sexes), many of them of solid social standing, dedicated to practical as well as spiritual ends. The Dames de la Charité (Ladies of Charity), for example, existed in many towns and larger parishes and had complemented, though they were no substitute for, the work of the Filles de la Charité. They visited needy families and distributed, possibly on no more than an annual basis, such scant relief funds as a parish possessed, or perhaps no more than cast-off clothing; or, they might help the daughter of a poor family to find a job in service. The women involved were sometimes married, were often widowed, with some social con-science, prepared to give a restricted number of hours per month to charitable endeavor, rather than dedicate their lives to the same. One of these associations, in the city of Besançon (see Figure 1), existed to provide layettes for poor mothers expecting babies and to give them some assistance in the months after the birth, when their earning power might be reduced by their physical debility and restric-tions imposed by breast-feeding a baby. This association had a continuous history through the ancien régime, the Revolution, and the nineteenth century. Yet such associations have almost entirely escaped the historian's attention.

It is difficult to summarize in a few short paragraphs the extent of the services proferred to society by women in the various branches of the religious life. The type of work can be subsumed under short headings: health (work in the hospitals and domiciliary assistance in the form of food and medicaments); institutional relief for the orphaned and the aged poor; education, extending to girls of all classes and village boys as well; social welfare, embracing categories as diverse as informal soup kitchens in time of harvest failure and associations to rescue young prostitutes from a life of vice; services to promote community or individual self-sufficiency, which might range from pioneering industrial enterprises such as spinning schools to providing crèche-type services for working mothers. Such a list must also include miscellaneous enterprises, such as ancillary prison services, or running sheltered accommodation for genteel widow geriatrics who could af-ford to pay. To get an idea of the quality and importance of the work involved we shall have recourse to a number of specific examples: the nursing sister in an *hôtel Dieu;* the teacher in a parish school; the *béate* (devotée) in Le Puy and the villages of the Velay helping the lacemaker to live on pitiful wages; and the quasi-industrial, even "entrepreneurial," nun who responded as her group saw fit to local problems.

The *hôtel Dieu* was a hospital intended for the sick whose family could not provide care. Many were founded in the Middle Ages and were the precursors of the modern hospital. If *hôtels Dieu* and *hôpitaux généraux* are taken together there may have been far more than 2,000 of them in 1789; certainly well over 100,000 people were hospitalized. Some catered to a mere handful of people, others to eighty to a hundred at any one time. In the course of the seventeenth century many *hôtels Dieu* were substantially overhauled, and as part of that process, the administrators or municipalities who had, or who gained control of them, invited or contracted with one of the new orders to fulfill nursing and (to a greater or lesser extent) administrative functions. The Filles de la Charité were often the first recourse of the hospital authorities unless there was a local alternative—though

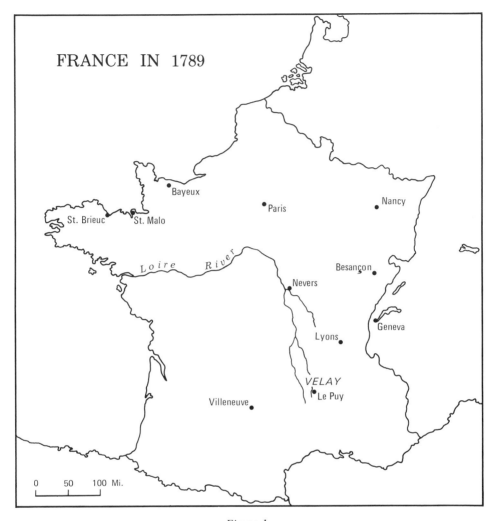

Figure 1

sometimes there were simply too few sisters to respond effectively. Hence, the Soeurs de Saint Charles de Nancy (est. 1652), or the Soeurs de Saint Thomas de Villeneuve (est. 1661), the Soeurs Hospitalières de Saint Joseph de Puy (est. 1686 and most common south of the Loire), or the Soeurs Chrétiennes de Nevers and innumerable other local groups might be called upon. The agreement between the sisters and the inviting administrators, often in formal contract, generally laid down provisions for the upkeep of the women and conditions of entry into the institution, as well as the extent of their authority over all personnel and internees. Usually, the invitation recognized that the sisters were coming to introduce order and authority into the institution, and although some administrators sought to keep some control over financial matters, generally they were prepared to cede financial autonomy and management of the funds and scope of activities to the women.

The sisters had to be guaranteed food, warmth, and clothing. By 1789, an annual payment of 150 *livres* per head was reckoned for their subsistence, which ensured modest comfort. The insane, those suffering from incurable, recognizably contagious, or infamous disease (by which was meant sexually transmissible) were excluded from the *hôtels Dieu*. There was an element of sense in such provision. The sisters were small in number and operating in a limited, sometimes medieval building, which would have made treatment of the violent mentally ill impossible. Contagious disease would have decimated sisters and patients alike, though a closer examination of what was understood by contagious reveals that whereas plague and smallpox victims were excluded from the institution, tuberculosis, typhus, typhoid, scabies, dysentery, and enteric fevers were accepted. The exclusion of venereal disease was on the grounds that the integrity, both of the institution and its personnel, needed to be preserved. Saint Vincent placed emphasis on the need to admit the indigent sick in which the condition of poverty was a substantial determinant. The sisters, however, were the arbiters of who should be admitted, and they gave a practical interpretation to the notion of poverty. They saw as eligible anyone who was not resident in his or her own home, for example, the migrant laborer en route to or from his place of seasonal work struck down with sunstroke, or the Lyonnais silk worker with tuberculosis. Such people were not without resources, but they were in conditions that precluded care. The rules applied more closely to the old with a terminal condition, requiring assistance beyond that which an *hôpital général* could give. Sometimes the nuns had to have an eye to the funds. Taking in sick or wounded (but not syphilitic) soldiers commanded fees from the war ministry. On the other hand, some of the *hôtels Dieu* had to receive foundlings, and the expense of these grew with the increased frequency of abandonment.

Once the patient had been admitted, diagnosis, surgery, and some treatment was the sphere of a surgeon, and sometimes a doctor, who were both paid fees for their services. Care, feeding, and medication were usually in the hands of the nursing staff. The pharmacy, its contents, and the mixing of medicines was one of the areas of contention between these medical men, intent on what they interpreted as medical progress, and the sisters. The latter were not trained in pharmacology nor to any extent were the doctors and surgeons. What the sisters disposed of was traditional lore that passed as a pharmacopeia: a limited range of medications, and a yet more limited budget. They had little faith in the power of medicine alone to cure, and in their thinking it ranked behind nourishment, rest, prayer, and cleanliness. Certainly they were not prepared to sacrifice the quality of their beef-tea to finance mere drugs. Indeed, the pharmacy-nun at the *Hôtel Dieu* of Saint Brieuc, an institution deeply in debt, believed that the first economy to be introduced to save the hospital was the abolition of all medication save rhubarb, a suggestion that looks more sensible if we take into account the other drugs at their disposal. They resented the doctors' assertions that they overfed patients. Fashionable medical thought believed the sick should be on a strict regimen, and deemed the seven cups of beef-tea provided by the sisters to be ''overfeeding.'' Given the weakened physical state of some of the patients, and the need of those with dysentery and typhoid for salted sustenance to prevent dehydration, it is difficult to accept the case of the medical men in this instance. However, it is undeniable that the sisters did stand in the way of autopsies, and hence the advancement of knowledge, in some of the larger hospitals. Their vision of the dying man was that of a soul preparing itself for immortality and needing an intact body, a belief they shared with at least ninety percent of the population.

The nursing sister was but one role of the nun in eighteenth-century France. Many of the women's orders, congregations, and associations were concerned in some way with education, though what was understood by this term varied considerably. At the end of the ancien régime it is calculated that about 35 percent of French women could sign their own names. There was a considerable difference, however, between female literacy rates north of the Saint Malo-Geneva line and those below, with the highest levels found in Flanders and parts of northeastern France. The ability to read, however, is unmeasurable and it is generally, if speculatively, assumed that more could do so than could write. More positively, we can make two observations. First, whatever the degree of female literacy, it was largely achieved through the teaching of the women's orders. Second, much teaching, to a broad social spectrum, concentrated not on literacy, but on skills that could generate self-sufficiency such as spinning, sewing, lacemaking and embroidery, along with knowledge of the catechism to allow the girl in question to resist heresy. Hence, the teaching orders could have more extensive impact than a consideration of pure literacy skills would suggest. Orders such as the Ursulines and local congregations ran boarding schools for the daughters of the social elite. However, on closer examination such fees as were paid by wealthy families were used for a less elevated tier of schooling, aimed at teaching poor girls to read and perhaps to write, but above all to work. A poor girl fortunate enough to be received into one of these establishments came by a limited educational package but acquired skills that were equivalent to an apprenticeship. Paradoxically perhaps, the Enlightenment's views on the education of the poor concentrated on the purely vocational and deemed literacy an unnecessary, even dangerous, extra, and hence accorded well with the intentions of many of these religious associations. The point of contrast was the emphasis given by the nuns to purely spiritual considerations.

Many of the houses of the religious congregations, which had a dual educational and charitable purpose, had original, local, and particular features that almost preclude generalization. Take, for example, the house of the Sisters of Charity at Bayeux. Invited to Bayeux in 1650 by the bishop to help care for the domiciled sick, to distribute relief during years of hardship, and to mobilize the wealthy women of the town to organize soup kitchens when food was scarce, the entrepreneurial activity of the next two generations of sisters proved quite remarkable. By the mid-eighteenth century they had introduced onto their premises or in hired adjacent buildings, the manufacture of soap, cloth, and lace. In the production of the first two items they could undercut any merchant in town. The profits allowed them to keep forty young girls of poor parentage between the ages of ten and seventeen, and to engage a further forty-five people in their miscellaneous productions and to help poor families with shoes for their children. Their enterprises flourished until the aftermath of the Seven Years' War (1756–1763), when the demands of inflated numbers of poor, a slump in lace production, and the debts arising from building a small chapel saw them in financial difficulties. However, sanctioned in the sale of a little property by the Intendant, they survived and by 1789 expenditures and receipts just about balanced.

More modest, yet equally effective, were the *béates*. The *béate* of the Velay represents one of the most original manifestations of Counter-Reformation enterprise. She was one of a limited number of women, enjoying no communal life and taking no vows, who dedicated themselves to fulfilling the economic needs of an entire job sector, those who worked in the lace industry. The idea was that of a widow, Anne Marie Martel, who in 1665, with the encouragement of the Bishop of Le Puy, set herself to gather and train women to meet the peculiar requirements of lacemaking.

While being a highly skilled craft, taking many years to acquire and perfect, the remuneration of the lacemaker was slight. The young girl of the Velay, a region with little other absorption for its woman-power, who took to lacemaking, probably could not maintain self-sufficiency during the learning period. Certainly she could not put aside any small profits from her labor that would allow her to accumulate a dowry after ten or more years and with the dowry find a husband. If, however, the girl who came into Le Puy from the country around was given free accommodation in a dormitory, paid only for the costs of her food and shared heating expenses, was helped to market the finished product, and then helped to put aside some of her profits from the sale, something, if perhaps not very much, could be saved. A *béate* was a pious widow or spinster, perhaps an accomplished lacemaker herself, prepared to run such a dormitory (possibly in a building given by pious bequest) and serve as cook and organizing agent. Theoretically independent of the marketing process, which was done through merchants, she could however keep an eye on transactions and advise the girl of the commercial value of her activities.

The *béates* organized themselves to maximize the profits a lacemaker might make. At the invitation of the village community who had to provide a simple, one-roomed dwelling, crowned by a bell, a *béate* would establish herself and organize a daily routine. At the first light of day a bell would arouse the village, and the young children and girls up to the age of twelve would come to the *béate's* house. The service was partly that of a crèche to keep the fingers of the prying toddler away from the mother's lace bobbins. The children, however, were taught their catechism and to sing hymns and the girls were schooled in the first steps in lacemaking. As the natural light receded the children returned home, and after an early evening meal, the bell sounded again and the village lacemakers gathered for a long work session in the *béate's* cottage. Light was provided by sharing the cost of candles placed in reflective globes too expensive for the lacemaker to purchase alone. Heating was usually provided by boxes containing charcoal embers, placed under the skirts at one's feet. This prevented the discoloration of the lace. Each lacemaker contributed a few vegetables or a bit of bread to a communal soup pot, thus providing a kind of late supper. The *béate* had no direct role to play in the economic aspects of the trade. This was carried out by the lacemaker herself, who negotiated with the distributors who were employed by the merchants to visit the villages. However, her services in maximizing potential earning power from lacemaking were widely acknowledged and without these services the plight of many families in this stark, virtually resourceless area would have been bleak indeed. The *béate* did nothing for female literacy, but she did much to foster a work skill, and to instill traditions of piety through chanting hymns and devotions.

Even so cursory an examination of the eighteenth-century nun reveals an immense range of activity and energy. However, while the range of services was impressive, indeed almost boundless, it should not obscure the limitations, in terms of comprehensive coverage of all those in need. The women with whom we are concerned were the executive arm of a particular social philosophy, according to which help to the needy was the responsibility of the individual Christian, intent on securing entry to the kingdom of God. It was not the concern of a coercive state obliging its citizenry to contribute effectively to the succor of the poor. The women were donors of funds, or raisers of money, or givers of time and energy in putting such resources to work. They operated, however, within the restricted confines of voluntary charity that could not, and certainly did not, expand with the demands made upon it. Indeed, magnificent as the principles underlying the social philosophy of the Counter-Reformation undoubtedly were, they were to a considerable extent weakened by demographic movements that broadened the base of the social pyramid more extensively than ever before. The number of those seeking help increased dramatically.

The inadequacy of voluntary charity in the long term to provide any realistic solution to social problems perhaps tended to deter those with the means to give. Enlightenment philosophy certainly deemed the entire notion of private charity as the origin of a group of social parasites, and this critique, too, may have stemmed the flow of bequests upon which many of these religious and philanthropic associations depended. It is perhaps useful to draw an analogy between the efforts and intentions of a Sister of Charity in ancien régime France, and those of Mother Teresa and her associates in modern Calcutta, which are so widely publicized. In individual terms, their efforts were of critical worth. Viewed in more general terms, they were a frail panacea to the problems of poverty, touching only an infinitesimal proportion of those in need. Nevertheless, until the state deemed and proved itself in a position to assume responsibility for social welfare—which presupposed greater economic growth, an increase in state resources, and a simultaneous reduction in the demand factor—they represented all there was to be had in the way of help.

Their efforts, therefore, need to be assessed by criteria other than their impact on France's massive social problems; or put another way, we should recognize that, limited though that impact might be, when the Revolution dispensed with their nursing and welfare services, the loss was keenly felt and bitterly resented. The mayor of Toulouse in 1816 demanded of a protesting crowd whether they would like a return to "the charity of the *philosophes*," thus evoking a period in which the efforts of the religious orders, associations, and voluntary services had been removed. When a number of nuns fled from persecution to London during the Revolution, they were struck by the absence of any association or institution to help poor and orphaned children and promptly set themselves to organize one.

The resources they could muster were puny and the effect of their presence on the generality of the deprived young can only have been minimal. When Napoleon reestablished the nursing and teaching sisters in poor houses and girls' schools, he consciously allowed the state to shelter behind their endeavors, minimizing state expenditure and transferring responsibility. The women accepted this because they interpreted their vocation as Christians as the solace of the poor and afflicted. For had God not made the poor the means whereby the wealthy might obtain salvation? The elimination of the problem remained in his hands, not theirs. They were his agents in his absence, and would be judged by what they did with what they had at their disposal, rather than by their total impact upon the situation. Such are the criteria whereby their work should be assessed.

The dismantling of their work by the Revolutionary assemblies, theoretically prepared to assume responsibility of the poor, and the ensuing chaos and dislocation, were to provide the incentive behind the rapid expansion of associations, congregations, and new religious orders characteristic of the nineteenth century. The executive arm of Catholic social policy, with its emphasis on patronal responsibility and Christian duty, again lay with "women religious." Their influence only began to recede as the state provided alternative services, staffed by salaried female nurses and teachers, and as the professionalization of both teaching and medicine gave careers to lay women endowed with qualifications laid down by the state. The process was far from swift or clear-cut and it must not obscure the fact that whether state- or church-organized, women were the personnel, and the notion of vocation remained attached to both teaching and nursing until perhaps the second half of the twentieth century. Only then did the vestigial notion that the teacher and nurse had dedicated their persons to social, not family, obligations, begin finally to disappear.

SUGGESTIONS FOR FURTHER READING

Fairchilds, Cissie. *Poverty and Charity in Aix-en-Provence, 1640–1789*. Baltimore, 1979.

Farmer, D. H. *The Oxford Dictionary of Saints*. Oxford, 1978.

Gueudré, M. de Chantal. *Histoire de l'ordre des Ursulines en France* [History of the Ursuline Order]. 2 vols. Paris, 1957–1960.

Hufton, Olwen. *Bayeux in the Late Eighteenth Century*. Oxford, 1967.

———. *The Poor of Eighteenth-Century France, 1750–1789*. Oxford, 1974.

Jones, C. *Charity and Bienfaisance: The Treatment of the Poor in the Montpellier Region, 1740–1815*. Cambridge, 1982.

LeGoff, T. J. A. *Vannes and Its Region: A Study of Town and Country in Eighteenth-Century France*. Oxford, 1981.

MacManners, J. *French Ecclesiastical Society Under the Ancien Régime. A Study of Angers in the XVIIIth Century*. Manchester, 1960.

4

The "Science" of Embryology Before the Discovery of the Ovum

Maryanne Cline Horowitz

History textbooks rarely include studies of women's biological and physiological role in human reproduction. Yet prevailing scientific paradigms influence normative forces that directly affect women's chances in life. When Aristotle defined woman as an "infertile male" and declared her "passive" because man contributed the formative influence in reproduction, he established a close link between biological essence and social experience. It is ironic that although women were increasingly defined in terms of their biological role, the learned scientific authorities misrepresented women's function in reproduction until the early nineteenth century. Maryanne Horowitz examines the biological controversies in the seventeenth and eighteenth centuries that pitted "spermaticists" (who were inspired by Aristotle's views) against "ovists." The debates centered on a range of issues. Did females produce semen? Were they a distinct sex or only imperfect males? What were the means by which the sex of a child was determined?

Drawing on scientific treatises, anatomical illustrations, and instructional manuals of the day, Horowitz analyzes the debate among male scientists during the great era of scientific experimentation. She includes William Harvey, who pioneered research on the human ovum; Anton Leeuwenhoek, whose microscopic studies only confirmed his belief that the sperm was the true source for the embryonic form; and Albrecht von Haller, representative of an opposite, ovist position. Scientific "progress" had to wait until Karl von Baer's discoveries of 1827 and even these were not picked up and incorporated into the scientific corpus for twenty-five more years. The lag was so great that well into the nineteenth century Aristotelian views still showed up in vernacular treatises on midwifery. This chapter makes us question the assumption that science, in contrast to art or philosophy, is value-free.

No one knew for certain that the female ovum existed until Karl Ernst von Baer's microscopic studies of 1827. From ancient through early modern times the subject of female contribution to the formation of the embryo in its mother's womb was misrepresented. Aristotle and Galen, whose rival theories of embryology both attributed to the father's seed the major contribution to the characteristics of the offspring, were the dominant authorities on reproduction quoted by theological, philosophical, and medical writers throughout the Middle Ages and Renaissance. The Renaissance publication of the classics and the proliferation of books to a wider and wider readership of men and women expanded public knowledge of the ancient "science" of embryology. Concurrently, the exclusively male scientific community, through animal dissections and experiments, had finally reached a serious intellectual quandary concerning the process of human reproduction. This chapter presents the conflicting scientific hypotheses that preceded von Baer's important discovery of the ovum and the consequent recognition of woman's role in embryonic development.

This debate parallels the well-known "Scientific Revolution" in physics and astronomy, in which the Ptolemaic theory of an earth-centered planetary system was overthrown by the scientists Copernicus, Galileo, Kepler, and Newton. From the sixteenth through the nineteenth centuries, the Aristotelian–Galenic theory of a sperm-centered embryological process, too, was overthrown by scientists investigating the capacities of the female reproductive organs. We shall follow this scientific revolution through its five major stages: the Aristotelian–Galenic tradition, William Harvey (1578–1657), Anton Leeuwenhoek (1632–1723), Albrecht von Haller (1708–1777), and Karl Ernst von Baer (1792–1876).

Despite the advancement of knowledge within the scientific community, the Aristotelian and Galenic theories continued to dominate the popular vernacular treatises on midwifery that proliferated from the sixteenth through the nineteenth centuries. The simple confusion in popular manuals parallels the much more erudite confusion among scientists in the seventeenth and eighteenth centuries. Aristotle believed that the childbearing woman provided only the location and the sustenance for the reproduction of the human child. The father was the true parent in that his semen provided the form, impetus, and direction of the embryo's growth. On account of woman's lack of semen, Aristotle defined her as an "infertile male." Assuming the exclusively material nature of her contribution to reproduction, he viewed femaleness as "material" and "bodily." Due to the inability of the female to bear young without the efficient, formative, and telic influence of male semen, he defined females as "passive." Unaware of anything as minuscule as an ovum and unwilling to hypothesize a human equivalent to animal eggs, he attributed to the visible male semen the sole source of human generation.

Aristotle's negative stereotypes of the female, which were still current in the early modern period, had an appearance of "scientific" respectability. Perhaps most disturbing of all was his presentation of the female body as a variant of the model of the male body. Women's menstrual fluid he viewed as a stunted form of semen. He defined the birth of a female child as the birth of a child whose surplus blood was distorted in development, leading to the later production of menstrual fluid instead of semen. The same semen, depending on conditions in the mother's womb, might produce a male or a female child: thus, by definition, a female child was a "mutilated male." At least, however, Aristotle's belief that the same seed, depending on circumstances, could grow to be either a male or a female laid the foundation for his very important metaphysical conclusion that men and women are of the same species.

The competing theory emanating from classical sources was the theory of Galen. He had accepted Hippocrates' view that both the males and females produce seed, both stronger seeds (source of males) and weaker seeds (source of females). If strong seeds came from both the mother and father, the child would be male; if weaker seeds came from both the mother and father, the child would be female; if a stronger one came from one parent than the other, the child's sex would depend on which seed prevailed. The stereotype of the female as "weaker" pervaded the Galenic writings as well as the Aristotelian. Like Aristotle, Galen utilized a male model for the female body. What we now call "ovaries," Galen called "testes." Going beyond Aristotle's observations, he discovered vessels within the female body. His illustrations of them showed the "testes" to be internal organs resembling the male's external testicles in the same way as, in his view, the uterus was an inverted penis.

Galen's major advance over Aristotle, while attributing generative power to women, nevertheless perpetuated many of the same stereotypes of inferiority. Both Aristotle and Galen viewed females as colder than males and designated their embryonic location as the colder, left side of the womb. Warmth was superior to coldness, and the male, produced in a superabundance of warmth, was viewed as biologically superior to the female. For Galen, as well as for Aristotle, man provided the "active" component in the formation of the embryo. A major difference between the two theorists, however, was that for Aristotle no material part of the embryo came from the male seed, whereas for Galen both the male seed and the female seed contributed materially to the embryo. This distinction opened up paths to further hierarchies: for example, the male semen was thought to produce the important heart of the embryo while the female semen produced the nutritive umbilical cord.

Galenic embryology, which utilized many Aristotelian principles, pervaded the textbooks in the medical schools of early modern universities and served as the starting-point for the seventeenth-century biological controversies. The issues included the classical question of whether or not females, as well as males, produce semen and the means by which the sex of the child is determined. By the turn of the seventeenth century a minority of medical writers, influenced by the experimental anatomists, expanded the debate to ask whether the male and female sex organs are comparable or are distinct, and whether woman is an imperfect version of the male or is equally perfect in her distinct sex. Answers were diverse and were often eclectic in their sources. Renaissance scholars had made available full editions of the classics of Aristotle, Hippocrates, Pliny, and Galen, as well as modern volumes of the anatomists such as Andreas Vesalius (*Humani corporis fabrica,* 1543), whose illustration of the male human body has been reprinted in textbooks as representative of the Renaissance discovery of human nature, and Gabriele Fallopio (*Observationes anatomicae,* 1561), who discovered the "Fallopian tubes" which bear his name.

Fallopio's descriptions of female anatomy were a major source for medical authorities who defended the new view that both sexes in their specific functioning are distinct and perfect. While Fallopio himself continued to compare male and female genitalia under the Galenic assumption that the organs were the inverse of one another, André De Laurens (1558–1609) in 1593 represented the dominant modern trend in the medical profession with a functionalist argument. Du Laurens argued that the male sex organs and the female sex organs are distinct and perfect; and by the seventeenth century, medical textbooks no longer assumed that the genitalia exist on one continuum upon which the female version might be judged an imperfect version of the male.

On the issue of whether the female secreted semen, there was diverse opinion surprisingly among both Galenists and neo-Aristotelians. The dominant view was the Galenic one that women secrete semen which is colder and less active than the male's and that both seeds contribute to both the form and the matter of the embryo. While research proceeded on the way in which menstrual blood provided the matter for the developing embryo, traditional religious associations of menstruation with the curse on Eve and uncleanliness continued to appear in medical books. The dominant new trend, however, was to view menstruation as a harmless, natural flow from the body.

The debate over what caused an embryo to be male or female was a medical topic with clinical implications. The natural curiosity of parents to know the sex of their future child opened up a market for midwives and doctors, as well as for charlatans and diviners. The Pythagorean theory that attributed a male child to location on the right side of the woman's womb and to a secretion from the right testicle might be combined with either Galen's theory, which stressed temperature and the conjunction of distinct male or female seeds, or with Aristotle's theory, which stressed the diet, climate, and strength of mother and father at the time of conception. Not until 1956 was a test devised that was truly scientific, namely amniocentesis; but predictors of sex have always had a market and some credibility, for, unless stricken with terribly bad luck, about half the time their prediction was accurate.

Prediction of the sex of a child in early modern times often relied on the left-right continuum, on the timing of the first fetal movement (the warmer males moved earlier than the cooler females), the relationship of the time of conception or the time of the last birth to the movements of the moon, or a variety of Hippocratic tests of the mother's urine, saliva, or blood. There was steady demand for help in ensuring a male offspring. A popular treatise, *The Compleat Midwife's Practice Enlarged* (1659), helped both to predict the sex of an offspring and, more importantly, to prescribe recipes for copulation that would lead to a male offspring. Recommendations included eating hot and dry meats, holding back from intercourse until the seed was well-developed, and positioning oneself so that the seed fell in the right side of the womb. It is a gross misnomer to call these "old wives' tales," for most of the theories were established and promulgated by male medical authorities, and even when utilized by a midwife at the request of a wife, often were catering to the societal pressure for male offspring.

Proof of the continuing negative influence of Aristotelian authority was the eighteenth-century forgery known as *Aristotle's Masterpiece*. It is a good example of how Aristotle's name continued to grant legitimacy to an array of ideas, some of which directly contradicted his own biology. The editions produced in the eighteenth and nineteenth centuries varied, showing some impact of rival modern theories of reproduction on the dominant traditional phraseology coming from Aristotle and Galen. The ancient theory that the seed of man is the efficient cause of generation runs into problems with the observation of seminal vessels in the female. However, the tract describes the testicles of woman as two eggs that are there merely to receive man's seed, and then presents another view that the testicles of woman are for the generation of seed. Fallopio's discovery and the work of later scientists, such as William Harvey, in no way ended the debate in the lagging popular literature between the Aristotelian one-seed theory and the Galenic two-seed theory.

Harvey's *De Generatione Animalium* of 1651 reported on his research on hens and deer and made some extrapolations to the human species. In his modification of Aristotle, he was influenced by Hieronymus Fabricius (1537–1619), who held that the female organs were stimulated by the semen of the male to produce eggs. In drawings such as those of Jacob Rueff's popular *The Expert Midwife,* the Aristotelian amalgam of semen and menstrual blood appears in oval shape as an egg; the succession of drawings shows the human embryo in formation. Harvey modified those illustrations by denying that the semen is physically in the egg, and suggesting that the embryonic egg derived from a minuscule egg not yet observed in the ovaries. Both Fabricius and Harvey wanted to explain how a hen, without any contact with a rooster, might produce unfertilized eggs. Harvey posited that parallel circumstances existed in the human womb. He observed the production of the eggs of hens in their ovaries, and could find no trace of semen in the uterus. He rejected the view that the egg was a mass of material produced after copulation; rather he attributed to the female organs the capacity to produce eggs. For Harvey, as for Fabricius, the sperm never reached the uterus physically, but rather acted from afar to determine embryonic development. In dissecting deer that had recently mated, he found no semen in the uterus, and concluded that there was no physical contact of female egg and male seed. In metaphoric language he compared the male semen to a magnet that attracts from a distance, like a star that exerts a "spiritual" influence on earthly beings.

Recently, Carolyn Merchant has argued that the dichotomy between active/passive and spiritual/material in Harvey's descriptions of male semen and female egg reflected and perpetuated both an Aristotelian mental framework and the sexual biases of his English society. Harvey's popularization of the adage "Ex ovo omnia" ("All beings come from eggs") in his frontispiece gave some recognition to the female generativity in the ovaries and inspired some scientists to become "ovists"; but overall, his work further accentuated the amazing power of the male semen to form an embryo without material contact.

Experimentation on mammalian ovaries in the 1660s and 1670s led several researchers to further substantiate the production of female ova before fertilization, while experimentation on semen led to the observation of the spermatozoon. What we now call the Graafian follicles were mistaken by some scientists as the true eggs, an error that delayed the true discovery of the ovum for well over a century. The more detailed illustrations of embryonic development, produced with the aid of a simple microscope, that appeared in the 1673 book of Marcello Malpighi (1628–1694), ushered in the preformationist viewpoint: "So admirable is every Organ of this Machine of ours framed, that every part within us is entirely made, when the whole Organ seems too little to have any parts at all." In the

1680s, Leeuwenhoek, who also did microscopic study of the Graafian follicles, denied that they were ova. He believed that the ovum provided only nourishment for the sperm, which was the true source of the embryonic form. His examination of human semen in the 1670s led him to observe what he called "animalcules," tiny organisms that moved with a swish of their tails.

Leeuwenhoek's detailed descriptions of what, since von Baer, we have called "spermatozoa," combined with his lack of observation of an ovum, confirmed his belief that each "animalcule" in the semen contained the full formative structure of the embryo. While hesitating at first on preformationism, in 1718 he described the spermatozoon of a sheep that contained a full description of the organs of the adult within it. In a letter to the German philosopher Leibniz in 1716, he suggested the following source of sex distinction:

> Moreover, all the animalcules of male semina [of all animals, it seems] agree not only in size but also in shape or conformation; except that some years ago I thought I observed some difference at the tail of a number of animalcules, near the body itself. This observation aroused in me the suspicion that the animalcules too differ in sex and are distinguished as male and female. Whence it would follow that if after marital copulation a male animalcule should reach that place in the matrix provided for the reception of these animalcules, a male would be born; but if a female should have taken possession of that place, a female would be born. By this explanation, the received view would fall to the ground; namely, that if the male semen has prevailed over the female, male offspring will be born; if the female semen has prevailed over the male, female offspring will be born.

This "scientific" description aroused hilarity among the community of scientists, and was used to ridicule Leeuwenhoek's spermaticist position. Nevertheless, his view served to undercut existing assumptions. He challenged the Galenic two-seed theory completely, by allowing for the production of both female and male beings from the male's seed alone. His belief that the animalcules are material embryos in miniature also discredited Harvey's modified Aristotelian theory of the spiritual, not material, formative impact of the male seed. Furthermore, his spermaticist position encouraged analogous but inverted claims to be made by ovists studying the so-called miniature egg, the Graafian follicles.

An exemplar of the ovist position is the Swiss physiologist Albrecht von Haller (1708–1777). Like Leeuwenhoek, he came to reject epigenesis in favor of preformationism, but von Haller believed the embryo-in-miniature to exist in the prefertilized ovum. In 1766 he wrote, "No part of the animal body is created after another and all are created and appear at the same time." His faith in no way inhibited his remarkably accurate narrative of embryonic growth. The semen in fertilizing the ovum calls up nourishment from the female body to bring about embryonic development. The goal and form of the embryo, which in the Aristotelian system were derived from the male's seed, and in the Galenic system were derived from the seed which had prevailed, are in this ovist position present fully and completely in the female egg. Von Haller's views gained wide distribution in Diderot's *Encyclopedia of the Arts and Sciences* (1751), an influential enterprise of the French Enlightenment.

One of the problems with the ovist, as with the spermaticist, position was the necessity to admit that if the full human being exists in miniature within one seed or egg, then the embryo's future children are likewise there in miniature ad infinitum. The theory of a box within a box corresponded in painting to the portraiture of a mirror reflecting a mirror reflecting a mirror ad infinitum in miniature. Antonio Valisnieri (1661–1730) suggested that the entire human race was within the ovary of Eve; Nicolaus Hartsoeker (1656–1725) made light of the controversy by attempting to calculate when the store of minuscule human beings that might have been contained within Eve's ovaries would be depleted.

Of the positions that allowed for only one sex to be the true "parent," the ovist position was obviously more disturbing to the male medical profession, and the satires of ovism far exceed those on spermaticism. Some historians, such as Joseph Needham, have been reluctant to conclude that the emergence of the ovist position corresponded with the greater visibility of women in Enlightenment society and the increased appearance of feminist tracts. Others, such as Ian Maclean, see anti-Aristotelianism and attention to the ovaries as feminist. Must we thank only the chickens under the scientists' observations for the openness of the ovists to consider accrediting to women the major impact on embryology? The ovist position, much like Jean-Jacques Rousseau's *Discourse on the Arts and the Sciences* (1749), questioned the glib assumption of scientific progress by viewing the post-Aristotelian versions of embryology as myths. The ovist position came closest to the natural notions of primitive peoples who identify the female as the life-producing force in the universe. Trobriander Islanders observed by the anthropologist Bronislaw Malinowski in the twentieth century went even further in their unawareness of a connection between the sex act and procreation, attributing to the female the sole role in reproduction. The ovists who initiated the preformationist position in the seventeenth century were met by a backlash of spermaticists, and out of this dialectic emerged the "egalitarian" epigenesist embryological paradigm of the modern period.

While scientific societies were offering prizes for the discovery of the ovum, the German scientist von Baer reported in a famous letter of 1827 that his own lack of interest in prize-seeking had deterred him from directly seeking to find the ovum by an examination of the ovary. Instead, he claimed to have accidentally noticed a yellowish little body in every Graafian follicle of the ovaries of a pregnant dog, that later he identified more fully through a microscope. He emphasized that the embryo derives its origins from an ovum formed in the ovary long before fertilization. Von Baer's observation and proper identification of the ovum were not noticed at first, but some years later received significant recognition through a prize from the Paris Academy and translations of some of his writings into French and English.

The elaboration of the roles of the ovum and the spermatozoon in embryology was the cumulative effort of nineteenth-century investigators. Three years before von Baer's discovery, Jean-Louis Prévost (1790–1850) and Jean-Baptiste A. Dumas (1800–1884), investigating the mammalian ovum, concluded that fertilization follows coitus by some days, and that the "animalcules" in semen were responsible for fertilization. It took another half-century of research for the modern view of conception to be fully established. Von Baer's discovery of the ovum ushered in comparative studies revealing the variation in the relative size of these eggs in different animals. In 1854 George Newport (1803–1854) made a significant break-through with his observation of a spermatozoon entering a frog's egg. At first it was believed that larger eggs were multicellular, but in 1861 Karl Gegenbaur (1826–1903) gave evidence that each egg was one cell. At first it was not known how many spermatozoa were necessary for the fertilization of an egg. In 1876 Oskar Hertwig (1849–1922) observed the actual fusion of the male and female nucleii within the egg of a sea urchin, and by 1879 he showed that only one spermatozoon entered the ovum of a starfish. Parallel investigation by botanists in the sexual reproduction in plants affirmed the basic similarity at the cellular level of all life and the essential features of the reproductive process. Ovism and sper-maticism were overthrown, and embryology was placed on a modern scientific basis.

Von Baer's discovery of the ovum led to the consequent recognition of the combined contribution of the mother's ovum and the father's sperm to the concep-tion of a human embryo. Nineteenth-century research on the ovaries encouraged woman's active, formative role in the embryological process to be taken seriously; and as experimentation proceeded on a sound scientific basis, the debate between the eighteenth-century spermaticists and ovists was forgotten. By the mid-twen-tieth century ideas derived from the Aristotelian–Galenic "science" of embryol-ogy were disparaged as "old wives' tales"; in that misnomer, the general public lost knowledge of the significant scientific revolution in embryology that took place between the sixteenth and the nineteenth centuries, among the international community of scientists. Through the work of women's historians, a significant episode in the history of embryology will enter the mainstream of Western history.

SUGGESTIONS FOR FURTHER READING

Bullough, Vern. "An Early American Sex Manual, Or, Aristotle Who?" *Early American Literature* (Winter 1973): 236–246.

Farley, John. *Gametes and Spores: Ideas About Sexual Reproduction, 1750–1914.* Balti-more, 1982.

Horowitz, Maryanne C. "Aristotle and Woman." *Journal of the History of Biology* 9, no. 2 (Fall 1976): 183–213.

——— "The Image of God in Man—Is Woman Included?" *Harvard Theological Review* 72 (1979): 175–206.

Irwin, Joyce. "Embryology and the Incarnation: A Sixteenth-Century Debate." *Sixteenth Century Journal* IX, no. 3 (1978): 93–104.

Maclean, Ian. *The Renaissance Notion of Woman: A Study in the Fortunes of Scholasticism and Medical Science in European Intellectual Life* (Cambridge, 1980), pp. 28–46.

Merchant, Carolyn. *The Death of Nature: Women, Ecology, and the Scientific Revolution.* San Francisco, 1980.

Meyer, Arthur William. "Old Ideas Regarding Sex, Fertilization, and Procreation." *Essays on the History of Embryology.* Stanford, 1931.

————. *The Rise of Embryology*. Stanford, 1939.

Morsink, Johannes. "Was Aristotle's Biology Sexist?" *Journal of the History of Biology* 12, no. 1 (Spring 1979): 83–112.

Needham, Joseph. *A History of Embryology*. New York, 1959.

Rich, Adrienne. *Of Woman Born*. New York, 1977.

Roe, Shirley A. *Matter, Life and Generation: Eighteenth-Century Embryology and the Haller-Wolff Debate*. New York, 1981.

Smith, Hilda. "Gynecology and Ideology in Seventeenth-Century England." In Berenice A. Carroll, ed. *Liberating Women's History: Theoretical and Critical Essays*. Urbana, IL, 1976.

II

WOMEN IN INDUSTRIALIZING AND LIBERALIZING EUROPE

Overview, 1750–1890

Historians customarily divide the vast sweep of human experience they are charged with recording and interpreting into periods that are short enough to be manageable and that are framed by dates of significant events. Thus, the nineteenth century, which is the primary focus of Part II, is often dated 1789 to 1914, years that mark respectively, the outbreaks of the French Revolution and of the First World War. Both events are assumed to have created, by the depth and extent of their impact on society, historical "watersheds" that changed the course of all that occurred thereafter. The traditional approach to history, as we pointed out in the Introduction, focuses heavily on revolutions and wars, for it is concerned above all with sudden, dramatic, often violent, changes in political structure and authority, territorial boundaries and geopolitical power.

In considering the history of women in the modern era, we are faced with a more difficult problem of periodization. Standard markers of change may have affected women's lives little, if at all, and then only gradually, for women rarely participated in political or military struggles. Furthermore, defined primarily in terms of personal roles, they often clung to familiar, family patterns long after socioeconomic changes had altered external circumstances. Yet change in women's worlds took place and we know that by the mid-nineteenth century, the lives of many women differed profoundly from those of their foremothers. The "New Woman," who is sometimes, as we will see in Part III, greeted as a product of

95

the First World War, appeared in Parisian circles in the 1830s and in Russian literature in 1862, when Vera, in Chernyshevsky's novel *What Is To Be Done?*, demanded a room and an income of her own. Votes for women in national elections, often portrayed as a reward for women's contributions to the war effort, in fact capped a struggle waged over many decades, with notable victories as early as 1869 in the Wyoming Territory of the United States, 1893 in New Zealand, and 1906 in Finland.

Today women and men live in an interconnected, dynamic, and constantly changing world. In contrast, people in the seventeenth and early eighteenth centuries lived in small, relatively static communities, rarely venturing more than a few miles from the place of their birth, or seeing a crowd larger than it took to fill a country church on Sunday. While the processes of change have taken place at varying rates in varied places, nevertheless, as the social historian Peter Stearns puts it, "The basic fact of European history since 1750 has been an unprecedented social upheaval. . . . A new kind of society has been formed, as different from its predecessor as agricultural society was from the hunting culture with which man first began to fight for survival."[1] Conceived most broadly, this picture is, of course, correct: a so-called modern world has indeed replaced premodern society. But the change was neither sudden nor synchronized and there was much dynamism in the old that influenced the character of the new world.

For our discussion of the changes in women's lives in Part II, we take as a convenient starting place 1750, and as a closing point, 1890. The year 1750 symbolizes the commencement in some areas of Europe of the types of economic, ideological, and social reconstruction that ultimately reformed the lives of most women (and men) of the Western world as much as the event often hailed as the birthmark of the modern age, the French Revolution of 1789. The date 1890 points to the closing of the era of laissez-faire and beginning of a monumental move toward greater state intervention that established a new context for women's lives. The emphasis in Part II is on the complex, interrelated series of events that go under the headings of the Industrial Revolution and the French Revolution, as well as the demographic, agrarian, transportation, and ideological changes that surrounded those two great transformations. The Industrial Revolution, which began around 1750 in England, and later moved in spreading arcs westward across the North Atlantic and eastward across Europe, encompassed numerous economic developments. Most importantly they included innovations in the organization of production and distribution of goods. The French Revolution, a subject of intensive investigation and analysis ever since 1789, was one of many "democratic revolutions" that, beginning in America in 1776, saw rights of political participation extended to ever-widening segments of the population.

This "Dual Revolution," as the cumulative changes have been called, depended on the interaction of various socioeconomic and political factors. Historical demographers, charting population change over time, have found in recent centuries transitions from patterns of high mortality and high fertility to low fertility and low mortality. In western Europe these shifts caused a late eighteenth-early nineteenth-century "population explosion" because mortality declined more rapidly than fertility before ultimately leading to the relatively slow and stable growth patterns that today characterize most advanced industrial nations. So profound are the effects of these changes that they are collectively designated a Demographic Revolution. Inextricably intertwined with population size, agricultural production was also altered due to factors such as the consolidation of relatively unproductive small holdings, the extension of lands under cultivation, the application of new chemical fertilizers, and later the utilization of new machinery. Termed an Agricultural Revolution, forces of change in the countryside stood in a complex relationship to the processes of industrial growth. In geographic areas in which small landholdings had been consolidated (for example, in England and Prussia), more and more people were forced off the land. As "free labor," they had to find work in urbanizing areas where, especially after the development of the factory system, increased employment was available for landless people. In these cases, rural areas contributed workers for urban industry. In turn, the growing need for food in urban areas acted as an incentive for agricultural development. This meant that some regions, like Bavaria in central Europe, experienced a re-ruralization in the course of the nineteenth century, becoming actually *more* agrarian than it had been a century earlier. Furthermore, the unprecedented movement of goods and people was facilitated by another revolution—the so-called Transportation Revolution. Canals were dug, roads were paved, and increased numbers of steamships and locomotives were constructed, opening up new jobs in iron and steel works and spurring on the development of heavy industry.

Finally to our list of "Revolutions," we must add the Ideological. The decline in the religious world view and loss of confidence in the church by some intellectuals that dates back to the Renaissance and Reformation produced, by the eighteenth century, a sense among the educated elite that society had progressed from the "dark ages" of the medieval period to an Age of Enlightenment. Many believed that through rational thought and the scientific method human intelligence could discover the laws of nature; and by applying them to social structures, could reform society for the greater good. Like the Renaissance humanists, the Enlightenment philosophers stressed the importance of education; in knowledge, not faith, lay the path to virtue. These philosophers sought to accumulate knowledge about everything in the natural world. They also applied critical thought to human institutions. After centuries of repression of unpopular or heretical views, Voltaire (1694–1778), the best-known *philosophe* of the age, championed total freedom of thought and speech. His contemporaries, Diderot (1713–1784) and d'Alembert (1717–1783), set out to compile in their thirty-five volume *Encyclopedia* all useful philosophic and scientific knowledge. Social thinkers of the nineteenth century went further: they devised schemes for the reconstruction of all human institutions, including along with religious, political, legal, and economic structures, personal relations and the family as well. As we will see in more detail shortly, Robert Owen, Henri Saint-Simon, and Charles Fourier invented new ways for men and women to live and to govern themselves in harmonious communities, and they expected that, once convinced of the reasonableness of new ways, people would hasten to adopt them. Near mid-century, in 1845, Karl Marx established a new agenda for social critics by declaring that the point was not merely to understand the world, but to utilize scientific knowledge of social laws to change it.

Reviewing the many "revolutions" in this period, we may ask what special meanings they held for women of the Western world. What rights did the political revolutions that destroyed absolutism and changed subjects into citizens bring to women? How did the agrarian changes affect women's roles as participants in rural marketing and manufacture? How did the industrial revolution transform "women's work" in the age-old tasks of production and reproduction that were essential to family survival? Did decreased infant mortality and declining fertility reduce the burden of childbearing and lighten the cares of childrearing? Did the rise of science free women from the inherited "curse of Eve," or did secularized thought simply reformulate older notions of women's inferiority? In which ways did wealth, age, marital status, and geographic location condition women's experiences? Were the lives of women truly revolutionized by the onset of the new society?

Industrialization and Women's Work

The industrialization of western Europe was a long and complex process in the ways that human beings transformed raw materials into the commodities necessary for life. As we have seen in Part I, it began with increased trade, with commercialization, with the development of a regional, national, and in some cases international market economy that stimulated the growth of cottage industry, rural manufacturing, and urban centers. By the end of the nineteenth century massive changes in population had taken place, both in numbers and in location. A European population of approximately 190 million in 1800 grew to 500 million by 1900—despite the emigration of over forty million Europeans, largely to North America. Differences in birth and death rates shifted the relative size of population eastward from France, the most populous European nation at the dawn of the nineteenth century, to Russia, where the crude birth rate was the highest in Europe by its end (at 49.3, double that of France at 21.3). These changes between nations were paralleled by movements of people within territories. Over the course of the century the number of people living in large cities (over 100,000) increased tenfold, growing from three to eleven percent of the aggregate population. The growth of urban centers created social needs that governments provided only slowly, after long struggles between laissez-faire and interventionist forces. Ultimately, however, municipal, regional, and national authorities created and extended their police forces, mail and rail services, census bureaus, public health agencies, and the like. Political leaders also accepted new responsibilities for people's education, creating the school systems necessary to produce a literate industrial work force.

Despite the many factors tending toward change, and the degree of alteration that, in the perspective of a century, appears so striking, on the scale of an individual life—on average very short (less than forty years) in our period—most change came in small steps. Ordinarily people who left the land migrated first to villages and small towns. Most workers who entered factories followed along the path of their kinfolk who had preceded them and who helped them to find jobs and housing. Most families who became wage earners in early industrial capitalism continued to farm small plots. Proletarianization (the dispossession of peasants of their lands and artisans of their tools and workshops) created a new self- and class-consciousness only after traditional forms of work and family life had evolved into new patterns of living.

Although James Watt's invention of the modern steam engine in 1769 and its adaptation to railroads half a century later are sometimes used to mark the beginnings of the Industrial Revolution, the early developments that most affected the lives and work of ordinary people came in textile manufacturing, the first major industry to be reorganized. Inventions such as the "flying shuttle" in 1733 and the "spinning jenny" in 1764 raised productivity drastically, quickly doubling, then multiplying by factors of twenty, thirty, one hundred, the output of a single worker. While woolen cloth had long constituted the most important product of textile manufacturers, the new methods were first applied to production of cotton cloth, for which there was a vast latent demand in England, on the Continent— and indeed, around the world. Early in the eighteenth century fashionable ladies had begun to add variety to their silk, linen, and woolen wardrobes by importing fine chintzes and calicoes from India. But ordinary people wore "homespun," coarse cloth that was usually made of wool and was in short supply. One costume usually sufficed for everyday use until it wore out; another "Sunday-best" might be set aside for church. Europe's mushrooming population provided a ready market for new, cheaper fabrics.

For a time, the first workers to adopt the new speedier methods of production in spinning and weaving enjoyed greater earnings while continuing to work in their homes. Within a few years, however, as increased wages attracted new workers to spinning, competition for work drove down profits; and the introduction of new machines, too large for workers' cottages and too expensive for their resources, impelled textile workers to seek employment in the new factories that began to dot the countryside. Located alongside rivers that provided water power, the first factories were often small, dark, and poorly ventilated. Later, steam power permitted construction of still larger and more complex machines and bigger factories with more specialized operations, which could be built at some distance from the older sources of power and labor.

The earliest factory labor forces were dominated by girls and young women. Not only were spinning and cloth production traditionally "women's work"; young females constituted a reserve that was relatively underutilized in agriculture and that could be hired for about half of a man's wage. By the 1830s, textile centers, such as Lowell, Massachusetts; Lyons, France; and Manchester, England employed tens of thousands of women. In many cases working conditions were poor. The women who extracted silk from cocoons in the factories of Lyons for fourteen to sixteen hours (less time for meals), six days a week, had to thrust their hands into near boiling water and suffered from pain and sores that tended to form under their fingernails. Silk dust penetrated their pores and lungs, producing high rates of skin disease and tuberculosis. Cotton mills likewise were filled with dust; and in cases where production required processing with water or steam, workers were compelled to spend hours in damp clothing and humid air. Machinery sometimes required uncomfortable or dangerous manipulations. A young English woman, who had started factory work at age nine, complained about

> always having to stop the flies [cylinders] with my knee. I could stop it with my hand, but I had to hold it with my knee while I piecened [spliced] it. It was having to crook my knee to stop the spindle that lamed me as much as anything else.

An older woman, who worked in a coal mine, described graphically the physical hardships she endured.

> I have a belt round my waist and a chain passing between my legs, and I go on my hands and feet. The road is very steep, and we have to hold by a rope, and when there is no rope, by anything we can catch hold of. There are six women and about six boys in the pit I work in: it is very hard work for a woman. The pit is very wet where I work, and the water comes over our clogs always, and I have seen it up to my thighs: it rains in at the roof terribly; my clothes are wet through almost all day long. . . . I have drawn till I have had the skin off me; the belt and chain is worse when we are in the family way. My feller (husband) has beaten me many a time for not being ready. I were not used to it at first, and he had little patience. I have known many a man beat his drawer.

Young workers also suffered from factory discipline. Zealous overseers used leather straps to apply frequent "lickings" to children who fell asleep on the job.[2]

The employment of women and children in English factories gave rise to demands for protective action by the state. Though doctrinaire liberals and some industrialists opposed all intervention, by the 1830s legislation was passed limiting the employment of young children, and the Factory Acts of 1842 and 1844 also prescribed a maximum work day for women. French leaders likewise sounded the bell of alarm. After Dr. Louis Villermé's famous report on the physical and "moral" costs of unbridled industrial labor, French leaders of many political views began to call for "English legislation." However, laws comparable to the British legislation of the 1840s waited until the 1880s and early 1890s in France and Germany, and until the early twentieth century in the United States.

Some countries took avenues other than legislation for the protection of their girls and women. For example, in Lowell, Massachusetts, cotton mill owners who wanted to attract a labor force of young women from the New England countryside built dormitories where their workers could be housed and fed at reasonable cost and receive suitable familial and moral support. In France, where many poor women who migrated alone to cities for work could afford only the most miserable of accommodations—often sleeping two or more to a bed of straw—*internats,* or boarding-houses, blended the Lowell plan with a convent-like regime to provide a kind of dormitory life and close supervision. By 1881 an estimated 1,110 of these establishments housed working-class children, of whom 80 percent were girls. Jules Simon, whose 1860 work *L'Ouvrière (Woman Worker)* was the most famous nineteenth-century account of the effects of industrialization on working women in France, estimated that these institutions produced 85 percent of the Paris shirt market. While the *internats* were highly profitable enterprises, they won praise for providing working-class girls with a substitute home from which they could, after some ten years' residence, leave with a sufficient dowry to found a new family. To critics they represented "nothing but commercial enterprises founded on the exploitation of children."[3]

Despite this evidence, recent research by social and women's historians has provided a needed corrective to the once-popular notion that working-class families were torn apart by the demands for factory labor. Not only did many textile-manufacturing families continue to work together as a unit in the early factories, but in cases where women did take factory employment apart from kin, they were most often young and single. The nursing mother separated all day from her infant, forced to tend machines while "the milk pours from her breasts, so that her clothing drips with it"; and the babies quieted at home by opium-laced cordials, described so passionately by Friedrich Engels in 1844, were not typical of women workers' experiences or of family life. In textile cities, however, there was indeed a great demand for female labor, for it was cheap. A family endowed with daughters might, at least during their prime years as mill workers, become relatively prosperous.

The increasing employment of women, which in the view of Engels "unsexes the man and takes from the woman all womanliness," scarcely turned the workers' world topsy-turvy. Such images were overdrawn, often created by social reformers intent upon convincing lawmakers to abandon their laissez-faire principles and pass protective legislation. Joan W. Scott and Louise A. Tilly, in an important study that draws upon occupational and demographic data from systematic samples of urban households in England and France, demonstrate that throughout the nineteenth century, traditional forms of female employment continued to dominate women's wage-earning activity. In 1851, the largest group of female wage-earners in England, fully 40 percent, worked as domestic servants. In 1866, 40 percent of the female labor force in France was employed in agriculture. Moreover, no more than one-fifth of the total female labor force in England, and one-tenth in France, worked in textile manufacturing. Outside of textiles, tobacco, and food processing, relatively few women worked in factories at all. Furthermore, in the major cloth-manufacturing centers such as Roubaix, France, where in 1872 over half the labor force worked in textiles, relatively few *married* women were employed outside their homes—about 17 percent. In the textile center of Lancashire, England, three-quarters of women workers were single.[4]

Although factory work, then, was not *typical* female employment in the nineteenth century, women's lives were altered by the processes that reorganized their work, whether removing the work to factories or, as Barbara Franzoi shows (Chapter 6), providing increased opportunities for wage-earning employment at home. In the first place, the symbiosis of married women's labor in production and reproduction, whereby women provided the daily necessities for family survival and gave birth to new generations of producers as well, was distorted by the redefinition of work that spread with the growing dominance of factory production. Work was recognized solely as "paid labor" and much of women's work remained unpaid. This enhanced the economic value and increased the autonomy of single women who found work outside the home, but it marginalized married women's work at home, even that done for wages. Second, factory manufacturing increasingly displaced much of the production done at home for the family's own use. In the course of time, mass production of soaps, yarns, and cloth, for example, encouraged their consumption "ready-made." New industries for ready-made goods proliferated in all European cities. In late nineteenth-century Britain and Germany, hundreds of thousands of women did "slop work" (low-skilled, repetitive piece work) in "sweatshops." In France, half of the female industrial labor force remained "isolated," that is, homeworkers. Domestic industry allowed women to continue contributing to family survival, but even in these households, family schedules were increasingly regulated by the factory whistle. Berlin home industry garmentmakers in the last third of the nineteenth century organized the rhythm of family life according to their husbands' work schedules, ensuring men leisure time even if it meant for themselves sewing for pay well into the wee hours of the morning.

While the internal cohesion of the preindustrial family and village should not be exaggerated, in the long run the advent of agricultural and industrial reorganization, with its increasing scale of production and growth in market economies and market mentalities, led to a slackening of kinship ties and community solidarity. It also restructured family roles. The movement of traditional women's work out of the home created a conflict between the two primary facets of women's lives—one that remains today as a problem for "working mothers" and "dual-career families." Furthermore, as early as the eighteenth century, men had begun to encroach on the domain of women's work. In textile factories a roomful of female operatives might be supervised by one or two men. Even in the countryside, the shift to market-oriented production narrowed the traditional female economy. In Bavaria, for instance, to the extent that dairy farming centered on the needs of the household, women obtained the necessary know-how on the farm itself. But market production required the mastery of new knowledge not necessarily related to the work processes themselves. And this was acquired by men from trade associations and agricultural institutes that were set up in rural areas. In short, industrialization and commoditization accelerated the process whereby the labor of women became subsidiary to that of men, even in work traditionally deemed feminine.

Women and the "Rights of Men"

Before, during, and after the French Revolution, women's primary role was support for their families. For the leaders of all parties that contended for power through the protracted period of struggle in France—the aristocrats, the radical Jacobins, the moderate Girondins and the *sans-culottes* (without breeches, or common people)—politics was the province of men. But politics cannot be separated from the culture and social arrangements in which it is grounded and which in turn it shapes and reshapes. Revolutionary leaders in late eighteenth-century France, indeed, intended to reconstruct society and create a new "man." They drew on ideas that contained powerful notions not only about the division of public political power but also about individual rights and responsibilities that were pertinent to the lives of all people. As we saw in the Overview to Part I, the seeds of "enlightened" thought about women's as well as men's rights were planted by English political liberalism (natural rights philosophy) in the seventeenth century. While the association of political rights with property ownership might work against women, the concept of "natural rights" contained the germ of equality. Indeed, John Locke, to strengthen his argument against patriarchal government and its logical extension, absolute monarchy, went so far in theory as to grant mothers "equal Title" to their children.[5]

Locke's ambivalence regarding women's rights echoed through the work of eighteenth-century philosophers. The "Age of Reason" saw a magnificent flowering of new secular thought which, embodied in the American Declaration of Independence as well as the French Declaration of the Rights of Man and Citizen, shaped liberal democracy in the Western world. Sometimes also called the Age of Ideas, the Age of Humanism, or the Age of Neo-Classicism, the century that culminated in the French Revolution is most popularly called the "Age of Light," or The Enlightenment, to signify the illumination produced when ancient Greek and Renaissance ideas were rekindled in the context of the seventeenth-century scientific revolution. More popularizers than original thinkers, the *philosophes* spread the ideas of Bacon, Descartes, Newton, Locke, and others. With full confidence in the power of human reason, they defined as "natural law" the principles that govern animal and human life, including "laws of justice and equity." Distinct from the "positive law" of nations, natural law was held to be perpetual and immutable, either given by God (according to some), or inherent in the material universe (according to others). Opposed to the church, to monarchy, and to all arbitrary forms of hierarchy and rule, the *philosophes* set as their goal to bring the laws of the state and the structure of social institutions into agreement with nature. Who was to remake the laws and institutions? "The only true sovereign is the nation," wrote Diderot. "There can be no true legislator except the people." For Jean-Jacques Rousseau (1712–1778), "sovereignty" resided in the "general will," a collective being created by a "social contract" with "absolute power over all its members."

The extent to which such ideas influenced the revolutionaries of 1789 (and other political leaders) has long been the subject of lively debate among historians and political scientists. From the publication in 1790 of Edmund Burke's *Reflections on the Revolution in France*, conservatives have held the political rationalism of the *philosophes* responsible for rending the organic fabric of traditional society and letting loose the twin demons of disorder and destruction. Liberals have emphasized, on the contrary, the *philosophes'* contributions toward development of the democratic institutions that foster political liberty and economic opportunity for the "common man" in most Western nations. Even Marxists, who deny the possibility of freedom in class society, credit the *philosophes'* ideas for replacing prejudice and privilege with a "kingdom of reason" designed to usher in a "democratic bourgeois" republican regime. Other analysts deemphasize the role of ideas, and stress the economic background of the French Revolution: bankruptcy of the royal treasury due to the expense of supporting the American Revolution; bad harvests, a bitter winter, widespread unemployment, high bread prices; resentment by various classes of high taxes or seigneurial dues; the ambitions of merchant or professional groups for greater economic as well as political power. The many perspectives on causes are matched by multiple interpretations of outcomes, showing the complexity of the relationship between politics and society.

The facts are simpler. In 1787 the Parlement of Paris rejected the King's proposals for new taxes, demanding that the Estates-General, a representative body that had not met since 1614, be summoned. It was composed of three bodies: the First the clergy, the Second the nobility, and the Third everyone else. Following traditional procedural rules, each Estate would cast one collective vote in the assembly; the vast majority, over 90 percent of the population, could then be outvoted, two to one. When denied their petition to vote by head rather than by order, the Third Estate proclaimed itself a National Assembly and voted to establish a new constitution for the country. As King Louis XVI tried to mobilize enough strength to regain his prerogatives, rumors of an aristocratic conspiracy fed on political and economic tensions to produce a "Great Fear" throughout the countryside. Dismissal of a reform-minded minister sparked riots in Paris, establishment by its populace of its own government and militia, and on July 14, the famous destruction of the Bastille, a prison that symbolized royal despotism.

The events in France, which began as attempts at reform, quickly progressed into social revolution. Every class played a role. Lawyers, office-holders, and members of the liberal professions led the creation of a new political culture, but marketwomen and artisans from the streets and shops of Paris emerged at critical junctures to accelerate the pace of revolution. Clergy who resisted secularization, loyalist peasants and aristocratic *emigrés* who sought foreign intervention against the revolutionary government contributed countervailing forces. Regicide and war, military conscription, scarcity of food and inflation, all intensified the level of conflict. Although revolutionary fervor peaked during the so-called Reign of Terror—between October 1793 and July 1794—constitutional changes, popular uprisings, and disorder continued until, in 1799, Napoleon Bonaparte assumed power by military coup. He, of course, carried the revolution with his Grand Army all the way to the steppes of Russia.

In a brief summary it is impossible to do justice to the constructive aspects of the revolutionary experience. These include the ending of feudal remnants that oppressed peasants and stymied economic development; the creation of a constitutional government balancing executive and legislative powers; the adoption of the Declaration of the Rights of Man and Citizen, establishing civil equality among men (including Jews); the enactment of new family laws allowing for civil divorce and inheritance rights by women; the defense of equality against inherited privilege. Most significantly, the revolutionaries in France replaced an absolute monarchy grounded in divine right with a republic based on the consent of the governed. The flames of the French Revolution lit a beacon for oppressed peoples everywhere—and cast a shadow of revolution over the entire nineteenth century.

It created a new political vocabulary and established a new agenda for rearranging social and economic relationships. Henceforth many people would imagine the world anew and seek to close the gap between what was and what could be. The revolutions in America and France were followed by numerous others in countries and city-states across Europe. The Chartist movement in England, led by workers demanding universal manhood suffrage, abolition of property qualifications for membership in Parliament, and other political reforms; the revolutions of 1848 and subsequent nation-building in central Europe; and the experiments with liberalization in Russia—these events ultimately brought political emancipation to most classes of *men.* The abolition of absolutism in relations between kings and subjects and between masters and servants might be expected to facilitate liberalization of social relations between the sexes. For women's rights, however, separate battles had to be fought. The Declaration of the Rights of Man did not encompass the female half of "mankind."

During the past decade, historians of women have reexamined the work of both the Enlightenment philosophers and the French revolutionaries. Mme. de Pompadour, Mme. Geoffrin, Mlle. de Lespinasse and other Parisian *salonières* contributed moral and financial support to the Encyclopedists; and a few joined their opponents. The Encyclopedists themselves, however, divided on the question of women's rights—the Huguenot nobleman Jaucourt penning entries in support of equality of the sexes in marriage; Desmahis, the dramatist protégée of Voltaire, reemphasizing misogynist views of women as vain, deceitful, and emptyheaded. The thirty-one entries on "woman" or topics beginning with that word include many contradictory opinions, some of which themselves cannot easily be categorized as "for" or "against" improvement in women's status. Overall, the Encyclopedists, like the *philosophes* more broadly, tended to see women as physically delicate, psychologically timid though passionate (a potentially dangerous combination), and socially destined for motherhood. Interestingly, the *Encyclopedia*'s seventeen volumes of text and eleven volumes of plates offer no reference to the salons, an institution of significance as we have seen in the Overview to Part I, both to women of the seventeenth and eighteenth centuries and to the philosophers themselves. There is, moreover, little discussion in the text of women at work, although the illustrations reveal women working in a large number of occupations, including many that were normally associated with men, such as glassmaking, papermaking, and gold and silver processing.

In their more fundamental task of defining natural law—the purported basis of social institutions—many eighteenth-century philosophers were divided in their assessments of the nature of women. The *philosophe* perhaps most famous for his support of enhanced women's rights is the marquis de Condorcet (1743–1794), while for his defense of traditionally restrictive roles, the best known is Rousseau. Condorcet, a mathematician and philosopher, was a leading member of the liberal nobility who supported the goals of the American Revolution and later of the Third Estate in his own country. Influenced perhaps by his experiences in America as well as by his relationships with educated women, he dealt with women's rights in several works. Writing even from prison in a society torn apart by social conflict, he envisioned a basis for reconstruction that included the "admission of women to rights of citizenship." Condorcet recognized the incompleteness of the revolution. The revolutionaries had

> violated the principle of equality of rights, in tranquilly depriving the half of the human race of that of assisting in the making of laws; in excluding women from the right of citizenship. . . . Either no individual of the human race has genuine rights, or else all have the same; and he who votes against the right of another, whatever the religion, colour, or sex of that other, has henceforth adjured his own.

Alleged conditions of female disability, such as "pregnancy and passing indispositions," he rejected as a justification for denying women rights, since "nobody ever dreamt of depriving people who have the gout every winter, or who easily catch cold."[6]

Despite the harmony of Condorcet's position on women's roles with the basic principles of the Enlightenment and the Revolution, he won few allies. Rousseau, on the other hand, won widespread support, as Barbara Corrado Pope shows (Chapter 5). He tapped several strong currents: traditional misogyny; distrust of the power of royal mistresses and the artifices of aristocratic ladies (dressed fashionably in tall, elaborate coiffures so that as they passed "you could see nothing but a forest of feathers, rising high above the heads and nodding to and fro"); and the romanticism that envisioned "natural woman" as the companion of "natural man." Defining the female role narrowly, for purposes of reproduction, Rousseau assigned women to their "proper" calling of childbearing and childrearing. But Rousseau added a new language to the discourse on women's subordination, because for him their differences entailed disabilities that precluded their participation in the "general will." Since participation in the general will required the transcendence of personal interest, and women, by Rousseau's definition as well as by custom and law, were dependent on personal relations, they could not exercise the highest duties of citizenship.

Rousseau's theory reflected the political reality of eighteenth-century Europe. Although exceptional women such as the Hapsburg Empress Maria Theresa of Austria (1740–1780) and Catherine II of Russia (1762–1796) exercised power over great countries, they owed their prerogatives to their inherited, aristocratic status. Both women tempered their power with Enlightenment ideals; but neither effected any change in attitudes, customs, or laws regarding their sex as a whole any more than had Elizabeth I of England two centuries before. Indeed, the laws codified by Catherine—one of the notable achievements of this "Enlightened Despot"—subjected women to the absolute authority of men. Empowered by the laws of every European country to prescribe and enforce rules for their families and households, men also represented their dependents in the political world. However, if most women had few formal political rights, they could exercise certain customary rights. Because the obligation to feed their families fell heavily on women, they might, during times of economic distress, participate in direct and highly political action such as bread riots and resistance to taxation. During the revolutionary upheaval in France women were active politically in old as well as new ways. Some women took their demands into the marketplace and streets. Others wrote political tracts, formed political clubs, and called into question the very basis of political power.

Consciously responding to the revolutionaries in France whose political double standard, like Rousseau's, violated their own principles, two unusual women quickly penned eloquent defenses of women's right to equality in the new society. In 1791, Olympe de Gouges, a butcher's daughter whose writings had gained her access to the French court, paraphrased the famous *Declaration of the Rights of Man and Citizen* in a radical manifesto that called on women, as "mothers, daughters, and sisters, representatives of the nation," to constitute themselves a national assembly. Asserting in terms resonant of Rousseau that "woman is born free and remains equal in rights to man," she redefined the general will explicitly to include female citizens. Like her antagonists, she catalogued women's defects but blamed them on their state of subjection to men. She prescribed "an invincible means of elevating the soul of women; it is for them to join in all the activities of men." Despite Olympe de Gouges's stirring call to her sisters, her voice went largely unheard for the next century and a half. Perhaps because she soon paid with her life for her unfeminine political activity, guillotined in 1793 at least partially "for having forgotten the virtues that suited her sex," her work remained obscure.

Across the Channel, Mary Wollstonecraft, an Englishwoman who first answered Burke's *Reflections* with her *A Vindication of the Rights of Men* (1790), was similarly indignant that revolutionary republican heroes who set out to reconstruct society instead reinforced patriarchal patterns of the past. She challenged the French leaders to examine the causes and consequences of women's situation. In the preface to her *A Vindication of the Rights of Woman (1792),* Wollstonecraft stated that

> If women are to be excluded, without having a voice, from a participation of the natural rights of mankind, prove first, to ward off the charge of injustice and inconsistency, that they [lack] reason—else this flaw in your NEW CONSTITUTION will ever shew that man must, in some shape, act like a tyrant, and tyranny, in whatever part of society it rears its brazen front, will ever undermine morality.

Wollstonecraft, a former governess and teacher whose wit and pen won her a place among the Enlightenment-inspired Philosophical Radicals in Britain, issued a stinging, point-by-point critique of Rousseau's treatise on female education, extending his blueprint for men's education to women, in the common interest. For, she wrote, "Till women are more rationally educated, the progress of human virtue and improvement in knowledge must receive continual checks. . . . Let woman share the rights and she will emulate the virtues of man."[7] Quickly moving through several editions and translations, the *Vindication* came to be considered the beginning of the modern women's rights movement, though Wollstonecraft herself, after dying in childbirth, was vilified for her unconventional life. Known to the leaders of the nineteenth-century struggle for women's rights in several nations, by mid-twentieth century she, too, was largely absent from the historical record, to be rediscovered for us by feminist historians in the late 1960s and the 1970s. Between 1970 and 1975, five new biographies of Wollstonecraft appeared in the United States.

Many others, before and after Condorcet, de Gouges, and Wollstonecraft, enjoined the leaders of society to include women in the new rights of citizenship. Abigail Adams, most famous as the wife of one American president and mother of another, is now well-known for rebuking John Adams and his fellow "Founding Fathers" for ignoring women's rights in the new United States Constitution. In Germany, Theodor von Hippel, in the same year that Wollstonecraft's second *Vindication* appeared, revised his popular treatise on marriage to reproach the revolutionaries in France who, in their new constitution, had "opted to forget one half of the nation. . . . All human beings have equal rights—all French men and women should be citizens and free." Agreeing with the German philosopher Immanuel Kant that no human being should be used merely as a means, he challenged Rousseauean principles. "Men, do you really believe that half the world exists merely for your pleasure, for your own desires, to satisfy your selfishness? Animals function; human beings act.—Why should a woman not be allowed to pronounce the word I?"

The challenge of revolutionary reconstruction not only inspired renewed debates about women's rights and abilities. Some women participated directly in the political events in France. Early in 1789, they joined men in submitting *cahiers,* or lists of grievances, to be delivered to the King. Working women petitioned for protection of their means of livelihood from competition, from encroachment by men. Others called for "free schools where we can learn the principles of our language, religion, and ethics," although they explicitly rejected instruction in science, for it might "inspire us with a foolish pride and lead us toward pedantry." They also asked for paid midwives in the countryside. Later they sent delegations to the National Assembly, began to address the political clubs directly, and formed separate women's clubs, the most famous being the Revolutionary Republican Women Citizens led by Pauline Léon, a chocolatemaker, and Claire Lacombe, an actress. None of the specifically feminist proposals submitted to the Assembly received serious consideration.[8]

The women's clubs were short-lived, dissolved by the Jacobins in the fall of 1793, possibly for their support of the *enragés,* who demanded extreme economic measures, or because the women transgressed social conventions of feminine behavior, donning the red cap of the revolution, debating politics in public, and attacking women in the marketplace who failed to wear the republican tricolor. The leader of the Paris Commune greeted a delegation of women with the admonition:

> Since when have people been allowed to renounce their sex? Since when has it been acceptable to see women abandon the *pious* duties of their households, their children's cradles, to appear in public, to take the floor and to make speeches, to come before the senate?

Robespierre's Committee of Public Safety counseled women who wanted to be republicans to dress simply, work hard—at home—and give only moral support to the revolution.

Robespierre's prescription for women, like Rousseau's, was in tune with the material and emotional needs of most people. Faced with conditions that threatened the sustenance of their families, women have always utilized every means at hand to find food and the revolutionary decade was no exception. Whether subject or citizen, the first concern of women was securing subsistence. Thus, the thousands of marketwomen, housewives, and working women who marched to Versailles in search of bread in October 1789 ("Let them eat cake" was Marie Antoinette's famous reply), were far more typical of women engaged in political action than any who spoke in political clubs or signed petitions. The march to Versailles exemplifies a characteristic form of women's collective action, the "bread riot." During the eighteenth and nineteenth centuries, as national markets prevailed over local needs and authorities ceased to control foodstuff prices, angry women, sometimes armed with knives and sticks, led mobs to attack mills, millers, machinery, or other ostensibly appropriate targets. "The bread riot," Olwen Hufton points out, "was female, or rather, maternal, terrain."[9]

After the Thermidorian coup in July 1794, which marked the end of the "social–democratic" phase of the revolution, autonomous public activity by women was forbidden. In May 1795, the National Convention decreed that women be excluded from its meetings and allowed to watch from a gallery only if accompanied by a man. The negative reaction to political participation by women demonstrates the limited impact of the French Revolution on social relations between the sexes. When we incorporate the experience of women, we can no longer simply hail as progressive a political process whereby traditional or informal power and privilege were replaced by formal rights of citizenship granted only to men, or even informal protest replaced by organized political parties that excluded women. As we shall see in Part III, the Russian Revolution, one of the most consequential events of the twentieth century, also failed to bring about fundamental changes in social relations between men and women.

Women, the Idea of Progress, and Utopian Socialism

The reaction against revolutionary change in women's social and political roles that began in France in the mid-1790s was strengthened by the accession to power of a great military leader, Napoleon Bonaparte. For the Corsican-born conqueror turned emperor, women contributed to the nation above all new soldiers. Often praised by champions of democracy for having "opened careers to talent," that is, for replacing inherited status with merit as the criterion for selection of army officers and other leaders, Napoleon became infamous among nineteenth-century feminists for several provisions of the influential Napoleonic Code of 1804, once lauded for having established civil equality among all men. Feminist critics objected strenuously to many articles, particularly those that required married women to "obey" their husbands, to take on their spouse's nationality and accept his domicile, and those that denied them legal status in court. They criticized regulations that prohibited lawsuits by unwed mothers to establish paternity of their children, thus denying them recourse for child support; that gave fathers exclusive authority to administer their minor children's affairs and to withhold consent to their marriage, even to imprison them for "correction," without the mother's consent. They rejected as well the provision that decreed adultery a crime only if committed by wives. For these laws, individually and collectively, made women second-class citizens, indeed hardly participating members of the new French nation. Moreover, during the ensuing decade, Napoleon's victorious armies carried his code of laws across the Rhine into the German lands and southward into the Italian peninsula. The influence persisted; in the 1860s, after the unification of Italy, the new government drew on Napoleon's Code. Napoleonic laws concerning women affected even the Louisiana Territory of the United States and the statutes of subsequent state governments. In France, although feminists condemned the Code for a century and a half and publicly burned it during solemn events celebrating its centennial in 1904, French people escaped its influence very slowly, beginning with revision of maternal authority and married women's control of their own earnings in 1907, and rights to initiate paternity suits in 1912.

Napoleon was overthrown by the combined armies of Europe in 1815. The ensuing two decades, following on twenty-five years of upheaval, were largely ones of conservative reaction, of "restoration." For most women as well as men, maintaining home and family continued to be the highest priority. Revolution had bred war; and as Olwen Hufton points out, "war strikes at the family: it takes fathers and sons and what death does not destroy can be left to the effect of long separation. This was certainly the hard lesson of the French Revolution." In the end, women looked backward to more settled times and renewed their fervor for the church. The church not only symbolized stability and continuity, it centered around the family. "The church," Hufton notes, "stood for [the family's] integrity, its sanctity; the hallowing of birth, marriage, death; the cement of something much more intrinsic than the social system." Even Napoleon had recognized the power of the church and come to terms with it in his Concordat of 1802.

Nevertheless, the old regime was never to be restored. Although England, Austria, and Russia, among other European countries, guarded against renewed revolutionary outbreaks by enforcement of repressive laws—for instance, in England the "Six Acts" of 1819 restricted mass public meetings and the Metternich decrees of the same year imposed censorship of the press and of university life in all the German states—industrial development continued and new ideas flourished. Not all the agents and armies of the Holy Alliance and the Concert of Europe (formed by the victors of Waterloo to maintain order on the Continent) could stamp out the spirit of change that spread across Europe in the early nineteenth century.

Prominent among the thinkers promoting change whose ideas had been shaped in the revolutionary upheaval and the developing industrial system were Henri Saint-Simon (1760–1825), Charles Fourier (1772–1837), and Robert Owen (1771–1858), founders of modern socialism. Believers in a universal (natural) law of progress, these men, known as "utopian socialists," went beyond criticism of existing privilege and exploitation to invent new systems of social organization. Most important for our concerns, they and their followers included in their contemplated reconstruction of society changes in women's roles and in relations between the sexes. Saint-Simon, who proposed that the rulers of his new order be scientists, intended to base a rationalized utilitarian social structure on the ethos of early Christianity. But, he said, "The true Christianity must render men happy on earth as well as in heaven." His key was "moral science." Acknowledging that human beings were not equal in capacity, Saint-Simon considered their differences to be beneficial, for society was an organism of many parts, all functioning, ideally, in harmony. Work appropriate to capacity was the first law of Saint-Simon's "New Christianity." Furthermore, since "love was the fluid which coursed through the body social," the followers of Saint-Simon, who after his death set about proselytizing throughout Europe, envisioned a critical role for women. "Who else," they said, "throughout the common ages, stained with blood, rust, and tears, has won man over to peace and love, if it is not woman?" Indeed, one of their primary goals became the reversal of centuries of Christian repression of sexual love and its concomitant degradation of women. Following Saint-Simon in his denial of the Christian dichotomy between body and soul, they proposed to liberate the instincts, to "rehabilitate the flesh." Led by Prosper Enfantin, a former engineering student turned banker, they organized expeditions to North Africa and the Middle East to search for a lost "Female Messiah" who would emancipate not only women but indeed the whole human race.[10]

Not all Saint-Simonians accepted Enfantin's conception of complete equality of the sexes, which was based in a rejection of the "politics of individualism" that he considered the cause of greed and inequality. This perspective led to one of his most controversial propositions—a denial of monogamy—labeled by its opponents (who eventually sent Enfantin to prison) as "free love." It also caused schisms among the Saint-Simonians. But Enfantin's ideas attracted women, some two hundred of whom regularly attended the lectures that were given almost daily by the Saint-Simonians after the July Revolution of 1830. In 1831, 110 working-class women enrolled as "faithful adherents." Although attracted originally less by consciousness of themselves as women than by interest in the emancipation of workers, these women developed a new gender awareness and eventually founded an autonomous women's movement. They published a newspaper, which in successive issues announced in its title the advent of "The Free Woman," "The Apostolate of Woman," "The Woman of the Future," "The New Woman," and "The Emancipation of Woman," before finally becoming *The Tribune of Women.* Its editors and contributors used only first names, declaring, "If we continue to take men's names we shall [continue to] be slaves." While some of them put the new sexual emancipation into practice, and others left the movement in disagreement with Enfantin's radicalism on this issue, most of the "new women" simply rejected ideas that conflicted with the reality of their lives. As historian Claire Moses points out, they recognized that the "love without marriage" advocated by Enfantin posed far greater dangers to them than to the Saint-Simonian men, most of whom would find places as industrialists, scientists, and managers in the new economic order, while they continued to labor as seamstresses for wages inadequate to maintain themselves, let alone also children.

Eventually, indeed, many Saint-Simonian men became leaders in the development of new railways or invention of credit banks and other commercial or industrial ventures that multiplied during the heyday of economic liberalism. During the second quarter of the nineteenth century, the rich got richer, perhaps following the advice of the French minister Guizot, who asserted that a country's political power belonged of right to the men of fortune who owned and exploited its resources. Meanwhile, as urban slums mushroomed, worker rebellions led to violent clashes. Some intellectuals began to assert that social peace could be achieved in industrial society only by reconstructing its economic and social foundations. They hoped voluntarily to draw people into new communities carefully planned to ensure a total harmony of interests.

One of the earliest social, or "socialist" thinkers, Charles Fourier, an eccentric bachelor banking clerk, proposed a new order composed of "phalansteries," where men and women, carefully selected to assure a full complement of 1,620 different naturally occurring personalities, would be assigned to perform work so perfectly matched to their passions that socially useful labor would be perceived as play. A change of task every two hours or less would relieve workers of the "torment" of their present twelve- to fifteen-hour days spent at tedious jobs, and allow them freedom to express their "butterfly" and other passions. Thus work would bring pleasure, even dirty work such as spreading manure, which would fall to youngsters because of the "natural penchant of children for filth." A potential murderer would be reformed by assignment to work in the butcheries. Fourier was so confident that a wealthy benefactor would appear to endow his scheme that for twelve years he went home everyday at the announced hour of noon to wait. Although he died unrewarded, even before his death and for decades afterward, Fourierist communities were established in Europe and North America.

To Fourier, the phalansteries, governed according to laws of association, represented an evolutionary improvement over societies based on individualistic competition, which he considered "the mother of all social crimes." From earlier chaotic stages of "savagery," "patriarchalism," "barbarism," and "civilization," human beings would progress through "simple association" to the highest stage of perfect harmony, called "compound convergent association." A measure of the level of progress in all societies was, he proclaimed, the status of women, a criterion later adopted by Karl Marx and other important thinkers. Thus like the Saint-Simonians, Fourier looked to a future world in which women would enjoy equality with men. Fourier's own passion for equality extended to the provision of identical clothing, education, and employment opportunities for both sexes. (Indeed, no occupation could have fewer than one-eighth members of either sex.) Individual families would give way to collective living, with communal responsibility for child care and housework.

If Fourier's scheme for social progress represented the vision of a lonely genius, an English utopian who set out to reorganize society, Robert Owen, was just the opposite, a successful businessman respected for his economic contributions to the community. After a spectacular rise from draper's apprentice to manager of a cotton mill employing 500 workers (by the age of 18), Owen bought the largest mill in Scotland and embarked upon an experiment to disprove the myth of competitive individualism that his own career might have reinforced. Paying higher wages and providing better working conditions than his rivals, furnishing good homes and schools for his work force, he made New Lanark more productive and profitable than competing enterprises. Workers themselves adopted his ideas, later replacing Owen's paternalistic management with their own cooperative direction. Like Fourier, he also inspired experiments in communal living in the United States and elsewhere.

Following the Saint-Simonians, the Owenites attracted considerable female interest. Mutually reinforcing contacts between the groups included the translation of articles from *The Tribune of Women* for publication in Robert Owen's journal, *The Crisis,* by an English Saint-Simonian turned Owenite, Anna Wheeler (1785–1848). Wheeler was closely associated with yet another "utopian," William Thompson (1775–1833), an Englishman who reorganized his 700-peasant estate in Ireland into a model scientific farming community. He also left his body to medical research, and his skeleton, library, and estate to the cooperative movement he founded. In concert with Wheeler, Thompson worked out the ideas he published in 1825 as the *Appeal of One-Half of the Human Race, Women, against the Pretensions of the Other Half, Men, to Retain Them in Political, and Thence in Civil and Domestic Slavery.* The Thompson–Wheeler *Appeal* was an attack on James Mill, the famous Utilitarian who, with Jeremy Bentham, adapted the ideas of the French *philosophes* to English society, calling for government by an educated middle class to procure "the greatest good for the greatest number." While proposing "universal suffrage," Mill had nevertheless rejected female enfranchisement, arguing that the "rights of men" included the interests of women. Thompson and Wheeler exposed the fallacies of Mill's position and protested his "pretensions," as indeed did his son, John Stuart Mill, whose own eloquent defense of women's rights, *The Subjection of Women,* co-authored with Harriet Taylor and published in 1869, eclipsed the *Appeal* in fame and far-reaching influence.[11]

Another woman of the "utopian" era, who also drew on Saint-Simonian and Fourierist ideas, deserves recognition as a forerunner of later feminist and socialist thought. Flora Tristan (1803–1844) was the daughter of a Peruvian army officer and a bourgeois French mother, who learned only in adulthood that she would be denied social status and inherited wealth because her parents' religious marriage had not been paralleled by the civil ceremony required to establish its legality; that is, she was an illegitimate child of an irregular union. Furthermore, she was twice a pariah, for she also had deserted an abusive husband, whom she could not, under the law of France (from the Restoration in 1815 until 1884), divorce. Traveling alone to Peru, where she vainly sought an inheritance from her father's substantial estate, and to England, where she met Owen and Wheeler and studied the social circumstances of women and urban workers, she used her uncommon experience as the basis of a "utopian synthesis of socialism and feminism." Feeling herself to be Mary Wollstonecraft reincarnated, she also used her pen to make a living writing passionate accounts of her experiences that established her reputation as a novelist and social critic. She felt herself called to tour France, bringing to workers and women her scheme for their liberation. In 1843 she published her *Workers' Union,* proposing to reorganize both work and family along Fourierist lines. The "absolute equality" of men and women, she believed, was essential to the emancipation of the working classes and the moral transformation of human society. For every community she planned education for the children of the working classes and refuge for the old and homeless. No one would suffer the ostracism and poverty she had endured.[12]

During the first half of the nineteenth century, currents of romanticism inspired an intense concentration on the self that resulted in both "dandyism," or extreme elegance in men's fashions, and the poetry of Byron, Shelley, and Keats. The literary *Sturm und Drang* period in Germany, the Jewish Hassidism of Eastern Europe, the Gothic revival in architecture, and the music of Chopin and Liszt all reflected rejection of the extreme rationalism of the eighteenth century. At the same time, romanticism also affected the more socially-oriented founders of the new science, the "social science" defined by Thompson and Wheeler as "the science of promoting human happiness." All of the forward-looking political ideologies of the nineteenth century—utilitarianism, liberalism, anarchism, socialism, feminism, Saint-Simonianism, Fourierism, Marxism—shared the conviction that human beings could perfect the social world. Common to many of these systems of thought and political movements was the belief that (in words taken from the conclusion of the Thompson–Wheeler *Appeal*) men could and must be persuaded to take "the most certain step towards the regeneration of degraded humanity, by opening a free course for justice and benevolence, for intellectual and social enjoyments, by no colour, by no sex to be restrained." Until its last decades, the nineteenth century was dominated by a passion for progress, by belief in a *law* of progress. The French sociologist Emile Durkheim spoke for Saint-Simon and generations of his spiritual descendants when he declared, "The supreme law of progress of the human spirit carries along and dominates everything; men are but its instruments." Women were both the agents and the beneficiaries of this historical current.

The "Woman Question"

Articulation of the "woman question," as debate over women's roles was called expressively in the nineteenth century, reached a zenith in the wake of the "Dual Revolution" and its political and social consequences. Intertwined with the "social question," or the debate about class relations and the condition of the poor, it led to an unprecedented outpouring, in all the languages of the Western world, of articles, books, sermons, theses, poetry, and painting concerned with the "place" of women. While changes in household functions altered the productive and educative roles of the family in society, the transformation of men's and women's work within familial boundaries created a split between reproduction and production that affected everyone. Men adapted by increasingly withdrawing from shared domestic labor to take on paid employment outside the home. Indeed, by the middle decades of the nineteenth century, some workingmen, principally tailors and other craftsmen, organized against work for wages at home, for they could obtain better working conditions and higher pay in workshop and factory employ.

In the case of women, the development of a commercial and industrial economy made ancient questions about their proper pursuits more acute and more complex. Tension developed between normative expectations and real experience. Even though the ideology of domesticity, which, as Barbara Corrado Pope shows (Chapter 5) was expounded and popularized by Rousseau and attracted adherents throughout society, the needs of working-class and some middle-class families for additional income made the gainful employment of women imperative. Women's ongoing productive activities for the home or for exchange defied the new normative divisions of work and home life inherent in the ideology. Furthermore, while the theory of natural rights led to new emphasis on individual liberty, equality, and self-fulfillment, the nearly simultaneous "discovery" of childhood led to increased demands for nurturance over longer periods by mothers. As a result, although the reality of women's lives defied any simple normative standard, discussions of women's roles and rights contained contradictory prescriptions. At stake were answers to such questions as whether women should be educated and if so, why and how; whether women had a "right to work" and if so, where and when; whether married women should enjoy rights to individual ownership of property or income; whether femaleness should entail permanent political disability.

One of the areas of greatest concern and conflict was education. Basic to the Enlightenment spirit and the liberal thought of the eighteenth and nineteenth centuries was a belief in the power of education. By defining human beings as rational animals capable of free will, Enlightenment philosophers tended to reject the Christian assumption of original sin that put human beings in everlasting need of salvation. Instead they emphasized human malleability, attributing to environment great influence in determining behavior. They were in large part, to use the modern term, environmentalists. Faith in education was fundamental to their belief in progress. In the 1760s, the French physiocrat Nicholas Baudeau (1730–1792?) pointed out the necessity of educating women. "National education [would be] imperfect in every respect if we were to abandon half the State to prejudice, routine, and abuse." Alluding to the example of ancient Sparta, where girls received rigorous training, he concluded that "Daughters of the Nation," would make "worthy wives for the Great Men" of France only if properly educated.[13]

During the nineteenth century, movements to establish public schools and to increase access to them by children of all classes were established in England, France, Germany, the United States, and many other countries. The motives of the founders were mixed. Some were compelled by new theories on child development (such as Rousseau's) and moved to found child-oriented programs, such as the first kindergarten, founded in Germany in 1837 by Friedrich Froebel. Others were concerned primarily with the need of representative governments for an educated citizenry. Some advocates of education represented privileged groups who, fearing the potential of illiterate and untrained people for crime and social unrest, considered the terms "working classes" and "dangerous classes" virtually synonymous. A "penny press" brought new information and expectations to the expanding populace, making it imperative for the leading classes to create a "schooled society" committed to emergent national norms in language, manners, and morals, especially to the values of hard work and self-discipline (the "work ethic").

The education of women could hardly be ignored in this effort although the push for female education, like so many responses to the situation of women in a changing society, contained contradictory elements. Educational reformers sometimes assumed that women, as mothers and the first educators of the young, were naturally disposed toward conservativism and patriotism. Educated women would exert a "calming influence" on men and hence promote social stability. Others, primarily anticlericals, hoped that improved education would free women from the sway of the church.

The systems of local, secular schools established by many European countries during the nineteenth century were rarely supported either by the populace or the municipal authorities to the extent envisioned by their founders. One important reason lay in the limited availability of trained teachers and of funds to pay them. It is not surprising, then, that arguments regarding the superior capacities of women as educators of young children helped to overcome the opposition of conservatives to publicly funded schools for girls and that the first female colleges were teacher training institutes. Rousseau might consider a "female wit" a "scourge to her husband, her children, her servants, to everybody" and Joseph de Maistre, a leading French conservative of the Restoration period, insist the female schools were unnecessary because girls were meant for "a life of retreat and shall be solely concerned with familial needs." But if girls were to be educated, certainly they should be taught by women. As Kreszenz Rapp, a German teaching candidate wrote in 1807 in her qualifying exam, girls

> require a softer, gentler treatment than boys, because nature plants in the girls' hearts the seeds of gentleness and timidity, a noble gift of their sex. . . . Who can understand/manage these feminine feelings, whose delicacy envelopes the entire being of the girls, better than one of their own sex? . . . Male teachers are less effective because their knowledge of female delicacy only comes from books.

Careers for women in teaching were justified as an expression of femininity and an extension of domesticity—women's "natural" nurturing role performed in another setting for a worthy public purpose. The teacher's role was "social motherhood."[14]

The increase in public schools, even for boys alone, created a new demand for large numbers of literate teachers; and if they could be paid low female wages, so much the better. In 1814, the southern German state of Bavaria created a teacher training institute for women. In the United States, prior to the Civil War, following the example of such pioneer educators as Emma Willard, Mary Lyon, and Catharine Beecher, female teachers began to replace male. In Massachusetts, which led in the transformation, women constituted two-thirds of the teacher corps by 1842; and by the 1880s, this was true for America as a whole. A comparison of average wage rates in various states of North America offers suggestive information on the rapid rate of change:

State	Year	Men	Women
Michigan	1847	$12.87	$5.74
Indiana	1850	12.00	6.00
Massachusetts	1848	24.51	8.07
Maine	c. 1848	15.40	4.80
New York	c. 1848	15.95	6.99
Ohio	c. 1848	15.42	8.73

Similarly, in the Vosges department of eastern France, the average annual income of male teachers in 1839 was 487 francs; of female, only 380.[15]

The motivation for change was different in England. The first colleges for women, Queen's and Bedford, date from the late 1840s. Established to elevate the status of governesses and other "ladies," they opened the teaching profession to women in order to meet an urgent need for "respectable" employment for impecunious middle-class spinsters. It was said that "every lady is and must be a teacher—of some person or other, of children, sisters, the poor." One of the pioneers of female education in England was Barbara Bodichon (1827–1891), whose father had founded a "Ragged School" for the education of poor children, where he employed a teacher trained at Robert Owen's New Lanark School. He gave his own children an Owenist education as well as an early introduction to the work of Mary Wollstonecraft. In her own school, established in 1854, Bodichon drew also on the ideas of the educational reformers Johann Pestalozzi, Emanuel Swedenborg, and Froebel to apply the latest theories in child development. She carried the argument for female education well beyond a utilitarian standard of preparation for domesticity to insist on the importance of training for economic independence.

> Women want to work both for the health of their minds and their bodies. They want it often because they must eat and because they have children and others dependent on them—for all the reasons that men want work.[16]

Thus the question of female access to education and to employment as teachers shaded into a developing controversy over women's "right to work." Physicians and professors debated the purported deleterious effects on the female reproductive system of intense, sustained mental exertion, some alleging that highly educated women would suffer sterility. The underlying ideology of domesticity also affected attitudes toward the roles of working-class women, for whom hard physical labor remained the common experience. In the 1860s and for the rest of the century, organized working men repeatedly placed "the woman question," or its variant, "the industrialization of women," high on the agenda at their trade union and political party conferences. Largely artisans in threatened handicrafts, they faced new competition from national and international markets, reduced wages and unemployment due to the mechanization and centralization of their industries, and, in some cases, for the first time they began to see women other than family members entering their workshops. They could draw on an older guild tradition of sex role divisions that reserved the production of goods for exchange to artisans alone (or their widows) and assigned women housework or service in other peoples' households. Perhaps also partly because, as skilled workers, they could better afford to support families than could the untrained day laborers who rarely participated in workers' councils, these workingmen called for the elimination of industrial work by women. By a large majority in 1866, members of the International Workingmen's Association, largely English, French, and Swiss artisans, passed resolutions declaring that woman's place was at home, that man's role was to'support her. Furthermore, they declared that women should give birth to numerous offspring (ideally four children at two-year intervals) and remain at home to raise them. Every good woman, they insisted to a protesting minority, would find a husband. The followers of the German working-class leader, Ferdinand Lassalle (1825–1864) agreed.

Working-class men who condemned industrial work for women argued that they intended thereby to improve the moral and physical condition of families, class, and nation. They supported, however, gainful labor by married women at home in the traditional ways that Barbara Franzoi depicts (Chapter 6). Recent research shows that this marginalization of women workers often led to their exploitation as pieceworkers in sweatshops. In other cases, as Donna Gabaccia shows among the Italian peasantry (Chapter 8), domesticity represented not a new cultural norm for ladies but a measure of decline in wage-earning opportunities. In rural populations such as Sicily, families required female contributions to move "beyond subsistence." When rural entrepreneurs responding to shifting markets reorganized the structure of agricultural industry and women lost cash-generating labor, they became fully dependent on inadequate male wages. Some women thus "unemployed" into full-time housewifery faced male hostility; others emigrated to the United States.

The developing feminine ideal, expressed at mid-century by numbers of working-class men, also denied women access to full membership in a society where labor was increasingly the criterion of social value and the mark of personal identity. Paule Mink (1839–1901), a young Polish-French woman later active in the Paris Commune (1870–1871) and in the founding of the French Workers' Party, responded to the workers:

> By denying woman the right to work, you degrade her, you put her under man's yoke and deliver her over to man's good pleasure. By ceasing to make her a worker, you deprive her of her liberty and, thereby, of her responsibility. . . . Certainly there will come a time—and I hope it is not too far off—when our honor will come primarily from our work, where no one will be worth more than he produces. Then what will woman's role be if, inert and passive, she is entirely at the disposal of her husband? If she is forbidden to think of work? If she has no future apart from marriage? And if she is deprived forever of liberty and a life of her own?[17]

Some of these debates pitted the men who followed the Frenchman P.-J. Proudhon (1809–1865), the father of philosophical anarchism, against the supporters of Karl Marx (1818–1883), the founder of "scientific socialism." Proudhon defended the family-centered ideal of the peasant-proprietor and artisan-merchant that rejected concentrated, capitalist industry, credit and exchange banking, centralized government, and female emancipation. Marx alternatively looked toward increasing industrialization and centralization as means to greater abundance and more equitable distribution of work and wealth. He saw the participation of women in "social production," or work outside the home, as a necessary step toward achievement of a just and "classless" society. According to Marx, despite its evils in the short run, under capitalism, ultimately,

> modern industry, by assigning as it does an important part in the process of production outside the domestic sphere to women, to young persons, and to children of both sexes, creates a new economical foundation for a higher form of the family and of the relations between the sexes.

Although Marx went beyond the utopian socialists to develop a more sophisticated historical and philosophical analysis of political economy and the "social question," he unfortunately narrowed his vision to exclude serious attention to the "woman question." The promise implied in the words above he never kept; that is, he failed to include forms of the family, relations between the sexes, and social reproduction in his systematic analysis of labor, class, and capital. Perhaps his own bourgeois background blinded him to the realities of women's economic and social contributions. Perhaps his need to appeal for support to workingmen increasingly attracted by artisanal and bourgeois notions of separate spheres and the "family wage" made advocacy of sexual equality a political liability.

Shortly after Marx's death, his close colleague, Friedrich Engels, extended the analysis and directly shaped the emerging European social democratic interpretation of the woman question. In *The Origin of the Family, Private Property and the State* (1884), Engels traced the subordination of women to the institution of private property and men's concern for accumulating and preserving wealth. Only through participation in "social production" could women escape subjugation; the key lay in abolition of the monogamous family and restoration of a higher form of early communalism in which women were no longer economically dependent on men. Engels's work was widely read, translated, and serialized in the international socialist press. Today, aided by the new feminist theorizing, we can see the limits of Engels's monocausal interpretation of women's subordination. By anchoring the issue of sex-based, social asymmetry in the material fact of private property, he failed to appreciate the complex links among women's roles—in sexual relationships, in the family, in religious institutions, as well as in political and economic activities—and their subordination to men. This made him and his followers, many of whom truly expected the emancipation of women to follow directly upon socialist revolution, unduly optimistic about the possibility of change.

Following Marx and Engels, most Marxists failed to acknowledge the unpaid household labor of women as productive activity, and they neglected the effect of family values and experiences on workers' consciousness. Nonetheless, social democrats offered women more attention than other political parties of the day. The exploitation of working-class women by capitalist employers was a recurrent theme in socialist literature and socialists gave strong support to protective legislation. Ambivalent about women's right to work, they nevertheless inscribed women's rights on their banners and at least in theory—and to a limited degree in practice—opened their ranks to all, "without distinction by sex." In nineteenth-century Europe, the woman question and the social question were entwined. But the "marriage" of two social movements for reform, feminism and socialism, was stormy and the partners unequal, as we shall see below.

Efforts to obtain advanced education and improved employment opportunities for women were largely the work of a small group of mostly middle-class women who recognized the contradictions between Victorian ideals and the circumstances of women's lives. Nowhere was the incongruence greater than in the simultaneous apotheosis of the married woman and mother as the moral guardian of the family and her total lack of legal authority in marital and parental matters. If men had "rights" and women only "duties," as the title of an English pamphlet suggested, how could the latter ensure family welfare in the event of masculine malfeasance? Did women's invisible contributions to material and social success merit no reward? What would become of the increasing numbers of "redundant women" destined not for the blessings of matrimony but for enduring spinsterhood? The "woman question" defied simple answers.[18]

Domesticity and Demography: Women and the Family

Women today may look back to Charles Fourier, John Stuart Mill, and Karl Marx, to Mary Wollstonecraft, Flora Tristan, Barbara Bodichon, and Paule Mink as defenders of the "second sex" and their rights as individuals. But women of the nineteenth century, who perceived themselves primarily as members of families, more likely aspired to achieve the new kind of femininity expressed in the work of the poets Coventry Patmore, whose poem "The Angel in the House" gave the ideology of domesticity a new symbolic expression, and Alfred Lord Tennyson, whose verses perfectly captured the doctrine of "separate spheres":

> Man for the field and woman for the hearth:
> Man for the sword and for the needle she:
> Man with the head and woman with the heart:
> Man to command and woman to obey;
> All else confusion.

Tennyson's dichotomous presentation of the sexes illustrates the phenomenon analyzed recently by a historian of German women, Karin Hausen, who suggests that in the nineteenth century the "character of the sexes" previously defined by particular household duties—field and hearth, sword and needle—came to be understood in terms of essential and universal attributes of male and female. We should not overestimate the newness of Hausen's formulation, for Aristotle spoke of woman's essentially weak character mirroring her imperfect nature. Now, however, as economic changes spurred the evolution of the European family toward a unit bound by needs of affection and consumption rather than production, the doctrine of separate spheres became normative. Concerted efforts were made to impose it on the working classes, and especially "to educate the women of the lower strata of society for their 'destiny as wife, housekeeper, and mother' . . . as the best solution to the social question."

Sibylle Meyer's study of "conspicuous leisure" among the wives of civil servants in the German Empire (Chapter 7) provides a telling example of the tensions posed by the new ideal feminine role. Meyer shows that perfect housewives who "determined the atmosphere of the household through their character, not their work," existed only in imagination. In reality middle-class wives led active, productive lives that paralleled and supported their husbands' increasingly routinized and disciplined labor. They kept careful accounts of every item purchased, every gift given or received, even every visit paid to or by themselves—a kind of "commercial balance sheet of home and social life." Yet they strove to maintain an *appearance* of ladylike idleness commensurate with their husbands' status. Indeed the leisure of its women, even more than the occupation of its men, served to validate a family's claim to middle-class standing.[19]

The process of change in women's familial roles was uneven and complex. Bourgeois women in the north of France maintained a "premodern" view of their roles up to the end of the nineteenth century, emphasizing ties to church and family bloodlines. For these Catholic and convent-educated daughters of the propertied classes, marriage was a "solemn duty." According to historian Bonnie G. Smith, they had "no illusions of love and romance." They recognized the economic basis of marriage and clung to the power they derived from their role in reproduction and sexuality, in supplying the "cord of life" that bound together the generations—and their estates—even though frequent childbearing exacted a high price in chronic illness and maternal mortality.[20]

For most women of all classes, marriage continued to be the only honorable—indeed often the only available—career throughout the nineteenth century. But slowly its purposes and significance was changing. Facing the fateful decision of choosing a mate—a decision that would determine, in a real sense, her life course—a twenty-one-year-old Frenchwoman, Stéphanie Jullien, wrote to her brother in 1833, "This is not child's play, this is a matter of my whole life, of my future, of my happiness. . . . To decide my fate once and for all, my whole destiny! I don't dare do it." She worried lest her prospective young husband fail to establish himself sufficiently and she questioned the nature of *his* character and *his* commitment. "Who can assure me that he will succeed? And if he loves me now, how do I know that he will always love me in the same way? Perhaps I'll be paving the way for lots of trouble if I accept, but if I refuse, what will I do? . . . I don't have any calling, nor could I have one."[21]

Despite the idealization of domesticity, most women of all but the wealthiest classes continued to find marriage essential for economic (not emotional) security. For the urban poorer classes, often kept from legal wedlock by poverty (as well as state intervention where laws prohibited the marriage of indigents), "common-law" marriage was commonplace in the nineteenth century. Middle-class moralists, however, disapproved, and some philanthropic groups, such as the Society of Saint Vincent de Paul, were formed to encourage poor people to marry and "legitimize" their offspring. And marriage rates increased as the century progressed. For the spinsters, however, destined by demographic imbalance or lack of dowry never to marry, other solutions were required. No longer able for the most part to retire to convents, less likely than single men to emigrate to the New World, unable to find respectable or remunerative employment, single women sought alternative forms of domesticity. Large numbers entered domestic service. A study of spinsters in mid-Victorian England shows that about 25 percent of single women in all age groups up to thirty-five to forty-four were employed as live-in servants. Older spinsters tended to live with siblings, especially spinster sisters and bachelor brothers. Sometimes spinsters formed what we today call "surrogate families," or cooperative living groups.

The difficulties of earning a living made life alone precarious for single women. In addition, they faced the societal disdain that Charlotte Brontë illustrates in her mid-nineteenth century novel *Shirley:* "Old maids, like the houseless and unemployed poor, should not ask for a place and an occupation in the world." They were not wanted by married relatives. Furthermore, all social life was closed to unescorted women. The French man of letters Jules Michelet felt that "the worst fate for a woman was to live alone. . . . She could hardly go out in the evening; she would be taken for a prostitute. . . . If she were late, far from home, and became hungry, she would not dare enter a restaurant. . . . She would make a spectacle of herself." As single women and widows in the nineteenth century led efforts to provide aid to unwed mothers, to care for foundlings, to rehabilitate prostitutes, to improve opportunities for education and employment for their sex, they also created a new social role for themselves. Some women, moreover, chose spinsterhood because they preferred the company of their own sex. Lifelong, emotionally as well as economically supportive, relationships among women provided them a not uncommon alternative to marriage. These "romantic friendships" also offered an important outlet for their erotic impulses.[22]

Most women, however, preferred to marry. Typically, they entered matrimony later than we might expect, usually only well into their twenties, on average about twenty-four or twenty-five, though with many specific variations. In rural areas, where young people still often had to await both parental permission and economic resources, women might not marry until their intended groom could convince his father to deed him a share of the family plot. Some parents resisted their children's marriages because the departure of grown children from the household meant the loss of labor power or wages essential to family survival. In 1835, when Villermé, while investigating working conditions visited cottage workers in the region of Tarare (near Lyons), he found that men married on average at the age of thirty, women at twenty-seven. Not only age at marriage but even the chance to marry at all depended on occupation. Thus, at mid-century in the textile cities of Roubaix, France (1861) and Preston, England (1851), all but 12 and 10 percent, respectively, of women married. But in the artisanal and commercial cities of Amiens, France, and York, England, 24 percent and 16 percent of women remained unmarried at fifty. Some women, of course, formed long-lasting "free unions," also called "concubinage" and "Parisian marriages," and contributed to the rising number of "illegitimate" children. Burgeoning rates of illegitimacy reflected the vulnerability of young women attracted to new urban centers by opportunities for employment. Particularly if they came from communities where premarital pregnancy routinely led to a wedding, they were very susceptible to promises of love and marriage. Separated from family and community, which in earlier times exerted pressure on reluctant bridegrooms, they might find themselves "with child" and deserted by their partner who, in an urban setting with considerable occupational mobility, could easily evade his responsibility.

Marital fertility, illegitimacy, and infant mortality have been the subject of extensive recent research by historical demographers. Social historians, including historians of women, find these records pregnant with meaning for the quality of women's lives. Using crude birthrates (births per 1,000 inhabitants), fertility ratios (number of children under five per number of married women, aged fifteen to forty-four), and infant mortality rates (deaths of infants under one year per 1,000 live births), they have reconstructed a world of reproduction in which women gave birth to numerous offspring and—especially in the working classes—saw half of them die. Birthrates and fertility rates declined steadily throughout the nineteenth century, a token perhaps of new attitudes about human control over their lives. Infant mortality, however, diminished only after the development of public health measures such as the purification of water and pasteurization of milk in the early twentieth century. The latter was particularly significant in reducing recourse to wet-nursing. The sending of the newborn to a rural cottage to be breast-fed diminished among the upper classes after the eighteenth century—at least partly because of the admonitions of Enlightenment philosophers. During the nineteenth century, however, this custom spread among the urban lower-middle classes. Wet nurses were also used by officials charged with the care of foundlings, the thousands of infants abandoned by their unwed or married, but impoverished, mothers. Many destitute women preferred abandoning their children to watching them suffer or die of hunger. This measure was in earlier ages a common recourse of poor families. "Abandonment," states Rachel Fuchs, "was a socially acceptable means to cope with an unwelcome child in an era without safe birth control or abortion, and without an effective program of aid to dependent children." Twenty percent of all babies born in Paris in the early nineteenth century (and over half of the illegitimate) were abandoned.

If the care of abandoned children created a widespread social problem, in France wet-nursing became so prevalent that it constituted a major "business," subject to regulation by law and government agency. Because mortality among nurslings reached scandalous heights—over 50 percent in some cases, up to 80 percent among foundlings—the government in 1874 adopted the Roussel Law, which put all infants nursed outside their homes for pay under state protection. Across the Channel, in 1871 an Infant Life Protection Society was formed, to combat the similar practice of "baby-farming." In 1911, legislation prohibited employment of mothers within four weeks of delivery—but enforcement was lax.

These responses of the state offer early examples of a new role for government in family matters.[23]

In the development of the modern family perhaps the most significant change has been the deliberate reduction of the number of children born to the average woman and a concurrent intensification of emotional ties between generations. Beginning with France in the late eighteenth century, followed by Sweden at mid-nineteenth century and much of Europe after the 1870s, most populations in the Western world have employed deliberate means to limit their fertility. It has been suggested that the ability to limit births, and hence to reduce economic obligations, has contributed to earlier as well as to increased rates of marriage. The source of these changes was not a new technology, as is sometimes assumed. Effective artificial contraceptive devices were not available until the twentieth century. Large-scale production of the condom, which was known in the sixteenth century, and the pessary and diaphragm, both invented in the nineteenth, was indeed possible after the discovery of the vulcanization of rubber in the 1840s, but widespread distribution came many decades later in the era of World War I. Therefore, some historians have assumed an increased practice of *coitus interruptus,* or withdrawal before ejaculation, a male-controlled method known since biblical days but not employed earlier on a scale large enough to affect overall population growth. More recently, historians such as Angus McLaren have pointed to female agency in control of family size, through abortion as well as infanticide and abandonment or neglect. In the nineteenth century, it appears, the mainspring of change was a new secularized attitude justifying human intervention in events previously attributed to nature or to God.

A movement to promote the new ideas and to spread knowledge of birth control practices began in the 1830s. Following an overture by William Thompson, who was concerned about potential population problems in his Mutual Cooperative societies, in 1823 the Utilitarian Francis Place published a handbill addressed "To the married of both sexes," which offered instructions in the use of a vaginal sponge as the means to avoid the "evil consequences of too large a family." It was distributed by a very young John Stuart Mill among others. In 1832 in the United States and in 1834 in England, an American doctor, Charles Knowlton, published his *Fruits of Philosophy, or the Private Companion of Young Married People.* Knowlton was fined and sentenced to jail but gained a considerable following in both countries. The impact on British popular opinion was most noticeable after 1877, when Charles Bradlaugh and Annie Besant reissued the Knowlton pamphlet, deliberately challenging the law that censored such material as "lewd, filthy, bawdry and obscene," definitely not fit "to be talked about among Christians." Publicity surrounding their trial made the subject headline news in the daily newspapers. As a result, hundreds of thousands of people learned about possibilities for fertility control; and many women wrote Besant begging for useful information. The jurors were "unanimously of the opinion that the book in question is calculated to deprave public morals," and found the defendants guilty. Although they escaped penalty on a technicality, Besant nevertheless was deprived of custody of her daughter, the judge fearing Besant's influence on the child's morality. Criminal prosecution of advocates of contraception continued for decades in all the states of Europe and in North America. Nevertheless, many women demonstrated their support. In Amsterdam in 1882, when Dr. Aletta Jacob opened the world's first birth control clinic, hundreds of women lined up for help.[24]

In Europe the movement for birth control was called Neo-Malthusianism, in recognition that the limitation of births, deemed by the economist Malthus as the only way the working classes could avoid starvation, might be achieved by means other than the abstinence that he had recommended. "Family planning" was thus originally proposed as a solution to the "social question," as a means to reduce poverty by limiting the numbers of children to be fed. It would also raise the bargaining power, and hence wages, of workers through reduction of the ratio of labor supply to demand. However, it spread less quickly among the impoverished than among the propertied classes.

The deliberate reduction of fertility, by separating sexuality and reproduction, allowed for a new attitude toward sexual pleasure. But it is unclear what this meant to women. The most widely publicized opinion of the era was that women were essentially "passionless." Lacking in spontaneous sexual urges, they would, if protected from corrupting influences, remain chaste. Without lust of their own, they could easily refrain from sexual activity and indeed would so prefer, except for their naturally-occurring desires to please their husbands and to experience maternity. Believing ignorance the means to preserving innocence, parents should— according to the custodians of Victorian morality—insulate their daughters from all suggestive sights and sounds. Hence the euphemisms "bosom" and "bust" for breast, "limb" for leg (and the leggings once installed on piano posts), "second joint" (of a chicken) for thigh, and such circumlocutions as "private parts" and "down there" for vulva and vagina.

While no one will ever know, of course, how many women were so well-brought up by Victorian mothers that they went to their bridal beds ignorant of where babies came from (a Victorian ideal), the views of female sexual passivity expressed by the English physician Lord William Acton found their way into many medical texts and sex manuals in both England and the United States.

> There can be no doubt [he wrote] that sexual feeling in the female is in the majority of cases in abeyance, and that it requires positive and considerable excitement to be roused at all; and even if roused (which in many instances it never can be) it is very moderate compared with that of the male.

To Elizabeth Blackwell, however, who in 1849 became the first woman to earn a medical degree in the United States, it was clear that Acton's views reflected the false education of women by men. She pointed out that not only had women been taught to consider sexual passion as sinful; they also feared continual childbearing, with its inevitable companions, pain, uterine injury, or death from toxemia, hemorrhage, and "childbed fever." Blackwell maintained that sexual urges were just as strong in women as in men. The consequences of sexual expression, however, differed greatly.

To understand female sexuality in any period or place, it is essential to examine a complex set of circumstances—economic, social, legal, medical, and religious—which affects each woman's life. Overriding factors for most women in the modern world have been their economic dependency on men; their social subjection to a double standard that demands chastity of females while condoning, even encouraging, promiscuity in males; their liability before legal codes enacted and interpreted exclusively by men; their vulnerability to pregnancy and lack of control over related medical interventions such as contraception and abortion as well as parturition; their exposure to religious doctrines that deny female spiritual authority and preach submission to men as obedience to God. Most women experienced marriage, sexuality, and reproduction as a total phenomenon that dominated their lives. It also, symbolically, expressed female weakness in the face of male sexual as well as political and economic power.

The saying that for men, love is a thing apart, but for women, their whole existence, likewise reflected this reality. The decision to marry, as Stéphanie Jullien recognized, irretrievably marked a woman's life. And yet, as Charlotte Perkins Gilman noted, women brought to the "marriage market" were forced by social pressures to pretend indifference while men exercised the right of selection. Furthermore, once married, women lost their individual identity. From the moment of marriage, whether under English common law, the Frederician (Prussian) Code, Napoleonic Code, or the vestiges of Roman law, a woman's legal existence was subsumed within that of her husband. She became known in law as a *feme covert*, that is, a woman under "coverture." This meant that, unlike a *feme sole*, or single (adult) woman, she could not own or control property, earn wages of her own, bring suit or bear witness in court. As the English jurist William Blackstone put it, "By marriage the very being or legal existence of a woman is suspended, or at least it is incorporated or consolidated into that of her husband, under whose wing, protection, and cover she performs everything." In turn, a husband assumed all legal responsibility for her actions, debts, and contracts incurred before marriage and even, in some cases, crimes she henceforth committed. She was, like "wards, lunatics, idiots, and children," not held responsible for herself. Along with responsibility for his wife, a husband gained the legal right to control her property, appropriate her income, administer chastisement to her, determine where she lived, what clothes she wore and food she ate, as well as, of course, make all decisions regarding the upbringing of her offspring. (Only unwed mothers had rights to custody of their children.) [25]

The personal subordination of wives imposed by the law reflected not only a specific bias against women but an historical linkage between property and personal status. Legally unable to own property, married women thereby were deprived of many of the rights of citizenship. This system of marital law was suited to a patriarchal form of family based on inalienable landed estates and indissoluble sacramental marriage. With the evolution of the modern family based on a civil, matrimonial contract between presumably equal partners, and dissociated for the most part from inherited, legally entailed property, traditional marital and family law became increasingly obsolete and, especially for women, oppressive. The inconsistency between new attitudes about love in marriage and the laws of marriage, and between the latter and women's changing economic roles would spark some of the earliest efforts toward feminist reform.

Nationalism and Feminist Reform

If the first half of the nineteenth century is associated in the Western mind with a rising swell of democratic political reform, economic liberalism (laissez-faire), and romantic individualism, the second half is often seen as a cloud dark with belligerent nationalism, rampant materialism, and class conflict. While the advance of commercial and industrial capitalism continued throughout the century, creating an era of overall prosperity that lasted until the 1870s, the tide of liberalism in politics began to ebb much earlier and turned with the failure of liberal, democratic revolutions in 1848. Throughout Europe emerging nationalist movements had formed, some in reaction to Napoleon's conquests, with the goal of liberation from foreign domination, others bent on creation of unified nation-states from numbers of smaller, dynastic principalities. For many of the nationalists, the idea of "country" embodied the expression of a glorious unifying and humanitarian spirit. Through a spontaneous "rising of the people" or through reasoned argument and compromise, it would achieve its aims. While the movements toward nationalism in central Europe originated in an idealistic desire for liberation and liberal government, the achievement of national liberation and unification, however, fell to the force of arms. It was not the heroic poet Giuseppe Mazzini (1805–1872) of the Young Italy Movement, but the shrewd manipulator C. B. Cavour (1810–1861), who was aided by French arms, that brought success in the Italian peninsula; and the anti-liberal diplomat and chancellor, Otto von Bismarck (1815–1898), who used the "blood and iron" of the Prussian Army to forge a unified German state. They established a model of aggressive nationalism that came to dominate international relations.

Increasingly, national states began to intervene in people's lives, moved by concern for maintenance of social order and military power. The late nineteenth-century discussions of the social question and the woman question were never far removed from concerns about patriotic goals. Whether analyzing the French defeat by Prussia in the war of 1870 or the bloody end to the Paris Commune the following spring, Frenchmen were likely to point to national "decadence" or "degeneracy" as a cause. This sense of national decline was closely related to the reduced population growth termed "depopulation." While some blamed the population decline on the pattern of land inheritance that emerged from the revolutionary period (which ended primogeniture and reduced patriarchal power), others, as Karen Offen shows persuasively (Chapter 9), looked pointedly at the changing roles of women and pronounced feminism as the guilty factor. Late-century women's movements were profoundly shaped by the population debate and the rising tide of nationalism.[26]

Feminist thinking, which spread throughout Europe in response to renewed debate about women's place, also was integrally related to the social question and the intensifying class conflict of the late nineteenth century. The power of the new professional and commercial middle classes, strengthened by political and economic changes that followed the French Revolution, was embodied by the 1830s in the "bourgeois monarchy" of Louis Philippe in France, the reform movement in England, and the constitutional development of the German state of Baden, which had the most advanced parliamentary life in central Europe in the first half of the nineteenth century. By 1848, however, the potential power of the growing urban working classes created a specter of class conflict that made resolution of the social question more urgent. If the countries of Europe were not to split permanently into "two nations," to use Disraeli's famous phrase, then the less privileged classes must be integrated more fully into the national life, and some kind of consensus or class harmony achieved. Measures to accomplish this—to dispel the threat of revolution that hung over Europe—ranged from the freeing of the serfs in Russia in 1861 to the English reform acts of 1867 and 1884, which extended the vote to the (male) urban middle and working classes, and to the enactment of the world's first social security program in Germany in the 1880s. "Social scientists" developed schemes for social harmony, which in the French Third Republic took the political form of "Solidarism" and in late nineteenth-century England, of Fabian socialism. Karl Marx's "scientific socialism" and the many national political parties it spawned also sought to resolve the social question, but through the abolition of private property (i.e., capital) and a dialectical movement of class conflict that would result in the dissolution of the state rather than in schemes for limited redistribution of wealth through "welfare state" programs.

The rise of heavy industry and the continuing proletarianization of much of the labor force—male and female, urban and rural—contributed to the growing appeal of Marxist parties. Since the Marxists had inherited from the utopian socialists a rhetoric that included women's rights, many women who sought amelioration of legal, economic, and social injustice turned to the socialist movement for support. Although there were liberal feminist movements in France and Germany, continental feminism, to a greater extent than the Anglo-American variety, developed in tandem with the socialist movement for resolution of the "two-nation" problem—that is, for extending political and economic benefits to the working classes. Women ranging from Louise Michel and Paule Mink, heroes of the Paris Commune, to Clara Zetkin and Luise Zietz in Germany, Adelheid Popp in Austria, Anna Kuliscioff in Italy, and Alexandra Kollontai in Russia allied themselves with the left, convinced that only with the radical reconstruction of society could the masses of women achieve emancipation. Attainment of equality with men under capitalism would, they argued, only mean continuing exploitation—twelve or more hours of labor, six days a week, for wages insufficient to provide even essential comfort and security. However, these women—as well as some of their male socialist allies, like the Frenchman Jules Guesde and the German August Bebel, both leaders of the Second International, and the Bolshevik V. I. Lenin, founder of the Soviet Union—all supported many reforms designed to improve the position of women in society, even though for the most part they attacked bourgeois (that is, nonsocialist) feminism for ignoring other social and working-class needs.[27]

The first thrust of modern European feminism, as we have seen, developed in response to social upheaval during the French Revolution and called for equality for women on the basis of natural rights. Radical intellectuals such as Wollstonecraft and Fourier, social reformers such as Owen, Thompson, and the Saint-

Simonians, challenged established society to open new opportunities for women. Across the Atlantic, in the United States of America, women (and some men) came to embrace women's rights through participation in the anti-slavery movement, as well as the causes of educational advancement, temperance, moral reform, prison reform, and philanthropic developments. Often stymied in these reform efforts because of prejudices against females, American women began to advocate improvements in the condition of their sex. In both the United States and Europe, the first successful efforts were directed toward specific and limited reforms of sex-based inequities in the law. They date from the 1830s, when the British writer Caroline Sheridan Norton turned her pen against injustice wrought by marriage and family law. Perhaps because of the nineteenth-century apotheosis of "the family," the feminist "politics of the breach" (limited, step-by-step reform), focused first on improvement of women's status and enhancement of their authority in marriage and family. Norton brought the most notable case of the century before a wide public. Granddaughter of a famous writer, she was an accomplished novelist, wife of a successful political figure, and mother of three children. Estranged from her husband, who falsely accused her of adultery, she could not, under the laws of England, obtain a divorce. She was legally deprived of custody of her children, visiting rights, and the income from property she had inherited from her family and brought to the marriage. Forced to support herself by writing, she struck back by publishing pamphlets attacking the laws—although the copyrights to her work, of course, belonged to her husband. Norton's work is credited with helping to win passage of statutes in England that, in 1839, allowed courts to give mothers some rights to their children; and in 1857, permitted courts to dissolve marriages in cases of adultery by wives or adultery coupled with incest, bigamy, rape, sodomy, bestiality, or extreme cruelty by husbands.[28]

In the same year, a married woman's property bill was introduced into the English Parliament, to be passed only in 1870. German wives suffered without redress until 1900, and married Frenchwomen waited until 1907 to gain legal rights to their own earnings. Although socialists sometimes expressed disdain for feminist demands for property rights, from this campaign married women of all classes, increasingly drawn into the paid labor force, obtained greater power within their families as well as an increasing measure of independence.

By organizing and agitating for custody and property rights, women gained experience and built a base from which to launch other drives. As middle- and upper-class women won access to secondary and university education, they also sought admittance to occupations monopolized by men. After securing a foothold in teaching, they moved into other white-collar employment. For a small, pioneering minority of women access to the "liberal professions" became a focal point. Indeed, as the healing professions developed new standards and required advanced education in medical schools closed to female students, some women created opportunities in a new profession of nursing. One early leader was Amalie Sieveking, an upper-class German spinster who, as she rejected marriage, vowed to be "If not a happy wife and mother, then founder of an order of Sisters of Charity!" When with twelve other women she founded the Female Association for the Care of the Poor and the Sick in Hamburg in 1832, she renewed opportunities for her sex, which had diminished with the decline of religious orders. "To me," she told an audience a decade later,

> At least as important were the benefits which [work with the poor] seemed to promise for those of my sisters who would join me in such a work of charity. The higher interests of my sex were close to my heart.[29]

Sieveking's more famous successors, the Englishwoman Florence Nightingale and the American Clara Barton, organized nursing services on the battlefields of the Crimean War (1854–1856) and Civil War (1861–1865) respectively, and likewise set out to promote the interests of women. Nightingale, who transformed nursing from a menial occupation of lower-class, untrained, and sometimes dissolute servants into a profession of respectable, educated, middle-class "women in white," was deliberately seeking a means to escape the narrow limits of her own life as a proper spinster daughter in a well-to-do Victorian family. Feeling herself called by God to treat the bodies of soldiers fallen in a distant land, she broke the bounds of Victorian femininity. Like Barton, she proved that women could overcome not only hard physical labor but also the sight of blood and death.

Reform-minded women engaged men directly also on another battlefield, one which pitted them against the double standard of moral behavior and the male license for extramarital sexual behavior that it allowed. Beginning as early as the Jacksonian period in the United States, Victorian women drew on the age's increasing differentiation of sexual "character" to justify female intervention against prostitution. In 1834, women met in a Presbyterian church to form the New York Moral Reform Society. Resolving that "the licentious man is no less guilty than his victim, and ought, therefore, to be excluded from all virtuous female society," they launched a crusade against prostitution in New York City. It was, they declared, the "imperious duty of ladies everywhere . . . to cooperate in the great work of moral reform." In England, Josephine Butler led the Ladies' National Association to campaign successfully for repeal of the Contagious Disease Acts, and her example directly inspired a German movement to abolish state-regulated prostitution. The British legislation of the 1860s, which was intended to control the spread of venereal disease among soldiers, subjected suspect women to pelvic examination and possible involuntary hospital confinement, while ignoring male participants. French women also organized in the cause of "abolition"; that is, for elimination of a state-sanctioned system of "public women" who were required to undergo periodic examination and to obey regulations regarding their dress, housing, and social behavior. Many reform-minded women agreed with Flora Tristan, who labeled English brothels "temples that English materialism has raised to its gods!—the *male* guests who come there to exchange their gold for debauchery." While most women of her era preserved their respectability by disdain for "fallen women," Tristan laid the onus directly on men.[30]

If many women (and men) devoted themselves to improvement of the educational, employment, and social rights of women, others decided, as early as the 1840s in the United States and England, that equal participation in the political arena was prerequisite to all other reform. The English and American women's rights movements began at mid-century to organize for the conquest of the suffrage—although as we point out in Part III, without great success before the World War I era. In most countries, however, women and men whom we today call feminist for their advocacy of improvement in women's condition, avoided both rhetoric and action that smacked of individual rights. They tended to focus on issues designed to enhance women's performance of their traditional familial duties. In the American context, their work has been called "domestic feminism," since it purported to strengthen women's power in the home. Karen Offen, in a recent study of historical variations in feminism, traces this "relational" or "familial" feminism, which predominated in France but influenced women's movements everywhere, to Ernest Legouvé's concept of "equality in difference." One of the most influential writers on the woman question in nineteenth-century Europe, Legouvé blended Enlightenment thought on "natural" or biological law with appreciation of the historical contributions of women to human culture. Arguing for reforms in law and customs that would allow both sexes to fulfill their unique responsibilities, Legouvé posed a doctrine of separate but equal spheres in family and social life that promoted women's interests against the power of patriarchy.[31]

For others, who followed in the tradition of Tristan, Marx, and Engels, the woman question was subsumed within the social question; that is, they traced the oppression of all groups to the power of states organized primarily to protect private property and to preserve class inequality. Believing that the problems of women would disappear once the conflict of classes was resolved, they devoted their lives to movements for radical social and political change. In the 1870s, young Russians of both sexes formed study circles to prepare for social revolution. Sofya Perovskaya (1854–1881), one of the assassins of Tsar Alexander II in 1881, launched her career as a revolutionary with a quest for personal autonomy along with nine other women in the "Chaikovskii circle," a study group of idealistic, radical young men and women. For her, emancipation for women was part of a broader attack on authoritarianism in personal life and despotism in political affairs. Her contemporary, Anna Kuliscioff (1854–1925), cofounder of the Italian socialist party, believed socialism prerequisite to the "perfectibility" of all "whom the present order of things compromises materially or morally . . . workers, youth, and women." The French Marxist, Aline Valette (1850–1899), headed her weekly journal, *L'Harmonie sociale* with the slogan "The Emancipation of Women Lies in Emancipated Labor." In the last decades of the nineteenth century, as socialists and feminists organized to contend for political power, socialist parties possessed greater resources and appeared to some working-class women to be more congenial than feminist organizations dominated by middle- and upper-class women. When they attempted, however, to introduce "women's issues" into socialist programs for action (as distinct from party platforms), they were either ignored, rejected, or labeled "deviationists."

As socialist victories at the polls accelerated throughout most western and central European states and put impressive power into socialist hands in several nations, class rivalries intensified. It became essentially impossible for socialist women to maintain alliances with bourgeois feminists, who were officially their class enemies, or to support reforms deemed inadequate to promote the class struggle. The problem is exemplified by the conflict between two German socialists, Lily Braun and Clara Zetkin, over establishing household cooperatives to reduce women's domestic duties. For Braun, such arrangements would not only relieve the conflict between home and work created by female entrance into the industrial labor force, they would also create an institutional basis for the transition from capitalism to socialism. To Zetkin, the acknowledged leader of European socialist women, they represented nothing but "bourgeois reformism," band-aids for festering wounds. For Zetkin, as for most socialist men, alteration of the domestic division of labor could only follow, not precede, the revolution. Loyal to their class, they soft-peddled issues such as domestic arrangements, family power, or family planning that might pit working-class women against working-class men, even as they sought to improve women's position in the work force and to win for them basic individual rights. If nineteenth-century socialist feminists found their theories often compromised in practice by socialist resistance to new roles for women and to issues defined as "feminist," they continued to believe first and foremost that fundamental transformation of family and society was prerequisite to the emancipation of women. Therefore, their emphasis remained on social revolution. The rest, they believed, would follow. The Russian Revolution, as we shall see in Part III, proved them mistaken.

The importance of solving class conflict loomed large also for reformers who hoped to avoid the revolutionary confrontation envisioned by many Marxists. The French Solidarists, the English Fabians, the Catholic Center Party in Germany, and other political groups inspired by religious values sought solutions to the social question that were geared toward class and familial harmony rather than conflict. A common ground among political factions (including, in fact, socialist parties) that adopted irreconcilable positions on most other matters was the need to safeguard the reproductive potential of the working classes by "protecting" women. Catholic and socialist stood together in the interest of family stability and maternal fecundity. Despite the protests of feminists concerned to enlarge, not to restrict, women's right to work and of some employers and laissez-faire liberals, politicians of the left, center, and right joined to pass labor legislation restricting women's employment in certain industries and limiting their hours. Through these protective laws the state intervened to act, as it were, as guardian of female health and family welfare. Assuming that women's health and endurance were more fragile than men's, and their ability to organize for self-protection less developed, it enacted statutes deemed philosophically or constitutionally unacceptable when applied to men. Parliamentary speeches in favor of protective laws often evoked nostalgic images of the family-centered domestic industries of earlier times. Indeed, in many areas the new laws operated to revitalize home industries, but as we have noted, the working conditions in these late-century "sweatshops" were far from idyllic.

Nevertheless, for many lawmakers the passage of protective legislation was the ideal solution to the woman question: it would "protect" those "mothers" whose families (now or in the future) would require their active financial contributions. The century-long campaign for a wide range of women's rights would be, at least for a time, partially eclipsed by "reason of state," especially in the interest of nationalist rivalry and military conflicts. The debate would also be transformed by the new context of the welfare state. Most women in Europe would not become involved in the issues of women's rights at all, but would continue to fulfill women's duties. Even middle-class women who consistently fought as feminists for their sex would emphasize familial rather than personal needs. They even began in the last decades of the nineteenth century to narrow their scope to the vote in the interest of "social housekeeping." When the idealistic optimism with which the century began turned toward cultural despair at its end, women would be called on to rehabilitate society in their traditional role as moralizing mothers.

NOTES

1. Peter N. Stearns, *European Society in Upheaval,* 2nd ed. (New York, 1975), p. 1.

2. Thomas Dublin, *Women at Work: The Transformation of Work and Community in Lowell, Massachusetts, 1826–1860* (New York, 1979); Laura S. Strumingher, *Women and the Making of the Working Class: Lyon 1830–1870* (Montreal, 1979), esp. pp. 21–22. For younger Englishwoman, see excerpt from Parliamentary Factory Inquiry Commission (1833) in Erna O. Hellerstein, Leslie P. Hume, and Karen M. Offen, eds., *Victorian Women: A Documentary Account of Women's Lives in Nineteenth Century England, France, and the United States* (Stanford, 1981), p. 389. For older Englishwoman, Wanda Fraiken Neff, *Victorian Working Women* (New York, 1966), p. 72.

3. Bettina Berch, "Industrialization and Working Women in the Nineteenth Century: England, France and the United States," (Ph.D. dissertation [economics], University of Wisconsin, Madison, 1976), esp. pp. 157–159.

4. Engels, Friedrich, *The Condition of the Working Class in England,* tr. and ed. by W. O. Henderson and W. H. Chaloner (New York, 1958; German first edition, 1845). Louise A. Tilly and Joan W. Scott, *Women, Work, and Family* (New York, 1978).

5. On Locke's "equal Title," see Susan Moller Okin, *Women in Western Political Thought* (Princeton, 1979), p. 200.

6. Our summary of the Encyclopedists' views draws heavily on Abby R. Kleinbaum, "Women in the Age of Light," in Renate Bridenthal and Claudia Koonz, eds., *Becoming Visible: Women in European History* (Boston, 1977), pp. 217–235; and Sara Ellen Procious Malueg, "Women and the *Encyclopédie,*" in Samia I. Spencer, ed., *French Women and the Age of Enlightenment* (Bloomington, IN, 1984), pp. 259–271. Excerpts from the works of several of the philosophers appear in Susan Groag Bell and Karen M. Offen, eds., *Women, the Family, and Freedom: The Debate in Documents* I: 1750–1880 (New York, 1978).

7. Mary Wollstonecraft, *A Vindication of the Rights of Woman,* Norton Critical Edition (New York, 1975), pp. 5, 40, 194.

8. Jane Abray, "Feminism in the French Revolution," *American Historical Review* 80, no. 1 (February 1975): 43–62; *Women in Revolutionary Paris, 1789–1795; Selected Documents,* tr. and ed. by Darlene Gay Levy, Harriet Branson Applewhite, and Mary Durham Johnson (Urbana, IL, 1979).

9. Olwen Hufton, "Women in Revolution, 1789–1796," *Past and Present* 53 (November 1971): 94.

10. For the utopian socialists, see Albert Fried and Ronald Sanders, eds., *Socialist*

Thought: A Documentary History (Garden City, NY, 1964), pp. 82, 92, 97–98; Frank E. Manuel, *The Prophets of Paris* (New York, 1962), pp. 122, 127, 186–187, 229, 231, 241; Claire Goldberg Moses, *French Feminism in the Nineteenth Century* (Albany, 1984), pp. 10, 47–48, 52, 65, 92; Mark Poster, ed., *Harmonian Man: Selected Writings of Charles Fourier* (Garden City, NY, 1971), p. 258.

11. For the latest reprint, with an introduction by Richard Pankhurst, see Thompson's *Appeal . . .* (London, 1983). Also Barbara Taylor, *Eve and the New Jerusalem: Socialism and Feminism in the Nineteenth Century* (New York, 1983).

12. S. Joan Moon, "Feminism and Socialism: The Utopian Synthesis of Flora Tristan," in Marilyn J. Boxer and Jean H. Quataert, eds., *Socialist Women: European Socialist Feminism in the Nineteenth and Twentieth Centuries* (New York, 1978), pp. 19–50.

13. In Bell and Offen, *Women, Family, Freedom* I, pp. 73–74.

14. Rousseau and de Maistre in Moses, *French Feminism*, p. 241, n. 20 and p. 6, respectively; Joanne Schneider, "Enlightened Reforms and Bavarian Girls' Education: Tradition through Innovation," in John C. Fout, ed., *German Women in the Nineteenth Century: A Social History* (New York, 1984), p. 58; Persis Hunt, "Teachers and Workers: Problems of Feminist Organizing in the Early Third Republic," in *Troisième République/Third Republic* 3–4 (1977): 180. Also Mary Jo Maynes, *Schooling in Western Europe: A Social History* (Albany, 1985).

15. Kathryn Kish Sklar, *Catharine Beecher: A Study in American Domesticity* (New York, 1973), pp. 180–181 and p. 312, n. 34; Laura Strumingher, *What Were Little Girls and Boys Made Of?: Primary Education in Rural France, 1830–1880* (Albany, 1983), p. 17; Linda L. Clark, *Schooling the Daughters of Marianne* (Albany, 1984), pp. 13–17.

16. M. Jeanne Peterson, "The Victorian Governess: Status Incongruence in Family and Society," in Martha Vicinus, ed., *Suffer and Be Still: Women in the Victorian Age* (Bloomington, IN, 1973), pp. 17–18; Jacquie Matthews, "Barbara Bodichon: Integrity in Diversity (1827–1891)," in Dale Spender, ed., *Feminist Theorists: Three Centuries of Key Women Thinkers* (New York, 1984), pp. 90–123, esp. pp. 100, 102.

17. In Hellerstein, Hume, and Offen, *Victorian Women*, pp. 398–400.

18. Rita McWilliams-Tullberg, "Women and Degrees at Cambridge University 1862–1897," in Martha Vicinus, ed., *A Widening Sphere: Changing Roles of Women* (Bloomington, IN, 1977), pp. 120, 294, n. 11.

19. Karin Hausen, "Family and Role-Division: The Polarisation of Sexual Stereotypes in the Nineteenth Century—An Aspect of the Dissociation of Work and Family Life," in Richard J. Evans and W. R. Lee, eds., *The German Family: Essays on the Social History of the Family in Nineteenth- and Twentieth-Century Germany* (London, 1981), pp. 67–68; Lenore Davidoff, "The Rationalization of Housework," in Diana Leonard Barker and Sheila Allen, eds., *Dependence and Exploitation in Work and Marriage* (London, 1976), p. 136.

20. Bonnie G. Smith, *Ladies of the Leisure Class: The Bourgeoises of Northern France in the Nineteenth Century* (Princeton, 1981), pp. 53–66.

21. In Hellerstein, Hume, and Offen, *Victorian Women*, pp. 144–149.

22. Michael Anderson, "The Social Position of Spinsters in Mid-Victorian Britain," pp. 377–393 and Olwen Hufton, "Women without Men: Widows and Spinsters in Britain and France in the Eighteenth Century," pp. 355–376, in *Journal of Family History* 9, no. 4 (Winter 1984); Lillian Faderman, *Surpassing the Love of Men* (New York, 1981). See also Martha Vicinus, *Independent Women: Work and Community for Single Women, 1850–1920* (Chicago, 1985).

23. Rachel Ginnis Fuchs, *Abandoned Children: Foundlings and Child Welfare in Nineteenth-Century France* (Albany, 1984), esp. pp. 72–73, 277; George Sussman, *Selling Mothers' Milk: The Wet-Nursing Business in France, 1715–1914* (Urbana, IL, 1982).

24. *Medical History of Contraception* (New York, 1970, orig. 1936); Linda Gordon, *Woman's Body, Woman's Right: A Social History of Birth Control in America* (New York, 1977); Angus McLaren, *Birth Control in Nineteenth-Century England* (London, 1978); J. A. and Olive Banks, *Feminism and Family Planning in Victorian England* (New York, 1964).

25. Lee Holcombe, *Wives and Property: Reform of the Married Woman's Property Law in Nineteenth-Century England* (Toronto, 1983).

26. Karen Offen, "Depopulation, Nationalism, and Feminism in Fin-De-Siècle France," *American Historical Review* 89, no. 3 (June 1984): 648–676.

27. Boxer and Quataert, *Socialist Women.* See also Charles Sowerwine, *Sisters or Citizens? Women and Socialism in France Since 1876* (Cambridge, 1982).

28. Lee Holcombe, "Victorian Wives and Property: Reform of the Married Woman's Property Law, 1857–1882," in Vicinus, ed., *Widening Sphere,* pp. 3–28, and Holcombe, *Wives and Property,* pp. 50–58; also excerpt from Caroline Sheridan North, *The Separation of Mother and Child by the Law of 'Custody of Infants,' Considered* (London, 1838) in Bell and Offen, *Women, Family, Freedom* I, pp. 161–163. Also Moses, *French Feminism* and Patrick Kay Bidelman, *Pariahs Stand Up! The Founding of the Liberal Feminist Movement in France, 1858–1889* (Westport, CT, 1982).

29. Catherine M. Prelinger, "Prelude to Consciousness: Amalie Sieveking and the Female Association for the Care of the Poor and the Sick," in Fout, *German Women,* pp. 118–132.

30. Carroll Smith-Rosenberg, "Beauty, the Beast, and the Militant Woman," *American Quarterly* 23 (1971): 562–584; Judith R. Walkowitz, *Prostitution and Victorian Society: Women, Class, and the State* (Cambridge, 1980); Tristan in Hellerstein, Hume and Offen, *Victorian Women,* pp. 419–421, and *Flora Tristan's London Journal: A Survey of London Life in the 1830s,* tr. by Dennis Palmer and Giselle Pincetl (London, 1980).

31. Karen Offen, "Ernest Legouvé and the Doctrine of 'Equality in Difference' for Women: A Case Study of Male Feminism in Nineteenth-Century Thought," *Journal of Modern History* 58, no. 2 (June 1986): 452–484.

5

The Influence of Rousseau's Ideology of Domesticity

Barbara Corrado Pope

Beginning in the second half of the eighteenth century, a new ideology of domesticity developed that required a redefinition of the social sphere of women. The Swiss-born philosopher Jean-Jacques Rousseau, son of a watchmaker, played an especially important part in formulating and popularizing a conception of femininity appropriate to the new ideology. Called "the prophet of breast-feeding" and the "Dr. Spock" of his age, Rousseau disdained ladies of the Parisian salons, and had five children (whom he abandoned) by his common-law wife, a servant. Although he considered it immoral, he was lionized by "brilliant" society.

In the following essay, Barbara Corrado Pope uses textual analysis to trace the origin and the influence of Rousseau's works, which are credited with changing the course of Western cultural history. Despite the difficulty of demonstrating how ideas affect behavior, Pope finds evidence of the response to Rousseau by the literate public that bought and borrowed his books. She explains the appeal of his romantic portrayal of maternal love to women otherwise denied power and influence. She notes his impact on revolutionary men and on "bourgeois morality." She also shows his influence on the development of pedagogical theories and educational institutions. He was one of the earliest exponents of child-centered education. But his ideas on female education reflected narrow and biased views of women's roles.

Jean-Jacques Rousseau was a political theorist of stunning originality, an influential pedagogue, incisive social critic, fervent moralist, best-selling novelist, composer, dramatist, master stylist, and celebrated personality. He shared with his contemporaries, the male intellectuals of the Enlightenment, a breathtaking range of knowledge and talents. What made him stand out from them was his passion, for he expressed and aroused more emotions than any thinker of his age. He has been credited or blamed with being the forerunner of Romantic sensibility; the father of the French Revolution; the prophet of nationalism, democracy, and totalitarianism; the foremost promoter of the modern concern for the child; and a self-indulgent paranoiac. Such contradictory appraisals are due to the fact that he asked large questions about the fate of human society and gave provocative an-

swers to them. Most frequently his work is treated as part of the history of political theory, and therefore as ideas about the economic, political, and social activities of men. But Rousseau really had a larger agenda in mind: nothing less than
the moral regeneration of society. And he was quite conscious of the fact that this
ambitious project must involve women. If equality and democracy for men was
one side of his prophetic vision, subordination and domesticity for women was
the other side.

The source of much of Rousseau's passion was biographical. His autobiography, the *Confessions,* provides sufficient evidence to label his ideas and attitudes
about women as hopelessly confused and ambivalent. It reveals Rousseau as the
eternally motherless child who continually overestimated female power in a bla-
tantly patriarchal society and who, in his amorous adventures and writing, simultaneously elevated and denigrated real and imagined women. Yet we also know
that such ambivalence was not unique to Rousseau. Indeed, it is inherent in the
ideology of domesticity itself that so many of his readers found so attractive. The
immediate popularity of Rousseau's ideas derived, at least in part, from the breadth
and power of his writings about women. Their long-term attraction, however,
depended upon the course of great historical events and their consequences. The
French and industrial revolutions seemed to validate Rousseau's vision and they
provided the political and material bases to sustain it.

Rousseau's first explication of the virtues and benefits of domesticity appeared
in the preface to his *Second Discourse,* the *Essay on the Origin of Inequality*
(1755). In this tract Rousseau imaginatively recreated the transition that took "man"
from his savage or natural state into society, or his social state. The development
of language, cooperation, tools, families, and concepts of property were the major
catalysts of this transition, which would eventually lead to inequality in society
and all the vices (conformity, enslavement, and frivolity) attendant upon it.

The *Second Discourse* was a clear condemnation of the inequalities of rank,
wealth, and privilege that Rousseau, who had suffered from their absence, saw as
the source of social evils. But it was not a condemnation of society per se. Rousseau made it clear that savage man was amoral. He did not (as some of his critics
claimed) want to go back to a state of nature. But in order for social and political
man to overcome corruption, he would need the help of social and domestic woman.
To demonstrate this point, Rousseau referred both to his idealized notion of contemporary Geneva, his birthplace, and to his theoretical recreation of the distant
past. This theoretical work is the first adumbration of his sexual politics, which
explicitly posed an idealized domesticity against the urban sociability he had experienced in Paris and come to disdain.

In his dedication to "The Republic of Geneva," Rousseau specifically con-
trasted the "sweet lessons" and "modest graces" of the "amiable and virtuous
daughters of Geneva" to the "extravagance" and "puerile and ridiculous manners" acquired among the "loose women" of other cities. These loose women
with their "so-called grandeur" enslaved men, whose greatest asset should be
liberty. In contrast, Genevan women, whose "chaste influence" was only "exercised within the limits of conjugal union," ensured the happiness of men, respect
for law, harmony among citizens, and a tranquil family life.

In a single paragraph Rousseau thus foreshadowed hundreds of nineteenth-century works glorifying the effects of fully domesticated women upon men and decrying the influence of those who stepped outside the home. He also signaled changes in the meaning of the term "domesticity." When it was originally coined in France at the end of the seventeenth century, the term simply referred to the household and family economy and the tasks necessary to sustain them. One of the marks of modern European and American society is that domesticity increasingly lost most of its economic content and took on emotional and moral connotations. That is, domesticity passed from being a matter of household activity to being an ideology and moral imperative. When Rousseau asked in his dedication, "What man can be such a barbarian as to resist the voice of honor and reason, coming from the lips of an affectionate wife?" he posed a rhetorical question that would be repeated with endless variations by a myriad of Victorian authors. In the nineteenth century, as in this dedication, the answer would be so obvious that it did not have to be provided.

Unlike many Victorians, however, Rousseau did not think of women as naturally chaste or asexual. Quite to the contrary, he credited them with great sexual power because, as he explained in the theoretical body of this *Discourse,* he believed that they had "invented" romantic love. This invention, he contended, was a calculated strategy to make up for their physical weakness. It was also an important aspect of the transition from savagery to human society. Before that time, according to Rousseau, "savage men" only occasionally coupled with women to satisfy their moderate sexual desires. There was no great passion, no jealousy, no scheming or bloody quarreling until the development of love brought about exclusive attachments between men and women. Rousseau never doubted the power—or the beauty—of romance; in fact, he probably overestimated it. One of the major problems he strove to solve in his later works was how to channel this power and beauty in a way that would ensure the liberty of men and the good of society.

Rousseau's influential novel, *La Nouvelle Heloise,* and his educational treatise, *Emile,* dealt directly with the problems of romantic love, sexuality, and education. They were written at a feverish pace in the countryside during a time when Rousseau made his final break with Parisian society. This ugly period began with a beautiful dream of Julie d'Etang, the perfect woman—or at least a woman as perfect as the possession of a delectably tender heart could allow. Julie was the Nouvelle Heloise of his novel, who fell in love with her young tutor, Saint-Preux. She surrendered twice to his passionate pleadings and spent the rest of her life (and the next 600 pages) making up for her transgressions. She was a beautiful aristocrat of the Swiss type: thus sturdily Protestant, endlessly moralistic, and finally, very, very good.

When her parents did not approve of the match between the lovers, Julie chose filial duty over romantic elopement and reconciled herself to accepting the philosopher Wolmar as her husband. This older suitor was also very good and very wise, if a bit cold. Together he and Julie turned his estate into a productive and self-contained utopia where happy servants served kind masters and children received the best possible education. So confident was Wolmar of the goodness of the life that he had created through his benign paternal authority, that he invited

Saint-Preux to live at the estate. When Saint-Preux saw Julie again, he was more in love than ever, for the physical and spiritual consequences of motherhood had made her even more beautiful. One day she told him about her educational principles. Most of these would be more fully elaborated in *Emile*, with the major exception of Rousseau's portrait of the ideal mother-teacher, Julie. She had breast-fed her children, cared for them, integrated them into a life full of household management duties, and developed a strict, but tender plan for their upbringing. But, ideal woman that she was, she also knew her limitations. She followed her husband's guidance, and she knew that a man must take over her sons' intellectual and moral education. For this task she chose the adoring Saint-Preux, explaining to the tutor that

> My son will not always be a child; once his reason makes its appearance, his father intends to let it be exercised according to the stage of its development. So far as I am concerned, my work does not go as far as that. I nurse the children, but I do not presume to aim at making men of them. . . . I am a woman and a mother, and I can keep my proper place. Once again let me say: the duty that falls to me is not to educate my sons, but to prepare them for being educated.

On her part, despite her high moralism and discipline, Julie still loved her former tutor. But she never again gave in to her feelings. She lived (and finally died) fulfilling her duties. Her last great act was to rescue one of her sons from drowning. Subsequently, she caught a cold. Realizing that she could never be happy, torn as she was between duty and love, Julie gladly died.

Because this was an epistolary novel, the characters gave full vent to their ideas and emotions. Among the Rousseauean themes that they articulated were the delights and dangers of human passions, the necessity of marital fidelity to maintaining social order, the beauty of motherhood, the corruptions of Paris, the virtues of isolated country living, and the importance of education. Rousseau's contention that mothers should educate their very young boys until they were old enough to be turned over to men, and keep their daughters at home with them until marriage, provided one of the fundamental concepts of maternal education, which became a cornerstone of the nineteenth-century notion of domesticity.

La Nouvelle Heloise was, for the eighteenth century, a runaway best-seller. Readers bought the book as soon as it was printed, fought to obtain library copies, pored over it all night, and shed buckets of tears. They took Jean-Jacques into their hearts and eagerly awaited his next exhortations. These would be delivered in *Emile*, the story of a boy of that name and his tutor, who, when he appeared in dialogue, was called quite simply, Jean-Jacques. This was a sign that Rousseau was well aware of and wanted to foster that intimate relationship he had attained with his adoring reading public.

Jean-Jacques struck his major chord early. The book begins: "God makes all things good; man meddles with them and they become evil." The problem was how to shape the child, who is by nature good, into the adult male citizen capable of constructing and perpetuating a good and moral society. Rousseau's answer was to isolate the child and instill in him a capacity to learn and to know by allowing him to pick up only those lessons appropriate to the various stages of growth. This slow, careful development, first of the senses, then of the mind, and finally of the heart, Rousseau called a negative education, for Emile's tutor refused to teach things that the pupil should discover for himself. The first four books of *Emile* are filled with a compassionate concern for the child and respect for each stage of growth. Rousseau did not see children as ignorant and sinful (as did many of his contemporaries), but as innocent and eager to learn. He held and propagated the modern view of childhood. The climax of this natural education was the articulation of a "natural religion" by the Vicar of Savoy, who taught Emile that "man" can know God through observing his good and beautiful works.

The antithesis of Emile's education is the training given to his future wife, Sophie. This comprises most of the fifth book. While Emile learns independence and autonomy, Sophie is raised to be pleasing to men. Instead of natural religion, she gets catechism; instead of independence of soul, she learns that she must bow to convention. She is even allowed to retain her "natural" coquettishness in order to be able to kindle and rekindle her husband's physical passion. Her major duties are to be modest and chaste (or at the very least appear to be so), to bear children, to create and maintain the bonds of affection between a father and his children, and to make the home a place of charm and refreshment. In short, boys are raised to think and be at one with themselves; girls are raised to be relative to and supportive of men.

By the time Rousseau wrote *Emile* his ambivalence about women was acute. It was revealed in the *way* he wrote the book. When he spoke of *women* he seemed to be talking to men about a common problem. He asserted that they should only be taught enough reason to be able to choose between duty and respectable appearances, that, indeed, "woman is made to submit to man and even endure injustice at his hands." Sophie, however, was not the only female character in *Emile*. Looming over all was a devoted female readership, embodied in what Jean-Jacques called the "tender and anxious mother," to whom he *directly* and *respectfully* addressed his opening passages.

This famous overture was an attack on the custom of sending infants to the country to live with hired wet nurses. His vivid depiction of the abuses of this system focused on the practice of tightly swaddling babies so that the peasant nurses could ignore the infants' cries and physical needs while they went about their work. Rousseau passionately exhorted mothers to keep their babies at home, to breast-feed them, care for them, and love them. He implied that direct and constant maternal devotion was the only way to free babies from the crippling physical restraints and moral deprivations imposed by a corrupt and corrupting society. For the good of society, mother and child had to be inextricably bound together. "No mother, no child," he wrote, "their duties are reciprocal. . . . The child should love his mother before he knows what he owes her. If the voice of instinct is not strengthened by habit it soon dies, the heart is stillborn."

Yet, according to Rousseau, the ties that bind mother and child need not be constraining. As they liberate the child, they also empower the mother. "When mothers deign to nurse their own children," he wrote, "then will be a reform in morals; natural feeling will revive in every heart; there will be no lack of citizens for the state; this first step by itself will restore mutual affection.'' Good mothering, then, was the key to family love, revitalized morality, and male citizenship.

Rousseau's message had an immediate and long-term appeal to his readers, especially to women. Most seemed ready to forgive him for his ideas about Sophie and remember him as the creator of the divine (and seemingly powerful) Julie. Many of these readers were literate aristocratic and bourgeois women who, despite Rousseau's inflated opinions of their power, had very little ability to control their own fate. They certainly had not ''invented'' romantic love as a strategy to usurp male authority. But Jean-Jacques's emphasis on emotional bonding between family members might have seemed empowering to women who faced the harsh realities of arranged and loveless marriages based upon property. Legal, political, and economic equality were beyond their ken, but Rousseau eloquently expressed and seemed to legitimate their right to exert moral and emotional influence.

The most immediate and concrete consequence of the publication of *Emile* was the fact that many women at the royal French court and in the salons as well as in humble bourgeois homes began to breast-feed their own children and to raise them *à la Jean-Jacques*. Much of this change in behavior was temporary and fashionable. But other acts had more enduring consequences. A few women wrote educational manuals of their own, either in imitation of the master or to express their differences with some of his views. These books, including Louise d'Epinay's popular *Conversations with Emily* (1774) and Stephanie de Genlis's highly regarded *Adele and Theodore* (1782) were the immediate predecessors to the outpouring of mothers' manuals that were published in the first half of the nineteenth century in Europe and America. As Claire de Remusat wrote in her own *Essay on the Education of Women* (1821), Rousseau had gotten ''mothers on his side.''

Men took his ideas seriously, too, as the example of three famous educators in the English- and German-speaking world amply demonstrates. In Ireland, Richard Edgeworth (who with his daughter Maria wrote on educational theory) tried to raise his son in strict adherence to the precepts laid down in *Emile*. So did Johann Pestalozzi in Switzerland. Pestalozzi, still celebrated today as the founder of modern elementary education, even named his first-born Jean-Jacques. In England, Thomas Day, the future author of famous children's books, adopted two daughters, hoping to raise one Sophie worthy of becoming his wife. None of these experiments was a success, but the fervor with which they were carried out is a testimony to Rousseau's inspiration. Further, although these men came to reject some of the specific practical advice given in *Emile,* they all continued to advocate a ''natural education,'' which attended to the stages of development and individuality of each child. These were fundamental precepts that came to be attributed to Rousseau.

Rousseau's ideas also affected the men of the French Revolution. When the Jacobins declared a Republic of Virtue in 1792, they encouraged female loyalty by employing Rousseauean rhetoric. They contended in their speeches and newspapers that women had a grave responsibility to inspire and form male citizens. On the Convention floor the Jacobin Pierre Chaumette called on women to be ''the divinity of the domestic sanctuary.'' This phrase was a piece of Rousseauean prose that easily became a commonplace of Victorian expression. The Jacobins soon fell, but the Rousseauean condemnation of the world of sociability lingered long after. Indeed, it seemed validated by the events of the French Revolution. In continental Europe and England upper- and middle-class people who had been traumatized or threatened by the great social upheaval, searched for its causes. One interpretation common to both conservatives, who had lost power and privilege, and women, who had felt powerless, was that the Revolution was a punishment visited upon them because of upper-class immorality. They shared the Rousseauean and Jacobin critique of (especially female) sociability. Thus the Revolution saw not only the triumph of the new bourgeois class in economic and political matters, it also saw the triumph of what came to be known as "bourgeois morality," a code that put particular stress on family life, male authority, female submission and chastity, and "good appearances." This is an ethos that had been spelled out in *La Nouvelle Heloise* and Book V of *Emile*.

This ethos and Rousseauean ideas were partially institutionalized in the new law codes of Europe. The Prussian *Allegemeines Landrecht,* published in 1794, even had a provision making maternal breast-feeding mandatory. Much more far-reaching was the Napoleonic Civil Code (1804). In general, the Code recognized married women only in their domestic capacities: as the leisured wives of the urban and rural bourgeoisie or the busy housewives of the peasantry. This was a traditional vision with which Rousseau would have been familiar and to which he would have given his approval. What is ironic is that the modernizing world that finally emerged in the nineteenth century found his message even more compelling. This was the world of state-building, industrialization, and rapid urban growth, all processes that fostered the separation between public and private life, between the lives of men and the lives of women.

New educational institutions also fostered the separation between upper- and middle-class men and women. The Napoleonic *Université* offered both secondary and university training for men. Its founders conceived this uniform educational system as a way of integrating young upper- and middle-class men into the modern state as patriots, soldiers, professionals, and functionaries. It offered the classical training that was the hallmark of cultured and educated males throughout Europe and the United States.

The curriculum of girls' schools throughout the Western world was quite different. In private and church-run institutions as well as in the very few publicly funded secondary schools, upper- and middle-class girls learned catechism, sewing, and a smattering of the "agreeable" arts and academic subjects. Few girls spent more than a few years at school, so that they received most of their "training" from their mothers. Most men and women believed, like Rousseau, that girls should learn only those subjects appropriate to prepare them for their roles as wives and mothers.

Certainly Rousseau is not solely responsible for these unequal political and educational systems. Conservatives before and after the revolutionary period had assumed that training should fit people to their separate, unequal, and unchanging "God-given" stations. They did not need to read the democratic Jean-Jacques to rationalize their notions of inequalities. But Rousseau did provide a rationale for revolutionary and liberal men. When he substituted "nature" for "God-given" and insisted that women be trained only to fulfill their *natural* functions, he offered progressive men a way to justify their belief in innate sexual inequality while at the same time they asserted their own right to change or improve their social station. Rousseau had helped to make gender the only "natural" given.

His writings also helped to create and spread the notion that there should be an emotional oasis against change: the home. Industrial and political changes presented upper- and middle-class men with vast new opportunities to compete for riches and places. But opportunity also meant competition. Businesses rose and fell; the professions in most European countries were overcrowded. The home was perceived as a refuge against the ugliness of the city, against the reality of competition among male peers in an increasingly individualistic society, and against the possibility of working-class rebellion. As the home ideally became more distinct, private, and differentiated from the world outside, so did the concept of woman, its abiding spirit. Man had to be rational, forceful, and strong, but was sullied by his contact with the competitive and materialistic world. Woman was thought to be angelic, pure, but weak; morally superior, but physically and intellectually incapable of living outside the home. Men and women must be confined to separate "spheres."

Doctors, ministers, and intellectuals elaborated upon the notion of sexual difference throughout the nineteenth century. Jules Michelet, for example, simultaneously denigrated women as invalids and elevated them as angels in a series of popular books that he produced at mid-century. He based his theories of female instability upon what doctors all over the Western world were saying and writing about the explosive nature of the connection between women's minds and their reproductive organs. In the *Descent of Man* (1871), Charles Darwin set forth the theory that an increasing differentiation of the sexes was inherent in the natural selection process that had made human evolution possible. Nineteenth-century medicine and evolutionary theory even gave Rousseauean ambivalence a "scientific basis."

After the revolutionary era, many upper- and middle-class women embraced their "retreat into the home" and used Rousseauean ideas to enhance their status, particularly as mothers. In America, educators took quite seriously the notion that the foundation of a new and daring form of government required the formation of a virtuous citizenry and exhorted women to become "Republican mothers." In France during the first half of the nineteenth century, a veritable movement to foster maternal education occurred. In these, as in other Western countries, the chief tasks of the mother-teacher were the moral education of her children, the training of daughters for their domestic roles, and the creation of a pure home environment. In Germany, France, England, and America women wrote scores of books and practical manuals to support this cause. Many of these authors took issue with Rousseau on the matter of moral autonomy, which they claimed for girls as well as boys. They consistently used the high evaluation of maternity as a reason for giving women an education and taking them seriously. Men also supported the cause. The most popular book about maternal education was not a practical manual, but Louis Aimé Martin's *The Education of Mothers; or, The Civilization of Mankind by Women* (1834). This rhapsodic account of the importance of female spiritual influence was published and discussed in France, England, America, and Spain. Aimé Martin traced his ideas directly to the master, Rousseau.

Eventually the ideology of domesticity spread from bourgeois homes to the families of the poor. Fortified by their belief in female moral superiority, many women in the second half of the century took the message of educative mothering to the lower classes through charity work. The notion that women should function solely as wives and mothers spread in less direct ways as well. As more and more working-class men worked for wages, they insisted upon gaining a "family wage," which would allow them to keep their wives at home. Although few working-class families could subsist without the wife making some money, obviously domesticity had become an ideal to which many below the ranks of the bourgeoisie aspired. Wherever the message spread, however, it carried with it the inherent ambivalence that can be traced to Rousseau. There was a disapproval of women who would step out of their "proper" place, be they the ladies of eighteenth-century sociability or the women who sought a "male" education, careers, or suffrage a century later. The ideology of domesticity elevated women by taking seriously the emotional concerns that defined their wifely and maternal roles, but it acted to bind them more tightly to their homes and to an increasingly narrow definition of "womanhood."

SUGGESTIONS FOR FURTHER READING

Badinter, Elisabeth. *Mother Love: Myth and Reality* (New York, 1981).

Bloch, Jean H. "Rousseau's Reputation as an Authority on Childcare and Physical Education in France Before the Revolution." *Paedogogica Historica XIV*, no. 1 (1974): 5–33.

———. "Women and the Reform of the Nation." In Eva Jacobs, *et al.*, eds. *Women and Society in Eighteenth-Century France: Essays in Honor of John Stephenson Spink*. London, 1979.

Eisenstein, Zillah. "J.-J. Rousseau and Patriarchal Ideology: Liberal Individualism and Motherhood." In *The Radical Future of Liberal Feminism*. New York, 1981.

Graham, Ruth. "Rousseau's Sexism Revolutionized." In Paul Fritz and Richard Morton, eds. *Women in the Eighteenth Century and Other Essays*. Toronto, 1976.

Jimack, P. D. "The Paradox of Sophie and Julie: Contemporary Responses to Rousseau's Ideal Wife and Ideal Mother." In Eva Jacobs, *et al.*, eds. *Women and Society in Eighteenth-Century France*.

Keohane, Nannerl O. " 'But for Her Sex . . .': The Domestication of Sophie." *University of Ottawa Quarterly* 49, 3–4 (July–October 1979): 390–400.

Kerber, Linda K. *Women of the Republic: Intellect and Ideology in Revolutionary America*. Chapel Hill, NC, 1980.

Misenheimer, Helen Evans. *Rousseau on the Education of Women*. Washington, DC, 1981.

Okin, Susan Moller. *Women in Western Political Thought*. Princeton, 1979.

Rousseau, Jean-Jacques. *The Confessions*. Tr. by J. M. Cohen. Baltimore, 1953.

———. *Emile: or, on Education*. Tr. by Allan Bloom. New York, 1979.

———. *The Minor Educational Writings of Jean-Jacques Rousseau*. Tr. by William Boyd. New York, 1962.

————. *The Social Contract and Discourses.* Tr. by G. D. H. Cole. New York, 1973.

Schwartz, Joel. *The Sexual Politics of Jean-Jacques Rousseau.* Chicago, 1984.

Wexler, Victor G. " 'Made for Man's Delight': Rousseau as Antifeminist." *American Historical Review* 81, no. 2 (1976): 266–291.

6

". . . with the wolf always at the door . . .": Women's Work in Domestic Industry in Britain and Germany

Barbara Franzoi

The transformation of women's work was one of the most significant results of the industrial revolution. Many nineteenth-century observers such as Friedrich Engels (in his 1844 *On the Condition of the Working Class in England*) decried the reorganization that "tore" women from their families, confined them to factories, and turned thriving artisanal communities into "she-towns." Historians, however, now know that this was an exaggerated, even erroneous, portrayal. Most women, especially married women, continued to labor at traditional tasks in domestic settings. A more pervasive and permanent effect of industrial development was the marginalization of women's work and the feminization of domestic industry. In this study, Barbara Franzoi illustrates vividly the role of paid homework in the daily lives of working-class women. She draws our attention to the phenomenon of "sweatshops" and the close fit between the pressures on women exerted by their need for income, the imperative of the ideology of domesticity as it spread to the working classes, and the demands of industrial capital for cheap and seasonal labor.

Along with traditional sources, such as contemporary portraits of working-class life, Franzoi employs statistics taken from occupational censuses in England and Germany to analyze the changing sexual division of labor in trade and industry. Occupational census data, while often understating women's work, nonetheless contain useful demographic information on age and marital status of workers and indices of industrial organization. By focusing on women's work in industries that are labor—rather than capital—intensive and require little skill or training, Franzoi illustrates how household production in an industrializing economy plays an essential role in the complex process of capitalist development. Her work on nineteenth-century Britain and Germany provides a model useful for understanding change in Third World countries today.

The term "industrial revolution" is one of those catchwords that conjures up a host of vivid images, most typically of factories, machines, and overheated, overcrowded workrooms. Among Western economies, Britain and Germany often are singled out as models of industrial transformation. Britain, after all, was the home of the first industrial revolution and for a century was the mightiest industrial power in Europe. As the end of the nineteenth century, its economic supremacy was challenged by the newly unified German Empire. Too often, the spread of industrialization appears as a monolithic occurrence and the labor force is depicted solely as factory workers who are predominantly male. This is only half the story, for it neglects an integral component of industrial capitalism—domestic industry or work done in the home, in the main by women. Less visible than factories or smokestacks and the throngs that came and went through the factory gates, the industrialized economies of both Britain and Germany housed thousands of women and children who worked in kitchens, attics, and tenement basements at the fragmented tasks of industrial homework.

Emphasis on factory production and mechanization conceals the complexity of capitalist economic development. In the nineteenth century, capitalist expansion used both machine and hand labor. If the factory symbolized industrialization, it is important to understand that large groups of workers remained outside it, carrying on essentially traditional tasks in old industries and performing the new jobs created by industrial expansion. Capitalism sought to maximize production and minimize costs. In selected work processes and in specific industries such as ribbonmaking, silkweaving, and lacemaking, these ends could best be achieved by keeping manufacturing in the home, or by locating it there, as was the case with the clothing trades and tobacco products. Mechanization—the introduction of machinery—in one part of the work process often generated expansion of homework in another. Growth of large factories was frequently accompanied by a proliferation of small production units in homes and workshops where capital-saving, labor-intensive methods prevailed. Subdivision of labor separated the work process into tasks that could be performed easily by hand at home.

In *Life and Labour of the People of London,* Charles Booth, a British shipowner and social reformer of the late nineteenth century, described the intricate processes of subdivision in the paper industry and the resultant gender segregation of the work force.

> The men who cut the paper and cardboard for the boxes make use of machines, worked some by steam and others by hand. . . . Boys tend the scoring machines, which make cuts in the cardboard along the lines on which the card has to be folded. . . . Women and girls make the boxes from the materials prepared by the men and boys. . . . The material is cut and prepared, and then given out, usually to married women who have worked in one of the factories before marriage.

Booth's narrative also points up the close connection between the factory and domestic industry in the paper trade and suggests a high degree of interaction as women moved from one work setting to another. In needlemaking, too, centered in Worcestershire, England, an observer estimated that the production process was so finely subdivided that a single needle was worked on by 120 different people.

A second characteristic of industries that expanded into homework was irregular market demand. Factories and machinery saved costs only if they were geared for large-scale production most of the year. While many industries in both Germany and Britain experienced periodic uncertainties, consumer goods were especially prone to the vagaries of the market. Production runs varied from season to season, even from day to day. An elastic market required a flexible labor supply. A widow in London remarked:

> The slacks in the cloak business occur twice a year—that is to say, at the end of the winter and the summer season. . . . Now I shall have nothing from the warehouse not before next March; so I shall have to seek some other employment till then.

Whether this particular woman was available the following March did not really matter to the employer. The important consideration was a labor supply that was ready on short notice, that could be hired when needed, and did not have to be maintained when there was no work. There was always a flurry of activity in season or when rush orders forced workers to stay at their tasks for fourteen and fifteen hours a day.

Countless women were present in the industrial labor force, albeit employed irregularly, often in their homes. The basic reason was the fit between capitalism's search for abundant and cheap labor and women's need for wages. While society claimed that men were primary providers, in many instances men's wages were unreliable and inadequate for family support. Industry controlled women through the economic insecurity of men. Skilled men in heavy industry could earn a family wage, but that was the privilege of the minority. Unemployment and underemployment regularly depressed men's wages. Even if a man were steadily employed, his earnings alone were rarely enough to support a family. Women and children had to be available as compensatory labor. Because women worked from necessity, in many cases just managing subsistence, they were economically vulnerable. They accepted poor wages because there were no real alternatives.

The conditions of proletarian poverty forced women into waged work. In most laboring families women and children were expected to supplement total income. Women's involvement with paid labor traced a pattern of recurrent hardship ''with the wolf always at the door.'' Working-class women could not evade the hazards of marginality, for women formed a large part of the surplus labor force primarily because of their roles and responsibilities in the family. Most women who could do factory work were young and single, but marriage did not mean transition out of the labor force. Family ties limited the options available to women and required considerable juggling of work-place and schedules. Women's choices were limited and they were disadvantaged, but they were not completely powerless. Wives and mothers resisted outside work when they could; they preferred ways of earning money that were compatible with household routine. Therefore, for many women, the constraints of economic need coupled with family responsibilities made domestic industry the only possible alternative to destitution. However, the fact that domestic industry was often the most exploited form of labor further perpetuated the desperate condition of the working population.

A glimpse at wage levels illustrates the depth of female poverty. Especially for those who relied on their own earnings, such as widows and single women, it was a terrible situation. Women's wages, depressed in comparison with men's, were further jeopardized by income interruptions and rate changes. Women usually prefaced responses to questions about what they earned with complaints about the lack of steady work. While a skilled male worker in the German machine industry, for example, could expect regular employment at about 35 marks a week, women homeworkers averaged less than 12 marks even when they had work.

Wage reduction was the most effective way for industry to increase profit. Because most homework was paid by the piece, wage adjustments were simple, direct, and disastrous. Women were forced to work harder just to stay even. The scramble among employers and middlemen to undercut prices worsened at the end of the century, and women homeworkers were the unfortunate victims of that competition. Since women's unskilled labor had no real scarcity value, too many women seeking work compelled all of them to take industry's meager offerings.

Women's economic activity at home was almost always augmented by the labor of children, a condition that further gave industry an abundant and cheap labor reserve. Henry Mayhew, who compiled detailed accounts of the London working classes in 1849–1850, was quick to see the connection between poverty and exploitation. He observed that families escaped destitution only by putting children to work as soon as they were able to do simple tasks.

> From people being obliged to work twice the hours they once did, a glut of hands was the consequence, and the masters were led to make reductions in the wages. They took advantage of our poverty and lowered wages, so as to undersell each other, and command business.

The prevailing pattern of women's work at home reflected the more pervasive gender division of industrial labor. Certain "women's jobs" were created in factory-based, mechanized industries, but the real volume of women's work was found in areas related to traditional work roles. Women workers were concentrated in large numbers in trades connected to household jobs and in occupations related to consumer goods and foods manufacture. In London at the turn of the twentieth century, women made up 68 percent of all workers in the clothing trades. They constituted about 40 percent of upholsterers, 90 percent of quill and feather dressers, 65 percent of textile workers, 80 percent of jam, preserves, and sweet makers, almost 75 percent of chocolate and cocoa makers, and 60 percent of tobacco workers. Similarly in Germany, a profile of domestic industry shows that women were concentrated in specific trades. It demonstrates clearly that between 1895 and 1907 domestic industry absorbed great numbers and high percentages of women. By the end of the century, every industry in Germany experienced an expansion of female labor in homework. Textiles was the only occupation that showed an overall decline numerically, but here, too, the percentage of women employed at home expanded. The figures for Britain and Germany show that capitalist organization of work intensified the feminization of certain industries, principally textiles, clothing, and tobacco, and increased the feminization of domestic industry in all areas.

Percentage of Female Domestic Workers in Selected Industries
in Germany

Industry	Year	Percentage of Women
Metals	1895	7.2
	1907	13.5
Machines	1895	9.4
	1907	19.8
Chemicals	1895	68.6
	1907	86.6
Textiles	1895	46.0
	1907	59.2
Paper products	1895	38.3
	1907	54.3
Wood products	1895	17.4
	1907	42.4
Foods and tobacco	1895	44.6
	1907	62.6
Clothing	1895	56.2
	1907	68.6

Source: *Occupational Census of the German Reich, 1907.*

The clothing industry in both Germany and Britain encompassed all the defining features of women's work. The clothing trades were a prime example of the degree to which industrial capitalism penetrated the work experience of women, especially work done in the home. All kinds of sewing such as corsetmaking, hatmaking, the manufacture of ties, scarves, collars and cuffs, fine feather working, artificial flowermaking, even dolls' clothes fell into this category. While sewing was performed by women all over Germany and Britain, in its modern, capitalized form, it was really an urban industry concentrated in specific cities. In Britain the clothing center was London; in Germany, it was Berlin.

In Britain, the lineal descendants of the handicraft trades of tailoring and seamstressing were the "sweated" trades of plain sewers, shirtmakers, button-stitchers, and pelt sewers that were the refuge of women in dire need. It was largely manual labor, requiring minimal skills and little outlay in terms of space and materials. The clothing trades were ultimately flexible and goods could literally be picked up and put down as market demands dictated. The term, "sweating," was in use in England by the 1830s to describe a system of subcontracting in the tailoring trades that used agents for the distribution and collection of goods. Orders were obtained by offering the lowest possible prices and by undercutting competitors, which directly reduced wages paid to homeworkers. While the term was usually associated with sewing, it was not restricted to clothing. Any work done at home with little or no equipment, that used repetitive, manual labor, with simple or easily acquired skills could fall within this category. Descriptions of sweated workers tell the story of long hours for little pay, and the term conveys a graphic image of severe destitution and appalling exploitation. The poorest paid jobs and cheapest goods were called "slop work." Mayhew told his readers that he was saddened by what he saw in the rooms of London sloppers.

> I then directed my steps to the neighborhood of Drurylane, to see a poor woman who lived in an attic in one of the closest courts in that quarter. On the table was a quarter of an ounce of tea. Observing my eye to rest upon it, she told me it was all she took. "Sugar," she said, "I broke myself of long ago; I couldn't afford it. A cup of tea, a piece of bread, and an onion is generally all I have for my dinner, and sometimes I haven't even an onion, and then I sops my bread."

Decentralization in the clothing industry in Germany enforced the sexual division of labor and replicated the conditions of sweating chronicled in Britain. Not only did piece work and subdivision of tasks multiply the numbers of women working at home, but changing technology, especially the sewing machine, increased production and roughly evened out the quality of domestic-made goods. In Berlin, the prevailing method for handling work was the middleman system. Subcontractors either delivered goods directly to the homeworkers or distributed them at factories and workrooms. It was rare to find a clothing firm that did not employ countless numbers of persons working at home in addition to those in the factory. In 1906, in women's and children's clothes, 350 firms employed 52,000 homeworkers; 210 establishments making boys' and men's wear utilized 22,000 homeworkers; 320 firms making undergarments employed 47,000 homeworkers; 150 hatmaking and flowermaking ships employed 6,000 homeworkers; and 170 shoemaking establishments employed 2,000 persons working at home.

By no means peripheral to the practical reasons for the expansion of home industry was the implicit and overt resistance of men toward women workers. Eliminating the competition of low-paid female labor was perceived as the best guarantee for a family wage. Thus the negativism contained both economic and ideological components. Caught in the powerlessness of their own economic uncertainty, men blamed poor wages and insecure jobs on women. Capitalist expansion pitted men against women, factory labor against homework, simultaneously as men, women, and families depended on the earnings supplied by domestic industry. The thousands of women in domestic production were not obviously visible because they were in their proper place—the home. But the appearance of women in previously male-dominated industries and the proliferation of jobs done by homework were both a real and a symbolic threat. Criticizing women workers because they were poorly skilled and cheap, all labor unions addressed the problem of domestic industry. Because domestic industry was indeed competition, trade unions sought to organize women homeworkers, while at the same time, they agitated for restrictions on homework and even demanded its abolition.

Hostility from male-dominated trade unions was only one facet of collective resistance to women's paid labor. The prevailing nineteenth-century image of woman as wife and mother formed the ideological context for the social anxiety about women's work. Women's factory work was never fully condoned. The view that woman's place was in the home caring for her husband and children set certain limits on the way women engaged in paid labor and made women's work into a public issue. Employment outside the home was an elemental threat to social values and summoned a call of alarm that generated debate in Germany and elsewhere. As working women entered the public arena, their roles were sharply defined and efforts were made to bring industrial work into conformity with patriarchal values. Elaborating the dangers of the factory while embellishing the merits of work done in the home was one approach to solving the dilemma. Another was the development of protective laws governing women's work. It is instructive to recognize that labor legislation in the nineteenth century virtually ignored domestic industry. "Going out to work" was the critical problem. Most public and private alternatives to women's employment were directed at keeping them at home. If women in the working classes were supposed to work, they were not to be conspicuously present in the labor force.

In Britain, legal restrictions on the hours of work and employment of women as a distinct occupational group dated from the Factories Amendment Act of 1844. Prior to that time, chief emphasis in the development of protective legislation had been on child labor. In the 1830s and 1840s, there was growing public concern about the physical and moral effects of factory employment on women. Several medical witnesses called by the Select Committee on the Labour of Children in Factories in 1832 (the Sadler Committee) said those abuses were the greatest evils of the factory system. Creating a new category of protected workers provided a way to deal with several interrelated problems simultaneously. Segregating women assured industry that male labor would not be tampered with legally. Not only did industry defend its prerogatives, but male workers perceived the real benefits from putting female labor at a competitive disadvantage. The Short-Time Movement achieved success in 1847 when the hours of factory work for women and children were reduced to a maximum of ten per day, but the Act applied only to textile mills. The desire to protect women because they were the mothers of future generations was an important component of factory legislation. Concern about women's labor generally focused on the effects of married women's labor on the family and on the health of the nation. Maternal breast-feeding became a metaphor for national strength: ". . . you cannot rear an imperial race on the bottle."

Charles Booth's investigations of the London poor brought to light important information about the marital composition of the labor force and the degree of destitution that drove women to seek paid work. Booth's narrative made it clear that not only single women and widows worked, but married women with children worked as well, and that most women were not in factories. In the 1890s, largely as a result of Booth's disclosure and the urging of his associate, Clara Collet, it was publicly acknowledged that there was special need for inquiry into home industry. The newly created Women's Industrial Council collected statistics and information. Domestic industry was officially "discovered." Ameliorative solutions stressed education, domestic skills, and self-improvement. Reform efforts were conventional middle-class remedies. Their implementation did little to relieve economic distress and in practice, actually limited chances for any real change. There was some reluctance to provide help because married women's work was thought to bring out latent male laziness and to erode the man's sense of responsibility. One observer commented that ". . . a dislocation of trade which throws the married woman out of work may even result in increased steadiness in the part of the husband." The problems and solutions of female labor were set in the context of women's "true role" and the damage that work outside the home was said to cause. It is no surprise that domestic industry was idealized as the appropriate way for women to earn.

The themes and social policy measures were much the same as Germany confronted women's industrial work at the end of the century. In the 1870s, the first official investigation of industry focused on factory work, child labor, and women. The report raised the question of whether the government should restrict or prohibit women's factory work, and at once responded with economic justification for female labor, moderated by proposals for protective measures. Conceptualization of the woman worker as a social problem was based on the premise that women had special moral and social responsibilities as wives and mothers. While protection was adopted by most major political parties in Germany, the Catholic Center Party was the most important source of agitation for prohibition and restriction. Catholic motivation was preservation of the family. A factory inspectorate, set up by the Imperial government, collected statistics on women's work and supplied much of the information for the development of protective laws. In 1891, major labor legislation stipulated general conditions for all factory workers and mandated specific regulations for children and women. Child labor under fourteen was prohibited and children were required to attend school until that age. Daily work time for all women workers, married and single, was limited to eleven hours a day. Married women with family responsibilities were allowed an extra half hour at mid-day break. Maternity leave of four weeks following delivery was provided unless the woman chose, with medical permission, to return sooner.

In Germany, there was no official investigation of domestic industry in the nineteenth century, although many studies analyzing its nature were published in economic journals and trade union reports. Domestic industry remained unregulated until 1911. Evidence suggests that a major effect of regulation of women's factory work and the prohibition of child labor was expansion of their labor in domestic industry. Employers used traditional work forms as a way to circumvent changes in the employment and education laws. And women moved away from regulated factory jobs into lightly restricted and uncontrolled industries because they could not afford the "cost" of protection.

Several brief comments about women's work in contemporary Third World countries will confirm that the effects of capitalist expansion are not bounded by time and geography. Remarkable parallels emerge as women are drawn into the developing economies of Africa, Asia, and Latin America. Asymmetrical growth, much of it directed by Western models and multinational corporations, structures an uneven economy. It results in a capital-intensive industrial core usually referred to as modern or the "formal" sector, and the "informal" sector that includes a large variety of activities based on the labor of women in a casual, intermittent, and marginal way. It was assumed by development planners that the informal sector would become redundant and would be absorbed as modernization progressed. This has not happened.

The activities in the informal sector are not traditional or transitional. They are essential responses to the capitalist system. The informal sector is labor-absorptive; it sustains large numbers of persons, mostly women, at low levels of living. The sector acts to maximize production at minimal cost. Handicrafts, cottage industry, trading, food preparation and sale, tasks closely related to agriculture in rural areas, small-scale manufacture in urban centers; these are the kinds of income-generating activities that fall into the informal sector. They require little capital outlay, low-level skills, few tools, little or no mechanization, and minimal technology. The jobs are flexible, fluid, and can be carried out individually or with family assistance. Where Third World women work in industry, they are usually concentrated in textiles, clothing, and electronics factories, many of which have a multinational connection. These industries actively seek out female labor because women are more docile, more dextrous, and less likely to organize. Ultimately, the basic reason for the prevalence of female labor is women's willingness to work for less pay. The ingredients are very familiar, indeed.

Domestic industry did not decline in the nineteenth century. It expanded. Homework was a nucleus for capitalist development. The pattern is replicated in contemporary Third World economies. Cheap, abundant labor in the form of women's work served important functions for economic growth. Romantic notions we may have about the family workshop do not fit the realities of industrial homework. Sweatshops and slop work comprise the dramatic testimony of hardship and inequity produced by capitalist transition. As societies moved from traditional to modern methods of production, women were forced into a condition of constant adjustment. They devised ways to survive that were adaptive, preservative, and flexible. Under the impact of industrialization, women seem to change less than men, but the continuity should not be read as an expansion of choices. Rather, it is the result of diminished options. Paradoxically, women's strategies for coping turned on the very hindrances that blocked escape from limited opportunity and economic constraint.

SUGGESTIONS FOR FURTHER READING

Alexander, Sally. "Women's Work in Nineteenth-Century London; A Study of the Years 1820–50." In Juliet Mitchell and Ann Oakley, eds. *The Rights and Wrongs of Women*. Harmondsworth, England, 1976.

Booth, Charles. *Life and Labour of the People of London*. New York, 1970, orig. 1889.

Boserup, Ester. *Women's Role in Economic Development*. London, 1970.

Franzoi, Barbara. *At the Very Least She Pays the Rent: Women and German Industrialization, 1871–1914*. Westport, CT, 1985.

———. "Impact of Economic Change on Women in Developing Countries." In *Global Interdependence: Case Studies for the Social Sciences*. Princeton, 1986.

Hewitt, Margaret. *Wives and Mothers in Victorian Industry*. London, 1958.

Mayhew, Henry. "Labour and the Poor" (1849–1850). In Anne Humphreys, ed. *Voices of the Poor: Selections from the Morning Chronicle*. London, 1971.

Pinchbeck, Ivy. *Women Workers in the Industrial Revolution*. London, 1930.

Quennell, Peter, ed. *Mayhew's London*. London, 1951.

Safa, Helen I. and Eleanor Leacock, guest eds. ''Development and the Sexual Division of Labor.'' *Signs* 7, no. 2 (Winter 1981).

Samuel, Raphael. ''Workshop of the World: Steam Power and Hand Technology in Mid-Victorian Britain.'' *History Workshop* (Spring 1977).

Tinker, Irene, Bo Bramsen, and Mayra Buvinic, eds. *Women and World Development.* New York, 1976.

Yeo, Eileen and E. P. Thompson. *The Unknown Mayhew.* New York, 1971.

7

The Tiresome Work of Conspicuous Leisure: On the Domestic Duties of the Wives of Civil Servants in the German Empire (1871–1918)

Sibylle Meyer
Translated by Lyndel Butler*

The absence of scientific historical research on women until recently permitted image and myth to pass for factual description of women's lives. Among the most persistent misconceptions was the popular picture of the typical Victorian lady as a woman of leisure. Freed from demeaning physical labor and sustained mental effort, the model middle-class wife and mother supposedly passed her days in ornamental pursuits, indulging in piano playing, china painting, fancy dress, and lavish entertainment. With a legion of servants at hand to attend to every necessity including infant and child care, she herself became an ornament reflective of her husband's class status.

This familiar but false image may be traced to the confusion between prescriptive and descriptive literature. Victorian novels and advice manuals portrayed women's lives as their authors wanted them to be. Recent research based on studies of occupation, household income, wage levels, and the like, reveals that even in mid-Victorian England, relatively few families of the "middle class" (a term ill-defined) could afford to hire a host of servants. Most often the mistress of the house had to make do with one servant, usually an early adolescent working-class or country girl who was ignorant of middle-

*This chapter first appeared in German under the title "Die mühsame Arbeit des demonstrativen Müssiggangs. Uber die häuslichen Pflichten der Beamtenfrauen im Kaiserreich," in Karin Hausen, ed., *Frauen suchen Ihre Geschichte. Historische Studien zum 19. und 20. Jahrhundert* (Beck'sche Schwarze Reihe, Band 276) Munich, 1983, pp. 172–194. It has been translated by Lyndel Butler. We thank the Beck Publishing House for permission to translate and publish an abbreviated English version of the article. Consult the German version for the notes and sources; we have included only a few of the works in the list of suggested readings.

class styles and standards of living. As Sibylle Meyer shows in this study of civil servants' wives in Imperial Germany, housewives themselves worked hard to satisfy the increasingly stringent requirements for the governance of a well-ordered household—all the while striving to maintain the appearance of domestic tranquillity. "Conspicuous leisure" required that housework be viewed as the expression of love and devotion rather than as labor. Yet this hidden work by women might be the key to their husbands' success in the bureaucratic order. The social and economic history of housework has been of particular interest to German historians as well as to British and American Marxists and feminists. They demonstrate the interdependency of private and public life even in the heyday of "separate spheres."

In historical research, bourgeois women appear most frequently as idle ladies of the drawing room who supposedly occupied their time with piano playing, literature, fine needlework, and the next social invitation. They are seen as persons who determined the atmosphere of the household through their character, not through their work, and who delegated all housework to servants, whom they merely supervised. This myth of the idle bourgeois lady of the salon indeed has little in common with the everyday reality of most bourgeois women in the last third of the nineteenth century.

The work of middle-class women was structured by specific obligations that bisected their lives and subjected the two parts to different rules. In the public eye, they were to appear idle and were, through their alleged freedom from housework, to symbolize the social status of their husbands. Within the family they had to fulfill their domestic duties following the principle of maximum thrift—housework recognizes no leisure. This study examines the complicated daily work of wives of the educated middle class of modest income using the example of domestic social relationships to bring clearly to light the pressures caused by the combination of bourgeois lifestyle and bourgeois housework. My evidence is based primarily on Berlin and there, above all, on the wives of civil servants; however, it appears to have general validity for the urban educated middle class of the German Empire.

The occupations of the educated middle classes—most especially civil service—required continuous allegiance to the government; not only was one's labor claimed by the state, but one's entire personality. Occupational duties embraced the entire life of persons in these professions. In every context, behavior worthy of the state was demanded of them. Every appearance in public—alone or accompanied by a spouse—was a test of respectability and social acceptability. Even the private sphere of bourgeois families was determined by professional pressures that found their expression in the family's considerable expenditures for keeping up appearances in public. Respectability required a correspondingly appropriate dwelling, whenever possible in a better quarter of the city. The annual summer trip to the seaside was obligatory for middle-class families. Sons had to receive an appropriate education; daughters, an adequate dowry to assure a marriage worthy of their class.

A special symbol of the socially respectable position, the "idleness of the wife" also expressed the wealth of the family. All housework was supposed to be taken care of by an army of servants. Every form of work was considered inappropriate for middle-class women and violated the rules of etiquette. Instead, the occupations prescribed for bourgeois women were obligatory piano playing, knowledge of French language, literature, and conversation. These required skills were to come into play on social occasions and were, therefore, functional for maintaining middle-class appearances. Bourgeois women in public were expected to sparkle and to maintain appearances in order to provide their husbands with a backdrop of education, respectability, and economic power. Idleness became a central component of the woman's obligation to keep up appearances.

The pressure to keep up appearances extended into the "private sphere" of the bourgeois family and objectified itself in the floor plan and partitioning of the middle-class residence. The arrangement and functioning of the rooms corresponded to the attempt, on the one hand, to establish the relationship to the public with the formal rooms near the street entrance and, on the other hand, to shield the private rooms from the outside world. The size of the individual rooms reflected the orientation of the residence to the requirement of keeping up appearances. The formal rooms frequently occupied four to five times as much floor space as the housekeeping rooms: kitchen, larder, and servants' chambers.

Occasions to demonstrate the respectability of the husband and the leisure of the wife were offered primarily by calling at the house or by private invitation. As soon as the family moved to another city—regular transfers were a permanent part of the careers of civil servants—it immediately initiated "social intercourse" by "paying calls." The domestic visits took place in the drawing room, which was not usually used by the family, but served only the purpose of keeping up appearances for guests and callers. The other rooms remained closed to strangers. From the splendor of the drawing room and the apparent worth of each individual piece of furniture, the wealth and social acceptability of the family could be ascertained.

In order to decorate the drawing room as a status symbol, corners were cut in furnishing the other rooms, so that there was a considerable disparity between the quality of the furnishings of the drawing room and the rest of the residence. Luise Otto-Peters (1819–1895), a leading German feminist, late in the 1870s described this contrast between drawing room and other rooms: "In the one elegant furnishings were exposed to view, splendor and attempts to keep up the latest fashion; in the others shabbiness and anxious attempts to make do. . . ."

Social events underwent a formal patterning that was maintained through the inflexible constraints of norms to be meticulously heeded. As a rule, between twelve and sixteen persons were invited to festive soirées. The upper limit derived necessarily from the relatively small size of the middle-class residence. The sequence of events for the parties was prescribed in detail, and every guest was familiar with it. The company met in the drawing room, was introduced, chatted, and sat down together at the table for a festive dinner. After an elaborate bill of fare, at which everything was served that the family had to offer, coffee and tea were served, the group heard the hostess or the daughter of the house play the piano, and conversation continued.

The obligatory banquet always constituted the high point of the social evening. On the basis of the table decorations, the china and silver displayed, the menu, and the consummate service, the host family was scrutinized by its guests to determine its qualifications for membership in "polite society." For this reason the guests' eyes should be virtually blinded by the brilliance of the silver, the number of glasses, and the gleaming china. Along this line, homemaking manuals recommended: "The gleaming focal point of the dining room should always be the table; therefore, it demands plenty of light and brightness. To this end have all your treasures of silver chest and china cabinet polished as bright and clean as possible; let everything simply sparkle with cleanliness. . . ."

At that time an important attribute of prosperity was a complete and appropriately expensive tableware service that was the pride of every housewife, for china and silver were usually part of her dowry. In any case "society" must not notice if the family owned no such lavish table service and silverware. One possible way to hide the lack was to borrow dishes from parents and friends, and, if they also had none, then if worse came to worst, to turn to a rental agency. Hans Fallada (1893–1937), a popular German writer, describes this necessity at his parents' house: "We had to obtain glasses and silverware from a rental agency, but not the dishes, for we owned the Wedgewood service notorious among our acquaintances. . . ."

The service at a dinner party had to be faultless. The only servant of educated bourgeois families, the maid-of-all-work alone would have been overburdened with the preparation of foods, serving, pouring drinks, and cleaning up afterward. Besides, most of them were very young girls from the country and not familiar with the strict rules of serving. Difficult "incidents" could arise that would destroy the painstakingly contrived arrangements. Thus the manuals on housekeeping recommended: "Since few servants understand faultless service, one hires a temporary servant, one from northern Germany who is a very well-schooled in fashionable usage." The temporary servant, who was engaged for one evening and with the maid took over the service for the soirée, appears to have been the rule in the family of the civil servant of that period. A male servant, who could only be afforded by the wealthiest families in the final years of the nineteenth century, was considered to be a sign of greatest refinement. The temporary servant became a favorite theme of contemporary family periodicals, which cynically portrayed the picture of a servant who could not find his way around strange quarters, who exploited the dependency of the family on his services, and purloined the leftovers from the expensive menus.

Such images caricatured the secret fears of the housewife that the temporary servant might behave badly or that the other guests might recognize him. "Isn't that the same one as at the privy counsellor's?" The housewife had to live in constant fear of the discovery of the elaborately arranged deception. It is easy to imagine how the furtive glances of the housewife clashed with the critical ones of the guests searching for *faux pas*. "One feared for the success of the evening. The guests, to whom all these situations were all too well-known, followed the course of the evening with almost fearful suspense."

The same women who, during the official dinner parties had to appear idle in keeping with their husbands' social positions, were at the same time responsible for the events of the evening and the comprehensive preparations. The appearance of refinement and the social deception, which was supposed to hide the lack of wealth, had to be arranged by the housewives. Days ahead detailed plans were worked out and the difficult undertaking of a table arrangement was begun. Every wife tried to create a special table decor, yet the accessorizing of her table should not be more sumptuous and more impressive than at all the other parties. In this vein one author advised in 1897: "In short, everything is permitted that is pleasing and there is only one law: within the limits of good taste, give your table the most individual touch possible." This principle became obligatory for the women.

Over the spotless white damask tablecloth, hand-embroidered or hand-painted table runners were spread—or as an especially extravagant variation—"the new unusual runners out of printed crepe paper" were used. Also the women, for the most part, painted the placecards and found endless fresh ways of informing the guests of the courses, e.g., "in the shape of small musical instruments such as tambourines, harps, or zithers, or apples, oranges, and flowers, decorated with the names, lying on the napkins, or as tiny palettes with figures painted in water colors."

The actual dinner party menu meant just as much painstaking preparatory work for the women. The rules of etiquette prescribed at least six courses, and their combinations were to be elegant, original, and distinguished through the use of luxurious ingredients and excellent preparation. Recommended menus for festive dinner parties were found in every contemporary cookbook or housekeeping manual, frequently also in women's magazines. The suggestions varied according to the projected readership. A simpler dinner party menu consisted of a bouillon with pastries or sandwiches as hors d'oeuvres, after which the two obligatory main courses, normally fish and a roasted meat dish, were served. Afterward, butter and cheeses followed, and the meal ended with a dessert. In more elevated bourgeois circles, three or four main courses were considered appropriate. The exaggerated value placed on these dinner parties increased even more the painstaking efforts already made by the housewives.

Not only the abundant menus, the faultless service, and the smoothness of the evening determined its success, but also the correspondingly decorative spatial backdrop of the drawing room. For this, not only short-term efforts were required, such as thorough cleaning and possible rearrangement of the room, but also long-term work in which women made part of the fittings for the drawing room. Many pieces of furniture, which would have been too expensive if purchased, were made by the women themselves or their apparent value was increased through artful adornment. Having conclusions about the wealth of the family drawn directly from the magnificence of the drawing room required establishing for the guests the best possible appearances.

Following the principle of obtaining the most decorative effect possible at the least possible expense, the women went to work and made artful pieces of decorative furniture. Accessories, wall decorations, glass paintings, hooked rugs that looked like real Persian carpets, table covers, piano throws, lamps, screens, tassels, pulls, and draperies were hand-sewn, embroidered, crocheted, and knitted. Out of four old carpet-beaters, they fashioned little tables for the drawing room. The handles were crossed and bound so that the lower parts formed legs, the four upper parts formed a small basket that was covered with embroidered cloth. The table legs were upholstered with plush or knitted covers so that no one could know that this apparently fine piece had been made out of old carpet-beaters.

The tremendous amount of trouble involved in the outfitting of a drawing room and in the preparations for the party were not to be noticeable to the invited guests. The more completely the housewife succeeded at this deception, the more certain appeared the professional promotion of the husband, assuring the material basis as well as the social reputation of the family. Guests of the house must not see the housewife engaged in physical work, or detect traces of this work on her. Thus soft, well-cared-for hands, on which one did not notice the daily work, were an attribute of class that women were concerned with keeping. As early as 1845 a housekeeping manual recommended:

> It often happens that even high-ranking ladies help at home with housework, and particularly with kitchen chores, scrubbing, etc., so that, above all the hands have good cause to become very rough, hard, and calloused. When these ladies appear in society, they are extremely upset at having such rough-looking hands. In order to perform the hardest and most ordinary chores, as for example, cooking, dish-washing, sweeping, and the like, and, at the same time, to keep a soft hand like those fine ladies who have no heavier work to do than embroidering and sewing, always keep a piece of fresh bacon, rub your hands with it just before bedtime, and you will fully achieve your goal. You will, as a result, have the inconvenience of having to sleep with gloves on, in order not to soil the bed.

The opposite pole to the elegance of the public facade was the meager everyday life of the family. Here everything had to be extremely economical in order, once or twice a year, to facilitate the contrived social appearances. The work fell to the housewife to carry out the strict requirement of compulsory, domestic thrift in all areas of housekeeping. Thrift here meant the reduction of expenditures required by the life of the family through the increase of unpaid work on the part of the wife—exploitation instead of expenditure.

The smaller the income of the husband, the more necessary to forego the work of servants; educated bourgeois families had to be content normally with one maid. The dominant interpretation since the period, that several maids could have carried out the entire work of the household on their own and the job of the wife consisted of overseeing the servants, misses the reality of most bourgeois women. It assumes a division of labor between the lady of the house and the housemaids corresponding to the separation of decision making from physical work. However, it is misleading and serves to buttress the dominant thesis of the ''idleness'' of the middle-class women. The housework to be accomplished was so comprehensive and so manifold that it could scarcely be completed by two women.

Housework required cooperation between all persons concerned, or at least required communication about the current task. This necessity was intensified when the normally very young maid-of-all-work brought no specific knowledge of housekeeping with her at the time she was hired and, therefore, had to be instructed by the housewife. In addition to the inhuman work pressure on the maid, which one cannot overestimate, the maid's arrival brought with it an increase in the work of the housewife. There was, indeed, a division of work between the two women, but it was not along previously assumed traditional lines of decision making and physical work. The division varied with the demands of the work to be accomplished at a given moment and was maintained through cooperation.

A generally ambivalent relationship resulted between the housewife and the maid. While the former worked out of "love," permanently and unpaid, the latter was poorly paid and could be let go at any time. On the other hand, both were required in the common work of the household and, in the process of accomplishing the everyday work of the family, depended on each other. They stood—although they belonged to different social classes—in a structurally comparable legal and material dependency on the man of the house. Subject to the familial, patriarchal power relationship, both of the women had to reach some mutual understanding in order to make their living and working situations as bearable as possible. Simultaneously the housewife served as mediator on behalf of the needs and interests of the man of the house. She had a concrete interest in maximizing the work accomplished by the maid; something that could only be achieved by applying continual pressure. Only the efficient functioning of the maid could ease the wife's schizophrenic life situation—appearing idle to the external world and not permitted, according to the rules of etiquette, to carry out any servants' work, such as she was, in reality, forced to do.

In those areas into which guests and callers could not peer, the housewives had to institute significant savings in order to free the means for keeping up external appearances. One very productive area for savings was the expenditures for physical care of the family, above all food, which, at the same time, was considered to be the foremost obligation of the housewife. How she dealt with groceries demonstrates the determining principles of housework in the bourgeois family. On the one hand, the woman must be extremely economical and satisfy the family with the cheapest ingredients; only by doing so could she cover the high costs of keeping up appearances. This demanded exact budgeting of household funds, shopping for the most reasonable items, differentiated food storage, and, above all, very economical cooking. On the other hand, the housewife was supposed to provide lovingly for the wishes of the husband and children. Their wishes also had to be taken into account in shopping and laying in foods, and special wishes were to be fulfilled by cooking. The housekeeping manuals emphasized the duties of the women to take the needs of the men as their highest goal; if they did not satisfy these needs, then an unhappy marriage was the result because "the way to a man's heart is through his stomach."

A festive roast appeared on the middle-class table only on Sundays and holidays, for roasts were "aristocrat's food." On workdays middle-class families had to content themselves with mixed dishes. Soups, which satisfied hunger and were inexpensive and quick to prepare, were the main component of the scanty everyday fare. Cookbook authors and manuals advised to thrifty wives simple fare which depended on the cooking of vegetables and meats in combination. For meat, the cheaper small cuts and internal organs of the animal such as feet, tongue, jowl, lungs, liver, heart, kidney, brain, and tripe were used. According to a popular author, even "in better houses the entrails were not scorned." As a consequence, cookbooks, which were aimed at a bourgeois class constrained by extreme thrift, abounded with recipes for dishes from cheaper cuts of meat.

Also crucial for cheap cooking was the reuse of all leftover ingredients and dishes. The leftover roast from Sunday was warmed up on Tuesday or Wednesday; leftover vegetables together with their liquids produced the next day's soup; sausage and pancake leftovers provided additions to the soup; dried bread became a new main dish as bread casserole. Tasty soups were cooked from the ribs of rabbits and poultry; the accumulated cores and stalks of vegetables appeared on the table again as mock salsify *(Schwarzwurzel)*. Goose gizzards, if they had been marinated long enough, boiled, and finally roasted, made a good side dish at supper; the peelings of lemons and oranges were finely chopped, extracted with vinegar, and finally were made into lemonade by adding sugar water.

Even the garbage from groceries, which was no longer fit to eat, found other applications in housekeeping. Sodium silicate served every purpose from preserving eggs to cleaning dirty tiles; damp used tea leaves cleaned the carpet, sauerkraut juice was a marvelous cleaner for brass items, and fresh coffee grounds cleaned cloudy glasses. The cooked-out pork skins and bones were kept cool in the waiting soap crock until the crock was full of leftover fat, back rinds, sausage skins, etc. Then the contents were sold to a soapmaker or, even up to the turn of the century, women made the soap themselves.

Nothing could be wasted, nothing thrown away. Empty cocoa boxes became the holders for cleanser, candle stubs, and matches. Small cardboard boxes later held herbs or powder. Old paper could be used to line cupboards, to clean knives and forks, and, above all, to polish lamps and stove tops.

> Of the many kinds of household leftovers, tins from bouillon make the best spice holders; one simply removes the labels, bronzes them, sews a broad colored ribbon—little ribbon scraps are appropriate here—around the neck of the tin, and writes the contents of the tin on this with ineradicable ink . . .

The most complete possible use of all leftovers demanded of the women ingenuity and experience, but, above all, it required extensive work.

The financial basis of the domestic work of the wife was the housekeeping money provided by the husband, and she was accountable to him for its use. All expenditures had to be proven; not even a penny could be missing from her bookkeeping. The housekeeping money was usually the only source of money under the control of the wife; the main part of the income and, if the occasion should arise, of the fortune, even her dowry, was controlled by the husband. The bookkeeping required of her assured the husband's control and characterized the internal familial power relationships making clear the complete financial dependence of the wife.

The husband was not required to give the wife access to information about his income or his wealth, a fact bitterly deplored by wives in many of their contributions to family magazines. Often the man could not accurately gauge the cost of the household and apportioned too little housekeeping money. Since contractual agreements on the amount of the housekeeping money were unthinkable, the housewife remained dependent on his estimate and often had to beg for every additional penny.

A widely recognized possibility for extending the limited housekeeping money was the cottage labor of the women even in the middle class. Only in this way, in many cases, could they come up with the everyday costs and the extra money for keeping up appearances. Bourgeois women prepared artistic embroidery, crocheted lace and insets, or sewed ready-made clothes at home. Numerous women sought purchasers for their textile handwork and handmade arts and crafts in the women's sections of the newspapers. The money they earned flowed into the household coffers to defray running costs or special expenditures. The homework of bourgeois women had to remain meticulously hidden from the public and frequently also from their husbands. If every form of housework was unacceptable for their class, then any form of paid work was also unacceptable. "Secretly, very secretly, so that no one will notice they [officials' wives] pick up handwork from the shops; secretly, very secretly, they carry it back again—No one should know or be allowed to find out."

The sharp separation of public and private spheres basically shaped the bourgeois lifestyle. The bourgeois housewife, nevertheless, accomplished the physical and psychological reproduction of the family members and supported additionally the professional career of her husband in two ways. On the one hand, she engineered the economy of everyday family life, which helped to cover the high costs of keeping up appearances, and, on the other hand, she made parts of the decor herself. These behaviors of the housewife followed an imminent rationality, which was determined through the constraints of middle-class life. Without the housework of the bourgeois wife providing the daily proofs of social acceptability and the consequent rise of her husband, the material betterment of the family would not have been possible.

Keeping up bourgeois appearances forced the invisibility of housework. Making this work invisible became in itself work, which had to be accomplished in addition to the normal domestic activities. This veiling of housework became its structuring element, and, along with the requirement of thrift and the needs of the family members, determined the work day of the housewives. What appears at first glance to be idleness is revealed, on closer examination, to be difficult and tiresome work.

SUGGESTIONS FOR FURTHER READING

Branca, Patricia. "Image and Reality: The Myth of the Idle Victorian Woman." In Mary Hartman and Lois Banner, eds. *Clio's Consciousness Raised: New Perspectives on the History of Women.* New York, 1974, pp. 179–191.

———. *Silent Sisterhood: Middle Class Women in the Victorian Home.* Pittsburgh, 1975.

Davidoff, Leonore. *The Best Circles: Women and Society in Victorian England.* Totowa, NJ, 1973.

Fallada, Hans (pseudonym for Rudolf Ditzen). *Little Man, What Now?* Tr. by Eric Sutton. New York, 1933.

Hellerstein, Erna Olafson. "French Women and the Orderly Household, 1830–1870." *Proceedings of the Western Society for French History* III (1976): 378–389.

Oakley, Ann. *The Sociology of Housework*. New York, 1974.

———. *Women's Work: The Housewife, Past and Present*. New York, 1976.

Smith, Bonnie G. *Ladies of the Leisure Class: The Bourgeoises of Northern France in the Nineteenth Century*. Princeton, 1981.

Strasser, Susan. *Never Done: A History of American Housework*. New York, 1982.

8

In the Shadows of the Periphery: Italian Women in the Nineteenth Century

Donna Gabaccia

Studies of women and work have tended to focus on urban occupations in factory, mill, school, and store. Except in Great Britain, however, most women (and men) resided in rural communities well into the twentieth century. Often bypassed by historians, though never by history, these peasants and villagers also experienced the effects of political and economic transformation. In this unusual study of southern Italian "women of the shadows," Donna Gabaccia describes a class for whom being unemployed signified not the fulfillment of a Rousseauean fantasy of ideal domesticity, or the achievement of a "conspicuous leisure" essential to urban middle-class status. For these women, lack of gainful employment meant debt and deprivation. The transition from a traditional subsistence economy to a market, or cash, economy, brought them not new opportunities and enhanced self-esteem but reduced status and increased dependency.

Generalizations about the effects of industrialization or "modernization" on women must be put to the test of evidence. By examining the effects of capitalist agricultural and industrial development on peasant women in Italy, this work shows a female experience significantly different from contemporary western Europe. Using census materials on female occupations and wage rates, records of landholdings, and accounts of changing agricultural techniques, Gabaccia first analyzes the sexual division and distribution of labor in several regions of Italy. She then demonstrates how political decisions affected economic developments that in turn remodeled women's work patterns. Italian unification, by facilitating the creation of a national and international market, ultimately forced women into "domesticity." Like Sibylle Meyer, Gabaccia provides a graphic illustration of the inadequacy of the concept of separate public and private spheres. Clearly, the daily lives and family relationships of these Italian women depended on distant decisions by political leaders. This analysis, too, has relevance for women in developing nations today.

Women in southern Italian life have been portrayed recently as "women of the shadows." That Italy's women should seem shadowy is not surprising. The women of the shadows are invisible not only as women, but as poor, often illiterate rural dwellers, as agricultural workers and peasants, and as residents of a region that became at most a minor power among Western nations. Thus, while historians have outlined women's new roles in the nineteenth century—as factory operative, as middle-class lady or her servant, as feminist—peasant women remain obscure. The very opposite of new, they seem left over from the Middle Ages, occupants of a traditional world untouched by the major events and transformations of the century.

In fact, as this essay will demonstrate, the women of the shadows (like other people without history) become visible precisely when we recognize that they too experienced political centralization, urbanization, and the rise of the factory system. As cities grew, the countryside fed and populated them, and as urban factories produced new and cheap products, the countryside often became an important marketplace for them. Change in the countryside might mean a new crop grown, an old trade abandoned, the search for a cash income, migration, or the loss of kin and neighbors to "better opportunities" elsewhere. Our task, then, is to outline the rural and, more importantly, the gender-specific consequences of the economic, cultural, and political transformation sometimes called "development" or "modernization." This is a worthwhile task. As late as 1890, most of Europe's population lived in the agricultural countryside, especially in Ireland, eastern Europe, the Balkans, and along the Mediterranean, but also in the hinterlands of England, Germany, and France. The average European woman of the nineteenth century was still a rural woman.

Firmly located in Europe's agricultural periphery, Italy has been viewed by scholars as a kind of "school for awakening countries" in today's Third World. To northern European visitors in the nineteenth century, the land seemed astonishingly backward: "almost oriental" was a favored (and telling) comparison. "Backward" is a value-laden expression of a simple reality: the Italian peninsula before 1890 little resembled the European nations which at the time proudly proclaimed themselves models for and pinnacles of human evolution. Although Italians formed a nation-state in the years after 1860, they did not yet share a strong national identity. Even more strikingly, Italy's economy showed few signs of following the example of industrializing northern neighbors. After the commercial and industrial successes of the Renaissance, central Italian industries actually declined through the seventeenth and eighteenth centuries. Modern industrialization began in earnest only around 1900, and only in a few central and northern areas. Until the 1950s, more than half of the Italian labor force worked in agriculture. The very importance of agriculture in Italy was sometimes taken as symbolic of the country's "backwardness." But however different from north European agricultural practice, Italy's agriculture and its countryside were not static and unchanging. Neither were the women of the shadows.

We know from studies of Britain, France, Germany, and the United States that new roles for women—"the lady" and "the mill girl"—accompanied industrialization. Recently, good studies of African, Latin American, and Asian women have told us more about the meaning of political and economic change in peripheral and agricultural regions of the world. In both cases, scholars discovered new forces that relegated women to domesticity. Clearly the policies of the nation-state or the dictates of colonial development agencies play an important role in domesticating women, often by excluding them from a male-dominated public world. (In nineteenth-century Europe, while increasing numbers of men obtained suffrage, women did not; in Africa, modernizing land tenure often meant limiting land ownership to male heads of nuclear families.) At the same time, the transition from a semi-subsistence (or household) economy to a cash (or wage) economy redefined the meaning of work.

Changing patterns in Italian women's work hint at the complexity of domesticity in an agricultural land. In the twentieth century scholars would be puzzled that so few very poor Italian women worked outside their homes. Cultural traits—a Muslim heritage in southern provinces or a more general male obsession with controlling female sexuality—often provided an explanation for the fact that Italian women, when compared to the French or British, rarely worked for wages. Italian culture, it seemed, demanded domesticity of its women. Some scholars even suggested that Italian men's insistence on female domesticity posed an insurmountable obstacle to agricultural or industrial development.

Actually, of course, the women listed in Italian censuses as "without profession and at home" were relative newcomers to Italy, as were housewives in other countries. Only where much productive work had left the household could the housewife exist. That transformation was incomplete in rural Italy in the nineteenth century. At the time of the first comprehensive Italian census in 1871, clerks found relatively few women "without profession"; they counted 50 percent of Italian women as active workers. The large number of working Italian women in 1871 reflected the continued importance for both Italian men and women of small-scale production for family consumption. Wage-earning in Italy (unlike Britain) was not yet central to defining male or female peasants as workers. Both Italian men and women, in a sense, worked in a domestic world.

What distinguished Italy from industrializing nations was that her women became more domestic in subsequent years. While rates of female labor participation in France increased (as women found wage-earning work as textile operatives or domestic servants), rates in Italy declined to less than 30 percent in 1901. This decline was partly an illusion, the result of redefining work as wage-earning; it tells us that Italian men largely claimed wage-earning for themselves. But it is also partially attributable to real changes in women's behavior. Women were less likely to be doing productive work with or without wages in 1901 than in 1871.

A major theme in Italian economic history is the slow decline of Italy's subsistence economy, and the equally slow but persistent growth of capitalist agriculture and industry. In fact, this is the trend of economic development in all western European nations in the nineteenth century: the transition from household production to wage-earning, from production for family use to production for the market, and from small-scale peasant and artisan production to large-scale capitalist production. Focusing on the women of the shadows, however, we might emphasize other themes.

The term subsistence production conjures up images of self-contained and pa-triarchal peasant and artisan families, working to provide themselves food, cloth-ing and housing, little affected by money and markets. To a degree, such families did shape reality for most Italian women in the early nineteenth century. It is unwise to exaggerate the self-sufficiency of such peasant and artisan households. And it is necessary to outline several important broad variations in how Italian men and women provided for family subsistence in the early years of the nine-teenth century.

In much of Italy, peasants enjoyed secure tenure to their land, either through ownership or traditional land rights; they worked small plots of land and grew their own food. If they lived close to a town, they might market any surplus there. By contrast, in parts of southern Italy, semi-feudal social relations persisted. Peas-ants enjoyed no secure tenure to the land; they cultivated different plots each year on large estates utilizing a three-field system. On their small plots they produced not only staple crops for their own food and garments (oil, grain, linen, sheep), but also a surplus that the estate manager marketed and used to pay land rents to the feudal lord. In areas like these, peasant family subsistence also rested on common rights to the use of land for gathering food and fuel and for grazing small animals. In addition, all over Italy peasant families combined production of food with production of cloth. Here, too, a distinction can be noted between regions with a cottage textile industry and regions where families produced cloth strictly for their own needs.

The division of labor between Italian men and women varied from region to region in the early years of the nineteenth century. In general, married men con-trolled access to land; few women inherited land or enjoyed rights to its usage. Where land tenure was relatively secure and where small villages were scattered through the countryside, women became an important part of the family work force in the fields, producing food for family consumption. Both men and women marketed small surpluses of eggs, milk, corn, cheese, and so on. Where large estates, herding, and extensive production for the market and concentrated settle-ment were common, women's agricultural labors were more clearly demarcated from men's. Women gathered, grazed small animals, and generally exploited common usage rights, while men raised grain and herded larger animals. Only at harvest time did women join men on the large distant wheat estates of Sicily, for example, and then mainly as gleaners. The fact that fewer women worked in the fields in such regions cannot be seen simply as a consequence of patriarchal con-cerns about women working outside the family group, although certainly that played a role. Employers' choices, as well as the very long distances (up to ten or fifteen miles) separating wheat fields from the large compact ''agrotowns'' of the Italian South, must also be considered.

Almost everywhere in Italy it was women's work at spindle and loom that clothed the family. Girls and mothers worked to produce the cloth and clothing that would become the dowry of daughters at the time of their marriages. (Sons inherited house and/or land.) Where cloth was produced mainly for family needs, men did little. But where cottage industry linked rural workers to city merchants, men might turn their hands in winter to spinning or (more frequently) weaving. In general, where women did little field work, men did little textile work. Local records in such areas might call men "peasants" but women "industrial workers."

The division of labor between men and women in all rural regions changed and became more differentiated in the course of the nineteenth century. The formation of the Italian nation-state can be cited as one important spur to changes in the rural world inhabited by the women of the shadows. Of course, Italy had no formulated plan for development as did colonial agencies or newly independent nations in the twentieth century. Still, the creation of a centralized state stimulated new markets, capitalist agriculture, and greater regional specialization. All in turn encouraged a new division of labor by sex. For women, the economic consequences of unification proved mixed. The legal ending of semi-feudal practices (in the southern provinces) and new inheritance laws after unification allowed small but growing numbers of women access to land. By 1881 more than a third of Italian landowners were female. At the same time, however, the end of feudalism rendered illegal women's gathering and grazing in precisely those areas where women did little field work.

The formation of the Italian nation-state allowed the growth of a unified national market for agricultural and industrial commodities. Through its changing tariff policy (free trade before the 1880s; protection for grain and industrial products thereafter), the state also regulated commercial ties between Italy and other nations. No other events more greatly affected rural Italian women than the import of cheap manufactured cloth and the growth of capitalist agriculture, producing new crops in new ways for markets far from the local piazza.

Historians have shown how the development of the textile industry in France and Britain meant wage-earning options for women. For women in the countryside, however, factory-produced cloth meant unemployment. Although there is much we do not yet know about the decline of Italian rural industries, it seems likely that some Italian women experienced unemployment earlier than others. By the 1880s, 80 percent of Italy's tiny population of female textile operatives lived in only three provinces (Piedmont, Lombardy, and Venice); their numbers and concentration grew substantially by the early twentieth century. In much of northern and central Italy in 1881, women had begun to abandon loom and spindle to purchase cloth. Furthermore, northern Italy's mill girls made up only one-tenth of the women who told census takers in 1881 that they worked as spinners or weavers. Large numbers of southern Italian women still produced cloth for their families, for local sale and for struggling cottage industries. But their numbers, too, were declining. And twenty years later, most women in Italy's South even purchased sheeting for their trousseaux.

The exact timing of Italy's declining rural industries is not yet entirely clear. It seems likely, however, that as cottage industry declined, so too did weaving at home for family use. Folklorists, like Giuseppe Pitré, a Sicilian, commented on the changing occupation of young girls, who no longer sat hours at spindle or loom producing cloth for their own trousseaux. The desire to purchase manufactured cloth probably itself became an incentive for some family members to switch their labors from subsistence agriculture to seek a cash income as either agricultural or industrial laborers. Since Italy's economy offered few rapidly expanding industrial opportunities for either men or women during these years, cash earned in agriculture became increasing important to many families.

Although individual women may have welcomed liberation from arduous work at the loom, the purchase of cloth also posed a problem. Where would the cash come from? We may never understand precisely how men and women struggled or cooperated to answer this question. But it is possible to describe the context in which differing answers emerged. The development of capitalist agriculture, the growth or decline of local male industries, and regional customs in defining men's and women's tasks all formed parts of that context.

Table 1 describes some representative Italian regions in 1881, and summarizes the work that women did in each (see map, Figure 2). It contrasts two areas where peasant agriculture remained important to three areas where large-scale capitalist agriculture developed fairly early. "Capitalist agriculture" assumed many forms in nineteenth-century Italy. Essential to all forms was the rural entrepreneur who contracted with individuals or families to produce crops which he sold at a profit. The three types of capitalist agriculture summarized in Table 1 represent a rough continuum from less to more capitalist. In the *mezzadria* ("classic sharecropping") system, the Tuscan entrepreneur owned land, houses, vines, trees, and animals; he contracted long-term with peasant families for labor. Peasants still owned some of their own tools, and they divided crops with the landlord, rather than receiving a money payment. The *latifondo* of western Sicily (and Apulia and much of Calabria) evolved from the semi-feudal estates described above. Here, the rural entrepreneur rented a large estate and found short-term sharecroppers (paid in grain) and day laborers (earning a cash wage). In the Po Valley, entrepreneurs owned large tracts of land and paid money wages and provided temporary housing for families of laborers.

Several patterns characterized Italian women's work by 1881. Where women had long worked in the fields (Turin, Abruzzi-Molise, Tuscany, and the Po Valley), they increasingly turned their attentions there as they abandoned their looms. This pattern became most obvious in areas with little capitalist agriculture, like Turin's hinterland. In both Turin and Abruzzi-Molise, women typically concentrated in subsistence production, raising food, while men took whatever wage-earning became available. Men's cash earnings bought property and cloth; women fed the family. In some areas like this, women constituted as much as 70 percent of the agricultural work force in 1881. Usually women also outnumbered men as Table 1 reveals. Men's quest for wages encouraged them to migrate elsewhere while wives, mothers, sisters, and dependent children of both sexes supported themselves on the land. Women in such regions had not in fact moved "beyond subsistence"—even though their work had changed. By 1901 many of the women agriculturalists in regions like these would be listed as housewives, for they worked without wages.

Capitalist agriculture meant different choices for Italian men and women. Women who abandoned their looms sometimes had a harder time finding work in the fields once rural entrepreneurs organized the conditions of employment. Previous habits

Figure 2. Italy in 1881 (Showing Regions Represented in Table 1)

also worked their influence: women in 1881 were far more likely to work among the Tuscan *mezzadri* than in *latifondo* Sicily. Still, the trend in all areas was similar and clear: growing numbers of men earned wages, providing the cash income that cloth (and other purchases) required, while large numbers of women already in 1881 found themselves listed in the census not as spinners, weavers, or peasants, but as housewives.

Sicily provides an extreme example of this second pattern of adaptation. By 1871, most men working in Sicilian agriculture already worked part-time as wage-earners on the large wheat estates. Their labors purchased food and (where necessary) paid rents or taxes, while women's spinning and weaving still clothed most Sicilian families. As cloth production at home declined, Sicilian women sought new work in the fields. (Within a ten-year period, Sicily's women ''indus-

TABLE 1.   Economic Development and Women's Work Patterns, 1881

| | Peasant Agriculture | | Semi-Capitalist Agriculture | | |
	Turin Hinterland	Abruzzi-Molise	Mezzadria Tuscany	Latifondo W. Sicily	Po Valley
Percentage of male peasants owning land	50%	59%	20%	18%	15%
Women as percentage of all agricultural workers	50%	40%	32%	16%	34%
Sex ratio	109	114	84	100	96
Women's work: Percentage of women aged nine and over working in					
Agriculture	50%	40%	32%	10%	19%
Textile/clothing production	6%	20%	8%	29%	10%
Housework	22%	23%	44%	44%	39%

Source: Direzione Generale della Statistica, *Censimento della Popolazione del Regno d'Italia al 31 Dicembre 1881* (Rome, 1884).

trial workers'' disappeared from local records to be replaced first by female ''peasants'' and then, rather swiftly, by ''housewives.'') Surprisingly, at first Sicilian women actually found work in the fields. In *latifondist* Corleone, for example, women made up almost 40 percent of the agricultural work force in 1881. Thus, not all Sicilian men adamantly forbade wives or daughters to work in the fields or to earn wages. Real agricultural changes, concurrent with the collapse of home textile production, may have helped undermine any male reluctance with hopes of new prosperity, for in the years following Italian unification new crops—especially grapes and oranges, but also nuts, fruits, and olives—began to replace wheat cultivation in western Sicily. These intensively cultivated crops grew conveniently close to town; furthermore, grape and olive harvests overlapped with the wheat ploughing that occupied Sicilian men. Thus, many Sicilian women in the late 1870s and early 1880s earned wages as grape, orange, and olive harvesters, providing the additional cash revenue that cloth purchase required.

During the 1880s, however, all of Sicily's major export crops suffered severe reverses on world markets, and the Sicilian adaptation collapsed in failure. Neither Sicilian men nor Sicilian women could return to subsistence agriculture as could landowning peasants in Turin's hinterland. Not surprisingly, men monopolized wage-earning opportunities in the ensuing crisis; former female agriculturalists as well as women newly liberated from the loom found themselves ''domesticated.'' The unemployed woman became a ''housewife.''

In claiming wage-earning for themselves, Sicilian men continued to provide food and rents; and in families where sons outnumbered daughters, men's cash earnings might also be diverted to cloth purchase. But in many families the wages of men would not stretch so far; the problem of cloth purchase in particular remained unresolved. Male migration was not a clear answer to this problem as it was elsewhere. Excluded both from the land and from wage-earning, Sicilian women could not easily support themselves and dependent children while men risked migration and the search for cash. A major challenge for Sicilians was the search for *female* employment. For this reason, Sicilian women were far more likely than other women to migrate. A number of studies of Sicilian women living in the United States point to the very large numbers of such women, even when married, who earned wages in one fashion or another.

Italy's sizeable population of housewives by 1900 included three groups of women: those who produced food without wages for their families, those whose labors in capitalist agriculture were subsumed under a family wage paid to husbands and fathers, and those who might best be considered unemployed textile workers or agricultural laborers. Although housewives, few became ladies. Most Italian men and women confronted domesticity in terms quite different from their counterparts in the middle- and working-classes of France, Britain, and Germany.

In many regions of Italy, housework continued the subsistence production practiced by peasant agriculturalists in previous centuries. While peasant men during the nineteenth century claimed wage-earning for themselves, wage-earning in no way carried with it social status, as did land ownership or secure tenure to land. Thus, the usual hope of male wage-earners was to return when possible to peasant agriculture, in part because of status considerations, in part because they could still achieve on the land a more comfortable standard of living than their wages alone provided. Obviously, the labors of wives and children on the land allowed many peasant men to pursue this hope. Furthermore, throughout much of the twentieth century the political and organizational efforts of Italian wage earners aimed at land reform. Eventually, land distribution enabled many formerly landless men to become peasant agriculturalists, involved simultaneously in production for family consumption and for the market. This means that in large parts of Italy the patriarchal authority of the father over a household economy persisted relatively unchanged. Indeed, capitalist agriculture incorporated patriarchal family traditions, for rural entrepreneurs adopted from peasant agriculture the employment of family work groups.

In other areas of Italy, however, like Sicily, housework evolved instead from women's unemployment. Domesticity and the relations between the sexes had a unique meaning in these regions. Sicilian proverbs, for example, praised housewives as efficient organizers of household consumption but also implied that most women were spendthrifts. Daughters were said to "rob the father"; brothers complained about burdensome sisters; proverbs simply wished unmarried girls dead. That domesticity might elicit male hostility is not difficult to understand. Unlike the food-producing women of the Abruzzi, the unemployed Sicilian women represented an immense cost to male wage earners. Rather than furthering men's hopes of mobility, a Sicilian woman represented a debt to be paid at the time of her marriage in the form of a dowry. Once Sicilian girls had produced their own dowries by weaving cloth and by earning with their spindles to provide for other necessities. Marriages united a girl's property (cloth, clothing, jewelry) to the house, furnishings, or bit of land owned by her bridegroom. As fewer girls labored at the loom or found agricultural wages, their fathers' and brothers' wages provided the dowry; in addition, families shifted formerly male-controlled properties, especially houses, to daughters. In doing so, they sought to compensate the bridegroom for acquiring an unemployable dependent. Men, meanwhile, married "with only their pants," but feared taunts that a wife's dowry stripped them of authority as head of the family. However blinded by their own assumptions, men like these could easily see domesticity as an important component of family poverty.

Scholars and feminists have long debated the complex and contradictory legacy of domesticity in industrializing nations. While imposing severe limits on women, domesticity also offered them an autonomous world of female solidarity and an exalted, morally superior sphere of their own. Modern feminism drew upon and reacted against both aspects of domesticity. Italian domesticity provided Italy's women of the shadows with different constraints and opportunities. Where housework continued to include subsistence production in agriculture, domesticity would never appear as an exclusively female realm as it did in England, France, Germany, or the United States—too many fathers and husbands returned to work and to rule in the domestic world. Furthermore, the status of domesticity, when it overlapped with subsistence production, was a superior one shared by the entire family, not a prerogative of women alone, but a class privilege. By contrast, in areas where peasants lived in large agrotowns far from their fields—as was true in Sicily—an urban woman's world (revolving around textile production) had preceded domesticity. Women's employment brought to this separate world none of the sentimentality associated with a lady's domestic "pedestal" in industrial nations. The most likely to be called housewives were the poorest women. Domesticity did not allow for family peace along traditional lines. Instead, it subjected women to increased male hostility even while it ironically placed in their hands more real property than in the past. Daughters bore the brunt of these changes; wives enjoyed the few benefits. Domesticity added new fuels to sexual tensions long burning in this part of the Mediterranean.

Note: I wish to thank Thomas Kozak, Tessie Liu, Jane Schneider, and Louise Tilly, as well as my editors, for their careful readings of an earlier version of this essay. The term "women of the shadows" is from Ann Cornelisen's book of the same name.

SUGGESTIONS FOR FURTHER READING

Caroli, Betty, Robert F. Harney, and Lydio F. Tomasi, eds. *The Italian Immigrant Women in North America.* Toronto, 1978.

Chapman, Charlotte Gower. *Milocca, A Sicilian Village.* Boston, 1971.

Cornelisen, Ann. *Women of the Shadows.* Boston, 1976.

Ets, Maria Hall. *Rosa.* Chicago, 1970.

Gabaccia, Donna. *From Sicily to Elizabeth Street.* Albany, 1984.

Neufeld, Maurice E. *Italy: School for Awakening Countries.* Ithaca, 1961.

Robertson, Priscilla. *An Experience of Women.* Philadelphia, 1981.

Schneider, Jane. "Family Patrimonies and Economic Behavior in Western Sicily." *Anthropological Quarterly* 42 (1969): 109–125.

―――. "Of Vigilance and Virgins: Honor, Shame, and Access to Resources in Mediterranean Societies." *Ethnology* 10 (1971): 1–24.

―――. "Trousseau as Treasure: Some Contradictions of Late Nineteenth-Century Change in Sicily." In Eric B. Ross, ed. *Beyond the Myths of Culture.* New York, 1980.

Yans-McLaughlin, Virginia. *Family and Community.* Ithaca, 1977.

9

Feminism, Antifeminism, and National Family Politics in Early Third Republic France

Karen Offen

The conflict between the developing ideology of domesticity and the increasing demand for female labor force participation continued throughout the period covered in Part II. By the end of the nineteenth century two discernible results were apparent: the movement for women's rights that today we term "feminism" and the reaction to it that we label "antifeminism." In the following study, Karen Offen shows how the development of both forces was shaped by the specific political context of *fin-de-siècle* France. She draws on the work of intellectual historians (who trace the history of ideas), including the study of *mentalités* (which seeks to situate ideas in their social context), on the political discourse and institutional structure of the period, and the demographic and economic factors that affected contemporary responses. Offen creates a new synthesis that shows that women's history extends beyond social history, to impact the most critical questions of the day. Thus it becomes a part of the total history of the period. Demonstrating a synthetic approach in her own work, she throws out a challenge to other historians, particularly to those who continue to limit their analysis to the supposedly "separate sphere" of political men in the public arena. They ignore the woman question, Offen contends, "at their peril." The message is instructive in reverse as well: the history of women cannot be divorced from the pressures of politics and forces of social and economic change.

To illustrate this truth, Offen draws on the history of French feminism. Inspired by the same French philosophical tradition that motivated the British and American feminist movements, leaders of the French women's movement were particularly sensitive to the dangers of political radicalism. Though largely republican, they divided on questions of religion and class. And whether Catholic or Protestant or Jew, bourgeois or working-class, they shared the peculiarly French loyalty to family, which embraces financial as well as personal affairs. Therefore arguments for women's rights as autonomous individuals attracted few; responsibility to family and/or society weighed more heavily than self-fulfillment. By the century's end, French feminists' response to national concern about "depopulation" and military potential strengthened their

resolve to confine their aspirations for women to "equality in difference."
Respect for a family ideal not unlike the vision of Rousseau gave a special
flavor to French feminism. It also foreshadowed the shape that welfare states
would take as government increasingly substituted for the family in the twentieth century.

The terms *féminisme* and *féministe* were of French invention. They came into use
in France during the last quarter of the nineteenth century, but only gained currency during the 1890s. By 1900 the words were in common usage in English,
German, and other Western languages. But at that time they meant something
different from what most people think they mean today.

French feminist demands, like those expressed in other Western nations during
the nineteenth century, were rooted in the language of Enlightenment political and
social criticism. The debate on the woman question had been going on in France
for many centuries, but during the eighteenth century its participants focused on
problems of women's inferior status in marriage and family law, and on their lack
of access to formal education. Indeed, one cannot overestimate the importance
throughout Europe of French Enlightenment debate on women, the family, and
education, exemplified by Rousseau's controversial antifeminist arguments for democracy among men coupled with the subordination of women. During the nineteenth century the debate grew even more intense, due in no small part to the way
women could themselves appeal to the ideological principles of the French Revolution—liberty, equality, fraternity—and to the concept of "rights" that French
republicans claimed to represent.

What was new to nineteenth-century debate on the woman question in France
was controversy over women's economic activity. At stake was a seemingly in-
soluble conflict between the emergence of paid employment for women *outside*
the household and a vision of the family, shared by French Catholics and anticlerical republicans alike, that precluded it. Echoing the counsel of the historian
Jules Michelet, some otherwise staunch republican men reacted adversely to the
concept of woman as "worker" and insisted that a "progressive" social structure
required male authority within the household itself. Others, more progressive,
argued for a thoroughgoing legal restructuring of the family that could emancipate
women and incorporate the notion of women as full-fledged economic beings.

French feminist demands during the later nineteenth century were thus shaped
within what was still a male-dominated political discourse with a fully-developed
range of political identities. Moreover, they were characterized by a distinctive
and quite conscious familial orientation, by an overt concern about maternity and
womanliness, and by an expressed acknowledgement of the national interest and
of women's particular contributions to the nation. This generalization holds particularly true for secular republican feminists, but it also applies, with few exceptions, to a broad spectrum of pro-woman advocates whose affiliations ranged from
social Catholicism on the right, to revolutionary socialists and syndicalists on the
left. Only the anarchists tended to be rigorously individualistic, but even most
French anarchists accepted the social implications of sexual difference and the

requirements of reproduction as sufficient rationale for role structuring, even when they attacked the existing property-based institution of marriage.

Fin-de-siècle French feminism can best be understood by Anglo-Americans as a non- or even anti-individualistic form of feminism, which I have elsewhere labeled "relational" feminism. It was based on a theoretical understanding of the relations between the sexes that insisted on their complementarity and interdependence and on a familial base. It posited distinct "manly" and "womanly" sexual natures, and argued for an equitable sexual division of labor in society and in the family. In its secular republican guise, advocates of "relational feminism" argued for a commitment by both sexes to sociopolitical solidarity in the interest of French national welfare. In contrast to today's feminism, French relational feminism was predicated on a combination of biological and cultural differences between the sexes. French feminists, female and male—Catholic, secular republican, and socialist alike—accepted the premises of this gendered system, but rejected the conclusions that had heretofore been drawn from them by such notorious patriarchs as Napoleon I, whose Civil Code had firmly consolidated French marriage and family law around male authority. Since the 1830s French feminists had called for a radical restructuring of these authoritarian laws governing marriage, for the reestablishment of civil divorce, and the revision of many other legal provisions that disadvantaged women. They also argued that women, precisely because they were different from men, must be enabled to make an equitable, yet distinctive contribution to the socioeconomic life of the nation.

During the early Third Republic (1871–1914), French feminist—and antifeminist—discourse was still tightly embedded in the prevailing national socioeconomic and political debates of the period. Not only was France immersed in the dramatic transformation that we now call urbanization and industrialization, but it was simultaneously experiencing a political transition from a highly centralized, authoritarian, and Catholic monarchy, based on an aristocracy of birth, to a more democratic, somewhat fragile, but still highly centralized anticlerical republic, based (as women's rights activist Maria Deraismes put it) on an aristocracy of sex. This double metamorphosis posed a fundamental challenge to the old hierarchical agrarian Catholic French family system and to long-established definitions of what it meant to be a man or a woman in that culture. Although other European nations were experiencing similar problems—and, indeed, Great Britain was providing all continental observers with the most conspicuous examples of urban and industrial problems to avoid—the French case reveals perhaps more than any other that much of the debate over what France had been and was to become was predicated on a politics of gender. Thus France offers an excellent case study of the way in which the social relationship of the sexes itself became a political issue. Moreover, the French case is one of international importance. The impact of French discussion on the woman question was not restricted to Francophone territory; many educated Europeans outside France, from Russia to Spain, and indigenous elites from the Middle East to North Africa and Latin America, attentively followed French public discussion on the woman question and adapted French arguments and solutions to fit their own needs.

French political history during the nineteenth century was marked by continual battles for control of the government. No regime founded in the wake of the French Revolution seemed able to survive more than 20 years. With the establishment of the Third Republic in the 1870s, the battles did not stop. The republicans, who wished to secularize French society, were ever on guard against the monarchists on their right who threatened to overthrow the republic and to reestablish the prerogatives of the king and the Catholic church. On the left, the republicans were under attack by anticapitalist socialists, who insisted that the republican revolution must deliver economic as well as civil and political equality (among men) before its work would be complete. The battle between the secularizing republicans and the monarchist Catholics was only laid to rest in 1904, when the republican regime effected the final separation of church and state by abolishing the government's century-old treaty with Rome. The confrontation with collectivist socialism continued well into the twentieth century.

The conflict between monarchy and republic immediately provoked questioning of male/female relationships and family structure, with the result that women's subordination to men within or outside the family became a very sensitive issue. Throughout the political struggles of the century, the men of both factions fought for a remarkable prize—control of the minds and hearts of women. In keeping with certain civic humanist notions about the importance of education for the training of citizens, a Rousseauean concern with the regeneration of national morality, and a firm conviction that the family (not the individual) was necessarily the cornerstone of the state, one of the first republican actions was to establish a full-blown state-run educational system. Central to their goals was control of the education of girls, not only at the primary level but also at the secondary level. The republicans believed firmly that the sexes should be separately educated, particularly after the age of ten, and that girls should not be taught by men but by well-educated women, themselves trained in republican teacher-training programs. By breaking the Catholic church monopoly on women's education, the republicans hoped to inculcate in future mother-educators, and in their children by extension, a thoroughly secular morality and a loyalty to the republic. By reestablishing civil divorce in 1884 (a longtime feminist demand), they also intended to demonstrate the state's full authority over the institution of civil marriage. These were reforms that enhanced the position of women in French society; they also served the cause of the secular republic.

As the republicans consolidated their hold on power, controversy over the further emancipation of women grew within French republican circles. In the 1890s this controversy became inextricably intertwined with two other factors, both of which could directly affect the political fate of any demands made on the republican government by the women's movement. These two factors were, first, the diminishing importance of the French nation as a world power, due in part (it was believed) to the declining birthrate, and, second, the combined threat of the growing antirepublican, monarchist-identified nationalist movement on the right, and the revolutionary socialist movement on the left. Partisans of the Third Republic correctly viewed both issues as potential threats not only to the continuation of the republican regime, but to the future of the French nation.

The population issue was closely connected to France's sense of its own diminishing international position. France was not the only European nation to experience a falling birthrate in the late nineteenth century, but it was the first to undergo such a decline, the beginning of which can be dated from the last quarter of the eighteenth century. In 1871, France's defeat at the hands of Germany underscored the relationship between population and national might, to France's great disadvantage. It was in the wake of defeat that socially conscious French physicians such as André-Théodore Brochard began to blame France's population problems on the women's maternal indifference, which resulted in high infant mortality, and his Parisian colleague Charles Richet began to blame them on "voluntary sterility." In the 1890s the birthrate figures became even more unfavorable. To demographers this was clear evidence of purposefully controlled fertility. Comparative studies subsequently revealed that, indeed, France had the highest percentage of persons married in western Europe, but these couples did not seem to be reproducing at a rate satisfactory to the republican nation-builders. Worse news came from the 1895 census, which revealed that there had been about 18,000 more deaths than births in France that year.

At this point, the second issue emerged. The leadership of the Third Republic came under attack from antirepublican nationalists. These enemies of the republican regime opposed the republic's parliamentary form of government; their ideal was based in an older, unreconstructed authoritarian notion of government that they equated with true French virility. They upheld old aristocratic institutions of the army and the magistracy against all criticism in the controversial Dreyfus case, and argued for the reinforcement of manly prerogatives throughout French society. Central to their vision was the formal subordination of women to men. The prolific nationalist writer Théodore Joran made the point clearly. He castigated feminism because "it allows women to envisage happiness as independent of love and external to love." "Good households," he wrote, "are those where the man considers the woman as an object made for his own personal pleasure and well-being and where the woman believes she ought to please her husband, to serve him, and applies herself exclusively to that end." The nationalist writers insisted, moreover, that feminism itself was "un-French," a "cosmopolitan," "international" import from England and America. It was well known that many members of the republican elite—including leaders of the women's rights movement—were Protestant, Jewish, and active in Freemasonry.

On the left, socialists also criticized the Third Republic. They offered a wide range of solutions to the woman question. The French Workers' Party was on record in favor of women's equality, but other groups took different approaches. These ranged from Aline Valette's advocacy of "sexualisme," based on explicit acknowledgement of women's reproductive function as "production," with the child as "product," to Madeleine Pelletier's insistence on abolishing the family altogether. Meanwhile, in 1892, French socialist deputies to the national legislature, led by Paul Lafargue (Karl Marx's son-in-law), proposed state subsidies for mothers.

In the face of these population concerns, coupled with overt hostility to female emancipation on the authoritarian right and the cluster of controversial ideas on the socialist left, French republican feminists understood that they would have to pursue their own agenda for change in a cautious and politically sensitive manner. Among the feminists' own favored political allies, the male Solidarist republicans, most men insisted—and the women agreed—that the claims of the nation must subordinate all individual claims. The deputies in this group did support a number of reforms that would ameliorate women's position in society by enhancing their assigned roles in the family—through liberalizing divorce laws, giving married women the right to control their own earnings, allowing all adult women to witness civil acts, or even to study in universities and professional schools—but always on the condition that the sexual division of labor in the family be respected. Their touchstone, one that had (and would continue to have) a long history in republican thought on the woman question, was "equality in difference." They were willing to consider women as moral equals but could not accept members of either sex acting as individuals in disregard of their functional context in the nation, which in this case was defined in terms of organic biology and the family. These men would never dream of supporting rights for women independently of— or in conflict with—their assigned maternal roles.

The family ideal envisioned by the Solidarist republicans was composed of two mutually complementary (and ostensibly equivalent) spheres of enterprise, the domestic and the public. The political analogy they liked to invoke was that of minister of foreign affairs and minister of the interior. The domestic sphere became identified with the female, and the public with the male, who even in this restructured version remained legally the head-of-household. This family ideal should not be confused either with the ancien régime patriarchal family insisted on by neo-traditionalist Catholic ideologues, nor with that inscribed by the Civil Code. It is still true, however, that distinctive socially imposed sex roles remained central to the Solidarist approach to sociopolitical organization at the end of the nineteenth century, a view reinforced by their own version of Social Darwinism. Republican Solidarists believed that universal marriage and a sexual division of labor in the family were key features in the social evolution of modern complex societies. Indeed, it was this system, and women's vital role in it, that enlightened republicans hoped to establish throughout France as a norm in order to accomplish the "regeneration" of France. Just as the citizen-conscript would replace the professional soldier as the basis for the new republican "nation in arms," so republican motherhood was to provide the cornerstone of a new secular national morality. "Maternity," as the dramatist Alexandre Dumas *fils* put it, "is women's brand of patriotism."

The arguments of republican feminists were shaped within, and in turn helped to shape, this discourse. They built on it to argue the women's case as one for justice. Their main argument dwelt on the point that the republican principles of liberty and equality should not apply only to men—that the republic must not be a *de facto* aristocracy of sex. This was certainly an appeal to which some republican men were sensitive. It is exemplified by Hubertine Auclert's exposition of the meaning of equality to the delegates at the 1879 Socialist Workers' Congress: "A Republic that keeps women in an inferior situation cannot make men equal. Before you men can earn the right to raise yourselves to the level of your masters, you are obliged to raise your slaves, the women, up to your own level." The appeal for justice still rang true in 1900, when Harlor, a journalist for the all-women's newspaper *La Fronde,* insisted at the International Women's Rights Congress that, "A society that declares *all* human beings born free and equal in rights contradicts its own principle if *all* are not offered the same conditions for development."

In a climate of political discussion sensitive to the population problem and to antirepublican nationalist activity, reformers gave strategic priority to the elimination of social penalties imposed on women by their reproductive role. They argued for generous protective legislation for women workers, for married women's right to control their own earnings, and for the restoration of paternity suits. In short, they reappropriated motherhood in order to argue for its restructuring. They argued for women's rights based squarely on women's claims on the nation as mothers of its citizens. This was not an argument that men in power could overlook.

Women's increasing economic activity outside the household proved to be the most prickly of issues for republican feminists and their allies. In addition to documenting the dropping birthrate, census reports since mid-century revealed that France had led all other Western nations with the highest percentage of women active in the labor force. The percentage of the female population employed in both agricultural and nonagricultural labor rose from 24 percent in 1866 to 38 percent in 1911. Of the several million women in the labor force, the number employed in the nonagricultural sector doubled between 1856 and 1906. Most of the women added to this sector worked in new types of unskilled or semiskilled jobs. The greater proportion of them were young and single, or older and widowed. Still, a sizeable proportion—some 40 percent by 1901—were married women with children.

What most appalled French social critics was that many of these married female workers, the bulk of whom lived in towns and cities, were farming out their newborn infants to other caretakers. Since mid-century this practice had contributed both to the spectacular growth of the wet-nursing industry and to the alarming rates of child abandonment and infant mortality among newborns in urban industrial centers. These tragic developments only increased public opposition to the employment of all women. Both doctors and economists insisted that French society's interests would be best served by enforcing the sexual division of labor and promoting the woman's dedication to her household and children, supported by the male breadwinner. From the 1860s to the 1890s Frenchmen ranging from the liberal Jules Simon to artisans active in the First International Workingmen's Association and Pope Leo XIII all argued that the "solution" to the "problem" of women's labor lay in paying men a "family wage." Men should *become* sole breadwinners. This was an argument that had long been made in England, but it was still relatively new on the Continent.

Feminists as early as the 1830s had objected to such an approach. Working-class women active in the Saint-Simonian movement and in the revolution of 1848 insisted repeatedly that women had a right to work as a guarantee of their independence. In her 1866 study, *The Poor Woman in the Nineteenth Century,* Julie Daubié argued that economic liberalism had deprived women, in the name of equality and liberty, of employments that formerly had been theirs during the old regime. Capitalism and the centralization that accompanied it were the culprits; this new economic system had no respect for what we now call "the rights of gender." In 1868 the socialist Paule Mink, countering the men of the First International, insisted that even though working conditions were often horrible, women required independent work to remain "free and intelligent creature[s]."

By the 1890s French debate on the question of women and work centered on the issue of protective (or restrictive) legislation for women workers. Following an international congress held in Berlin in 1890, most European governments embarked on a program of regulating industrial work. One of the first targets was the employment of women. Even the staunch liberal, Jules Simon, who headed the French delegation to the Berlin Congress, returned to France a convert to government regulation of women's work. After extensive controversy, legislation was finally passed in late 1892 that limited the working hours of women and children in all industrial establishments, and in particular prohibited night work for women. Feminist critics condemned the law in its entirety. Maria Pognon was unequivocal: "The 1892 law was made by antifeminists, who were concerned with reserving all the well-paying work for their constituents; this is the real truth!"

From the 1890s on, republican bourgeois feminists adamantly defended women's right to work against all critics. They denied charges that paid work for women was simply a means for individual aggrandizement, a manifestation of antisocial "egotism." Women went to work not for amusement, one feminist argued, but for survival. Republican feminists called for equitable pay and for married women's right to control their own earnings. But they listened carefully to the findings of doctors such as Adolphe Pinard, who ardently advocated enforced maternity leaves as a means to countering infant mortality among working-class women, and from 1900 on, some called for paid maternity leave and guarantees that working women could return to their jobs without penalty. They sought to ensure that measures designed to "protect infants" or to "preserve the family" were in fact beneficial to women themselves. Even as they demanded, as Nelly Roussel did, women's right to control their own fertility, they pressed for more maternity homes, and for day-care centers and nursery schools where working mothers could leave their children in safety. They advocated improved housing and a variety of social measures that would facilitate family life. At the same time they worked to overturn the law that forbade paternity suits by unwed women and for a law that guaranteed married working women control over their own income. They also continued to press for equal educational opportunity, with an eye to opening more professions to women; to this end, they called for establishment of the *baccalauréat* curriculum in the girls' lycées. They argued that all trades and vocations should be open to women, including the well-paid ones.

Many feminists advocated unionization as one solution for the problems of working women, and a few, such as Marguerite Durand, organized women workers in several trades. By 1911, over 100,000 women workers belonged to *syndicats* (unions). These numbers had tripled since 1900, yet women still represented less than 10 percent of the total union membership. Twenty-five thousand of these women belonged to the 162 all-female unions, many of which had been organized under social Catholic auspices. Male trade unions continued to resist admitting women as members. Some still feared that women's low wages would drag down their own, while others were concerned that if women were paid the same higher wages as men, they would be preferred to men by employers because they were more docile. Between 1890 and 1910 some fifty-six strikes by male workers to keep women out of their shops took place. Although the General Confederation of Labor (CGT) supported the case for economic equality and the full inclusion of women workers in men's unions, as partners in proletarianization, working-class sentiment lagged behind.

The problems that plagued a married working woman in early twentieth-century France were epitomized by the Couriau affair. Emma Couriau, a printer like her husband Louis, applied to join the local printers' union in Lyons. The printers had long been among the most militant opponents of women's employment. Their skilled trade was threatened by a combination of technological and organizational changes that allowed employers to recruit women at lower wages, and women had been brought in as strikebreakers during earlier printers' strikes. Not only did the Lyons local deny Emma Couriau's application, despite the fact she was already earning union wages, but its members expelled her husband because he allowed his wife to work. French feminists rallied behind the Couriaus as they appealed the decision at the national level. The leadership of the CGT ultimately supported Emma Couriau's right to work and to join the union, but many workingmen still grumbled about the employment of women and their inclusion in male unions.

Such incidents as this ultimately convinced French feminists that women's interests could not be advanced, even under a republican form of government, unless they could break men's hold on political power. It was then that French feminists began to organize for woman suffrage. Between 1909 and 1914 the suffrage movement became a force to be reckoned with. Unfortunately, the outbreak of war in 1914 precluded the long-awaited debate on suffrage in the Chamber of Deputies. At war's end France was among the few Western countries that did not enfranchise its women.

The war exacerbated the situation with regard to women's rights. More women than ever before, especially from the lower and middle bourgeoisie, were employed. Heavy war losses (1.4 million dead; over 3 million wounded) intensified French national anxiety over the birthrate. The war encouraged both the demand for women workers and for more babies. At the end of the war, nationalist pro-family and pronatalist associations (both Catholic and secular) joined forces to lobby against birth control and for tax initiatives and other measures to encourage family growth. In 1920 the republican government stiffened the laws against abortion, outlawed the spreading of contraceptive information, and established medals for motherhood. A symbolic gesture, the nationalistic rhetoric surrounding the medals was nevertheless revealing: the birthrate must be raised so that France could "retain the rank in which victory has placed us" and "permit us to harvest all its fruits." "The Republic ought to testify in a striking manner to her gratitude and respect toward those who contributed the most to maintaining, through their descendants, the genius and civilization, the influence and radiance of France." But neither the women workers nor the problems of motherhood went away. Nor did the birthrate go up. French women's demands and nationalist family politics would remain on a collision course well into the twentieth century.

SUGGESTIONS FOR FURTHER READING

Bell, Susan Groag and Karen M. Offen. eds. *Women, the Family, and Freedom: The Debate in Documents* II: 1880–1950. Stanford, 1983.

Boxer, Marilyn J. "Foyer or Factory: Working Class Women in Nineteenth-Century France." *Proceedings of the Western Society for French History* II (1975): 192–203.

———. "Protective Legislation and Home Industry: The Marginalization of Women Workers in Late Nineteenth–Early Twentieth Century France." *Journal of Social History* 20, no. 1 (Fall 1986): 45–65.

Harsin, Jill. *The Policing of Prostitution in Nineteenth-Century Paris.* Princeton, 1985.

Hause, Steven C. and Anne R. Kenney. "The Limits of Suffragist Behavior: Legalism and Militancy in France, 1876–1922." *American Historical Review* 86 (1981): 781–806.

———. *Women's Suffrage and Social Politics in the French Third Republic.* Princeton, 1984.

Hellerstein, Erna O., Leslie Parker Hume, and Karen Offen, eds. *Victorian Women: A Documentary Account of Women's Lives in Nineteenth-Century England, France, and the United States.* Stanford, 1981.

Hilden, Patricia. *Working Women and Socialist Politics in France, 1880–1914: A Regional Study.* Oxford, 1986.

Maruani, Margaret. "France." Alice H. Cook, Val R. Lorwin, and Arlene Kaplan Daniels, eds. *Women and Trade Unions in Eleven Industrialized Countries.* Philadelphia, 1984.

McDougall, Mary Lynn Stewart. "The Meaning of Reform: The Ban on Women's Night Work, 1892–1914." *Proceedings of the Western Society for French History* XII (1984): 404–417.

———. "Protecting Infants: The French Campaign for Maternity Leaves, 1890s–1913." *French Historical Studies* 13 (1983): 79–105.

McLaren, Angus. *Sexuality and Social Order: The Debate over the Fertility of Women and Workers in France, 1770–1920.* New York, 1983.

McMillan, James F. *Housewife or Harlot: The Place of Women in French Society, 1870–1940.* London and New York, 1981.

Mitchell, Barbara. "Revolutionary Syndicalism and the Woman Question." Abstract. *Proceedings of the Western Society for French History* VIII (1981): 436.

Offen, Karen. "Depopulation, Nationalism, and Feminism in Fin-de-Siècle France." *American Historical Review* 89 (1984): 648–676.

———. "Ernest Legouvé and the Doctrine of 'Equality in Difference' for Women: A Case Study of Male Feminism in Nineteenth-Century French Thought." *Journal of Modern History* 58, no. 2 (June 1986): 452–484.

———. "The Second Sex and the Baccalauréat in Republican France, 1880–1924." *French Historical Studies* 13 (1983): 252–286.

———. *The Woman Question in Third Republic France, 1870–1914.* Stanford, forthcoming.

Segalen, Martine. *Love and Power in the Peasant Family: Rural France in the Nineteenth Century.* Chicago, 1983.

Sowerwine, Charles. *Sisters or Citizens: Women and Socialism in France since 1876.* Cambridge, England, 1982.

III

WOMEN IN
THE ERA OF THE
INTERVENTIONIST STATE

Overview, 1890 to the Present

By the late nineteenth century Europe had reached a pinnacle of power and influence over much of the rest of the world. There was no question about European technological and military superiority. Historians might still debate the reasons why the industrial revolution began in England and not elsewhere—perhaps in the once technologically vibrant empires of the Far East (China) or Middle East (Ottoman Empire). But *that* it occurred in England and then spread to the European continent had enormous consequences. The industrial development of Europe meant a power dominance that Europeans were quick to exploit. Throughout the nineteenth century, for example, the threat of British gunboats sailing through the Dardanelles and pointing their modern weapons at the Topkapi (the Sultan's residence) repeatedly won economic and political concessions for the British Empire and its merchants in Ottoman territory. Not a shot was ever fired. In the last third of the nineteenth century, the Europeans gobbled up Africa, much of Asia, and many islands of the Pacific at a dizzying rate. Britain alone acquired 4.7 million square miles of territory between 1870 and 1900; France amassed 3.5 million and the new German Empire one million. By the turn of the century, nearly one-half billion non-Western people were under the control of Western colonial administrations, although not without protracted and often bloody resistance by native populations. For many ordinary Europeans, and certainly in the eyes of the ruling classes, such successes pointed to unmistakable moral superiority. While the Germans might challenge the British claim that "God was an Englishman," nonetheless there was broad consensus that "man was good, but Western man was better." Where did this leave women—the ones living in Europe but also those under colonial rule with whom ultimately their fate is joined? The twentieth century has linked the peoples of the world together, made all parts of it truly interdependent, and inaugurated a new era in world history.

The Europe of imperialism and industrial might had its own elites, not only of birth and status but increasingly of property and wealth. Victors in the struggle for success, they had overseen the unparalleled social and economic changes accompanying the emergence of the new industrial world that we have described in Part II. Furthermore, they had come to share a set of beliefs and commitment to institutional structures that provided a similar framework within which change took place in the various countries of Europe. Historians have called these beliefs "classical liberalism" or "the bourgeois synthesis," implying the existence of a dominant nineteenth-century world view that shaped attitudes toward political life and economic growth as well as family living and gender roles. Above all, the synthesis meant a commitment to laissez-faire economics. Left to its own devices, an unfettered market economy was believed to offer the best mechanism for economic growth and development as well as for the material welfare of the masses. Thus, the proper role of the state was as night watchman, safeguarding property, maintaining the rule of law, and defending the cause of its citizens abroad—essentially noninterventionist, except for the acquisition of colonies. The proper form of the state in western and central Europe included parliamentary institutions, acknowledging the claims of peoples to a more direct role in government. Parliamentary government did not necessarily mean democratic rule; the liberal notion of natural rights had not been transformed into democracy. France was ahead of the other countries in having effective universal male suffrage from 1871 onward. The new German Empire of Bismarck's creation (1871–1918) also instituted universal manhood suffrage but curtailed its impact by depriving Parliament of any real power or influence. In 1884, the England of Gladstone passed a suffrage act extending the electorate to about five million male citizens, but this represented only one-sixth of the total population, and in Italy as late as 1913 only seven percent of men could vote. Further east, institutions of representative government developed even more slowly; the Russian Tsar made concessions to parliamentary rule only in the face of popular unrest during the Revolution of 1905.

Liberal commitments, to the bourgeois synthesis, to parliamentary government, market forces, and private property, were matched by a truly optimistic outlook, a strong belief in progress, and an equally strong but potentially disruptive nationalist spirit. Furthermore, no one among the ruling groups questioned the significance of the patriarchal family for social stability. Its critical social function was facilitated, most agreed, by a proper and necessary sexual division of labor: men were breadwinners outside the home and women were homemakers. Those who adhered to the synthesis included not only the liberals per se, representing the middle classes of Europe—the captains of industry and commerce, many bureaucrats, and other well-educated professionals—but also many conservatives, large and middling landowners, who were rooted in the older world of agriculture and service. Overall, they were the beneficiaries of the processes of industrial advance.

Classical liberalism, however, faced serious challenges, and one central theme of twentieth-century history is the erosion of faith in the premises of this once influential world view. Pressure for broadening the suffrage and democratic rule was launched most dramatically by those left outside political power and influence in liberal Europe—by women and workers. Obtaining the vote became a key feminist goal in the early twentieth century, and suffragists could use liberal arguments of the natural rights and equality of all to their own advantage. This strand of feminism was individualistic, predicated on equality of opportunity irrespective of sex. In the years between 1915 and 1922, after protracted struggle, women in nineteen European countries and North America received the suffrage and won recognition of their right to participate in the public realm. Were women "emancipated" by the vote? How did they use their new potential to influence public affairs?

Feminists not only worked for their sex but forged alliances with workers—another outsider group—for greater social and sexual emancipation. The Russian Revolution of 1917 and Bolshevik political successes provide the most telling example of the rejection of classical liberal premises and institutions. In 1917, Russian Marxists were in a position to make good the century-old commitment of socialism to women's equality. What role did women play in the revolutionary upheavals? Did primarily ideological considerations or more pragmatic requirements of economic development shape Soviet policy toward its female citizens?

There were also more subtle ways in which classical liberal premises were being transformed in the early twentieth century. The appalling abuses of industrial development under laissez-faire principles—urban slums, child labor, long work hours in factories and workshops under unhealthy conditions, and poor sanitation—provided a rationale for growing government intervention into daily life. Based in part on an optimistic belief in the benefits of social manipulation, the nations of Europe took unprecedented steps in expanding the range and nature of public power. They moved beyond protective labor laws to offer health and disability insurance and old-age pensions, to enlarge municipal services and eventually to introduce unemployment compensation. These policies and other new public commitments have inaugurated the era of the welfare state. In the West, from Scandinavia through Western Europe to North America, it has become a commonplace assumption that governments now are committed to the "general welfare" by providing a wide range of social services. And under communist rule as well, with public ownership of the means of production, the state has taken an activist role in overseeing social and economic life.

This expansion of public authority has altered the relationship between women and the state. As educational and employment opportunities widened for women and legal changes improved their status and power, growing numbers began to appropriate for themselves the Western ideal of individual self-determination. However, these changes dramatically increased societal preoccupation with women's roles as childbearers and childrearers. One result was the development of new professional and governmental agencies that substituted public for traditional family constraints. The evolution of government intervention provided a new framework for women's lives in the twentieth century. The shift is so important that we have called Part III of this book "Women in the Era of the Interventionist State." The new reforms constituted not simply a neutral set of welfare policies, but a powerful force for influencing family life, gender, class, and social relationships. To what extent have public services benefited women? Conversely, in what ways has the welfare state limited women's autonomy? Given women's critical role in childbearing, must the Western ideal of individual autonomy be modified to ensure individual rights for women?

When seen from the perspective of women's rights, state intervention took on some menacing aspects. More and more women were having fewer and fewer children, a fact that did not escape notice by worried male politicians who equated population size with national power. The decline in fertility was a result of complex forces related to the pattern of women's gainful employment and the evolution of the modern family. In the pre-World War I era, it led to a population debate and a move by some politicians, organized pressure groups, and even feminists to encourage women to have more children for the sake of the nation—at times even to force the issue by seeking to outlaw abortions and prevent the sale and spread of birth control devices and information. How did European rivalries and imperialism reinforce race consciousness and societal preoccupation with women's sexuality and motherhood? What accounted for an explicit and growing antagonism between the sexes in the prewar period that was exacerbated by the First World War?

World War I was a shattering event that did a great deal to erode belief in Europe's ruling classes and their values. People asked what kind of society would sacrifice millions of its young men during four long years for such questionable gains. They inquired less intently about the effects of war on women. Yet women's lives were altered by both the world wars of the twentieth century. By disrupting the normal lines of power and social activity, war opened up unparalleled opportunities for women in work and family decision making and made their war experiences very different from men's. In contrast, the interwar years brought into question women's gains, especially their right to work. The decades of the 1920s and 1930s saw renewed efforts to remove married women from the work force as "double earners." At the same time, in many parts of Europe, but most successfully in Germany and Italy, fascist movements fed on post-war disillusionment and drew sustenance from their anti-feminist "Kinder, Küche, Kirche" (children, kitchen, church) ideal for women. Even women responded positively to this restrictive vision. Why did fascism appeal to numbers of ordinary European women? How did German National Socialism successfully combine sexism and racism in its program for women? Why did similar conditions yield radically different results in Scandinavia?

From the global perspective, the two world wars were but one great civil war from which Europe never recovered its former position of power and influence. In the post-1945 period, indeed, Europe became divided into two hostile ideological camps. Forced to give up most of its colonial territory, it was dwarfed by the superpowers of Russia and the United States and the rising economic might of

Asia. Did the reconstruction of Europe open up new opportunities for women? Have socialist experiments altered women's consciousness? Why did a women's movement reemerge in both Eastern and Western Europe in the 1960s and 1970s? Has a century of government intervention in individual and family matters fundamentally changed the roles of women in political, economic, and social life?

Women's Growing Participation in the Labor Force

By the late nineteenth century, a second cycle of economic growth was creating a new industrial and social landscape that altered women's position in the labor market. Although the earlier industrial economy had been subjected to periods of booms and busts, the Great Depression of 1873 to 1896 eroded the classical liberal commitment to free trade. Those depression years were times of declining prices and profits, and the response to the insecurities of uncontrolled markets was the antithesis of economic liberalism: an economic nationalism. The various countries of continental Europe passed restrictive tariffs and treaties (first proposed already at the end of the 1870s) that were designed to improve their competitive advantage at the expense of their neighbors. The climate became one of struggle and rivalry, and England, once the unquestioned economic leader, saw its position challenged by the economic successes of the new German Empire and also by those of its former colony across the sea, the United States of America. The following anecdote captures well the shock to the British of the shifting balance of economic forces. Shaking his pencil to reinforce a point he was making against unfair German competition during a debate, a member of Parliament only then noticed the inscription stamped on it, "Made in Germany."

State intervention in economic life through protective tariffs not only expressed growing national tensions, it also had important domestic consequences. By limiting foreign competition in the national market, government tariff policy reinforced a trend away from the family firm to large-scale enterprises. Businesses were growing larger and capital was being raised in new ways by joint-stock companies, which issued shares for purchase by the general public. Cartels and monopolies—agreements among businesses to fix prices, share profits, and control markets—flourished in the protected environment. This was particularly true in heavy industry, which was growing much more rapidly than the older consumer trades such as textiles. New jobs were opening up in metallurgy and engineering, as well as in the electrical and chemical industries; in the main these jobs were taken over by men. With the shift from consumer to heavy industry, there were fewer jobs proportionally for women in the manufacturing sector of the industrial economy.

Nonetheless, one of the most significant socioeconomic trends in the twentieth century has been the steady increase of women working outside the home—aptly dubbed "a subtle revolution." Figure 3 shows the growth in women's gainful employment in select countries between 1890 and 1975. While reflecting the dramatic rise in women's employment in Russia, Sweden, and the United States, and steady increases in Germany and the United Kingdom, it suggests only a modest

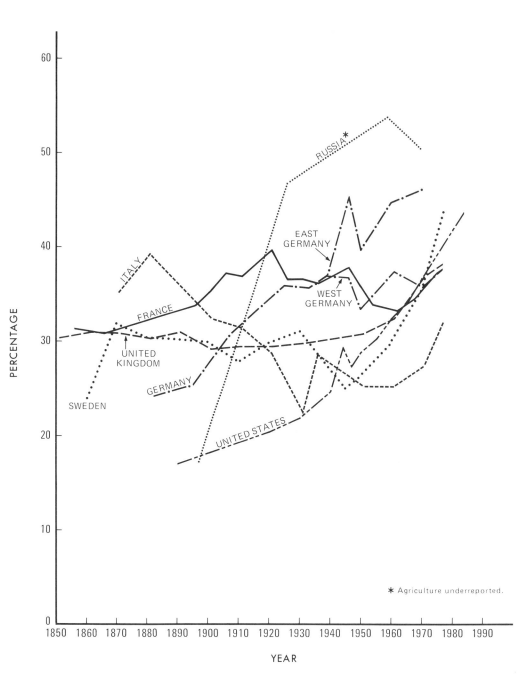

Figure 3. Women's Gainful Employment in Select Countries as a Percentage of Economically Active Population, 1851–1984. Sources: B.R. Mitchell, *European Historical Statistics, 1750–1975* (New York, 1975). OECD, *Labour Force Statistics: Demographic Trends 1950–1990* (Paris, 1979). U.S. Dept. of Commerce, *Historical Statistics of the United States, Colonial Times to 1970,* I (Washington, 1975) and *Historical Abstracts of the United States* (1985). U.S. Dept. of Labor, *Handbook of Labor Statistics* (Washington, 1983).

growth of gainfully employed women in France and (after a noticeable decline) Italy. The curve, however, masks an important shift. Agriculture employed large numbers of women in France, Italy, and Russia much longer than in the more industrialized nations of Germany, England, and the United States. In 1911, for example, 41 percent of French and 56 percent of Italian working women were recorded in agriculture; in Russia, an overwhelming 92 percent were recorded. Thereafter, wage-earning women in the agricultural sector declined steadily and were replaced by equal numbers going into the service, or tertiary, sector of the economy. Foreshadowing a likely trend for other nations, technological advances stimulated an ever-expanding demand for women in clerical and other service jobs, and the United States experienced yet a further increase of about 11 percent between 1975 and mid-1984. Figure 2 also shows clearly the greater utilization of female labor under the socialist regime in postwar East Germany than in capitalist West Germany.

The shift to service jobs has been the most important and long-term change in women's employment patterns. As industrial enterprises grew larger, they needed more typists, stenographers, and file clerks. As more and more goods were produced, manufacturers required enlarged systems of distribution. Increasing numbers of retail shops opened up in urban centers and they utilized young women for sales. As government expanded its services, it too employed new personnel as clerks, telephone operators, and low-level administrators. With industrial expansion, clerical work became routinized, requiring little skill beyond literacy, and the positions that opened up provided little chance for advancement. However, these jobs were coveted by daughters of the middle classes and of aspiring workers, for they were ''cleaner'' than manufacturing work, offered greater job security, and often carried with them the rewards of higher status such as paid vacations. They also provided opportunities for women of modest social backgrounds to meet and marry higher-status, white-collar men. Employers, in turn, found in young single women a cheaper, more compliant work force, whose youthful sex appeal might also enhance the business environment. The clerical labor force became feminized.[1]

The need for a literate clerical work force was a powerful stimulus driving the expansion of female opportunities also in education. Teaching became an important force for changing women's lives. With their certificates, daughters of the working and lower-middle classes earned admission to the world of white-collar employment and, often, to a culture more sophisticated than that of their origins. While it was generally the mid-twentieth century before female teachers won the right to equal treatment with male teachers, they were among the first professional groups to organize and to claim equal rights. Through the educational reform movement women learned organizational skills they could transfer to other causes, and teachers disproportionately filled the ranks of feminist movements. In France, organized lay teachers were among the most active of female union members.

Since World War II, we are accustomed to consider university training as prerequisite to careers in teaching. Earlier, however, certification as elementary school teachers required little more than secondary education (indeed, when most of the population could neither read nor write, mere literacy was the basic qualification). In the early twentieth century, teaching closely resembled clerical service, in qualifications, pay, and working conditions. As the requirements for teaching (first in secondary and later in all public schools) were increased to include university training, however, the schools ceased to offer women the same ease of admission that the office did. In contrast, the expansion of office employment opportunities was facilitated by the public schools, which offered courses in typing, bookkeeping, and stenography and sometimes even required that girls take them. Due to the vast expansion of demand during the Second World War, women with a secondary "business education" entered the office in record numbers.[2]

The Advent of Mass Consumption and the Smaller Family

Growth in the numbers of women in paid labor helped to generate an expanding market for labor-saving devices in the home. Made possible by the advances of earlier decades in cheap steel, electricity, and precision manufacture, a whole new range of reasonably priced, consumer-durable goods was being produced, including sewing machines, clocks, bicycles, furnaces, cast-iron stoves, improved cooking utensils and, later on, electrical appliances like toasters and vacuum cleaners. A series of "universal expositions" held in "Palaces of Industry" in capital cities of Europe between 1851 and 1900 had introduced urban society to the marvels that scientific and technological progress made possible. The aim of these events was to teach a "lesson of things." We owe the Eiffel Tower, for example, to the Paris Exposition of 1889. Material improvements were the capstone of a century of progress; mass consumption would fulfill dreams, "merchandise . . . fill needs of the imagination." By connecting "imaginative desires and material ones," the expositions created a new "dream world of mass consumption" that industry and commerce stood ready to serve. So successful was this strategy that by the early twentieth century, Europeans had become their own best customers.[3]

The anticipated economic benefits of industrial growth finally had begun to affect even lower-class families. Aggregate purchasing power was on the rise and real per capita income growing. This rise in living standards changed patterns of consumption in highly significant ways. Where once food, clothing, and housing had absorbed working people's total income, improved earnings and changing values were reflected in monies allocated for entertainment and other discretionary spending. Furthermore, with wages rising particularly in heavy industry, increasing numbers of working-class families could rely on the income of husbands and the wages of their grown children to meet the family's changing aspirations. More than ever before, daughters—rather than mothers—were out in the work force. By the early twentieth century a household division of labor that allowed married women to stay at home (but, quite probably, still engage in some wage work) was becoming as characteristic of working-class couples as of those of the middle classes. The onset of consumer mass society changed the nature of the family in the industrialized West, and promoted, as Tilly and Scott call it, the "family consumer economy," focusing on higher consumption levels.

The Western family was becoming smaller, and this was true among all the classes of Europe, not only those living in urban centers but those in rural areas as well. In part, the advantages of rising living standards prompted lower-class families to limit the numbers of their offspring as it had earlier encouraged the middle classes. Child labor laws and compulsory education helped to change their view of children. Young children no longer were seen as potential earners but rather as dependents, living for longer periods of time on the family income. Better diet and hygiene and public health measures such as municipal water and sewage disposal led to reduced infant mortality and improved the chances of each child for survival to adulthood. Shorter working hours allowed more time for family affairs and parents could begin to devote more and more attention to their children. Investment in the support and education of children now represented parents' hopes for a better future for their children and through them, for the family. Working-class culture also was beginning to center on family and home life. In Belleville, a poor district in Paris, it appeared to observers in the 1890s that "the working man's love for his children borders on being an obsession."[4]

New attitudes coupled with new material conditions produced a notable reduction in fertility levels, as Figure 4 reveals. It shows a steady drop in crude birthrates for selected countries in the twentieth century. In Germany overall fertility declined by 60 percent between the date of unification in 1871 and the early 1930s. The Nazi years (1933–1945) reversed the trend for Germany alone. The French had the lowest rates to begin with, 24.6 per thousand in 1880, and their population was growing at the slowest rate in all of Europe. In half a century (from 1851 to 1911) the population rose by only 3.4 million, from a total of 35.7 to 39.1 million people. Across the Channel in England the picture was similar. Marriages of the late 1860s, when they lasted more than 20 years, produced on average 6.2 births; those of 1915, only 2.4 children.[5] In the twentieth century, with the exception of a rise after the depression years and World War II, the number of births per thousand also has been declining.

These are aggregate statistics that mask differential fertility by class. In the early decades of the century, lower-class couples still had the largest families and struggled to get by. In certain regions of Europe, however, most notably in textile areas like Manchester, England, the Oberlausitz, Germany, or Roubaix, France, working-class families had few offspring. Here, the fertility decline expressed the real tensions that working women faced in balancing jobs and family responsibilities. These areas had uncharacteristically high employment of married women because of the low wages paid to men and women alike. Nothing affected women's decision to reduce the size of their families more than employment outside the home in the absence of day care and other household services. In general, the class and regional differences began to converge in the 1920s. Reduction in the amount of time women spend in childbearing has been one of the most significant changes in the female life cycle, especially in light of pronounced increases in longevity in the twentieth century. Most women in the West are no longer caught up in a long series of pregnancies followed by early death. The acceptance of new attitudes and practices that conscious contraception represents marks a major departure in human history. Along with women's increasing labor force participation, it makes possible revolutionary change in the history of women.

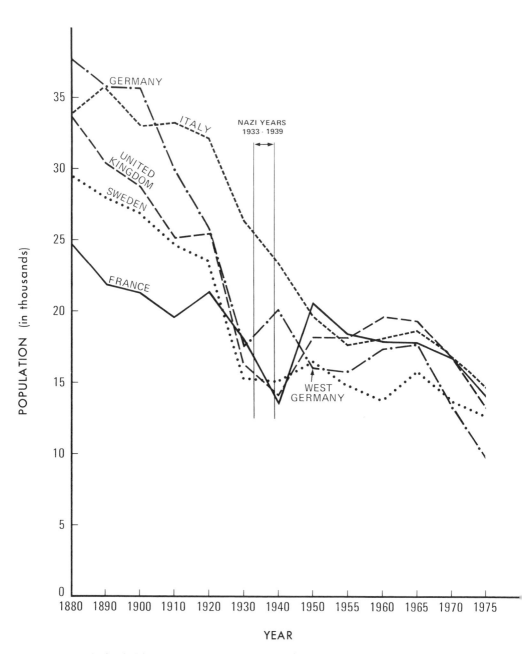

Figure 4. Crude Birthrates (per 1000 population) for Select European Countries, 1880–1975. Source: B.R. Mitchell, *European Historical Statistics 1750–1975* (New York, 1975), pp. 118–136.

Suffrage, Feminism, and Socialism

The emerging consumer society directed its appeal toward housewives and found in the single-family dwelling an expanding market for its goods. Each home would be equipped with its own washing machine, electrical appliances, and other new products. With reduced childbearing, housewives had greater time that could be spent in home management and consumption. For middle-class women in prewar Europe, this meant supervising servants and entertaining for business purposes. For lower-class women, it meant more time for careful marketing, canning, and home sewing. Consumption, however, might not be confined solely to the needs of each individual family, but might involve group purchasing in the interest of economizing. In England and Germany consumer cooperatives that bought in bulk and shared profits emerged in working-class precincts. Discussion in such groups inevitably moved beyond domestic and cooperative matters to questions of politics and class issues, and participation was often the first step in a woman's greater involvement in the outside world.

Whatever the reasons for political awakening, women seeking to change conditions still worked in a public arena that was unfavorable to their efforts. And this difficulty they shared with some of Europe's working classes, who also had no meaningful political voice. We have seen in Part II that feminist organizing began in the nineteenth century and sometimes grew out of religious, moral, and family concerns. Women in groups campaigned for temperance, against prostitution, and, in America, for the abolition of slavery. Single women, especially of the middle class, sought better opportunities for education and employment. The feminist call also, somewhat tentatively, had included the vote, but by the early twentieth century suffrage had been transformed into the key demand—seen as the vehicle to carry all the other reforms needed to improve women's position. The intensity of the campaign for the vote varied by country and reflected the overall political climate; it was strongest in Britain and America, two nations fully committed to natural rights philosophy. It was weaker in Germany, where that country's authoritarian structure and ambivalence toward natural rights dampened enthusiasm for suffrage; and in France, where it was caught up in conflicts of church against state, of individual rights versus family obligations, and of party politics and national politics.[6]

Suffragists were fighting for a basic principle: the right of women to citizenship in the nation-state. And in this push for democracy women could become the allies of workingmen who, in countries with property qualifications for voting, were also disenfranchised. The alliance of woman suffrage and women's movements generally with working-class or socialist parties was more characteristic of European nations than of America, where socialism was weaker and women drew energy for suffrage essentially from women's clubs and reform societies. American suffragists were militant at the end of the nineteenth century; they staged 480 campaigns in 33 states between 1870 and 1910, but with only limited results. The pioneer suffragists Elizabeth Cady Stanton, Lucy Stone, and Susan B. Anthony were being replaced by more conservative leaders such as Anna Howard Shaw and Carrie Chapman Catt. Although they still linked woman suffrage to reforms in women's and children's labor, some new leaders also saw in votes for women a key to preserve Anglo-Saxon supremacy against the hordes of immigrants who had moved to American soil, and as an antidote also against the vote by Negro men.

England had the most well-known and brash suffragists of the twentieth century, Mrs. Emmeline Pankhurst (1858–1928) and her daughters Christabel and Sylvia who, in 1903, founded the Women's Social and Political Union (WSPU). Despite an initial link with the Independent Labour Party (ILP), the WSPU appealed mostly to middle- and upper-class women. It was among the first of the pressure groups in Europe or America to recognize the importance of the media, and its members undertook outrageous acts to publicize their demands. Ministers were slapped or showered with eggs and tomatoes; "suffragettes" (as they were disdainfully labelled but soon called themselves with pride) chained themselves to lampposts, went on hunger strikes in jail, and, in the notable case of Emily Davison, who threw herself before the King's horse at the Derby, even died vainly for the cause. Across the Channel, the "French suffragette" Hubertine Auclert failed to forge an analogously audacious party.

Less well known among British suffragists, radical trade union women from the textile districts of Manchester and women in the Cooperative Guilds drew on their industrial experience to stress suffrage as a means to obtain legislation favorable to women wage-earners. These union women forged ties to other working-class organizations. Union women, including Mrs. Dickenson and Mrs. Cooper, Miss Reddish and Miss Silcock, worked hard for Labour candidates in the first two decades of the twentieth century in anticipation of labor support for woman suffrage. But a mutually beneficial alliance foundered over differences between those who favored adult suffrage (a call to enfranchise all adults and abolish property qualifications) and woman suffrage (enfranchising women on the same basis as men had been in an 1884 reform bill). In addition, some socialists argued that if a full manhood suffrage bill were easier to obtain than a limited woman suffrage bill, labor should work for men's votes. Suffragists favored the woman's bill as a first pragmatic step toward full adult suffrage; most male Labourites favored adult suffrage on principle, although chances of its success were dimmed by Liberal and Tory opposition. Amid the conflict, women suffragists helped Keir Hardie, a member of the ILP and leading male advocate of women's votes, conduct a survey inquiring what proportion of the women enfranchised by the limited (women's) suffrage bill would be working-class. When they found the answer to be at least 80 percent, limited suffrage could not be dismissed derisively by Labour as a "Ladies' Bill." The facts, however, failed to cement the alliance in the prewar era.

Continental women like Clara Zetkin in Germany, Madeleine Pelletier in France, and Alexandra Kollontai in Russia had similar difficulties in forging effective alliances with socialists and unionists as we have already learned in the Overview to Part II. In the first two decades of the twentieth century, these socialist feminists were urging reforms to ease wage-earning women's double burdens as workers and mothers. Unlike the fiery Polish-German radical Rosa Luxemburg, who "regarded her sex as irrelevant" and sought to channel all energies toward promoting the revolution, socialist feminists were unwilling to delay change until "after the revolution." Their platform included a call for reform in women's present circumstances. They supported maternity insurance and day-care centers, broadened apprenticeship training to lift women from low-skilled, poorly paid jobs, and equal pay for equal work. In North America, Charlotte Perkins Gilman (who considered herself a socialist) drew architectural plans for kitchenless houses in restructured neighborhoods to overcome patterns of urban space that isolated women and made their domestic work invisible.[7]

But increasingly, socialist women also felt a need to support the bourgeois feminist call for the vote. To demonstrate their position on this issue they pressed for a special day, a woman's day, to be set aside to publicize the issue of women's vote, which had been monopolized effectively by middle-class feminists. Responding, the Socialist Party of the United States set up a Woman's National Committee to plan demonstrations for the suffrage. The first was held in New York City on March 8, 1908, although subsequently, American socialists designated the last Sunday in February as National Woman's Day. In Europe similar efforts were underway, spearheaded by socialist feminists of the "Second International," an official grouping of socialist parties, trade unions, and political associations. At the women's conference of the International that met in Copenhagen in 1910, Clara Zetkin and Luise Zietz pushed the idea of an International Woman's Day, although they did not specify a date. The first was held in Europe on March 18, 1911 and it became a tradition in socialist circles. It was officially declared March 8 by Lenin in 1922, because Russian women five years earlier, following the American lead of celebrating the last Sunday in February, had precipitated the first Russian Revolution of 1917 on February 23 by Gregorian calendar (March 8 in the West). Setting aside a special day gave prewar socialists the opportunity to work for, and not just pay lip service to, women's causes. In the Austro-Hungarian Empire, for example, over 300 demonstrations for woman suffrage were held in 1911 and socialist delegates to the parliament for the first time openly called for the women's vote.[8] But in the main, most male and many female socialists remained skeptical about feminist activities and still saw them as diversionary and potentially harmful to working-class unity. Since the late 1960s, International Women's Day has been resurrected in the nonsocialist West as a common celebration and affirmation of feminist causes and solidarity.

The Welfare State and Motherhood

By clamoring for political and economic change (and even questioning the existing sexual hierarchy), working-class organizations posed a real and recognized threat to Europe's ruling classes. Despite a shared rhetoric of revolution, however, not all were revolutionary; many merely wanted a greater slice of the public pie. It was just this combined pressure "from below," however, that convinced many former laissez-faire politicians to institute reforms and redistribute some of the benefits of economic development more equitably. In this fashion, liberalism was transformed into its twentieth-century variant, the welfare state. Germany was the first industrializing country to adopt national welfare programs for wage-earners. Under Otto von Bismarck's guidance, factory workers obtained health insurance in 1883 and accident insurance in 1884; five years later, an old-age pension scheme was passed. The timing of these reforms, which directly influenced passage of similar prewar legislation under Solidarist influence in France during the 1890s and under the liberal governments of Herbert Asquith and David Lloyd George in England between 1906 and 1916, says much about the motives. Bismarck was quite explicit in his hope to wean workers from socialism through welfare capitalism. He sought to suppress the political party of the working class, the German Social Democratic Party (SPD), by securing anti-Socialist laws that were on the books from 1878 to 1890; at the same time, the welfare reforms were a carrot designed to win workers' loyalty and promote socially integrative and conservative sentiments. Increasingly, the nations of Europe and the United States have followed Bismarck's lead, instituting progressive income and inheritance taxes to defray the costs of the wide-ranging social services. Germany expanded its commitments during the 1920s, providing unemployment insurance for the first time. The United States followed during the dislocations of the Depression, with Roosevelt's New Deal legislation in the 1930s. So, too, did the Scandinavian countries, where social democratic parties assumed power and cooperated with conservatives to enact broad-ranging welfare legislation.

Welfare provisions and other forms of state regulation are powerful instruments that can shape modern societies along certain lines. Their effects reach far beyond people's "welfare" and "the public good," for they express assumptions about work, proper family life and gender behavior as well as class ties; therefore, they structure class and gender relationships. For example, social services such as day care, which allow some educated married women to hold well-paying jobs, at the same time exacerbate class differences by offering child-care employees notoriously low wages. However, welfare legislation has helped to avoid class conflict, as Bismarck explicitly intended it should, and this has been done partly by reinforcing traditional gender relationships. In the observation by a Danish author that "what the workers needed was not a revolution but a neat Danish home," lies an unspoken premise that the home be kept neat through woman's work. Benefit plans that offer extensive maternity insurance but deny money for abortion reinforce pronatalist values and limit women's alternatives; the same is true of rules that deprive a single mother of public child support if she cohabits with a man. She is deprived of her position as head of household and the man is forced to support the (fictitious) family. While this policy reduces expenditures of public funds, it reinforces women's dependency on men.[9]

Other historic examples of assumptions embedded in the laws are found in the early protective legislation for wage-earning women that was promulgated in Germany, France, and elsewhere. The dominant belief behind this legislation was that a woman, above all, was a mother responsible for her family, and that the state had a duty to help the wage-earning woman fulfill this critical role. In 1891, German legislators passed a law that gave the married working woman a one-and-one-half hour noon break—so she could rush home and cook the noon meal for her family; and they gradually reduced her work day, including closing by 2:00 p.m. on Saturdays, so she could have time to clean her home and do the wash on the weekends. Similarly, in 1917, France adopted a five-and-a-half day work week (the so-called English week) in clothing manufacture (where most women in industry worked), advancing as the primary justification the need of women for time off Saturday afternoon to shop, clean house, and prepare their families for church on Sunday. Whatever the stated intent of these special laws, the actual impact was to reinforce women's double burdens in wage and housework. Unpaid housework, however, was not recognized as socially useful labor and housewives have received no independent claim to pensions or health insurance in the welfare states of the West.

The social definition of women as mothers and homemakers, then, has profoundly shaped the laws providing services in the emerging welfare states. It helps account for the remarkable similarity of welfare provisions throughout the West, despite different national traditions and levels of economic growth and development. The political uses made of "motherhood," however, are highly complex. As we will show below, the woman-as-mother model provided a rationale for prewar efforts to intervene into people's lives and force some women, but not others, to bear children. In the interwar years, that same image was at the root of fascist antifeminism in Germany. But it also motivated socialists in Scandinavia in the 1930s to expand welfare services and to provide greater opportunities for women as mothers and workers.

Motherhood, Feminism, and Racism

The population debate that involved women's reproductive capacities represents the distinctive context for early twentieth-century feminists, an arena unlike that faced by their foremothers in earlier eras. It strengthened a "domestic" or "familial" feminism, based on the nineteenth-century principle of "equality in difference," which accepted the sexual division of labor but sought to elevate and highlight the special contributions that women made to the family and society by their uniquely feminine intervention. Feminists could best gain the support of male politicians and public figures when they argued their cause in terms of women's social contributions as mothers and wives, as Karen Offen's case study of the debates in France in the early Third Republic shows (Chapter 9).

In some instances, women themselves sought to appropriate motherhood and make it the basis of a more radical feminist philosophy. This was the case of the German Society for the Protection of Motherhood and Sexual Reform, an influential organization admired by feminists outside of the Second Empire. The Society had been founded by Ruth Bre in 1904 and later was taken over by Helene Stöcker, a Berlin advocate of changes in sexual and marriage practices. Its program was inspired by the writings of the Swedish social and educational reformer and essayist, Ellen Key (1849–1926). Key sought to restructure society in ways that would put motherhood at the center stage of public life. While Key was active in the prewar period, her ideas on motherhood directly influenced the characteristics of the emerging welfare state in Scandinavia in the interwar era. Like Key, Society members were dedicated to elevating motherhood regardless of marital status and sought to extend municipal services to young, unmarried mothers and their children. They set up counseling centers to deal with sexual problems and advocated legal equality for "illegitimate" children. At the same time, they adopted a Neo-Malthusian argument (one favorable to birth control and medical self-help) and fought for the right of women to reject having children under adverse circumstances. The members agitated for the availability and diffusion of birth control information and devices as well as for the decriminalization of abortion laws.[10]

Such goals were controversial; battle lines were drawn. For some groups, the requirements of national growth and strength overrode a woman's right to control her own body. Anti-Malthusian leagues, adopting pronatalist positions, proliferated in prewar Europe and sought official ban on the sale of contraceptives and sex information literature. Nationalist politicians who blamed women's wage work outside the home for the steady fertility decline sought to remove married women from gainful employment in the expectation that then they would have more children. This proposal was debated on numerous occasions (although never enacted) in the parliamentary chambers of France and Germany. It was an antifeminist position that strongly resonated among some workingmen who felt particularly threatened by women's presence in the work force. The German-National Commercial Employees Union, for example, a union of male white-collar workers that had been organized in the early 1890s to oppose the "degenerative" forces of the modern age, set out to stem the "invasion" of female elements into their profession. Its members openly advocated limiting women's work in service occupations.

Other organizations echoed the turn-of-the-century concern with "race." For them, absolute population decline was less significant than the question of which groups in society were having the most children. Taking their cue from the prominent Social Darwinist notion of life as a deadly "struggle for existence," their answer was unequivocal—the "unfit." Increasingly, the term "race suicide," popularized in the United States by President Theodore Roosevelt, entered the European vocabulary. The prewar population debate shaded inexorably into open discussion of forced sterilization and other eugenic programs under the guise of devising a "science of producing the finest offspring." The "fit," it was feared, were failing to reproduce and only government intervention could reverse the alarming trend.[11]

Imperialist rivalries contributed to the preoccupation with motherhood. The European powers, which had forced open the doors to China and Japan, now feared what the German Kaiser, William II, termed a "yellow peril," an imaginary horde of Asians inundating Europe. Imperial crises turned into debates over the nation's human stock and revealed considerable class fear and racist sentiment. Britain's Boer War (1899–1902) offers a prime example of these connections. (England has the dubious distinction of being the first of the modern nations of the West to become embroiled in battle with a smaller but determined group of anticolonial fighters defending their homeland, the Boer in the Transvaal, South Africa). Recruitment of English soldiers from working-class neighborhoods and subsequent investigations of workers' living standards had revealed appalling conditions and poor health and raised fears of lower-class "degenerates" swamping civilized peoples by simply outbreeding them. This outcry came at a time when Labour was beginning to organize working-class people, and class antagonisms, compounded by hatred of the Irish, were running high. Turn-of-the-century England was deluged by books and articles with such revealing titles as *The Problem of the Army, Fertility of the Unfit, Physical Deterioration*. Their aim was twofold: to encourage passage of public legislation designed to curb indiscriminate breeding of lower-class peoples, and to turn middle- and upper-class women into bearers of higher quality citizens. Motherhood of the "fit" was seen by a vocal group as the nation's salvation. It was also posed as a solution to the fears of prewar anti-Semites in Europe of "rule by foreign Jews."

If imperialism fueled the population debate in Europe, it had, of course, a very direct and disruptive impact on the lives of native peoples of areas that fell under European colonial rule. Luise White (Chapter 10) shows how Kenyan women coped with changes in their rural areas as a result of the incorporation of much of black Africa into the European-dominated world economy. She develops a fascinating connection between the world economy and forms of prostitution, by showing what draught, famine, cattle diseases, and a shift to cash cropping meant for wealthy agriculturalists and their daughters, who were expected to help their families out economically.

The African case is not an isolated one. With the spread of white settlements across the Australian continent, for example, a traditional and delicate power balance between aboriginal men and women of the Northern Territory was upset. Colonial administrators and pioneering settlers brought with them their own class and cultural biases, which included restrictive notions about the proper roles of women in society. In the case of Australia, a road was located through the very center of a spectacular area of rocks in the desert. Known as the Marbles, in precolonial times it had been a taboo area for men and the site of women's rituals and celebrations. With construction of the road, however, the area was considered contaminated and no longer accessible for ritual purposes. "Sorrowfully, the women claim they can still hear the old people crying from the caves." Also, consultations to work out settlement patterns took place between aboriginal and white *males,* and women were bypassed in the process of political negotiations.[12]

The New Woman

In the early twentieth century, some radical men and women experimented with new living patterns and sexual relations that went beyond the wife and mother ideal. Older certainties were breaking down at a bewildering rate. The Newtonian universe that had been the model of the physical world for two centuries was coming apart. It had rested on two erroneous assumptions: that both time and space were absolute no matter where one stood in the universe. A young German patent officer, Albert Einstein (1879–1955), destroyed those certainties by his theory of relativity put forth first in the paper, *The Electrodynamics of Moving Bodies* (1905). He showed how time and space were relative to the observer and proved that relativity could not be removed. This finding was soon translated by segments of public opinion into a philosophy of relativism of values, mores, and behavior.

Equally significant was the refutation of the optimistic Enlightenment notion of human nature by the work of Sigmund Freud (1856–1939), the Austrian founder of psychoanalysis. For about 200 years, liberal educated opinion had struggled with the Christian notion of original sin, emphasizing the human capacity for rational self-determination. But Freud, uncovering unconscious aggressive and sexual drives, showed that human beings, while endowed with the potential for reason, also possess strong instinctual drives that conflict with the demands of social existence. He was deeply concerned with the tension between the individual and civilization and believed that civilization had been able to emerge only by repressing basic human instincts, particularly the sexual drives. In Freud's more complex view, human beings might achieve a reasoned existence, but only by bringing instinctual drives to consciousness, and guiding them through rational choice. This integration of rational and irrational was difficult to achieve.

Like many other thinkers whose work is seen to define an age, Freud was not alone, nor even the first social analyst to develop a theory about the dominant role of instinctual drives in human experience. The "recovery of the unconscious," as it has been called, drew also on the philosophical works of Friedrich Nietzsche and Henri Bergson, and other intellectual leaders who rejected positivism and emphasized instinct, introspection, and intuition. Studies of sexual science—or sexology—formed a part of this broader analysis and Freud's work on sexuality was preceded by that of Havelock Ellis and Richard Krafft-Ebing. However, Freud's influence on attitudes, behavior, and culture, as well as on science, has been so far-reaching that the founder of psychoanalysis has been compared to Copernicus and Darwin, and the twentieth century labeled "The Freudian Century," signifying a new, truly revolutionary concern with the inner self and its impact on human behavior and social history.

Along with demonstrating the importance of sexual drives in personality development, in dreams, in both conscious and unconscious expression, Freud pointed out the harmful effects of repressed sexuality. Women as well as men suffered numerous physical and emotional illnesses because of unexpressed sexual needs. To the extent that Freud sought change, he wanted to free people from the repressive morality and constraints of Victorian society that caused suffering among his patients. Countering Victorian notions that women were "passionless," he recognized female sexuality as a powerful force, and supported those who defended women's rights to sexual satisfaction. Female frigidity was not innate but socially constructed. The popularizing of his ideas inaugurated a so-called sexual revolution and initiated a debate about the sexually emancipated woman. But Freud, whose views of women reflected his own cultural milieu, was a poor guide, for, like Aristotle and Aquinas, he accepted a male model of human being and depicted women as lesser men. His views were used by his followers to reinforce older stereotypes of female passivity.

The Freudian view of the development of female psychology defined woman as born deficient, that is, like a "castrated man," she was a "mutilated creature," a being without a penis. Jealousy based on "penis envy" underlay female psychic development, which followed one of three possible avenues toward adulthood. Some girls repressed their sexuality and became frigid; others refused to accept the fact of being "castrated" and developed a "masculinity complex," characterized by a persistent preference for a childish clitoral masturbation over mature vaginal intercourse and sometimes by lesbianism; and a third, or "normal" group, accepted their "femininity." In this case, through the process of sexual maturation, a girl rejected her mother, longed for her father, and achieved true femininity only after marriage and the birth of a child, who served as her substitute for the long-desired penis. Such sexual differentiation was reflected in personality types from infancy onward. That these ideas could not sustain a movement for equal sexual freedom is clear, for optimal female development required motherhood. Radicals of both sexes nonetheless embraced them in their efforts to experiment with new sexual and marital possibilities, and in the long run, Freud's discovery of powerful, aggressive, sexual instincts in both sexes contributed to movements for sexual liberation.

Other men and some "new women" of the late nineteenth century heralded female emancipation in marriage, culture and society. The most famous literary proponent of female individualism in that period was the Norwegian playwright, Henrik Ibsen (1828–1906). While rejecting the label "feminist," Ibsen believed in the right and the duty of women as well as men to individual development, and recognized that "a woman cannot be herself in the society of the present day, which is an exclusively masculine society, with laws framed by men and with a judicial system that judges feminine conduct from a masculine point of view." In 1879, Ibsen shocked society by producing his now-famous, then infamous, play, *A Doll's House*. Nora, wife of Helmer and mother of three, commits two acts that violate male standards. First, in the interest of her husband, she forges a document; then, stunned by his lack of understanding of her motives into recognizing that he treats her as a "silly child," as his "little lark," she walks away from home, husband, and children to fulfill a duty to herself that she sees as "sacred." Before slamming the door, Nora tells Helmer, "I believe that before all else I am a human being."

In the early twentieth century, bohemians in Greenwich Village and Montparnasse and avant-garde playwrights associated with Germany's naturalist theater wrote, argued, and lived in an atmosphere charged with excitement—and ambivalence—centered on the characteristics of the new, sexually-emancipated woman. In France, Victor Margueritte's novel *La Garçonne (The Bachelor Girl,* 1922) sold 20,000 copies in four days, 300,000 in its first year, over a million by 1929, although—and no doubt because—it showed a young woman adopting male standards of sexual behavior. Men of solid bourgeois standing, ranging from Léon Blum, later prime minister of France, to Judge Ben Lindsey of Denver, Colorado, published books advocating forms of "trial marriage." It was an exciting era for those involved even if its immediate impact on the masses of women was minimal. Many ideas were proposed; almost all could agree that some measure of freedom in love was essential to self-development and some even advocated birth control because it permitted the separation of sexuality from reproduction. Emma

Goldman (1869–1940), the Russian–born American anarchist, said it probably better than most. The modern woman would achieve emancipation

> First by asserting herself as a personality, and not as a sex commodity. Second, by refusing the right to anyone over her body; by refusing to bear children, unless she wants them; by refusing to be a servant of God, the State, society, the hus-band, the family, etc., by making her life simpler, but deeper and richer. That is, by trying to learn the meaning and substance of life in all its complexities, by freeing herself from the fear of public opinion and public condemnation. Only that and not the ballot, will set woman free, will make her a force hitherto un-known in the world, a force for real love, for peace, for harmony; a force of divine fire, of life-giving; a creator of free men and women.[13]

The fundamental goal of individual self-determination that was part of Gold-man's philosophy remained unrealized. The Freudian revolution helped to bring about a change in sexual mores, but it did not include the socioeconomic trans-formations needed to underpin female sexual independence. Indeed, most of Freud's followers of both sexes rejected the revolutionary potential of his work and, at worst, used it to reinforce demands for social adjustment to conservative values. Henceforth, however, people in the West were more willing to talk about sex and many came to regard sexual pleasure as a legitimate pursuit.

The sexual experimentation and "free love" that began shortly before the war constituted a "sexual revolution" only for the few. Most surely were horrified by new sexual roles and relationships, including most women. Actresses refused to play Nora and even self-proclaimed radical men expressed considerable ambiva-lence about the prospect of women's emancipation. Both before and after World War I, changing relations between the sexes generated fears of deteriorating val-ues and contributed to a pervasive sense of cultural despair.

World War I and the Russian Revolution

In retrospect, that Europeans plunged headlong into war in 1914 seems inevitable. Prior to 1900 nationalist rivalries could be played out in imperial conflicts in far-off lands. But once there was no more territory left to conquer, the focus returned to the Continent and settled on disputed claims in eastern Europe. There was a noticeable absence of will to avoid war. Indeed, there was a discernible cultural strain among men that positively welcomed war as the ultimate test of the fittest of nations and the fittest of men—a virulent expression of Social Darwinism. The heroes of Italian poet Gabriele d'Annunzio exemplified Nietzsche's "Superman," seeking fulfillment through striving for power and dominance. The Frenchman Georges Sorel idealized violence as a catharsis that might arouse mankind to its highest levels. Expressed in art and philosophy, Sorelian sentiments constituted a revolt against reason, science, and modernity. They were echoed in Germany in the "exaltation" of August 4, 1914, when the overwhelming majority of German parliamentarians voted for war credits and "war [seemed to] signify a release from an intolerable past, a final escape from the emptiness of bourgeois life."[14]

This is not to say that all Europeans acquiesced in war. International peace movements were gathering strength in the early decades of the twentieth century: the Hague Convention of 1899 created an international court of arbitration, and the Second International desperately fought nationalist sentiments and passed resolutions exhorting the world's working classes to reject a call to arms. Furthermore, many feminists and socialists alike thought that as women became more publicly aware, the force of maternal love would be a natural barrier to armed struggle. These expectations failed to materialize. Indeed, some socialist leaders joined wartime cabinets and most feminists deferred suffrage campaigns in order to mobilize women in patriotic causes. However, some notable prewar suffrage leaders maintained their pacifist principles. A well-known Frenchwoman, Hélène Brion, defending herself in court against a charge of treason, declared "I am an enemy of war because I am a feminist. War represents the triumph of brute strength, while feminism can only triumph through moral strength and intellectual values. Between the two there is total contradiction."[15]

World War I was a catalyst accelerating technological, political, and cultural change. It was the first three-dimensional war, fought on land, in the air, and under the sea. It reshaped the map of Europe and ruptured people's lives, yet it had a very different meaning for the men and women of Europe. Young men were called on to give their lives for their country; back home, women assumed unprecedented responsibility for the continuity of economic and social life. As men went off to the front, women took over many social functions that previously had not been open to them (and, after the wartime emergency, would once again be closed). In England, women undertook "men's work" as chimney sweeps, truck drivers, farm laborers, cementmakers, and steelworkers. As ticket collectors on English buses, they were labeled "Superwomen." As "Molly the Munitions Maker" they further disproved the "fiction of women's incapacity." By tens of hundreds of thousands, the "munitionettes" earned higher wages than before; and they won new attention from men's trade unions. During the war, the number of English-women employed increased by 1,345,000, of whom nearly all either entered new occupations or replaced men. At war's end, however, the prospect of five million returning soldiers in need of employment brought rapid displacement of women workers. Many women were happy to resume traditional roles; others protested. Eight days after the Armistice, on November 19, 1918, 6,000 union women marched to Westminster bearing signs, "Shall Peace Bring Us Starvation?" By 1919, 650,000 women were unemployed, of whom 150,000 received no compensation, many for having refused alternative work as domestic servants. Wartime gains disappeared in the postwar depression.

A similar story may be told of France. In March 1915, the Chamber of Deputies resolved "to utilize the feminine labour force to replace the military labour force wherever possible." Factories of all types turned to female employees: manufacturers of soap, drugs, explosives; producers of gas, electricity, and armaments; paperworks as well as metalworks. Transport companies hired their first female drivers, guards, and ticket-takers. Though fewer than their English sisters—perhaps because of the greater demand for women in French agriculture—Frenchwomen left their traditional employment for war work, some 684,000 in armaments factories alone. While some employers reorganized work processes especially to accommodate women, others found their performance identical to men's and, of course, their pay less. Men's concern that the employment of substitute female labor might permanently depress their own wages led to pressure for equal pay legislation. In July 1915, the first law in France establishing a minimum wage was enacted—quickly climaxing six years of debate—for women homeworkers in garmentmaking, many newly employed in the military uniform business. A decree of January 1917 required that piecework rates for women equal those of men in identical work. Nevertheless, although women's wages rose dramatically, up 400, 500, even 600 percent, rarely did women earn as much as their male counterparts. And most of the financial gains that women made were swallowed up by wartime inflation. After the war's end, as in England, Frenchwomen were encouraged to leave their war jobs. In an effort to prevent widespread unemployment among the returning soldiers, the government offered severance pay to women workers who voluntarily conceded their jobs—but only if they acted by December 5, 1918.

The situation was also very similar in wartime Germany. Indeed, in all the belligerent nations, unprecedented numbers of women undertook "men's work." What were the psychological reactions of women to their new opportunities? How did the wartime release of female inhibitions feed into postwar antifeminism? Sandra Gilbert (Chapter 11) describes very vividly this wartime world of men—and of the women left behind in England. Through contemporary fiction, she probes the underlying "battle of the sexes," a hitherto unacknowledged component of the war and of the postwar decade.

In one country, political upheaval during World War I introduced the most far-reaching changes in the status of women yet experienced anywhere in the Western world. The Russian Revolution of 1917 brought into the daily lives of millions of people questions previously dealt with largely in theory and discussion. Whether or not Russia would have succumbed to revolutionary onslaught without the dislocations of the war is a matter of considerable disagreement among historians. What is clear is that the tsarist government's commitment to industrial growth, dating from the 1890s, strained the traditional political and social system nearly to the breaking point. The Revolution of 1905 was one clear indication that the autocratic system could not accommodate industrial advance without changing its political and economic structure. War strained it even further.

The first Revolution of 1917, as we have seen, began on International Women's Day. Women textile workers were the first to go on strike, protesting deepening economic crises—lack of foodstuffs and other necessities, stagnating wages, rampant inflation—and the strike spread spontaneously, particularly after troops garrisoned in the capital of St. Petersburg mutinied. The story of the Provisional Government and Lenin's return from exile in a sealed train provided by the Germans has been told many times and need not be repeated here. For our interest concerns a number of related and less well-known areas. After Lenin successfully led the second, or Bolshevik, revolution in October 1917, a regime pledged to women's rights, reconstruction of the family, communal support of children, and other radical revisions of the social and gender hierarchy took over a backward land of about 128 million "souls." What was the Bolshevik attitude toward "the woman question?'' What reforms in women's position did the new Soviet regime seek? How did women respond to the proposed changes in sexual relationships?

Within weeks of wresting power, Lenin appointed the first female cabinet-level officer in the West, Alexandra Kollontai, to serve as Commissar of Social Welfare. Kollontai, who wanted to liberate women by abolishing the family that made them dependent on men, represented the radical wing of socialist feminism. But the force of tradition prevailed over the promise of sexual and social equality. Many women clung to familiar patriarchal forms of family life for purposes of subsistence. Rural women, for example, were hurt by the new government's failure to protect the rights of single women to land. During the period of the Civil War that followed the Revolution, many women alone (soldiers' wives and widows) were attempting to farm their family's allotment, while at the same time peasant men were demanding large allotments of village holdings and those of former landlords. By 1924, most peasant women who were heads of households had no land whatsoever and had been subjected to considerable humiliation and abuse when they protested the loss of property. This village conflict between men and single women reinforced women's conservatism; survival seemed to require reliance on traditional male-dominated institutions. And most Russian men agreed. Those women who profited from the Revolution were those who were willing to reject tradition, join the Bolshevik party, and enter politics. This took both ''daring and opportunity to move into the new elite. Most Russian women had little of either.'' [16] Richard Stites (Chapter 12) writes that all revolutions cheat their followers in some ways; although the Soviet regime proclaims full equality of the sexes, in practice, power, authority, and opportunity are tilted in favor of men (over women) as they are toward industrial workers (over peasants). This is not, however, to deny the very real gains made by Soviet women in education, employment, and personal development.

The Interwar Years

In most countries more or less severe political, economic, and social dislocations followed the war's end. Employment patterns returned to their prewar division into men's and women's work. At the same time, many of the governments acknowledged women's contributions to the war effort and to national life by passage of suffrage legislation, as Table 1 demonstrates. Nineteen countries in Europe and North America passed woman suffrage laws between 1915 and 1922.

Until the feminist reinterpretation of history that began in the 1960s, the decade of the 1920s was often described as the time in which women were ''emancipated.'' The woman question was solved. In many countries women had the vote and a few now sat and deliberated in parliament. Once life settled down after the period of demobilization, they again entered the work force at a rapid rate, even at the ''expense'' of male workers (as Germans contended). Reform legislation was codifying advances, such as the British Sex Disqualification Removal Act of 1919, which opened the higher levels of the civil service, the legal profession, and jury duty to women. Furthermore, the stuffy and quite ''proper'' prewar

TABLE 1. Timing of States Granting Women Suffrage in National Elections

State	Year	State	Year
Australia	1901	Hungary	1918
Finland	1906	Austria	1918
New Zealand	1910	Czechoslovakia	1918
Norway	1913	Luxembourg	1919
Denmark	1915	United States	1920
Iceland	1915	Canada	1920
Netherlands	1917	Belgium	1920
Soviet Union	1917	Ireland	1922
Sweden	1918	France	1945
Great Britain	1918	Italy	1945
Germany	1918	Yugoslavia	1946
Estonia	1918	Romania	1946
Latvia	1918	Bulgaria	1947
Lithuania	1918	Switzerland	1970
Poland	1918		

world had given way to a new climate of restless vitality and renewed sexual and cultural experimentation. For the single "working girl," according to a popular view, it was a crazy age of rising hemlines, bobbed hair, and new leisure activities that included marathon dancing and hand-holding or gum-chewing contests and forays into nightclubs and cabarets where ladies had once not dared to tread. While each specific element in the picture can be backed up by facts, the optimistic conclusions drawn about women's improved status require reassessment.

Some women certainly looked different; the maternal image, exemplified in the United States by the Gibson girl, with her upswept, constrained long hair, her full bosom, narrow waist, wide hips, and concealed legs gave way to the flapper, who boyishly flattened her chest with binders, discarded corsets, lowered her waistline, and displayed her legs in silk stockings. But the flapper dress was seen as a "sexual assault" on men accustomed to women as passive recipients of their sexual advances. Postwar literature, as Sandra Gilbert shows, featured woman as bitch. The only good woman was profoundly passive, chaste, and domesticated. For France, as the historian James McMillan concludes, "the First World War ultimately served to consolidate the domestic ideology." While Parisan fashion designer Coco Chanel dressed women in tailored suits, white shirts, and men's ties, the French government not only rejected votes for women in 1922, it began in 1920 to forge medals for mothers: for five living children, bronze; for eight, silver; for ten, gold. To emphasize the seriousness of its intent to raise the birthrate, in the same year the government also decreed mere advocacy of abortion a crime punishable by up to three years in prison and three thousand francs penalty. Somewhat lesser penalties—six months maximum—awaited anyone who "for the purpose of contraceptive propaganda, describes, divulges, or offers to reveal . . . the procedures for preventing pregnancy." On the losing side in this long struggle, French Neo-Malthusians observed, "The rights of women increase. But what is their great duty: to give birth, to give birth again, always to give birth. . . . Should a woman refuse to give birth she no longer deserves her rights." [17]

As if further inducement to maternity were needed, in 1930 Pope Pius XI presented an encyclical on Christian marriage, declaring contraception a "horrible crime" in the sight of God, who "at times has punished it with death." The physiological, social, and economic emancipation of women, as commonly understood, was characterized by the pope as a "*debasing of the womanly character and the dignity of motherhood and indeed of the whole family* [italics in original]." Through "false liberty and unnatural equality," women became "as among the pagans the mere instrument of man." Women's rights, according to Pius XI, must be adapted to the welfare of the family as authorized by God. The patriarchal family was "not changeable by public laws or at the pleasure of private individuals." [18]

Fascist Antifeminism and Alternatives to Fascism

The experiences of women during the 1920s in Germany offer another instructive case of the postwar reaction, although in many ways the history of women in the Weimar Republic (1918–1933) was distinct and not duplicated in the other countries of Europe. Germany embodied a profound contradiction. On the one hand, a republic had been created by revolutionary upheaval and abdication of the Kaiser in November 1918. The new constitution expressed the best of liberal principles pushed in the direction of democracy. Guaranteeing equality before the law and full political rights for women, as well as labor protection, it seemed to offer proof of the triumph of feminism—women were guaranteed equal access to public life. On the other hand, Germany became the home of the most antimodern, violent, and racist movement in interwar Europe—the Nazi movement (National Socialist German Workers' Party) led by Adolf Hitler. Fascist parties appeared in every country of Europe in the interwar years, although they took power longest in Italy under Mussolini (1919–1944) and in the Germany of the Third Reich (1933–1945). Fascism fed on a deep sense of malaise and discontent spawned by the war experience and growing rejection of parliamentary liberal government as weak, ineffectual, and pandering to the mediocrity of the masses. Furthermore, fascism everywhere was particularly attuned to masculine values: its call was for struggle, strength, and courage. In many cases, early fascist converts had been disoriented soldiers trying to recreate the comradery and mutual dependency that they had experienced in the trenches. The fascists were very much opposed to feminism. They felt that women's work and women's rights were part and parcel of the "degeneracy" of the modern world and they were bent on returning women to the home. Antifeminism was a central part of the Nazi ideology. Germany in the 1920s, therefore, offered a stark contrast between the claims of the Republic to uphold women's equality and the call of the fascists to send women back to the home. What were German women's reactions?

The uneven and incomplete nature of change in the direction of women's liberation accounted for the political responses of many women. In the first place, a majority of adult women lived off the earnings of their husbands or their children and did not work for wages outside their homes; the trend toward small families with their emphasis on domesticity was continuing. Of the approximately 11.5 million adult women who were working for their living in 1925, fully one-third were in a category of "helping dependents," women who acknowledged to the census taker their secondary economic role in a family business or farm. Their numbers had doubled since 1907. These small establishments, which had difficulty meeting the competition of larger businesses, increasingly were being forced to let the hired help go and rely on the labor of wives. The Republic's new labor laws establishing the forty-hour work week and regulating wages made hired agricultural labor unprofitable, thus increasing the burdens on peasant wives. These developments do not suggest economic advancement or "emancipation" for rural women.

However, during the Weimar Republic, the most bitter contest for jobs occurred in industry and service. It was erroneously believed at the time that women were achieving economic success—indeed their very emancipation—by displacing men. Recent research by Renate Bridenthal and Tim Mason has proven otherwise,[19] but the political significance of the contemporary view and the backlash that it created remains. What fascism has taught is that myths are important and real if they influence how people act. Even during demobilization at the war's end, there had been public outcry against women's work. It gathered momentum in the unsettled economic conditions of the early postwar period and resurfaced when massive unemployment, caused by the Great Depression of 1929 in the United States, appeared in Germany. In reality, it was the process of economic rationalization that made women's work seem threatening to men. In a burst of effort beginning in the mid-1920s, Germany attempted to discard old plants and equipment and to modernize both industry and agriculture in order to remain competitive in world markets. Rationalization entailed the introduction of labor-saving machines, standardization of parts, and a flow production design that moved goods more swiftly along an assembly line. The new machinery and techniques invaded not only the factories but even the offices. It meant that work became divided into smaller and simpler, more repetitive stages and permitted the hiring of unskilled, cheap labor—and the cheapest laborers were women.

Yet most newly hired women did not replace men; instead, they took jobs in expanding industries that had previously employed women and, now, as women's share of total jobs shifted from agriculture and domestic service to factories and offices, women's work was more easily observed. Furthermore, women as well as men suffered the adverse effects of rationalization. As the new processes led to "speedups" and work became more intense, the conditions of women's labor in many ways deteriorated. Since nothing was done to ease the lot of workers who were both wage-earners and homemakers, many women found it hard to combine paid labor in factories, offices, and shops with running a home. Is it any wonder, then, that the call to "return women to their homes" was favorably received by some working women?

The deteriorating material conditions of life during the Weimar period and the resulting class antagonisms also pushed some middle-class women's organizations in the direction of the Nazi camp. The case of the Housewives Union, part of the bourgeois women's movement in the 1920s, is a telling example.[20] The organization had been founded during World War I to advise housewives on wartime consumer problems and now, after the German Revolution of 1918, was determined to oppose the goals of the Domestic Servants Union, which was in the socialist camp. In the 1920s, housewives and servants fought to a standstill over the question of working time. The organization of domestics wanted to limit household work to defined hours rather than have it take up all available time, while housewives opposed any limitations. But more was at stake. The number of available domestics was declining because young women preferred regulated employment in offices or factories to working in someone's home. As economic conditions worsened, middle-class people were not as readily able to afford domestics, but the presence of a maid still was a requirement of middle-class status as it had been in the nineteenth century. Middle-class housewives thus faced the prospect of becoming their own servants. Their response was to propose a service year for every girl (which would increase the pool of available servants), claiming that housewifery was a profession and, like every profession, needed a regular sequence of training and apprenticeship. It was Hitler and the National Socialists who came close to realizing the Housewives Union's program when they introduced a general service year for all German girls. The Housewives Union reacted positively; "No earlier regime listened to us," said the last president of the Union, Maria Jecker, when her organization was "coordinated"—that is, disbanded and brought under National Socialist control.

The Nazi party offered alternatives to women's emancipation by glorifying domestic life and its daily routine. There is every indication that this "drive for domesticity" after the Nazis came to power, between 1933 and 1936, met with tacit approval of German women. The regime offered tangible benefits to women who stayed at home. As early as the summer of 1933, it provided interest-free marriage loans to young couples as long as the woman withdrew from gainful labor. The money was designed to be spent on furniture and household appliances and to stimulate the depressed economy. The government improved welfare and maternity services and offered family allowances, which increased with the birth of each child. At the same time, it suppressed the sale and spread of birth control devices and information and applied the older antiabortion laws much more strictly. Birth rates reversed themselves and rose slightly in the period (Figure 3). The controlled public media kept up a constant barrage of propaganda designed to praise and glorify mothers and wives and to enhance their self-respect. The policy was both sexist and racist, however, and reveals the same complex connection between sexism and racism that we saw develop in the prewar period over the population debate.

The glorification of motherhood, which received public support, found its necessary counterpart, from the Nazi perspective, in compulsory sterilization for the sake of racial purity.[21] A new statute in late spring, 1933, legalized eugenic sterilization and, in July, the Law for the Prevention of Hereditarily Diseased Offspring ordered sterilization for certain categories of people. All women were affected by the regime's dual policy: so-called Aryan women were hailed as "mothers of the race" and turned into breeders, and non-Aryans vilified as perpetrators of racial degeneration. The Nazis acted on their racist and sexist program with their usual efficiency. It has been estimated that in the six years preceding the outbreak of World War II, about 320,000 persons, or nearly half of one percent of the population, were sterilized. This figure does not include the Jews who were victims of mass sterilization for supposed medical experiments and exterminated through mass genocide (six million Jews were killed during the Hitler period) in concentration camps, but only those of "German" ethnicity. The victims of sterilization were evenly divided between women and men, and came typically from the lower classes. Of the women sterilized, it was servants, unskilled factory or farm workers, jobless housewives married to poor and unskilled workers, prostitutes and unmarried women who were overrepresented. These women deviated from the norm of acceptable gender behavior. Proper and orderly German workers of either sex were less likely to fall victim to sterilization; "race hygiene" contributed to the maintenance of the class structure as well as the affirmation of the Nazis' standards of proper gender behavior.

During the interwar period, a combination of factors—reaction against the disruptions and losses due to the "Great War," especially population decline, and economic pressure resulting from the "Great Depression"—tended to reinforce traditional domestic ideology. Retrenchment against gender role revision took place even in Soviet Russia, where during the 1930s the leader Joseph Stalin (1879–1953) presided over a temporary dismantling of the codes of law that had liberalized marriage and divorce regulations, legalized abortion, and strengthened women's roles in family and society. Similar demographic and economic problems led to a radically different resolution in Scandinavia. Sweden's neutral position on the northern frontier of Europe had left it less traumatized by World War I. Under the leadership of a remarkable couple, the sociologist Alva Myrdal and her husband, the economist Gunnar Myrdal, both socialists, Sweden moved to solve its population crisis by expanding economic opportunities for women so that, married or unmarried, they could successfully combine work and motherhood.

Putting into practice ideas advanced decades earlier by their countrywoman Ellen Key as well as by the American Charlotte Perkins Gilman and the Frenchwoman Madeleine Pelletier, the Myrdals used the argument that motherhood is a socially essential function worthy of the highest respect. They convinced Swedish legislators, conservatives along with liberals and social democrats, to enact laws ensuring freedom for mothers by legalizing birth control, abortion, and sex education and protecting the employment rights of pregnant women. To reduce the penalties of pregnancy, Key had demanded that married women be allowed to retain their names, properties, and positions, that parents share equally in duties and rights, and that sexual morality—so loaded against women and especially against single mothers—be centered on "reverence for the child." A measure of the Myrdals' success was Alva Myrdal's statement in the foreward to a 1962 book on *The Changing Roles of Man and Woman*.

As early as the 1930s, we had succeeded in convincing the Royal Commissions to accept the idea that a career for married women should be viewed as "normal." This was the time when the family role of women first came to be regarded as an ancillary, though highly important part, of her life-plan. The official formulation of the demand was not the "right of married women to work," but rather the "right of working women to marriage and motherhood." [22]

In Denmark, the economic and social crises of the depression years in the 1930s also reinforced the case for expanded welfare services. Led by social democrats, who dominated a coalition with radical-liberals, the welfare state was pushed forward. Reform legislation was passed that broadened social services, including health and unemployment insurance and social security, instituted educational reforms, and curbed the economic might of business monopolies. Through increased social expenditures, the Danish government promoted a higher standard of living and a new degree of equality. This established the basis in the post-World War II period for the Scandinavian countries to take the lead in converting "women's rights" into "parents' rights," by reorganizing the workplace to allow men a greater share in home and family responsibilities, and by amending the maternity leave policy to permit fathers time off for infant care. Few men, however, take advantage of these opportunities to transcend sex role divisions.

Mobilizing Again for War: Women, Mothers, and Work

Europe could not avoid another war, because right from the very start the Nazi regime in Germany was bent on aggression. It solved the unemployment crisis by embarking on a massive rearmament program and its response to social tensions was the call for territorial aggrandizement *(Lebensraum),* not internal social and welfare reform. By 1936, however, the regime faced a dilemma, which grew in magnitude as the country embarked on war in September 1939. There was a labor shortage for heavy industrial work and the most obvious source of new recruitment was the married woman who had been encouraged to stay home. Would ideology or economics prevail? Would the regime channel married women into industrial jobs and later war work? The Nazi government was sensitive to what it thought popular opinion wanted. It believed that its ideological stance on women reflected the views of most German families; and, later, it strongly felt that men would fight harder if they knew their wives were not working long hours in munitions and other factories. In stark contrast to Britain, or America, or the Germany of World War I, the Nazi regime took only ineffective measures to mobilize women for the war effort. It made up the shortfall by conscripting laborers from the eastern and western territories it had conquered and transporting them to factories in Germany as forced labor and by exploitation of the inmates in concentration camps.

In contrast, the governments of England and America worked hard to ensure that women did their part for the war effort. The British adopted compulsory registration of women in March 1941, after it was clear that an enormous labor power shortage was developing. From December 1941 onward, women were selectively conscripted into industry, administration, and the armed forces, although British officials favored voluntary compliance and only used compulsion as a last resort. By 1943, it was impossible for a woman under forty years of age to avoid war work; in September of that year, all women under 51 years were required to register. Between September 1939 and May 1942, the number of British women in industry alone increased by 1.1 million; by 1943 there were 1.5 million women in the engineering trade, whereas prior to the war their numbers had been minuscule.

The results were similar in the United States, although the government did not institute civilian conscription but rather embarked on an ambitious propaganda campaign and relied on high wages to sell war work to women. The mass press was particularly important in this effort. The government's main channel of communication with the media was the Office of War Information (OWI), which put out a *Magazine War Guide* informing publishers and writers about the themes that Washington agencies considered useful to the war effort: democracy's struggle, the attitudes of good Americans, the importance of meeting production goals. The OWI was deeply involved in the move to recruit women into the labor force, particularly into prewar male jobs that were short of workers. Magazines were encouraged to publish romances in which women who entered defense industries found fulfillment and the admiration of desirable men in performing such important work for the nation. They changed the typical prewar fiction story that described irreconcilable tensions between marriage and career to show how married women in war work successfully combined both family and labor responsibilities. The recruitment strategy varied by class. For example, magazines like the *Saturday Evening Post,* which had a middle-class readership, invariably depicted working women in positions of leadership over male subordinates, making courageous and timely decisions. Middle-class women needed to be persuaded to take the step down the social ladder and enter the blue-collar work world, which had less status than their own middle-class lifestyle. Female authority maintained middle-class superiority, despite the loss of status. By contrast, the tales in *True Story,* read by working-class people, rarely showed women in nontraditional positions or those that carried authority. Its readers in real life were unlikely to be found in management roles or professional jobs; also, such portrayal might place working-class women in a position to compete with working-class men. Rather, the themes encouraged working-class women to identify with and be proud of the important contributions of their class. These differences aside, the portrayal of women's war work made it clear that women were not intended to become a permanent part of the labor force. The American symbol of war work, Rosie the Riveter, proved she could do the job but everyone knew that she was working "only for the duration." [23] Despite the intended message, however, there is some indication that in the United States—if not the other belligerent nations—the war experience was an important one for *married* and *older* women. After the war, to be sure, women once again were shifted to low-skilled and traditional female jobs. But more and more married women would find a permanent place in the labor force.

European Reconstruction

The European war came to a close with the fall of Berlin in May 1945. Germany lay in ruins, occupied by the four victor powers of the United States, the Soviet

Union, France, and Britain. The Allied policy of unconditional surrender had meant a land and air battle to the finish. This war, as all wars, took a heavy toll on male life. Population figures for Germany tell part of the story, and their impact on social relations lasted long after the physical scars of war were removed by the rebuilding of demolished cities. Death claimed 3.7 million German soldiers during the Second World War; another 11.7 million were confined in prisoner-of-war camps in 1945. After the war, there were 1717 women for every 1000 men in Berlin; in the 1950s the ratio was 1353 to 1000, and over one-third of all West Berlin households were headed by a woman. It is hardly surprising that before reestablishment of central government in 1949 much of the work of daily survival lay in women's hands. Berliners tell of female communities and solidarities, of great ingenuity in mastering the arts of barter in the black market, and of endless waiting in lines for food or official papers. Small subsistence gardens sprang up in every nook and cranny, and women grew a variety of foodstuffs for their own family's use as well as for exchange. They took all manner of makeshift jobs. With the return of men came a return to "normalcy." The family of husband, wife, and children reemerged as the norm of private living, and females who headed households (widows with children) were mislabeled "single." Dwellings in new government-subsidized apartment buildings were often reserved for the normative family. When wage labor was reestablished, after being subordinated to exchange through barter in the period of occupation, differentials by sex reappeared.

With economic recovery, however, a significant change took place in the character of women's gainful employment in Europe as well as in the United States. Service jobs continued to expand, outpacing employment options in industry and opening up the largest area of new positions for women. Most striking, *married* women's employment rose to levels unparalleled during any previous period of Western industrial development. This reversed the trend of the beginning of the twentieth century, when even lower-class wives were staying at home if the collective income of their households (from husbands and children) was sufficient to permit them to do so. In the post-1945 period, if the household needed added income or had targeted a special goal such as a better home or a longer vacation, the mother, rather than her children, went out to work. Table 2 captures these changing patterns that reflected new aspirations for families in the United States. Comprising less than one-sixth of the female labor force around the turn of the century, by 1970 married women made up two-thirds of the female work force, accounting for 40 percent of all married women in the country. A similar rise in married women's employment has also occurred in Western European countries in the post-World War II period. Between 1963 and 1975, the labor force participation rate of married women in Sweden increased from 47 percent to 66 percent; in the same years in West Germany it rose from 33 to 39 percent.[24] In part, the postwar trend expresses the more important role of continuing education in family calculations; parents of all classes now want their children to spend considerably more time in school, including technical or university training. In addition, a growing number of divorces, beginning particularly in the 1960s and 1970s, has pushed married women with small children back into the work force; it has forced older women to search for jobs in a market still geared to the sex appeal of youth.

TABLE 2.   Marital Status of Women in the Civilian Labor Force in the United States,
1890–1970

	Percent Distribution of Female Labor Force			Female Labor Force as Percentage of Female Population		
	Single	Married	WW**	Single	Married	WW
1890	68.2	13.9	17.9	40.5	4.6	29.9
1900	66.2	15.4	18.4	43.5	5.6	32.5
1910*	60.2	24.9	15.0	51.1	10.7	10.7
1930	53.9	28.9	17.2	50.5	11.7	34.4
1940	49.0	35.9	15.0	45.5	15.6	30.2
1950	31.9	52.2	16.0	46.3	23.0	32.7
1960	23.6	60.7	15.7	42.9	31.7	36.1
1970	22.5	62.3	15.0	50.9	40.2	36.8

*Data unavailable for 1920.
**WW = widowed or divorced.
SOURCE: U.S. Department of Commerce. Bureau of the Census, *Historical Statistics of the United States: Colonial Times to 1970*. Part 1 (Washington, DC, 1975), Series D 49–62, p. 133.

While once it was thought that the emergence of women's movements in the 1960s in the West "caused" the growth in women's labor participation, the reverse probably is more correct. As more women went into the labor force, the strains and stresses associated with balancing work and family responsibilities provided the context for the reemergence of concern with the woman question. The conflict between individual and social concerns strikes hard at the working mother.

Socialist countries have even higher proportions of women in gainful employment than do Western Europe and the United States. According to the national census of 1970, 92.5 percent of all adult women held jobs in the Soviet Union. Comparable figures for Western European nations in the same year were 48 percent in France and West Germany, nearly 30 percent in Italy, almost 60 percent in Sweden, and 50 percent in the United Kingdom. In addition, nearly 50 percent of all women between 15 and 64 years were gainfully employed in the United States. More than Western Europe and the United States, the industrial development of the Soviet Union relied heavily on female labor; the leisured housewife was not an accepted social alternative. The Soviet development pattern originated from a mix of necessity and ideology. Huge numbers of men died in the two world wars (in the Second World War alone, about 20 million Russian soldiers lost their lives). Furthermore, the country faced innumerable deaths at the time of the Great Civil War (1918–1920) and paid a high price in human life for its collectivization of agriculture and rapid industrialization after 1928. Soviet Russia had to rely on the labor of women for its push to become a modern, industrial society. Between 1928 and 1975 the female labor force in the Soviet Union grew from 2.8 million to 53.7, representing an increase from 24 to 51.5 percent of all industrial, clerical, and service workers.[25] At the same time, the socialist leadership has acknowledged the importance of integrating women into wage labor outside their private households. There are also high rates of female labor participation in other Eastern European countries.

It is a common interpretation in the noncommunist West that women in socialist nations such as the Soviet Union or East Germany are "doubly burdened." Nearly all adult women work long hours for wages outside the home but, because socialist society has failed to challenge traditional family sex role divisions, they are nearly solely responsible for running the home. In addition, with production goals determined by the state rather than the market, women have insufficient labor-saving devices to ease the burdens of housework, and due to shortages of consumer goods, must spend far more time shopping than their counterparts in the West. Furthermore, while pay differentials by sex are not as pronounced as in the noncommunist West, women tend to be overrepresented in many of the low-skilled and poorly paid jobs.

Not enough attention, however, has been given to how *women* in socialist societies perceive their work day and evaluate their own lives. Maria-Barbara Watson-Franke, an anthropologist, offers a new look into the question of altered female consciousness in the German Democratic Republic (Chapter 13). She argues that Western analysts inappropriately have projected onto socialist societies a typically liberal concept of the self that stresses individualism and autonomy as well as individual self-determination. Her study shows that in the East German society "woman's space" has expanded because of the widespread participation of females in gainful labor. Women have taken into the work force the values of intimacy, responsibility, and social connectedness that have developed out of their family lives and social experiences.

Contemporary Currents

By the 1980s, in both the socialist and nonsocialist countries of the West, the woman question once again stood at a center stage of public discussion. From very different traditions and contexts, many women had come to disquieting conclusions about their lives. In the decade of the 1960s, public concern in Europe and the United States about the Vietnam War, student protest movements on both sides of the Atlantic, civil rights riots in American cities, a general strike in France, combined to produce a heightened sense of alienation among the younger generations. Many young Germans were disturbed by the materialism of their parents and their complicity in, and silence about, the Nazi past. Youth in France and the United States attacked bureaucracies that seemed too rigid to respond to their needs. These protest movements in Western Europe and America provided the context for the founding of new women's movements. In New York City, tens of thousands of women marched on August 26, 1970, in celebration of the fiftieth anniversary of the suffrage amendment. In France, in the same year, women achieved public notice at a demonstration at the Tomb of the Unknown Soldier by laying down a wreath dedicated to the one who was more unknown than the soldier—his wife. Dormant feminist movements reawakened in many countries of the Western world. The socialist countries have not allowed the formation of autonomous women's movements; their systems of single party rule preclude independent political action. Nonetheless debate is occurring at the workplace, in the underground press, and in fictional literature, about ways and means to improve women's situation.

What is remarkable about contemporary feminist thought is an apparent convergence of views. Feminist writers and thinkers in both the West and the East have moved beyond the conception of woman as "the Other." In a highly influential work in 1949, Simone de Beauvoir had argued that under patriarchy women were defined by their differences from men; throughout history, attitudes and institutions based on these biological differences had constrained them to second-class status. For her pioneering role in the renaissance of mid-twentieth century feminism, Beauvoir has been likened to Mary Wollstonecraft. Called the "thinking woman's woman," she took an active role in the French women's movement of the 1970s and she is known to women everywhere.[26] After several decades of discussion and debate, feminist thought in socialist and nonsocialist countries has come to reevaluate the differences, seeing, for example, the social and cooperative values associated with women as opposed to individual and competitive values attributed to men as a source of women's strengths.

Women's liberation movements, however, face challenges in the last decades of the twentieth century. As this book has shown, the effort to transform public and private lives along lines of greater sex equality has not followed a simple, linear progression, nor will it in the future. The absence of a viable, independent women's movement in socialist countries is a liability, and the decline of the birthrate in the labor-short countries of Eastern Europe and the Soviet Union may encourage governments to adopt pronatalist policies that infringe on women's rights. In the United States, the Equal Rights Amendment has not passed as of 1986 and feminist gains have provoked considerable backlash, astutely orchestrated by the Moral Majority and other ultra-conservatives. The status of many women has declined, due to restrictions on social welfare programs created by the liberal state. Some well-educated women, however, have attained new access to high levels in government, business, and education. They may serve to improve the chances for other women in the future. It appeared in 1981 that women had made a significant breakthrough in France. After a majority of women voted for and helped elect the socialist François Mitterrand to the Presidency, he reciprocated by creating a Ministry of Women's Rights, headed first by Yvette Roudy. But the socialist government has not been able to realize its program of job creation, growth, nationalization and the redistribution of wealth. To the extent that socialism is called into question in France, so might its ally, feminism. History rarely produces clear-cut, permanent victories of an ideology, a party, or a movement. But if women, strengthened by the knowledge of their own past, actively participate in the debates and issues of the day, they will directly shape the future course of history.

NOTES

1. Louise A. Tilly and Joan W. Scott, *Women, Work, and Family* (New York, 1978); Ann Douglas, *The Feminization of American Culture* (New York, 1977).
2. Susan Bachrach, *Dames Employées: The Feminization of Postal Work in Nineteenth-*

Century France (New York, 1984), pp. 61, 119 n. 19; Persis Hunt, "Teachers and Workers: Problems of Feminist Organizing in the Early Third Republic," *Third Republic/Troisième République*, nos. 3–4 (1977), pp. 168–204; James F. McMillan, *Housewife or Harlot: The Place of Women in French Society, 1870–1940* (New York, 1981), p. 55; Linda L. Clark, *Schooling the Daughters of Marianne* (Albany, 1984), p. 73; Lee Holcombe, *Victorian Ladies at Work: Middle-Class Working Women in England and Wales, 1850–1914* (Hamden, CT, 1973), p. 46.

3. Susan Strasser, *Never Done: A History of American Housework* (New York, 1982), pp. 67–84; Rosalind H. Williams, *Dream Worlds: Mass Consumption in Late Nineteenth-Century France* (Berkeley, 1982), pp. 58, 65.

4. Lenard R. Berlanstein, *The Working People of Paris, 1871–1914* (Baltimore, 1984), p. 141.

5. John E. Knodel, *The Decline of Fertility in Germany, 1871–1939* (Princeton, 1974), pp. 246–247; Angus McLaren, *Birth Control in Nineteenth-Century England* (New York, 1978), p. 11; Karen Offen, "Depopulation, Nationalism, and Feminism in Fin-de-Siècle France," *American Historical Review* 89, no. 3 (June 1984): 649–652.

6. Jill Liddington and Jill Norris, *One Hand Tied Behind Us: The Rise of the Women's Suffrage Movement* (London, 1978), pp. 136–137; Amy Hackett, "The German Women's Movement and Suffrage, 1890–1914: A Study of National Feminism," in Robert J. Bezucha, ed., *Modern European Social History* (Lexington, MA, 1972), pp. 354–379; Steven C. Hause with Anne R. Kenney, *Women's Suffrage and Social Politics in the French Third Republic* (Princeton, 1984); Eleanor Flexner, *Century of Struggle: The Woman's Rights Movement in the United States* (Cambridge, 1959); Ellen Carol Dubois, *Feminism and Suffrage: The Emergence of an Independent Women's Movement in America 1848–1869* (Ithaca, 1978).

7. Marilyn J. Boxer and Jean H. Quataert, eds., *Socialist Women: European Socialist Feminism in the Nineteenth and Early Twentieth Centuries* (New York, 1978); Jean H. Quataert, *Reluctant Feminists in German Social Democracy 1885–1917* (Princeton, 1979); Dolores Hayden, *The Grand Domestic Revolution: A History of Feminist Designs for American Homes, Neighborhoods and Cities* (Cambridge, 1981).

8. Temma Kaplan, "On the Socialist Origins of International Women's Day," *Feminist Studies* 11, no. 1 (Spring 1985): 163–171.

9. Jennifer G. Schirmer, *The Limits of Reform: Women, Capital, and Welfare* (Cambridge, 1982); Elizabeth Wilson, *Women and the Welfare State* (London, 1977).

10. Cheri Register, "Motherhood at Center: Ellen Key's Social Vision," *Women's Studies International Forum* 5, no. 6 (1982): 599–610.

11. Richard J. Evans, *The Feminist Movement in Germany 1894–1933* (London, 1976), pp. 120–130, 178–182; McLaren, *Birth Control*, pp. 141–154, 188.

12. Diane Bell, "Women's Business is Hard Work: Central Australian Aboriginal Women's Love Rituals," *Signs* 7, no. 2 (1981): 314–337.

13. In Leslie Fishbein, "The Failure of Feminism in Greenwich Village before World War I," *Women's Studies* 9, no. 2 (1982): 281.

14. Fritz Stern, *The Politics of Cultural Despair: A Study in the Rise of the Germanic Ideology* (New York, 1965), pp. 256–257.

15. Susan Groag Bell and Karen M. Offen, eds., *Women, the Family, and Freedom: The Debate in Documents,* II: 1880–1950 (Stanford, 1983): 271–272.

16. Barbara Evans Clements, "Working-Class and Peasant Women in the Russian Revolution, 1917–1923," *Signs* 8, no. 2 (1982): 215–235.

17. McMillan, *Housewife or Harlot*, pp. 191–192.

18. Bell and Offen, *Women, Family, Freedom,* II, p. 310.

19. Renate Bridenthal, "Beyond 'Kinder, Küche, Kirche': Weimar Women at Work," *Central European History* VI, no. 2 (June 1973): 148–166; Tim Mason, "Women in Germany, 1925–1940: Family, Welfare and Work," Parts I and II, *History Workshop* (Spring 1976 and Autumn 1976), pp. 74–113; pp. 5–32.

20. Renate Bridenthal, "Class Struggle around the Hearth: Women and Domestic Service in the Weimar Republic," in Michael N. Dobkowski and Isidor Walliman, eds., *Towards the Holocaust: The Social and Economic Collapse of the Weimar Republic* (Westport, CT, 1983), pp. 243–264.

21. Gisela Bock, "Racism and Sexism in Nazi Germany: Motherhood, Compulsory Sterilization, and the State," *Signs* 8, no. 3 (1983): 400–421; Renate Bridenthal, Atina Grossmann and Marion Kaplan, eds., *When Biology Became Destiny: Women in Weimar and Nazi Germany* (New York, 1984).

22. In Shari Steiner, *The Female Factor: A Study of Women in Five Western European Societies* (New York, 1977), p. 245.

23. Leila J. Rupp, *Mobilizing Women for War: German and American Propaganda, 1939–1945* (Princeton, 1978), p. 181; Maureen Honey, "The Working-Class Woman and Recruitment Propaganda during World War II: Class Differences in the Portrayal of War Work," *Signs* 8, no. 4 (1983): 672–687.

24. Mary Kinnear, *Daughters of Time: Women in the Western Tradition* (Ann Arbor, 1982), p. 180.

25. Gail Warshofsky Lapidus, ed., *Women, Work, and Family in the Soviet Union* (New York, 1982); "Comparative International Statistics," No. 1519, *Statistical Abstract of the United States* (Washington, 1984), p. 872.

26. Simone de Beauvoir, *The Second Sex,* tr. by H. M. Parshley (New York, 1953, orig. 1949); Hester Eisenstein, *Contemporary Feminist Thought* (Boston, 1983).

10

Prostitution, Differentiation, and the World Economy: Nairobi 1899–1939

Luise White

With European industrialization, imperialism, and the rush for colonies in the second half of the nineteenth century, the focus of Western history must necessarily broaden to areas outside of Europe. The political and economic situation in much of the rest of the world was profoundly influenced by the rise of the West and by European military and technological superiority. And it has created a cruel dilemma that is of crucial significance to Third World countries: how to appropriate the fruits of industry, science, and technology, and at the same time preserve the unique values, culture, and ways of life of the particular nation.

Luise White takes us outside Europe to Kenya, a British colony in East Africa, in the first third of the twentieth century. The rural population was already differentiated into "rich and poor and everything in between" and was facing continuous pressures as a result of increased white settlements, crop failures, cattle diseases, and the introduction of cash crops into the countryside. Prostitution in Nairobi was one response by daughters to a sudden decline in the economic fortunes of their wealthy families. The form it took was determined by the economic needs. One of White's most innovative points is that sexuality is not just a "personal and private matter" but can be shaped by forces other than personal desire. It is best described "by the language of family and kin." Prostitutes worked as daughters, accumulating for their fathers what they had been unable to do through the more traditional method of marriage. Prostitution, therefore, is not marginal or aberrant, but economically rational behavior, as the Frenchman Dr. Louis Villerme recognized in his 1847–1848 study, when he labeled it "the fifth quarter" of women's day.

White's pathfinding study rests on oral interviews. Oral history is a rewarding approach for uncovering contemporary women's experiences, a corrective for biases and omissions in written texts. As White has noted elsewhere, "people are excellent chroniclers of their immediate past, however unheroic, illegal, or unpleasant that past might have been." She worked as well with more traditional historical documents in the archive of the colonial office, using fruitfully the records of the Medical Department, heir to records of the Contagious Diseases Act, that dealt with medical regulation of prostitution and housing.

We tend to think that sexual relations are personal and private matters. While we may read dozens of books advising us on how to achieve intimacy, we generally believe that decisions about who sleeps with whom, where, for how long, and under what kinds of encouragement are the results of passions so personal that they cannot be studied systematically. We believe this partly because we see matters such as sexual attraction and choosing a partner as timeless qualities, where choice is personal, so personal as to make any serious inquiry difficult, if not pointless. But how do we know what is personal and what is not? Perhaps if we look at those sexual relations that are the most furtive—conducted in alleys and doorways not because either party likes it better that way, but because those are the only spaces available for such acts—we can see people brought together by forces other than their personal desires. Perhaps we can begin to observe people who occasionally sleep together because of cattle diseases, falling food crop prices, and increased cash crop production.

In this essay I want to look at two forms of prostitution that developed in Nairobi, Kenya between 1899 and 1939. Both forms, or ways for women to conduct the sale of sexual access to themselves, emphasized brief sexual relations with customers rather than night-long fictions of matrimonial bliss, and both forms were known for the aggressiveness with which women sought their customers. All the labor forms, in Nairobi and presumably elsewhere, were determined by specific crises in rural society and the women's relationship to housing in the town. In Kenya there is no evidence, oral or written, of anything that could be even vaguely construed as pimping: when women prostitute themselves, they retain all their earnings. How a woman prostitutes herself—with which form—indicates the urgency with which she requires money. In Kenya the women who walked the streets (*watembezi* in Swahili, widely spoken in Nairobi) were precisely those women who took the pennies from sex conducted in doorways back to the stunted agricultural economies of East Africa, and enabled their families to recoup some of the losses the world economy had forced upon them. It was the women who quietly waited in their rooms for men to come to them (*malaya* in Swahili), the ones who provided the widest range of domestic services, including cooked food and bath water, and had the most discreet and circumspect of relationships, who accumulated capital for themselves, and most definitely not for their families.

Nairobi was founded in 1899 at the foot of the fertile highlands that were to be taken over by white settlers. Built around a swamp where no one had lived before, everyone who came there, black or white, female or male, was a migrant of some sort. Europeans came to settle because Kenya offered more opportunities than they might otherwise inherit in their homes; African men came because their inheritance was substantially delayed (by the untimely combination of natural disaster and European conquest), and because they were forced to do so. From 1902, a tax was levied on married men, payable in coin that could most easily be obtained by working for Europeans. Young African men were observed to work to pay their fathers' taxes (polygamous men had higher tax rates), and then work to enhance their own inheritance. They left the wage labor force once they married, and to secure a still larger supply of male laborers, in 1910 a tax was introduced on all males over 16.

Why did women come to Nairobi, and why did they become prostitutes? We know that they became prostitutes because there were simply no jobs for women then or in the next forty years. Some came to set themselves up as independent heads of households. "In those days," said one widow, "I didn't get another husband; there was another way to make a living then." Another woman said, "At home, what could I do? Grow crops for my husband and my father. In Nairobi, I could earn my own money, for myself." But most women came to help their families. By the end of the nineteenth century those families were primarily agriculturalists already differentiated into rich and poor and everything in between. In almost all those families women and livestock were the traditional elements of wealth, exchange, reproduction, and, of course, status. They could be exchanged for each other and they could reproduce more like themselves. They were integral elements in the cycle of family formation and they were at the same time investments. Thus, men with many wives could produce more daughters and grain with which to exchange for livestock, and young men would work for their fathers so that they would eventually be given the livestock with which to wed. The most valuable livestock was cattle, then sheep, then goats.

In the 1890s, a devastating series of cattle epidemics swept through Eastern Africa. By 1897, central Kenya was struck by drought, famine, and smallpox. It had the effect of turning the world (and its values) inside out—with as many as 60 percent of all the local cattle dead, famine devalued the remaining cattle and, indeed, everything but foodstuffs. Agriculturalists dominated, and men with many wives could find no one to marry their daughters and thus replenish their herds. Virtually an entire generation of wealthy men faced an end to their way of life. All the available evidence points to the fact that these men's dwindling status and wealth was restored and restocked by their daughters' prostitution. These women already knew that permanent sexual access to them had an exchange value; they simply transformed the location and control of the work so that they sold repeated sexual access to themselves to many men. Thus, as early as 1899 daughters of the hardest hit pastoralist people, by all accounts the Masai, were observed to be the "loose women" in Kenya's rudimentary townships, and by 1909 some 300 Masai *watembezi* prostitutes were arrested in Nairobi.

How do we know that these women were the daughters of wealthy fathers? How do we know they were not impoverished young women who sought through prostitution to better their own lives? First of all, we know that in the years before World War I, prostitutes earned roughly between four and eight times what male wage-earners did (partly due to the low value of the currency at that time), so that any rapid gains accruing to the older generation would almost have to have come from prostitutes' earnings. Secondly, we know because these women, the *watembezi,* left prostitution once the requisite number of livestock were acquired. Those women who came from impoverished households also came to Nairobi, and the best evidence I have indicates they and they alone became *malaya* prostitutes.

The pre-World War I interaction of the colonial state, the Masai, and other pastoral peoples provides an excellent example of a sequence of destocking, prostitution, and livestock acquisition. Masai herds were decimated in the epidemics of the 1890s and their economy seriously undermined; Masai women seem to have been active in prostitution even before Nairobi was established, and in the early years of this century they were said to dominate Nairobi prostitution. Meanwhile, pastoral peoples in western Kenya, an area largely unaffected by the cattle epidemics, raided British installations (see Figure 5). The British led Masai soldiers in punitive expeditions against the Kipsigis and Nandi, and by 1905 it was estimated that 55 percent of Nandi cattle had been taken to Nairobi. The Masai soldiers were paid in goats that they parlayed into cattle (at rates of about fifteen goats per cow), just as prostitutes' profits were invested in livestock. In 1911, when Masai herds were said to approach their nineteenth-century levels, there was a noticeable Masai retreat from prostitution and wage labor. By 1907, however, colonial officials began to observe an increasing number of Kipsigis and Nandi women entering prostitution, replacing the Masai women and accosting men on settlers' farms and on the streets of Nairobi. These women, too, were said to buy livestock with their earnings, at rates that were at least double what the Masai had

Figure 5. East Africa in 1905

paid, as white settlement brought about a demand for meat that slowly began to raise the value of cattle. According to contemporary male authors, by 1909 Nandi women were "notorious" throughout Kenya and by 1913 "the most enlightened" Nandi were those prostitutes who had returned home after a few years in Nairobi—presumably they knew the most English and belonged to the wealthiest families.

What were these women doing? They were doing through prostitution what in better times they would have done through marriage: stock their fathers' herd and keep livestock values competitive. They had to restore their fathers' property— cattle, not daughters—to its earlier level of prestige. That they were doing this in the streets, in alleys, loudly, aggressively, testifies to the urgency with which monies were required. For despite how disrespectful the *watembezi* form looked, despite its emphasis on brief sexual encounters in less than sensual surroundings, the means of accumulation was anything but disorderly: it was aggressive and swift by design; it matched high risks with high profits. It would then seem that anything more than occasional *watembezi* prostitution was not caused by dire poverty; it was the response of relatively wealthy families to a sudden decrease in their wealth. Young women became streetwalkers not as a survival strategy, but to help their families maintain previous levels of differentiation—and most of these women did not just survive, they prospered.

During World War I prostitution in Nairobi changed. The *watembezi* form still dominated, indeed it took on a revitalized dimension in pursuit of British and South African troops during the war, but its practitioners tended to be long-term residents of Nairobi, not immigrants from newly impoverished societies. "It was extra money, we went to pick beans and had a man in secret; sometimes a woman would go . . . just for the men," said a teenage woman who had been born in Nairobi. World War I *watembezi* were on the whole older than the young women who had sought men on the streets and back alleys of the prewar city. Wartime *watembezi* earned large sums, but they saved their cash or bought urban real estate. They could not have bought cattle with their earnings had they wanted to, so successfully had pastoralist fathers and daughters managed to reconstruct and reestablish the value of their herds.

Unlike pastoralists, many East African cultivators prospered from the events of the 1890s and the coming of colonial rule. Not only were they able to sell grain at exceptionally high rates of exchange to other Africans, they fed the European expansion into East Africa as well. Until World War I, African agriculturalists dominated local and export markets, and many of the Kikuyu farmers in central Kenya became wealthy. Until the ravages of military conscription during World War I and the rapidly increased white settlement after the war, the Kikuyu had sent relatively few sons into wage labor and fewer daughters into prostitution. The combined weight of white farmers' land-grabbing, and legislation introduced to prevent further white farmers' labor shortages, reduced many Kikuyu farmers to resident laborer status on European farms. Nevertheless, many Kikuyu "squatters" and cultivators on their own farms were able to produce and sell surplus crops. By the mid-1920s the increased production of maize and rice in other parts of the country began to erode the profits Kikuyu farmers could get for potatoes and millet in Nairobi. The price of potatoes, for example, had increased by 57 percent between 1924 and 1928 and the prices of other Kikuyu crops had risen as well: fewer people bought them. By 1928, both Kikuyu chiefs and *malaya* prostitutes in Nairobi complained about married Kikuyu women coming to town as if they were selling vegetables, but prostituting themselves with workingmen in the alleys of the African areas, and returning to their homes before dark. It seems very likely that these Kikuyu *watembezi* were not acting out of any immorality or personal insecurities; they were engaging in prostitution so that they could maintain the standard of living that only a few years before they had obtained solely through the sale of their farm produce. This *watembezi* prostitution was not about any preference for sex conducted in doorways and bushes, but about keeping a standard of living buoyant in the face of declining food profits.

Cattle diseases and state-sponsored destocking do not qualify as an incursion of the world economy into peoples' private lives. Rising crop prices are facts of life for farmers all over the world, and are not a unique characteristic of colonized peoples. To see how the world economy influences what we think of as intimate behavior, we have to look at those crops introduced specifically by colonial powers for the specific reason of making their colonies pay off: cash crops. Coffee, tea, cotton, sugar, and tobacco are a few examples. Among critics of imperialism, cash crops have an importance almost unmatched by any other colonial introduction: they are almost never edible crops; they take up arable land that might be better used for food crops; they are often produced on plantations and concentrate local labor in such a way as to remove people from food production. They are often produced at gunpoint. This list could go on for pages, but the most significant thing about cash crops is that they draw producers into a worldwide system of supply and profit and loss that is determined by conditions far outside the country producing the coffee, tea, or sugar. Unlike mining—the wholesale extraction of a country's wealth—cash crop production pits various countries' producers against each other. Coffee growers in Kenya do not compete with each other, they compete with coffee growers in Brazil and Colombia and Sumatra. The amount they pay their workers in each of these countries has nothing to do with how hard these men and women work; it has to do with the competitive value of their coffee crop relative to that of coffees produced thousands of miles away under different conditions. The only real influence local producers have on profit is quantity, but this can backfire when demand drops. In most colonies it was a crime for Africans to uproot their cash crops when prices were low and plant food crops instead. Some scholars have argued that cash crop production enabled Africans to resist the depredations of wage labor, but this argument fails to tell us what happens when the cash crop is not wanted, or is overproduced, or is deemed obsolete by the production of synthetics. The introduction of cash crops made African cultivators as dependent on the health and stability of world markets as they were on the rainfall.

It is this kind of dependence that determines not only who becomes a prostitute, but the duration of the services prostitutes provide. The process does not happen overnight, but it does happen with great clarity. In 1903 the German colonizers of what was to become Tanganyika (when it was handed over to the

British at the end of World War I) introduced coffee to the Haya people on the western shore of Lake Victoria, a thousand kilometers (600 miles) from the sea. They did not concentrate coffee in plantations, but gave some to every large farm. Before the War, coffee did well in the fertile hills of Bukoba, but it was not until the worldwide boom of the 1920s that Haya producers began to see spectacular profits. By the mid-1920s the wealthier Haya were almost heady with success; they hired laborers from the neighboring Belgian colonies to come pick their coffee and "squat" on their land, and as Christians they ceased exchanging their daughters for livestock and requested and received a cash bride-price, which by about 1927 was the equivalent of $175 or more. Unlike many African peoples, the Haya permitted divorce, and fathers returned the bride-price in full. Thus, in 1930 when the world price of coffee dropped a staggering 90 percent, Haya producers were in trouble; it was not even worth their while to ship their produce to the coast, but they had laborers living on their farms who demanded payment nonetheless. Although the problem lay in cash crop production, the solution was found in women. Young wives were divorced and fathers repaid the bride-price, shifting the problem back on themselves—a generation of fathers now had to come up with cash to repay their own increasing debts and refurbish the foundations of a sagging cash crop economy. How the decision to solve this problem was made within individual households is not known, but within two or three years Haya women in their early twenties appeared in large numbers on the streets of Kampala (Uganda), Dar es Salaam (Tanganyika), and Nairobi.

Haya women did not walk in the streets in these towns; instead they rented rooms in the African areas and sat outside their houses and solicited men from there. This was called the *Wazi-Wazi* form, from a slang term for Haya common in Nairobi. Haya women scandalized the more sedate and circumspect prostitutes of these areas, who saw such open solicitation and aggressive behavior as a threat to their respectability and their profits. Haya women were known for shouting out their prices to men, and they took these men into the four-by-eight foot rooms they shared with other Haya immigrants for brief sexual encounters, for which they received just about 17 percent of the world price of raw coffee beans. Between 1930 and 1935 the world price for a thirty-five-pound bag of coffee beans varied between three and seven shillings. In those same years, *Wazi-Wazi* prostitutes in Nairobi charged fifty cents—one half of one shilling—for sexual intercourse. *Malaya* women were justifiably upset since this had the overall effect of lowering the price for brief sexual relations for all prostitutes, at a time when most *malaya* prostitutes earned perhaps a third more than male laborers did. *Wazi-Wazi* prostitutes were also said to fight with the men who refused to pay them and call on their neighbors for help—practices unheard of by both *malaya* and *watembezi* women in 1930s Nairobi. An old woman born near Nairobi in about 1900 said that the biggest change she observed in her lifetime was that after the mid-1930s "women beat up men." According to a younger *malaya* woman, cash was so important to a Haya woman that she "would risk her blood to get her money." Indeed, it was so important to Haya women that they were reputed to send money home each week or month, and if a Haya woman died in Nairobi her friends would take her body and her money the hundreds of miles back to Bukoba. Why did Haya women do all this? Clearly because the advantages and opportunities of being a daughter of a well-to-do coffee-growing family outweighed the disadvantages of being a prostitute in Nairobi.

How did the colonial state respond to streetwalkers and *Wazi-Wazi* women? While it was not in the interests of public order that women be allowed to call out a price to men as they returned from work, there were few arrests of *watembezi* prostitutes in colonial Nairobi, and none of Haya women. More than any other kind of political entity, colonial states do not act with one voice, let alone motivation; they mediate between different and competing interests—the government at home, the settlers it must protect, the African leaders who make ruling easier, and the Africans who must be made to work in colonial enterprises, but in ways that do not antagonize any of the groups above. Although we might think that no state encourages prostitution, these particular interest groups had nothing against it. In Nairobi and other cities, the presence of prostitutes and the amenities and cooked food they sometimes offered, made the task of getting urban Africans back to work day after day somewhat easier. It also reduced African wages just enough to keep them at work a few months longer than they otherwise would have stayed. Moreover, the colonial police were busy with the Africans the state made into criminals, those Africans who broke the law by spending more than a month looking for work in Nairobi, or leaving an employer before their labor contract had expired. The state knew about Haya and *watembezi* women, but found them more of a service than an offense. The values of accumulation and entrepreneurship subsidized solid, Christian, patriarchal households on the western shore of Lake Victoria and helped extend the laboring time of hundreds of badly needed unskilled African workers in Nairobi.

No new forms of prostitution emerged after 1939. While the *watembezi* form dominated World War II prostitution, it did so under special circumstances, only some of which could be identified as young women's family labor. That no new forms emerged after the mid-1930s is especially significant, and may well mark a point of transition in East African agricultural history. The biggest change in African colonial history has nothing to do with barbarism and civilization, nothing to do with tribe and nation. It has to do with a transition around the issue of Africans' participation in wage labor. In most of Africa in the era before World War II, wage labor was a means by which Africans could supplement their farm production. It was not something they relied on solely for their subsistence. The monies earned working enhanced farming, however unwillingly and hesitantly that labor was originally undertaken. By World War II, in those areas where most men were migrant laborers, wage labor became the means by which most people subsisted, and farming itself was dependent on the cash migrant laborers brought home. So atrophied were the agricultural systems of these parts of Africa that women farmers could not plant maize or cotton or beans unless their husbands, working on tea estates in Kenya or the docks of East Africa, sent them the money to buy seeds—even subsistence required an assist from wage labor. These areas also sent a steady stream of prostitutes to towns, but they went as independent accumulators, not as daughters bailing their families out of trouble. Elsewhere, African agriculture took off in ways that colonialists had not full expected—and in fact were to complain about—and these families did not have daughters who became prostitutes. That no new forms of prostitution emerged after 1939 testifies to the impoverishment of the poorest peasant households; they continued to have crises, but they no longer attempted to solve them—if they could be solved at all—from within the family.

Note: Virtually all the information in this essay comes from my unpublished Ph.D. thesis, "A History of Prostitution in Nairobi, Kenya, c. 1900–1952" (Cambridge University, 1985) which, in turn, was based primarily on 170 interviews conducted with women who had been prostitutes in Nairobi between about 1909 and 1960, and twenty-six men who had visited prostitutes between 1917 and 1960; these interviews were conducted by myself and my assistants, Paul Kakaire and Margaret Makuna, without whom the research would have been impossible.

SUGGESTIONS FOR FURTHER READING

Bujra, Janet M. "Women 'Entrepreneurs' of Early Nairobi." *Canadian Journal of African Studies* IX, 2 (1975): 213–234.

Cooper, Frederick. *From Slaves to Squatters: Plantation Labor and Agriculture in Zanzibar and Coastal Kenya, 1890–1925.* New Haven, 1980.

Hay, Margaret Jean and Sharon Stichter, eds. *African Women South of the Sahara.* London, 1984.

Mwangi, Meja. *Going Down River Road.* London, 1977.

Petrik, Paula. "Capitalists with Rooms: Prostitution in Helena, Montana, 1865–1900." *Montana: The Magazine of Western History* 31 (1981): 28–41.

Vail, Leroy and Landeg White. " 'Tiwani, Machambero!' Forced Cotton and Rice Growing on the Zambezi." *Journal of African History* 19 (1978): 239–263.

van Onselen, Charles. "Prostitutes and Proletarians." *Studies in the Social and Economic History of Witwatersrand,* I, *New Babylon.* New York, 1982.

Walkowitz, Judith R. *Prostitution and Victorian Society.* Cambridge, 1980.

White, Luise. "A Colonial State and an African Petty Bourgeoisie." In Frederick Cooper, ed. *Struggle for the City: Migrant Labor, Capital, and the State in Urban Africa.* Beverly Hills, 1983, pp. 165–191.

———. "Prostitution, Identity, and Consciousness in Nairobi during World War II." *Signs* 11, no. 2 (1986).

11

Soldier's Heart:
Literary Men, Literary Women,
and the Great War

Sandra M. Gilbert

From the ancient Greeks on, the theme of war has figured prominently in Western historiography, but as is true of the historical tradition generally, the literature saw war mainly from the male perspective. This is changing now, as women's historians and literary critics take up the topic. Sandra Gilbert's chapter on the Great War—World War I—is an excellent case in point. As Gilbert shows, the war functioned in many ways to liberate women, but "ended up emasculating [men], depriving them of autonomy, confining them as closely as any Victorian women had been confined." This unusually sensitive study of "war images" is based on literary fiction, the poems and novels of male modernist writers like D. H. Lawrence and Ernest Hemingway, and the works of female authors like Radclyffe Hall, Alice Meynell, Madeline Ida Bedford, and Virginia Woolf. Literary fiction and poetry are excellent sources for reconstructing an historic era. The fiction of a period reflects the prevailing spirit of the times, for the authors themselves were eyewitnesses to what was going on. As artists, they were particularly sensitive to underlying social and sexual tensions and had the creative power to express them. We could even say that in the days before psychology developed as an academic "discipline," writers were society's major interpersonal and social psychologists. They dealt with themes like eroticism between men and men and women and women, which polite society handled only with great restraint. In their work, Sandra Gilbert, a literary critic, uncovers a true "battle of the sexes" that accompanied the battles of the Great War. These tensions, furthermore, directly fed into the mood of anxiety, self-doubt, and intensified misogynist resentment which, "in the words of Rebecca West, was 'strikingly the correct fashion . . . among . . . the intellectuals' " in the postwar period.

*This chapter is an abbreviated version of an article by the same title that appeared in *Signs: Journal of Women in Culture and Society* 8, no. 3 (1983): 422–450. We thank Sandra M. Gilbert for her willingness to help revise and shorten it. Full citations are in the *Signs* article. We thank the University of Chicago Press. Copyright © 1983 by the University of Chicago. All rights reserved.

As we have all been told over and over again, World War I was not just the war to end wars; it was also the war of wars, a paradigm of technological combat which, with its trenches and zeppelins, its gases and mines, has become a diabolical summary of the idea of modern warfare—Western science bent to the service of Western imperialism. That this apocalyptic Great War involved strikingly large numbers of men as well as shockingly powerful technological forces, moreover, has always been understood to intensify its historical significance. The first modern war to employ now familiar techniques of conscription and classification in order to create gigantic armies on both sides, World War I, as we have all been taught, virtually completed the Industrial Revolution's construction of anonymous dehumanized man, that impotent cipher who is frequently thought to be the twentieth century's most characteristic citizen. Helplessly entrenched on the edge of No Man's Land, this faceless being saw that the desert between him and his so-called enemy was not just a metaphor for the technology of death and the death dealt by technology, it was also a symbol for the state, whose nihilistic machinery he was powerless to control or protest. Fearfully assaulted by a deadly bureaucracy on the one side, and a deadly technocracy on the other, he was No Man, an inhabitant of the inhumane new era and a citizen of the unpromising new land into which this war of wars had led him.

Of course, as we have also been taught, these many dark implications of World War I had further implications for twentieth-century literature. From D. H. Lawrence's paralyzed Clifford Chatterley to Ernest Hemingway's sadly emasculated Jake Barnes to T. S. Eliot's mysteriously sterile Fisher King, the gloomily bruised modernist antiheroes churned out by the war suffer specifically from sexual wounds, as if, having traveled literally or figuratively through No Man's Land, all have become not just No Men, nobodies, but *not* men, *un*men. That twentieth-century Everyman, the faceless cipher, their authors seem to suggest, is not just publicly powerless, he is privately impotent.

Obviously, however, such effects of the Great War were in every case gender-specific problems, problems only men could have. Never having had public power, women could hardly become more powerless than they already were. As for private impotence, most late Victorian young girls were trained to see such "passionlessness" as a virtue rather than a failure. Yet women, too, lived through these years, and many modernistic writers seem to suggest that, oddly enough, women played an unusually crucial part in the era. In D. H. Lawrence's 1915 "Eloi, Eloi, Lama Sabacthani," for instance—a representative, if somewhat feverish, wartime poem—the unmanning terrors of combat lead not just to a generalized sexual anxiety but also to a sexual anger directed specifically against the female, as if the Great War itself were primarily a climactic episode in some battle of the sexes that had already been raging for years. Drawing upon the words Christ cried out as he died on the cross, the creator of Clifford Chatterley here presents the war metaphorically as a perverse sexual relationship that becomes a blasphemous (homo)sexual crucifixion. As battle rages and death attacks, the speaker assumes, in turn, the terrifying roles of rapist and victim, deadly groom and dying bride. Lawrence's perversely revisionary primal scene is made even more terrible, however, by the voyeuristic eyes of a woman who peers "through the rents / In the purple veil'' and peeps ''in the empty house like a pilferer.'' Like the gaze of the Medusa, her look seems somehow responsible for male sufferings.

Can this be because the war, with its deathly parody of sexuality, somehow suggests female conquest? Because wives, mothers, and sweethearts were safe on the home front, did the war appear in some peculiar sense their fault, a ritual of sacrifice to their victorious femininity? Through a paradox that is at first almost incomprehensible, the war that has traditionally been defined as an apocalypse of masculinism seems here to have led to an apotheosis of femaleness. If we reflect upon this point, however, we must inevitably ask a set of questions about the relations between the sexes during this war of wars. What part, after all, *did* women play in the Great War? How did men perceive that role? More specifically, what connections might there be between the wartime activities of women and the sense of sexual wounding that haunts so many male modernist texts? Most importantly, did women themselves experience the wound of the war in the same way that their sons and lovers did?

If we meditate for a while on the sexual implications of the Great War, we must certainly decide, to begin with, that it is a classic case of dissonance between official, male-centered history and unofficial female history. For not only did the apocalyptic events of this war have a very different meaning for men and women, such events were in fact very different for men and women, a point understood almost at once by an involved contemporary like Vera Brittain, who noted about her relationship with her soldier fiancé that the war put ''a barrier of indescribable experience between men and the women whom they loved.'' The nature of the barrier thrust between Brittain and her fiancé, however, may have been even more complex than she herself realized, for the impediment preventing a marriage of their true minds was constituted, as we shall see, not only by his altered experience but by hers. Specifically, I will argue here that as young men became increasingly alienated from their prewar selves, increasingly immured in the muck and blood of No Man's Land, women seemed to become, as if by some uncanny swing of history's pendulum, ever more powerful. As nurses, as mistresses, as munitions workers, bus drivers, or soldiers in the ''land army,'' even as wives and mothers, these formerly subservient creatures began to loom malevolently larger, until it was possible for a visitor to London to observe in 1918 that ''England was a world of women—women in uniforms,'' or, in the words of a verse by Nina Macdonald, ''Girls are doing things / They've never done before . . . All the world is topsy-turvy / Since the War began.''

''All the World is topsy-turvy / Since the War Began''; that phrase is a crucial one, for the reverses and reversals of No Man's Land fostered in a number of significant ways the formation of a metaphorical country not unlike the queendom Charlotte Perkins Gilman called Herland, and the exhilaration (along with anxiety) of that state is as dramatically rendered in wartime poems, stories, and memoirs by women, as are the very different responses to the war in usually better-known works by men. Sometimes subtly and subversively, sometimes quite explicitly, writers from Alice Meynell to Radclyffe Hall explored the political and economic revolution by which the Great War at least temporarily dispossessed male citizens of the patriarchal primacy that had always been their birthright while granting

women access to both the votes and the professions that they had never possessed. Similarly, a number of these artists covertly or overtly celebrated the release of female desires. In addition, many women writers recorded drastic (re)visions of society that were also, directly or indirectly, inspired by the revolutionary state in which they were living. For, as Virginia Woolf put it in a crucial passage from *Three Guineas,* "So profound was [the] unconscious loathing" of the daughters of educated (and uneducated) men for "the education" in oppression which all women had received, that while most "consciously desired [the advancement of] 'our splendid Empire,' " many "unconsciously desired" the apocalypse of "our splendid war."

Not surprisingly, however, the words as well as the deeds of these women reinforced their male contemporaries' sense that "All the world is topsy-turvy / Since the war began" and thus intensified the misogynist resentment with which male writers defined this Great War as an apocalyptic turning point in the battle of the sexes. Not surprisingly either, therefore, the sexual gloom expressed by so many men as well as the sexual glee experienced by so many women ultimately triggered profound feelings of guilt in a number of women: to the guilt of the female survivor with her fear that "a barrier of indescribable experience" had been thrust between the sexes, there was often added a half-conscious fear that the woman survivor might be in an inexplicable way a perpetrator of some unspeakable crime. Thus, the invigorating sense of revolution, release, reunion, and re-vision with which the war paradoxically imbued so many women eventually darkened into reactions of anxiety and self-doubt as Herland and No Man's Land merged to become the Nobody's Land T. S. Eliot was to call "death's dream kingdom."

From the first, World War I fostered characteristically modernist irony in young men, inducting them into "death's dream kingdom" by revealing exactly how spurious were their visions of heroism, and—by extension—history's images of heroism. Mobilized and marched off to the front, idealistic soldiers soon found themselves *im*mobilized, even buried alive, in trenches of death that seemed to have been dug along the remotest margins of civilization. Here, all the traditional categories of experience through which the rational cultured mind achieves its hegemony over the irrationality of nature were grotesquely mingled, polluting each other as if in some Swiftian fantasy. From now on, their only land was No Man's Land, a land that was *not,* a country of the impossible and the paradoxical. As Robert Graves notes, "The average life expectancy of an infantry subaltern on the Western Front was, at some stages of the War, only about three months," so that a universal sense of doom, often manifesting itself as a *desire* for death, forced the wild man soldier to ask, with the speaker of one of D. H. Lawrence's poems, "Am I lost? / Has death set me apart / Beforehand? / Have I crossed / That border? / Have I nothing in this dark land?" (see Figure 6).

With no sense of inherited history to lose, on the other hand, women in the terrible war years of 1914–18 would seem to have had, if not everything, at least something to gain: a place in public history, a chance even to make history. Wrote one former suffragist, "I knew nothing of European complications and cared less. . . . I asked myself if any horrors could be greater than the horrors of peace—

Figure 6. Hospitalized Veterans in England (Reproduced with permission of the Trustees of the Imperial War Museum, London.)

the sweating, the daily lives of women on the streets. . . ." Ultimately, such revolutionary energy and resolute feminism, together with such alienation from officially important events, was to lead to a phenomenon usefully analyzed by Nina Auerbach: "Union among women . . . is one of the unacknowledged fruits of war," and particularly during World War I, there was "a note of exaltation at the 'Amazonian countries' created by the war, whose military elation spread from the suffrage battle to the nation at large." For, of course, when their menfolk went off to the trenches to be literally and figuratively shattered, the women on the home front literally and figuratively rose to the occasion and replaced them in farms and factories. Picture after picture from the Imperial War Museum's enormous collection of photos portraying "Women at War" illustrates this point. Liberated from parlors and petticoats alike, trousered "war girls" beam as they shovel coal, shoe horses, fight fires, drive buses, chop down trees, make shells, dig graves (see Figure 7).

Though it may be a coincidence, then, there is ironic point to the fact that Charlotte Perkins Gilman's *Herland,* with its vision of a female utopia created by a cataclysm that wiped out all the men, was published in Gilman's feminist journal *Forerunner* in 1915, and at least one feminist noted the accuracy of a cartoon in *Punch* depicting two women who "did not think the war would last long—it was too good to last." When the time came for demobilization, many women wept at the ending of what they now saw as the happiest and most purposeful days of their lives. For despite the massive tragedy that the war represented for an entire generation of young men—and for their grieving wives, mothers, daugh-

Figure 7. Women's Land Army Workers in England (Reproduced with permission of the Trustees of the Imperial War Museum, London.)

ters, and sisters—it also represented the first rupture with a socioeconomic history that had heretofore denied most women chances at first-class jobs—and first-class pay.

Inevitably, the enthusiasm and efficiency with which women of all ranks and ages filled in the economic gaps men had left behind reinforced the soldiers' sickened sense that the war had drastically abrogated most of the rules that had always organized Western culture. From the first, after all, it had seemed to the man at the front that his life and limbs were forfeit to the comforts of the *home* front, so that civilians, male and female, were fictive inhabitants of a world that had effectively insulated itself from the trenches' city of dreadful night. Ultimately, this barely veiled hostility between the front and the home front, along with the exuberance of the women workers who had succeeded to (and in) men's places, suggested that the most crucial rule the war had overturned was the rule of patrilineal succession, the founding law of patriarchal society itself. For as the early glamour of battle dissipated and Victorian fantasies of historical heroism gave way to modernist visions of irony and unreality, it became clear that this war to end all wars necessitated a sacrifice of the sons to the exigencies of the fathers—and the mothers, wives, and sisters.

That such a generational conflict was not just associated with but an integral part of the sexual struggle fostered by the war is made very clear in a poem by Alice Meynell, a long-time suffrage fighter, who accurately foresaw that through one of the grimmer paradoxes of history the Great War might force recalcitrant men to grant women, the stereotypical peacemakers, a viable inheritance in patriarchal society. In fact, her "A Father of Women" seems almost to explain the sexual anxiety of D. H. Lawrence, who actually lived with her family during part of the war, for the speaker of this verse answers some of the questions Lawrence had asked in "Eloi, Eloi, Lama Sabacthani": "Our father works in us, / The daughters of his manhood. Not undone / Is he, not wasted, though transmuted thus, / And though he left no son." She goes on to tell "The million living fathers of the War" that they should finally "Approve, accept, know [us] daughters of men, / Now that your sons are dust." Ostensibly so calm and sympathetic, her last phrase can be read almost as a taunt, though it is certain she did not intend it that way. You have killed your sons, she seems to say, so now your daughters will inherit the world.

Even the most conventionally angelic of women's wartime ministrations must have suggested to many members of both sexes that, while men were now invalid and maybe in-valid, their sisters were triumphant survivors and destined inheritors. Certainly both the rhetoric and the iconography of nursing would seem to imply some such points. To be sure, the nurse presents herself as a servant of her patient. "Every task," writes Vera Brittain of her days as a VAD (Voluntary Aide), "had for us . . . a sacred glamour." Yet in works by both male and female novelists the figure of the nurse ultimately takes on a majesty which hints that she is mistress rather than slave, goddess rather than supplicant. After all, when men are immobilized and dehumanized, it is only these women who possess the old (matriarchal) formulas for survival. Thus, even while memoirists like Brittain express "gratitude" for the "sacred glamour" of nursing, they seem to be pledging allegiance to a *secret* glamour—the glamour of an expertise which they will win from their patients. "Towards the men," recalls Brittain, "I came to feel an almost adoring gratitude . . . for the knowledge of masculine functioning which the care of them gave me."

Not surprisingly, this education in masculine functioning that the nurse experiences as a kind of elevation is often felt by her male patient as exploitation; her evolution into active, autonomous, transcendent subject is associated with his devolution into passive, dependent, immanent medical object. In *A Farewell to Arms,* Hemingway's Frederic Henry clearly responds with a surface delight to being cared for and about by Catherine Barclay. Yet there is, after all, something faintly sinister in her claim that he *needs* her to make "unpleasant" preparations for an operation on his wounded knee and something frighteningly possessive in her assertion that "I get furious if [anyone else] touch[es] you." Similarly, in *The Sun Also Rises,* Hemingway's Jake Barnes, consoled by the nymphomaniac Brett Ashley as he lies limply on his bed, cannot forget that she "was a V.A.D. in a hospital I was in during the war" and fell in love with him because "she only wanted what she couldn't have," a line that ambiguously implies a form of perverse penis envy as well as a species of masochistic desire. More openly, Lawrence writes in "The Ladybird" about a wounded middle European prisoner who tells a visiting English Lady with whom he is falling in love that she must "let me wrap your hair round my hands like a bandage" because "I feel I have lost my manhood for the time being." Hopelessly at the mercy of his aristocratic nurse, this helpless alien adumbrates wounded males who also appear in works by women—for example, the amnesiac hero of Rebecca West's *The Return of the Soldier*, whom a former girlfriend restores by gathering his "soul" into "her soul"; and Lord Peter Wimsey, in Dorothy Sayers's *Busman's Honeymoon*, who is so haunted by memories of the war that he confesses to his bride that "you're my corner and I've come to hide."

Where nurses imagined by men often do seem to have sinister power, however, the nurses imagined by women appear, at least at first, to be purely restorative, positively (rather than negatively) maternal. The "grey nurse" whom Virginia Woolf describes in a notoriously puzzling passage in *Mrs. Dalloway* is thus a paradigm of her more realistically delineated sisters. Knitting steadily while Peter Walsh dozes, she seems "like the champion of the rights of sleepers" who responds to "a desire for solace, for relief." Yet even she is not an altogether positive figure. Like "The Greatest Mother in the World" depicted in Alonzo Earl Foringer's 1918 Red Cross War Relief poster—an enormous nurse cradling a tiny immobilized male on a doll-sized stretcher—Woolf's grey nurse evokes a parodic *pietà* in which the Virgin Mother threatens simultaneously to anoint and annihilate her long-suffering son, a point Woolf's imaginary male dreamer accurately grasps when he prays "let me walk straight on to this great figure, who will . . . mount me on her streamers and let me blow to nothingness with the rest." Does male death turn women nurses on? Do figures like the pious Red Cross mother experience bacchanalian satisfaction as, in Woolf's curiously ambiguous phrase, they watch their patients, one-time oppressors, "blow [up] to nothingness with the rest?" A number of texts by men and women alike suggest that the revolutionary socioeconomic transformations wrought by the war's "topsy-turvy" role reversals did bring about a release of female libidinal energies, as well as a liberation of female anger, which men usually found anxiety-inducing and women often found exhilarating.

On the subject of erotic release, a severely political writer like Vera Brittain is notably restrained. Yet even she implies, at least subtextually, that she experienced some such phenomenon, for while she expresses her "gratitude" to men from whom she learned about "masculine functioning," she goes on to thank the war that delivered their naked bodies into her hands for her own "early release from . . . sex-inhibitions." Significantly, too, as if to confirm the possibility that Brittain did receive a wartime sex education, Eric Leed records the belief of some observers that "women in particular 'reacted to the war experience with a powerful increase in libido.' " Was the war a festival of female misrule in which the collapse of a traditional social structure "permitted," as Leed also puts it, "a range of personal contacts that had been impossible in [former lives] where hierarchies of status ruled"? In their different ways, notorious heroines like Hemingway's Catherine Barclay and his Brett Ashley are set sexually free by the war, as are Lawrence's famous Connie Chatterley, his Ivy Bolton, and his Bertha Coutts, all of whom contribute to the impotence of his Clifford Chatterley and the anxiety of his Oliver Mellors.

Significantly, however, where men writers primarily recounted the horrors of unleashed female sexuality and only secondarily recorded the more generalized female excitement that energized such sexuality, women remembered, first the excitement of the war and, second (but more diffusely), the sensuality to which such excitement led. Thus, where most male writers—at least after their earliest dreams of heroism had been deflated—associated the front with paralysis and pollution, many female writers imagined it a place of freedom, ruefully comparing what they felt was their own genteel immobilization with the exhilaration of military mobility. In her "Many Sisters to Many Brothers," Rose Macaulay articulated their envy of the soldier's liberation from the dreariness of the home and the home front: "Oh it's you that have the luck, out there in blood and muck." To women who managed to get to the front, moreover, the war did frequently offer the delight of (female) mobilization rather than the despair of (male) immobilization. After all, for nurses and ambulance drivers, women doctors and women messengers, the phenomenon of modern battle was very different from that experienced by entrenched combatants. Finally given a chance to take the wheel, these post-Victorian girls raced motorcars along foreign roads like adventurers exploring new lands, while their brothers dug deeper into the mud of France. Retrieving the wounded and the dead from deadly positions, these once-decorous daughters had at last been allowed to prove their valor, and they swooped over the wastelands of the war with the energetic love of Wagnerian Valkyries, their mobility alone transporting countless immobilized heroes to safe havens.

For many women, moreover, but perhaps in particular for lesbian women like Willa Cather, whose inability to identify with conventional "femininity" had always made their gender a problem to them, the war facilitated not just a liberation from the constricting trivia of parlors and petticoats but an unprecedented transcendence of the profounder constraints imposed by traditional sex roles. Most dramatically, this transcendence is described in Radclyffe Hall's two crucial postwar fictions—her short story entitled "Miss Ogilvy Finds Herself" and her more famous *The Well of Loneliness*. In the first, the aging lesbian Miss Ogilvy remembers, as she is being demobilized, that her ambulance was "the merciful emblem that had set [her] free," and mourns the breaking up of the "glorious" all-female unit she has led. Similarly, Stephen Gordon, the "invert" heroine of *The Well*, feels at the outset of the war like "a freak abandoned on a kind of no-man's-land" (and Hall's metaphor is significant) but soon finds herself paradoxically metamorphosed into a member of a new women's battalion "that would never again be disbanded." For, explains Hall, "war and death" had finally, ironically, given "a right to life" to lesbians like Stephen, women who refused the traditions of femininity and the conventions of heterosexuality alike.

To be sure, specifically erotic release was frequently associated with such a right to life, for Vera Brittain's sex education was complemented by the romantic permission given, in various degrees, to heterosexual characters like Miranda in Katherine Anne Porter's "Pale Horse, Pale Rider" and to lesbian heroines like Miss Ogilvy and Stephen Gordon. In the first work, Porter's protagonist, falling in love with a young soldier, meditates happily on the "miracle of being two persons named Adam and Miranda" who are "always in the mood for dancing." As for Miss Ogilvy, she goes off on a vacation where Hall grants her a dream of unleashed desire in which, transformed into a powerful primitive man, she makes love to a beautiful young woman, enthralled by the "ripe red berry sweet to the taste'' of the female body. Similarly, Stephen Gordon meets her lover, Mary Llewelyn, when they are sister drivers in the allegorically named ''Breakspeare'' ambulance unit, and after the war they too achieve a ''new and ardent fulfillment'' on a honeymoon in Spain.

Perhaps more important than the female eroticism that the war energized, however, was the more diffusely emotional sense of sisterhood its ''Amazonian countries'' inspired in nurses and VADs, land girls and tram conductors. As if to show the positive aspect of the bacchanalian bonding that some male writers feared, women like Vera Brittain, May Sinclair, and Violetta Thurstan remembered how their liberation into the public realm from the isolation of the private house allowed them to experience a female (re)union in which they felt ''the joys of companionship to the full . . . in a way that would be impossible to conceive in an ordinary world.'' For Radclyffe Hall, too, the battalion of sisters ''formed in those terrible years'' consisted of ''great-hearted women . . . glad . . . to help one another to shoulder burdens.''

It is also, of course, true that the Great War produced for many men a ''front-line experience replete with,'' as Paul Fussell puts it, ''what we can call the homoerotic.'' From Herbert Read, who wishes one of his dead soldiers to be kissed not by worms ''but with the warm passionate lips / of his comrade here,'' to Wilfred Owen, who sends his ''identity disc'' to a ''sweet friend,'' imploring ''may thy heart-beat kiss it, night and day,'' male combatants frequently feel for each other ''a love passing the love of women.'' Significantly, however, where the liberating sisterhood experienced by women was mostly untainted by hostility to men—where it was, in fact, frequently associated with admiration for male soldiers or identification with male heroism—the combatants' comradeship seems as often to have been energized by a disgust for the feminine as it was by a desire for the masculine. The war between the front and the home front, that is, issued in an inextricable tangle of (male) misogyny and (male) homosexuality, so that Owen, say, reproaches female ''Love'' while praising beautiful ''lads.''

The male comradeship fostered by the isolated communities of the trenches, moreover, was continually qualified by rifts between men that were not just accidental but essential consequences of the war. Most obviously, the No Man's Land that stretched between allies and enemies symbolized the fragmentation of what Sigmund Freud called the ''wider fatherland'' in which, as Freud sorrowfully noted, European men no longer dwelt, though they had ''moved unhindered'' in it before the war. ''Strange Meeting,'' perhaps Owen's most famous poem, stunningly dramatizes this disintegration of male love, with its vision of brotherly doubles meeting in a ''dull tunnel'' where one tells the other that, ''I am the enemy you killed, my friend.''

But if the war forced men like Lawrence, Freud, and Owen to qualify their dreams of brotherhood by confronting the reality of No Man's Land and imagining themselves as nightmare citizens ''without a land,'' it liberated women to imagine a revisionary worldwide Herland, a utopia arisen from the ashes of apocalypse and founded on the revelation of a new social order. In a range of genres—poems and polemics, extravagant fantasies and realistic fictions—women writers articulated this vision repeatedly throughout the war and postwar years. Gertrude Atherton's popular fantasy, *The White Morning,* for instance, told a utopian tale of the takeover of Germany by a female army, while Dorothy Harrison, one of the protagonists of Sinclair's *The Tree of Heaven,* has a mysteriously epiphany when she is confined at Hollowell Prison as part of the prewar suffrage battle, an epiphany that turns out to be a proleptic vision of how women will get the vote in "some big, tremendous way that'll make all this fighting and fussing seem the rottenest game."

For many women such intimations of social change were channeled specifically through the politics of pacifism. From Olive Schreiner, whose meditation on "Women and War" had argued that the mothers of the race have a special responsibility as well as a special power to oppose combat, to Charlotte Perkins Gilman, whose Herland was an Edenically peaceable garden because its author believed women to be naturally nonviolent, feminist activists had long claimed that, in the words of Crystal Eastman, "woman suffrage and permanent peace will go together." Indeed, like the trade unionist Mrs. Raymond Robins, whose opinions were otherwise very different, Eastman had confidence that "it is the first hour in history for the women of the world. This is the woman's age!" Precisely because these thinkers were uniformly convinced of woman's unique ability to encourage and enforce peace, however, there is sometimes an edge of contempt for men implicit in their arguments. But it is in Virginia Woolf's *Three Guineas,* the postwar era's great text of pacifist feminism, that such hostility to men comes most dramatically to the surface, in the form of violent antipatriarchal fantasies paradoxically embedded in an ostensibly nonviolent treatise on the subject of "how to prevent war." Perhaps, Woolf even hints in an early draft of this New Womanly book of revelation, the devastation wrought by war is a punishment (for men) exactly fitted not only to the crime of (masculine) war-making, but to other (masculine) crimes. Even in the more subdued final version of *Three Guineas* she seizes upon the imperative to prevent war as an excuse for imagining a conflagration that would burn down the old male-structured colleges of "Oxbridge," representative of all oppressive cultural institutions, and substitute instead an egalitarian and feminist "new college, [a] poor college" where "the arts of ruling, of killing, of acquiring land and capital" would not be taught.

Later in *Three Guineas,* moreover, Woolf rebels even against the rhetoric of writers like Schreiner and Eastman, observing sardonically that "pacifism is enforced upon women" because they are not in any case allowed to offer their services to the army. Thus, most radically, she puts forward her famous proposal that "the daughters of educated men" should refuse to join their brothers in working either for war *or* peace, but should instead found a "Society of Outsiders" based on the principles that "as a woman, I have no country. As a woman, I want no country. As a woman, my country is the whole world." To be sure, Woolf recommends as part of this proposal a passive resistance to patriarchal militarism significantly similar to that advocated by many other feminist pacifists. But at the same time, with its calculated ex-patriotism and its revisionary vows of "indifference" to the uncivilized hierarchies of "our" civilization, her Society of Outsiders constitutes perhaps the most fully elaborated feminist vision of a secret apocalyptic Herland existing simultaneously within and without what she called in that volume England's "splendid Empire," a righteous and rightful woman's state energized by the antiwar passions the war produced in women. In some part of herself, therefore, Woolf may well have shared the apocalyptic delight that Hesione Hushabye bizarrely expresses when bombs begin falling at the end of Bernard Shaw's *Heartbreak House:* "Did you hear the explosions? And the sound in the sky: it's splendid: it's like an orchestra: it's like Beethoven." As patriarchal culture self-destructs, those it has subordinated can't help feeling that the sacrifices implied by "the sound in the sky" might nevertheless hold out the hope of a new heaven and a new earth.

Not surprisingly, then, even as they mourned the devastation of the war, a number of women writers besides Woolf felt that not only their society but also their art had been subtly strengthened, or at least strangely inspired, by the deaths and defeats of male contemporaries. Vera Brittain notes that when her fiancé, Roland, was killed, "his mother began to write, in semifictional form, a memoir of his life," and adds that she herself was filled "with longing to write a book about Roland." Again, in *A Son at the Front,* the tale of an artist-father whose art is mysteriously revitalized by the death of his soldier son, Edith Wharton offers an encoded description of a similar transformation of a dead man into an enlivening muse. Finally, in perhaps the most notable instance of female inspiration empowered by male desperation, H.D. writes in her roman à clef, *Bid Me to Live,* how the various defeats of her husband (Richard Aldington) and her male muse (D. H. Lawrence) transformed her autobiographical heroine, Julia, into a "witch with power. A wise woman . . . [a] seer, a see-er." No wonder, then, that when she later looked back on her experiences in two wars she revised and reversed the imagery Lawrence had used in his "Eloi, Eloi, Lama Sabacthani." "Am I bridegroom of War, war's paramour?" Lawrence's speaker had asked, and H.D. seems almost to have wanted to answer him directly. Tracing her own growth in an unpublished memoir called "Thorn Thicket," she declares mystically that "the war was my husband." And at the very least, if the war was not her husband, it was her muse—as it was Woolf's, Brittain's, Wharton's, and many other women's.

Given the fact that the war functioned in so many different ways to liberate women, it seems clear that more than simple patriotism caused some leaders of the women's movement quite early to recognize a connection between feminist aspirations and military effects. In 1915, for instance, *The Suffragette,* the newspaper of the English Women's Social and Political Union, was renamed *Britannia,* with a new dedication: "For King, for Country, for Freedom." At last, it must have seemed, women could begin to see themselves as coextensive with the state, and with a female state at that, a Britannia, not a Union Jack. And as we know, the female intuition expressed in that renaming was quite accurate; in 1918, when World War I was over, there were eight and a half million European men dead, and there had been thirty-seven and a half million male casualties, while all the women in England over the age of thirty were finally, after a sixty-two-year struggle, given the vote. Not too much later all the women in America over the age of twenty-one achieved the same privilege. For four years a sizable percentage of the young men in England had been imprisoned in trenches and uniforms, while the young women in England had been at liberty in farm and factory. Paradoxically, the war to which so many men had gone in the hope of becoming heroes ended up emasculating them, depriving them of autonomy, confining them as closely as any Victorian women had been confined. As if in acknowledgement of this, Eric Leed tells us, doctors noted that "the symptoms of shell-shock were precisely the same as those of the most common hysterical disorders of peacetime, though they often acquired new and more dramatic names in war: 'the burial-alive neurosis,' 'gas neurosis,' 'soldier's heart,' 'hysterical sympathy with the enemy' . . . what had been predominantly a disease of women before the war became a disease of men in combat."

Because women developed a very different kind of "soldier's heart" in these years, "wearing the pants" in the family or even "stepping into his shoes" had finally become a real possibility for them. Yet of course that triumph was not without its darker consequences for feminism. Because male artists believed even more strongly than their sisters did that soldiers had been sacrificed so that some gigantic female could sleep surrounded by, in Wilfred Owen's words, a "wall of boys on boys and dooms on dooms"; because they believed, with Hemingway, that a Lady Brett was a sort of monstrous antifertility goddess to whose powers the impotent bodies of men had ceaselessly to be offered up; because, finally, with Lawrence they "feared" the talents of liberated "poetesses" like H.D. at least as much as they admired them, the literature of the postwar years was marked by an "antifeminism" which, in the words of Rebecca West, was "strikingly the correct fashion . . . among . . . the intellectuals."

Inevitably, many women writers themselves internalized the misogyny that actuated such antifeminism. Heroines like Hall's Miss Ogilvy and her Stephen Gordon, for instance, who had been briefly freed by the war, ultimately succumb to the threat of a reconstituted status quo. Miss Ogilvy dies almost directly as a result of the sexual "dying" that climaxes her dream of erotic fulfillment, and Stephen Gordon is assaulted by "rockets of pain" which signal "the hour of our death" as she surrenders Mary Llewelyn to the male lover who she decides is Mary's rightful spouse. At the same time, the guilt of the survivor is specifically articulated by one former nurse who defines her culpable numbness in a dreadful confession: "She [a nurse] is no longer a woman. She is dead already, just as I am . . . a machine inhabited by a ghost of a woman—soulless, past redeeming." Most theatrically, perhaps, Katherine Anne Porter expresses in "Pale Horse, Pale Rider" this nurse's feeling (and what might have been a universal female sense) that if men are sick, they must have fallen ill because women are sickening. After her heroine, Miranda, down with influenza, has had a terrifying dream about her lover, Adam, in which "he lay dead, and she still lived," she learns that her disease has contaminated him, and indeed, he has died and she has lived, kept going by a "fiery motionless particle [which] set itself . . . to survive . . . in its own madness of being."

Eventually, therefore, repressed by what was still, after all, a male-dominated community, and reproached by their own consciences, many women retreated into embittered unemployment or guilt-stricken domesticity after World War I. "Generally speaking, we war women are a failure," confesses a character in Evadne Price's *Women of the Aftermath*. "We had a chance to make ourselves solid in the working market . . . and came a hell of a cropper in most cases.'' To be sure, as J. Stanley Lemons and others observe, women's ''peacetime levels [of employment] were [still] significantly higher than the prewar situation.'' Nothing would ever be the same again. But no war would ever function, either, the way this Great War had, as a battle of the sexes which initiated ''the first hour in history for the women of the world.'' World War II certainly was to be as much a war against women civilians as it was against male combatants, with a front indistinguishable from the home front. As Virginia Woolf anticipated in *Three Guineas,* in fact, it was to be a war whose jackbooted Nazis, marching for the Fatherland, enacted the ultimate consequences of patriarchal oppression, so that Sylvia Plath, protesting against her imprisonment in ''daddy's'' black shoe, would fear that ''I may be a bit of a Jew.'' In 1944, moreover, in her war-shadowed ''Writing on the Wall,'' H.D. was to return to Radclyffe Hall's definition of ''no-man's-land'' as a ''waste land'' for ''inverts'' (Hall) and ''hysterical women'' (H.D.) while more recently, in a revision of the metaphor that Hall's Stephen Gordon temporarily transcended, Linda Pastan was to see her own body as a ''no man's land'' over which sons and husbands battle, and in 1981 Adrienne Rich was to publish a poem which despairingly declared that ''there is no no man's land,'' by which she clearly means there is still no Herland. With Rich, all of these women would understand themselves to be participants in an ongoing ''war of the images'' whose possibly apocalyptic dénouement has not yet really been revealed, though the combats of the early twentieth century offered enduring possibilities of vengeance and victory, female anxiety and feminist ecstasy.

SUGGESTIONS FOR FURTHER READING

Auerbach, Nina. *Communities of Women.* Cambridge, 1978.

Borden, Mary. *The Forbidden Zone.* London, 1929.

Bradbury, Malcolm. ''The Denuded Place: War and Form in *Parade's End* and *U.S.A.''* In Holger Klein, ed. *The First World War in Fiction.* London, 1976.

Braybon, Gail. *Women Workers in the First World War: The British Experience.* London, 1981.

Brittain, Vera. *Testament of Youth.* London, 1979.

Cadogan, Mary and Patricia Craig. *Women and Children First: The Fiction of Two World Wars.* London, 1978.

Cook, Blanche, ed. *Crystal Eastman on Women and Revolution.* New York, 1978.

Cott, Nancy. ''Passionlessness: An Interpretation of Victorian Sexual Ideology, 1790–1850.'' *Signs* 4, no. 2 (Winter 1978): 219–236.

Fussell, Paul. *The Great War and Modern Memory.* New York, 1975.

Greenwald, Maurine Weiner. *Women, War and Work: The Impact of World War I on Women Workers in the United States.* Westport, CT, 1985.

Lane, Ann J., ed. *The Charlotte Perkins Gilman Reader.* New York, 1980.

Leed, Eric. *No Man's Land: Combat and Identity in World War I.* New York, 1979.

Lemons, J. Stanley. *The Woman Citizen: Social Feminism in the 1920s.* Urbana, 1973.

Matthews, Caroline. *Experiences of a Woman Doctor in Serbia.* London, 1916.

Nicolson, Nigel. *Portrait of a Marriage.* London, 1973.

Reilly, Catherine, ed. *Scars upon My Heart: Women's Poetry and Verse of the First World War.* London, 1981.

Schreiner, Olive. ''Women in War.'' In *Women and Labor.* London, 1911.

12

The Russian Revolution and Women

Richard Stites

Based on his wide experience researching and writing Russian history, Richard Stites offers a broad synthesis of women's place in the Russian revolutionary tradition and post-revolutionary society. His story begins with the reforming sentiments of the 1850s and 1860s, at a time of debate over the nature and course of the emancipation of serfs. He identifies mid-century as the first phase of women's participation in the reforming movements and identifies three influential, if distinct, approaches: the feminist, which was essentially a movement by women for women; the nihilist, which was a countercultural current stressing the personal values of equality; and the radical, which sought total emancipation of all through socialism. The second phase was inaugurated by the tsarist government's commitment to industrialization and shift to parliamentary politics. It saw the growth of political parties, and many on the left, including the Marxists, feared the feminist revival as diversionary. In 1917, however, the significance of the half-century debate over the woman question became clear. Women's equality was among the many promises made by the new Bolshevik leadership, as were workers' control over factory production, educational advances, and ethnic self-determination. Despite the regime's public commitment to women's rights, however, the persistence of older notions of women's subordinate role hampered greater strides toward gender equality, as did continuous priority dilemmas that placed women's issues secondary to other societal and developmental goals. Besides, the regime was poor and could not afford extensive social support. It was only in work—as wage earners in social production—that the possibility of individual independence was extended to Russian women. There was less success in transforming family relationships and role divisions within the family.

The participation of women in the Russian Revolution of 1917 was conditioned—both in its successes and in its failures—by a long and interesting prehistory. The explosive events of 1917 can be explained only partially by the physical, military, and social environment of the moment; to this picture must be added a legacy of images, beliefs, feelings, and attitudes shaped in the two generations preceding the Revolution: the Populist Revolt (1860–1881), an almost purely upper-class affair; and the Revolution of 1905 (1890–1914), a nationwide, all-class uprising. Recent scholarship on peasants, workers, nationalities, soldiers, sailors, and other groups has demonstrated clearly that long-standing attitudes and circumstances of life are as important as any other factor in the molding of revolutionary (and counterrevolutionary) behavior. The same applies to the history of women: although deep study of the social structure of women's lives among the working class has just begun, research on the development of women's consciousness and women's movements in the major revolutionary episodes of the nineteenth and early twentieth centuries indicates the main peculiarities of women's political activity in the great Russian Revolution of 1917.

Though there is evidence of the growth of various forms of "women's consciousness"—that is, a refusal to accept traditional social roles—in early nineteenth-century Russia, it is generally accepted by Western and Soviet scholars that the woman question as a social issue burst onto the public scene in the late 1850s and early 1860s. There is no consensus as to why this happened. Some have stressed the general atmosphere of a political "thaw" under a new, reforming tsar, Alexander II (r. 1855–1881), the deep shame over the Russian defeat in the Crimean War (1854–1856), and a sense of euphoria connected with the imminent emancipation of the serfs (1861). Some have also suggested that social and economic factors were at work: the specter of serf emancipation and the prospect that dependent females might now be thrown onto the economy might have awakened an impulse to prepare for economic and personal independence. But no less important than these was the emergence of a new generation of intelligentsia males whose social outlook—often described as "nihilism" or a sweeping negation of accepted values—included egalitarianism, an attack upon elitist manners and conventions, and a determination to practice their beliefs in everyday life. From such males, many of whom became radicals of the 1860s, came the first important writings on women's equality. The Russian radical scene was almost unique in its inclusion of a demand for equal opportunity for women among its earliest political and social programs. This appeal by nihilist and radical males coincided with a new stage of women's perception and self-perception and set the stage for a movement for the emancipation of women.

But just as the motivations and impulses were complex and diverse, so were the responses of the women themselves. Almost simultaneously, there arose three distinct approaches to the woman question: feminism, nihilism, and radicalism. Though there was much overlapping, shifting, and interlocking of these three currents at first, they eventually sorted themselves into separate ways. The feminists of Russia were in many ways similar to Western feminists. They sought not revolution or even personal sexual emancipation but rather a legal and moderate movement led by women on behalf of women. By social origin, the leaders and founders were upper-class—mostly of the nobility. One should not be tempted to construct a deterministic sociology of their mentality because of this: the early nihilists and radical women came essentially from the same background. If the feminist leader Anna Filosofova was the wife of a tsarist general, Sofya Perovskaya, assassin of the Tsar in 1881, and Alexandra Kollontai, a Bolshevik Com-

missar in 1917, were daughters of generals—all of affluent and successful families. But the feminists chose very consciously to define the needs of women as
something separate from general social struggle and the liberation of all the people. Their aims were modest and their achievements impressive: charity for poor
girls, mutual assistance to themselves, experience in self-directed activity in a land
where this was in short supply, and educational and professional opportunities for
those women possessing the talent and the energy for careers. Largely through
their efforts, universities and medical courses became available to Russian women
in the 1870s, a notable feat for any European country at that time.

Nihilism was not a political or a formal intellectual movement in the 1860s—
it was rather an ethos and a style of personal liberation. Like their male colleagues, nihilist women stressed their independence, their modernity, and their
contempt for the established order by means of physical appearance and symbolic
gestures: short hair, plain (sometimes dirty) clothes, a defeminized manner, ciga-
rette smoking, and brusqueness in speech. This was part of a countercultural revolt like those of nineteenth-century European bohemians, *fin-de-siècle* decadents,
or American hippies of the 1960s. Their values were equality, science worship, a
general belief in progress, and a moralistic disdain for old Russian ways and
customs—including religion, the family, and the highly stratified and visible class
system. Wives and daughters broke with their families, migrated to the big capital
cities—St. Petersburg and Moscow—enrolled in courses, joined circles and communes, and in general scandalized polite society. Many women who went through
this counterculture moved on to political radicalism and even terrorism. But many
of them did not. Nihilism was not coterminous with revolution for people of either
sex. Even among women who admired Nicholas Chernyshevsky's *What Is To Be
Done?* (1862)—a political novel and a utopia about women's emancipation—were
those that remained deaf to its radical message and contented themselves with
borrowing its devices (fictitious marriages, women's cooperatives, communes) for
personal, social, and sexual emancipation.

Nihilist and radical women are often linked in the study of the revolutionary
movement of the 1860s. But as far as women are concerned, radicals had more in
common with active feminists than with those nihilists (often accused of egoism)
who defined emancipation as a personal affair. Both the feminists and the radical
women had larger goals; for the former, emancipation of women of their own
class and assistance to many women of the urban lower orders (prostitutes, or-
phans, shopgirls); for the latter—emancipation of all the people, especially the
toiling peasants, through socialism. They also seemed to share an almost religious
sense of service and self-sacrifice. In a brilliant book on the subject, Barbara
Engel has analyzed the sense of religious devotion and service among radical
women of this generation and shown how their strategy of sacrifice and martyrdom—while extremely valuable in giving the revolution a symbolic halo—diminished their feminist sensibilities and led them to downplay or ignore special problems of the female population. This does not mean, however, that the feminist
impulse was absent among radical women. Engel has shown in detail how many
of the most active women in the populist movement of the 1870s went through an
important phase of consciousness-raising and womanly self-definition before turn-

ing the "personal" into the "political." Female revolutionaries also maintained what we now call networks of moral and psychological sustenance, a phenomenon that has survived strongly into the present.

But who were the radical women and what did they do? Most of the several thousand females who participated in the revolutionary movement between the 1860s and 1880s were from privileged Russian families—gentry, professionals, government officials, and military officers—with an increasing admixture of merchants' and priests' daughters, women of the lower classes, and Jews, Poles, and other nationalities. In the minuscule circles of the 1860s, women acted as adjuncts, recruiters, messengers, and were sometimes treated by radical men—such as Sergei Nechaev—in a rather manipulative way. In the 1870s, with the "Movement to the People," women came into their own, migrating into factories and into villages in search of the "socialist" peasant, propagandizing, and falling into police dragnets. Hundreds were arrested and incarcerated or sent into Siberian exile. An era of assassination was inaugurated when Vera Zasulich fired a shot at a high police official in the capital in 1877. When disillusionment with peasant revolutionary potential and fear of open exposure led a branch of the movement—the People's Will—to a campaign of terror in the years 1879–1881, women were even more prominent numerically, constituting about one-third of that body's all-powerful Executive Committee. It was Sofya Perovskaya, after the arrest of her comrades, who led the final assault on the Tsar that took his life in March 1881, after which she and her co-conspirators were hanged. But failure attended the symbolic victory: no revolution occurred, peasant socialism did not emerge, and the People's Will gradually disintegrated.

The Populist episode left a dual legacy for radical women: it encircled them with the aureole of martyrdom and revolutionary honor and it endowed them with a myth of moral courage and indomitable power. But it often led their followers to continue the "pure radical" notion of the Great Cause, to the detriment of feminist concerns; and it also failed to win women a place of equal power and creativity in the revolutionary movements.

The second phase of the revolutionary movement in Russia occurred in an altered social context. Russia's rapid industrialization added dramatically to the number of urban factory women, prostitutes, and domestic servants. Peasant women followed their menfolk—and sometimes went independently—into the work force in the cities, the slums, and the proletarian working-class quarters. Female domestics were the most ignored by social critics (and the least studied to this day), though they were very prominent in the urban housing revolution that erupted in Russia after the Bolshevik Revolution. The prostitutes became a veritable symbol—in the eyes of cultural observers—of the moral decadence that was overcoming Russian society. Factory women, as Rose Glickman's superb new study has shown, had to face hostility and abuse on two fronts: in the exploitativeness of the factory system itself; and in the home where male "proletarian virtue" did not always include decent treatment of wives and daughters.

The partially successful Revolution of 1905, which produced civil rights, a free press, a parliament, and dozens of new public institutions, also thickened the social and political texture of Russia. Into the maelstrom of revolutionary politics rushed peasants, workers, the middle classes, and national minorities of many levels of cultural development. To represent their interests and those of the forces of order and stability, a whole spectrum of political parties appeared, most of which deliberated openly in the Duma, or parliament, created in 1906. As might be expected, the parties that inscribed fatherland, faith, and tsar on their banners were wholly opposed to feminism and woman suffrage. Conservatives sometimes fudged the issue but were generally hostile. The Liberal Party (Kadets) divided at first—thinking other matters more important than votes for women—but grudgingly came round to support them. The parties of the left—the Marxist Social Democrats (both Bolsheviks and Mensheviks), the Socialist Revolutionaries, and the anarchist groups supported equal rights for women in principle, though only the Marxists proclaimed it publicly and unambiguously. But in practice many leftists often ignored the woman question or were simply hostile to it, seeing it (as did the Liberals) as a luxury, a special cause that should be subsumed under a grander perspective of all-Russian liberation and the destruction of the tsarist system. The radical generation of 1905 was distinctly less interested in living sexual equality in part because its cohort rested comfortably on the radical myth that these things had already been decided in the 1860s.

While women were accepted as equals in the parties of the left, as individuals they were much less prominent in the leadership than they had been a generation earlier. The steady influx into the socialist parties of workers whose attitude toward women was not as advanced as those of the intelligentsia may also have been responsible for a certain downgrading of the role of women. It must be kept in mind, however, that for many women who sought a role in political life, the socialist parties seemed the only genuinely hospitable home.

One development—but not the only one—that made some Marxists suspicious of what they called "feminist" concerns was the emergence of the Russian women's suffrage movement around 1905 outside the context of socialism and large-scale revolution. The feminist movement of 1905 was very complex. In one sense it was a continuation of "classical" feminism of the 1860s—a movement of women for women and emphatically not simply the female component of one of the opposition movements, and consequently, not ready to bury its separate cause under some larger cause as defined by men. This focus on *women* as a constituency that cut across class lines and the willingness of some feminist groups to accept a limited (property) suffrage was quite enough to besmirch it in the eyes of most Marxists as bourgeois. The charge was not wholly accurate (quite aside from the utter meaninglessness of the word "bourgeois" in any Russian context).

In the first place, almost all feminists—conservative, liberal, or "social"— saw women's emancipation as part of a larger cause also: the liberation of all oppressed peoples, but not via a simple formula of "proletarian" revolution or neopopulism. They upheld the revolution and supported a whole range of reforms that benefited everyone. Secondly, an important component of the feminist movement was specifically interested in the labor movement, working-class women, factory conditions, the right to strike, and so on. Some of these feminists were even socialist party members. But they usually found themselves rebuffed by party leaders who frowned upon "separatist" tendencies. By 1906, the feminists—rearranged and reshuffled several times—had parted company with the revolutionary movement and continued their fight for the vote. They did not get it until 1917, but in the course of their campaigning they continued what their mothers had started—building self-confidence, gaining organizational experience, and winning valuable reform for women in matters of education, law, and social protection.

The Populist tradition of "pure radicalism" and devoid of organized feminism continued into this era. It was very strong among those women who shared with radical men the belief that everything about the emancipation of women had already been said and that there was, therefore, no need for a special movement for women. For Maria Spiridonova, a fiery schoolteacher from Tambov province, the hallmark of a political woman was personal valor and action: during the 1905 Revolution she avenged the scourged peasants of her province by shooting dead the General who had led the punitive expedition against them. After ten years in exile she returned to European Russia in 1917 and became a leader of the ultra-radical left Socialist Revolutionaries. Through it all, she evinced no interest whatsoever in organized feminism, seeing herself as already the equal of men and seeing the Revolution as the focal point of her life. Vera Zasulich, ex-terrorist and now a Menshevik Marxist, shared this opinion: special meetings and organizations for women within Social Democracy were unnecessary. In many ways these women (and there were many more) harbored some of the shortsightedness of successful women of the past (monarchs and writers, for example) who viewed their own record as "proof" of women's ability and who thought that there was nothing more to be done about the matter. The multitude of professional revolutionary women of all parties in the revolutions of 1905 and 1917 who shied away from the suffrage movement distinguished the Russian experience from that of England where violence found a place inside the feminist movement itself. It also reinforced male notions that attention to women's problems was provincial and harmful.

The "proletarian women's movement" in contrast was an attempt to synthesize one brand of radicalism—Marxism—with feminism. Formulated by the German Marxist, Clara Zetkin, and adapted to Russian conditions by Kollontai and Nadezhda Krupskaya (Lenin's wife), this synthesis rejected "bourgeois" feminist movements of women for women, reaffirmed the alliance of men and women in the class struggle for a proletarian revolution, but insisted on the special needs and concerns of women within the proletarian movement. Working-class women in particular were beset by problems of illiteracy, low political consciousness, unequal pay, absence of maternity benefits, sexual harassment on the job, and even abuse from their proletarian husbands. The Marxist feminists believed that these concerns were real, that organized feminism—with its suspected class bias—could not alleviate them, and that male socialist leaders poorly understood them and gave them insufficient attention. In 1905, Kollontai, still a Menshevik, helped to launch a special campaign to enlist women workers in the Social Democratic labor movement and to fight the feminist organizations in Russia. This struggle culminated at the first Women's Conference in 1908 when the two currents confronted each other in a mood of hostility. Thereafter, feminism in all its parts declined rapidly. The Marxist women's movement revived on a very modest scale, in 1912–1914, when the Bolsheviks launched a newspaper called *The Woman Worker* and began celebrating the European Marxist holiday, International Women's Day.

Three years of bloody European war (1914–1917) threw many of these controversies into the shadows, reduced old organizations to shambles, and kept many revolutionary leaders out of touch with Russian reality. Thus, on the eve of the 1917 Revolution, the woman question, having won important successes in the last years of the monarchy, was practically dormant.

The revolutionary year 1917 was actually only eight months long. It began with the overthrow of the monarchy, was followed by an uneasy and undefined alliance of the "bourgeois" parties in the Provisional Government and the moderate socialist leaders in the Soviets (workers' councils), and ended in October with the Bolshevik seizure of power and the creation of a new revolutionary regime under Lenin. At no time did the women's struggle dominate the proceedings, but a struggle there was nonetheless. All the old factions went to war again. The urban uprising in the capital that caused the collapse of the monarchy was begun by a demonstration in support of International Women's Day; and both Mensheviks and Bolsheviks attempted to organize and recruit women workers throughout the year. The feminist organizations came out of the doldrums, united, and petitioned the Provisional Government for the vote—which they received along with sharpened barbs from the Bolshevik women's organizers for presuming to speak for lower-class women. All the rhetoric and the insults of 1905 were trumpeted again by both sides.

But the feminists found a fresh cause with an ironic twist: the Women's Batallions of Death. If women of the revolutionary tradition could shunt feminism aside in favor of the Great Cause of social revolution, other women could do the same for another Great Cause: defending the fatherland. In the summer of 1917, while regular troops were melting away during the Provisional Government's last and ill-fated offensive against the Central Powers, Russian women volunteers, organized into batallions, were trying to stiffen the lines against the invaders. In the last act of 1917, the dramatic but anticlimactic storming of the Winter Palace, headquarters of the Provisional Government, a unit from the Women's Batallions defended while Bolshevik Red Guards, some women among them, assaulted and took the palace.

For the Bolsheviks the moment had at last come when, after generations of postponement of "smaller" questions for the sake of the larger, these questions had to be faced and solved: "the day after the Revolution." But the day after the Revolution never came. As there had been in the past, there were always good reasons why certain things had to wait—equality, harmony, cooperation, abundance, social justice, all the furnishings of the utopian dream. The first inkling that the "revolution" was not over but only beginning was the Civil War (1918–1921), where perhaps as many as 80,000 women served in combat, medical, support, espionage, partisan, and administrative roles. For these women the Great Cause arose once again as the all-embracing mission in life, and not the rights of women. They fought, they suffered, and they died—sometimes horribly—as they had done in the struggle against autocracy, once again projecting an unparalleled image of nobility and sacrifice, an image reflected in the posters and stories of the Civil War. It was in fact one of the greatest sagas of women at war in modern times—a saga to be repeated in excruciating and terrible detail when Nazi Germany invaded Russia in 1941. But as in all the previous episodes of the revolutionary tradition, the women were more often deputies, auxiliaries, assistants, nurturers, and teachers, than the possessors of raw power and monumental stature.

This is not to say that the Marxist-feminist synthesis of the prerevolutionary years was forgotten or abandoned. Lenin proclaimed again and again the complete equality of the sexes in all realms of life—and was the first political leader in power ever to do so. His regime, with the assistance of women advisors, promulgated a series of measures that legalized equal pay for equal work; proclaimed full political, juridical, and educational equality; legalized abortion; and liberalized the divorce system, making woman a full partner in the family. More important than this, recognizing that laws do not make a social revolution and that the best arbiters of women's affairs were women themselves, Lenin blessed the launching of a new experiment in women's self-activity—the Zhenotdel, or women's section, of the Communist Party (1919–1930). Under the general leadership of Inessa Armand and Kollontai, the Zhenotdel attempted through a national network of women organizers to spread the news of the Revolution, to enforce its laws (especially against errant and brutal husbands), to give political education and apprenticeships to working-class and peasant women, to launch literacy classes, to campaign against prostitution (which was now outlawed), and to lift the veil physically and metaphorically from the faces of Muslim women of the eastern regions of the Soviet republic—groups that had been all but untouched by the currents of women's liberation thought before 1917. The energy of Zhenotdel leaders was prodigious and their social ambitions vaulting; but their organization always remained weak, their efforts underfinanced, and their aims held in dubious repute by many male Bolshevik leaders, especially after death of Lenin. Why?

All Bolshevik leaders proclaimed in principle the equality of the sexes, but most of them had no interest in the rapid emancipation of women. Those who did often thought in terms of what one scholar has called "mobilization for modernization"—the deployment of women's energies in modern productive labor for the sake of the regime or of society (the Great Cause once again). It would be easy and natural to attribute this to the "treachery" or "hypocrisy" of the Bolsheviks, but name-calling does not add much to historical understanding. All revolutions, in a sense, cheat their supporters and mass participants, just as almost all societies exploit their poorest and weakest members. The communist revolutions of our time in Yugoslavia, China, Cuba, Vietnam, and other places that have gone back on their promises to women are hardly different in this than previous revolutions, except that perhaps they promised more and thus found it more difficult to keep their word. Like many revolutionaries in Russia before them, the Bolsheviks interpreted "equality" as complementarity, specialization, or division of labor. Since there were no titles or rules of entry that mentioned gender, Bolsheviks came to assume that theirs was a community of equals even though some had more power, did more writing, or, after coming to power, had bigger rations. Bolshevism could not break—and to this day has not broken—with the deep conviction that women, though "equal" in valor and revolutionary consciousness, were by nature better at support, sustenance, nurturing.

In their public statements and symbols, Bolsheviks neither demeaned women nor put them on a pedestal (there is no equivalent to the French Marianne, symbol of the Republic, in Soviet heraldry). The posters, medallions, and symbols of the Revolution show man and woman, side by side, apparent equals in struggle and in labor. But a closer look at those symbols of the earliest months and years often shows women (sickle in hand) depicted as representing rural life, agriculture, the peasantry, fertility, while men (hammer in hand) represent the city, industry, workers, production. In a subliminal way, early Bolshevik symbolism reflected a view of women as passive, pliant, and reproductive. Although the Bolsheviks proclaimed from the very outset a moral and social alliance between peasants and proletarians, between town and country, the alliance was always an unequal one in favor of the urban over the rural.

From 1917 to the end of the 1920s Bolshevik men and women tried through public statements and institutions to reduce this dichotomy. But with the emergence of Stalinism in the 1930s, all but the thinnest of ideological pretenses were laid aside. Conservative divorce and abortion laws were issued, the Zhenotdel was abolished with the explanation that women were now actually equal to men and that its work was no longer needed—a palpable misstatement; wives of engineers and managers were publicly exalted for their work in beautifying the home and adorning their husbands' offices. The old ideal of the ascetic, thin-lipped, and determined women revolutionaries gave way to gushing images of supermothers and heroines of domesticity. If the early Bolshevik male leaders were conditioned by a cultural block to renege on the promises of women's equality, some of them at least had made an effort to recall these promises. With Stalin, an unabashed repudiation of old intelligentsia norms of political respect for women took place, and Soviet Russia reverted to many of the patriarchal attitudes and life patterns of the old regime. The heavily authoritarian style of politics under Stalin, the brutal warlike atmosphere of strife, and the economic imperatives set during the five-year plans were partly responsible for this; but so also was the industrial revolution of the early 1930s that pushed peasants into the cities and workers and lower-class urban elements up into positions of power and responsibility. With them came still unreconstructed attitudes toward women, the family, and sexuality. The result can only be called a counterrevolution in women's emancipation.

Post-Stalinist reform in the status of women was, like much else after 1953, partial and selective. On the one hand, the divorce and abortion laws were altered and certain legal and educational disabilities and inequities of women were removed. But attitudes and structures remained as in Stalin's time: women were to work in the economy and were expected to work a second shift as well in the home; they were segregated into lower-paying professions and into lower-paying ranks in all professions. Nothing except pallid and formulaic statements about male responsibilities and the ritual claims of equality was done to remove or diminish the strong Russian patriarchal attitudes toward women on the part of males.

In recent years patriarchalism has even been expressed in official and semi-official journals.

In retrospect, the Revolution—and the revolutionary movement that preceded it—seems a failure in respect to women's position in Russian society. This is not wholly true. Until a few years ago, Soviet women enjoyed certain rights and wide opportunities in science, technology, medicine, and other professions that were rarely found in the West. That gap has almost closed and women's activism in Europe and the United States has—to use a favorite Soviet expression—"caught up and overtaken" that of Soviet women. Yet there is ferment. Some of it is quiet and indirect—newspaper campaigns and lobbying for an upgrading of facilities that are central to women's lives. More recently, there are signs that a genuine independent feminist movement has arisen among dissident women, one group of whom has published an almanac of grievances and aspirations that is truly moving and reminiscent of bygone feminist currents in Russian history. For any new feminist movement that may emerge from this ferment, the lessons of the Russian Revolution are quite clear: "larger" issues and causes—however noble—cannot be permitted to swallow the women's issue per se or to dismiss the purely feminist emphasis; males will have to look hard at the reality of women's lives, a reality that is clearly visible behind the tatter of overused slogans and symbols. Ultimately everyone will have to recognize—as painful as that may be—the fact that revolution and revolutionary movements and regimes, however lofty and libertarian their ideals, often generate their own kind of authoritarianism in their solution to the ills of social history.

SUGGESTIONS FOR FURTHER READING

Atkinson, Dorothy, Alexander Dallin, and Gail Warshofsky Lapidus, eds. *Women in Russia.* Stanford, 1977.

Bergman, Jay. *Vera Zasulich: A Biography.* Stanford, 1983.

Clements, Barbara Evans. *Bolshevik Feminism: The Life of Aleksandra Kollontai.* Bloomington, IN, 1979.

Edmonson, Linda. *Feminism in Russia, 1900–1917.* London, 1984.

Engel, Barbara. *Mothers and Daughters: Women of the Intelligentsia in Nineteenth-Century Russia.* Cambridge, England, 1983.

Farnsworth, Beatrice. *Aleksandra Kollontai: Socialism, Feminism, and the Bolshevik Revolution.* Stanford, 1980.

Glickman, Rose L. *Russian Factory Women: Workplace and Society 1880–1914.* Berkeley, 1984.

Lapidus, Gail Warshofsky. *Women in Soviet Society.* Berkeley, 1978.

Mamonova, Tatyana, ed. *Women and Russia: Feminist Writings from the Soviet Union.* Tr. by Rebecca Park and Catherine A. Fitzpatrick. Boston, 1984.

Stites, Richard. *The Women's Liberation Movement in Russia: Feminism, Nihilism, and Bolshevism 1860–1930.* Princeton, 1978.

13

"I Am Somebody!"—Women's Changing Sense of Self in the German Democratic Republic

Maria-Barbara Watson-Franke

Reflecting the onset of the cold war, the redrawing of the European map after World War II divided Germany into two separate countries, and several generations of Germans now have grown up under different social and political systems. Maria-Barbara Watson-Franke offers an innovative approach to the women's situation in the German Democratic Republic (GDR). An anthropologist, she did not adopt the typical method of anthropological research, onsite fieldwork, but rather bases her insights on an interpretation of texts (magazines, interviews, fiction) "created and collected by people living in the GDR." In the last few decades there has been fruitful dialogue between history and anthropology concerning the ways in which the social world is related to the cultural world. Watson-Franke's research illustrates how a society that restructured its priorities to stress women's contributions to social production over domestic concerns affected the social personality—willy-nilly, we are tempted to add. She points to the emergence of a new sense of self that derives from joining a deep involvement in the public world of work to the values of intimacy from family as well as broader social relationships. There is good indication that GDR women "look at themselves as selves and perceive the man as an-other person." This new self-image, however, breaks with the tradition of Western individualism, which has valued individual autonomy, initiative, and separateness. As we have shown throughout this book, such an ideal was never possible for most women and if it functioned at all, it did so because women (or other men) provided social support for the free-standing individual. Recent experience in the GDR points up for us that changing social behavior entails revision in cultural norms and affects personal consciousness.

This study deals with women living in a socialist society, the German Democratic Republic (GDR). It focuses on the development of a new female self-image due to women's extensive involvement in gainful employment and their responsibilities for family life. While scholars in the West have seen only the negative aspects of such "overburdening," they have overlooked the actual effect of the double day on women's sense of self. Crucial to understanding the situation is the public socialist position that women are to be rewarded for combining traditional and nontraditional skills and roles.

We have no systematic research on how socialist women *themselves* perceive their new lives, and East Germany is no exception. This is partly due to the difficulties surrounding the collecting of materials; their interpretation also poses formidable challenges to the Western scholar. Anthropological fieldwork in the traditional sense—involving prolonged periods of time spent in relatively close contact with the informants—has not been carried out among GDR women. Although I know the GDR from personal observation, I will follow an approach similar to the "study of culture at a distance," a research strategy developed by United States anthropologists (Margaret Mead, for example) in the 1940s. The main body of data on which this paper is based has been created and collected by people living in the GDR. It comes from the news media, literature, and interviews with GDR women published in the GDR. Data interpretation, however, can only bring meaningful results if the original context is taken as a framework of interpretation. This means that the Western researcher must be familiar with the different meanings of terms and concepts in East and West. For example, East and West understand "self," "change," and "emancipation" differently.

In a socialist society the social-centered sphere is heavily emphasized. The socialist self is manifested in a personality that has individual characteristics which are experienced within a specific social context. Powerful social institutions like the state, the work collective, and the party are understood as the leading forces in the process of personality formation. And though human beings remain responsible for their self-development and the dominant role of social institutions does not absolve them of their individual responsibilities, it is the social-centered aspect of the personality that is clearly given primary significance. While this may seem oppressive to a Western observer, it creates a new situation for women, who are now publicly encouraged to participate actively in the social sphere through participation in social production (i.e., gainful employment).

The socialist tradition thus suggests that the Western concept of self with its strong individualistic emphasis cannot be uniformly applied to the understanding of all human experience. In a different context, the anthropologist Hsu voiced this same criticism and offered instead a concept of intimacy that creates an understanding of self that places greater significance on the social factors and group-related experiences. According to Hsu's model, the interaction between the self-centered and the social-centered spheres of intimacy should lead to the development of a new sense of intimacy in women. This becomes clearer, perhaps, when we use a different terminology. Having traditionally lived in the privacy of the domestic sphere, women are now expected to act in the public world. They bring their sense of self developed in the privacy of their relationships and homes to the public sphere of work. At the same time, new attitudes acquired in the workplace are brought back to the home. The result of this is that women, who have always felt at home in the domestic sphere as their place of intimacy, now carve out new territory in the public sphere which provides them with new links of communication and expands their experience and scope of intimacy.

The lives of East German citizens of both sexes have been radically transformed as compared to the prewar era and to contemporary development in West
Germany. Not only has the structural framework of society changed—now the
state owns the means of production and the economy is centrally planned—the
pattern of social participation within this framework also has changed. Women
now participate more actively in the public sector of the new society than before.
As a result, essential changes also have occurred in the minds of the people, but,
as GDR scholars have pointed out, women seem to be more affected by and more
involved in these changes than men, and women are quite aware of this difference. We will pursue these changes by looking at the impact of work, motherhood, and marriage on women's self-consciousness.

Socialist ideology emphasizes the importance of the work collective as well as
the family. While a person cannot fully develop as a mature personality if one of
these two is missing, one of the cornerstones of modern socialist thinking is the
view that "work is the most important sphere of personality development." Work
is defined as paid employment outside the home. GDR sociologists stress the
liberating effects of women's participation in the labor force, which means more
than merely the financial rewards but also an independence that changes women's
outlook on life and their views of themselves, and of men. The claim that woman's self-esteem is increasing through her involvement with a work collective and
that she feels a need for this involvement has been supported by research on the
motivations of female and male workers. The relationships within and to the collective, and the social aspects of the working situation in general, hold greater
significance for women than for men. While women's role in gainful employment
is seen as central, the problem of the devaluation of women's work in the home
has not been resolved by socialist ideology. Housework is not defined as productive labor. Solutions are sought by efforts to minimize the amount of housework,
which reduces the problem to a time issue, but does not solve it.

The socialist concept of work ethics, moreover, cannot be divorced from
motherhood. Work and motherhood emerge as the most important experiences in
a woman's life with respect to self-development. Motherhood is usually not discussed as a separate topic but within the context of family life. Marriage is seen
as desirable, but it is not an absolute precondition for successful socialist living
nor for the existence of the family. However, work is essential and is believed to
make the woman a better and more resourceful mother. The socialization of children in the family setting has a very important place in socialist thinking. It is
looked on as one of the most creative and responsible tasks in society, a process
that is important for the personal growth of the children as well as adults. While
this view includes both mother and father, women are (still) seen as more involved
in social reproduction and therefore particularly in need of society's support. By
providing both material and psychological support, society reinforces the tradition
of women as nurturers and caretakers of the young, but with the understanding
that they do it as *working* mothers.

Socialist social scientists are sensitive to the tension created by women's involvement in production and reproduction. That women's "double" and actually
"multiple" days create problems has been acknowledged by scientists and party

officials alike. Various ways of reducing women's workload have been considered: part-time work, the one-child family, and childlessness. However, these possibilities are not seen as acceptable since they are in direct opposition to the goals of the socialist state, which is pledged both to increase the birthrate and to maximize women's participation in social production on all levels.

Yet another solution is rethinking gender concepts to include new roles for men. One commentator pointed out, "In our society . . . we do not know the problem of the working man and father. But there is the problem of the working woman and mother—we've got plenty of that." The call for a new father image is one attempt to initiate such changes. This evolution will not be realized easily, since socialist ideology has so far focused on the "new woman," which has obviously led to a discrepancy in women's and men's outlooks and personal growth. However, the changes in women's lives that have triggered changes in their self-concepts will now force men to make adjustments. In fact, GDR women call for changes in men, as we will see shortly in the collection of Maxie Wander's *Protokolle*.

Marriage is encouraged in the GDR as a means to create a stable, constructive, balanced union between adults. The dramatic increase of women in the labor force, leading to greater economic independence of the majority of women, has, however, changed the conditions of marriage. GDR authors emphasize the new freedom of true choice which overrides economic considerations for entering a relationship. "The woman does not found a family any longer in order to be provided for, and the man does not look any longer for a housekeeper but a companion." Since economic security is no longer the guiding motive for marriage, it is likewise no reason to continue with an unsatisfactory relationship. This point is stressed by GDR authors when they discuss the high divorce rate. The increasing number of women initiating divorce is interpreted as a change in women's roles and self-concepts. This development is facilitated by the legal situation which makes life for unmarried women easier in the GDR than in West Germany. It supports the argument that marriage, while highly desirable from a social as well as a personal perspective, does not have the same potential significance for self-formation as work and motherhood.

This prioritizing of women's three roles—as worker, mother, and wife—is reflected in the mass media of the GDR. Even though the media "are committed to the eradication of sex-differentiated childrearing," some magazines explicitly address one sex rather than the other. One example is *FÜR DICH (FOR YOU),* a popular GDR magazine "for women" (as the subtitle says), which appears weekly at newsstands all over the GDR. *FÜR DICH* addresses women-specific and general concerns, but "women-specific" must be understood from the perspective of a socialist society. The magazine regards women as autonomous members of society, rather than as beings defined by their relationships to men. Its function is not to provide a source of escapism, and it features mainly nonfictional material. It illustrates well the new social norms that are changing women's self-concept.

Cover photographs give cues to culturally defined norms. The anonymous fashion model representing an ideal type rather than a particular human being, so typical of Western women's magazines, is almost never featured. The majority of the covers show women whose names and occupations are stated, an indication of the strong interest in women as individuals and workers. This format also makes it easier for the reader to identify with the persons portrayed and the messages they convey. A few covers show men, alone or with women. The title "Family Happiness," for example, can be interpreted as an attempt at redefining traditional concepts, for instead of showing a "whole family," it portrays a man with a child.

Fashion features appear in each issue. While all fashion photographs show attractive people, they do not transmit the image of women as sex objects. In the few instances in which female and male models appear together, the women are not shown in seductive poses or in situations that suggest helplessness. They are not particularly young. The males appear not as aggressive or overpowering, or as victims of feminine charms. In general, fashion poses present clothes as a form of self-expression, not as examples of consumerism. Clothes are not meant to serve as a cover-up or a means of manipulation. Captions explain how these fashions fit women's occupational needs as well as personal taste. That women's working activities outside the home are so prominently brought into the fashion pages strengthens the image of women as producers rather than consumers. Furthermore, one of the most striking aspects of *FÜR DICH* is the almost total absence of advertising, which strongly contrasts with the West. The extremely rare advertisements that do appear encourage people to buy books and insurance.

Considering the importance of women's skills as homemakers in the German tradition, the scarcity of material in the section on "Home Economics" is remarkable. Cleaning and/or decorating the home are not topics of interest. Suggestions for food preparation take up very little space. As a rule, recipes for individual dishes, such as a soup or dessert, are printed. There are no presentations of lavish parties or huge family dinners, and there is no encouragement to use food as a means to manipulate others. However, there is also no indication that food preparation in the home could be equally a man's job.

While difficulties resulting from women's multiple involvements are usually acknowleged, the magazine stresses the idea that women successfully combine all their tasks. The question of "career-or-housewife?" which produces guilt, doubt, and tension in many Western women, is not even asked. Like most magazines of its type, however, *FÜR DICH* offers its readers various opportunities to voice their opinions and present their own questions. There is a column on "Do-It-Yourself" types of problems, a "Pedagogical Adviser" answering questions on socialization, and an intimate column entitled "Between the Two of Us." In one revealing case, the paper invited readers and experts to respond to a letter by the leader of a work collective who was faced with the irresponsible actions of one of its members, Ute.

Ute worked in a factory that produced women's clothes. Her collective specialized in sewing sleeves for women's suits. The factory goal had been to produce one hundred suits above the quota, but Ute, though a highly skilled seamstress, made this impossible by her indifferent attitude toward her work. She frequently stayed away from work or showed up late, thus causing disruption in the work flow of her team. The leader, furthermore, was irritated with her, since

Ute's behavior caused the whole collective to earn a bad reputation in the factory. The factory already had dealt with this problem in various ways. There had been open discussions with the whole collective, confidential meetings with supervisors, one warning, one reprimand, and substantial wage reductions. None of these measures had changed Ute's attitude. The leader asked for Ute's dismissal for pedagogical reasons, because "Ute's 'unparalleled' indifference served as a negative role model." The party organization and one of Ute's co-workers believed, also for pedagogical reasons, that Ute should remain.

FÜR DICH interviewed Ute in her home. She seemed somewhat embarrassed to face journalists at home when she should have been at the factory. But she had had a busy day: she had taken the children to the child-care center, had gone shopping, and was now sewing. Today her husband was coming home a little earlier and there was still work to be done before his return. She defended her conduct: "I do not take anything away from anybody. This is my own business."

The magazine asked its readers if they favored her dismissal or retention and wanted to know how their respective collectives acted in a similar situation. Of 47 replies printed, 19 supported her termination, while 28 were in favor of retention. The magazine then invited a group of experts to discuss this problem. This group supported retention, citing the pedagogical significance of the collective for the development of the socialist personality, the importance of attitudes toward work, the value of work as a school for socialist thought, the impact and significance of human relations at the workplace, the role and function of mentors, the importance of reward as opposed to criticism, and the significance of self-education for self-development. The outcome overwhelmingly stressed the socialist work ethic—which regards the work collective as instrumental in forming new socialist personalities—over the practical goal of meeting the quota. Ute obviously had not yet reached the stage of the ideal socialist personality, whose personal goals coincide with those of society at large. In the socialist frame of reference, Ute's tendency occasionally to favor traditional tasks in the home over work at the factory did not speak in her defense.

Literature also plays an important part in our understanding of the changing process of self-development. As the prominent East German writer Irmtraud Morgner says: "One can change existing customs only by showing how strange and inappropriate they have become. . . . A change of mores is a creative process of society as well as of the individual, a process which brings about discoveries. Through literature . . . one can provoke people to make such discoveries, especially the discovery of oneself."

The short story "Turnip Festival," which takes place on a collective farm, provides a telling example of Morgner's assumptions. The author introduces witches as powerful, constructive women (fear-inducing to men). Turned into a woman himself (although he still possesses his male mind and memories), the hero-turned-physically-into-heroine receives a first-hand introduction to the women's world. His discoveries are illuminating. Women do harder physical work than men: they harvest the turnips in the fields while the male head of the collective shuffles papers in his office. The woman worker whom he always detested as a nagger in male days turns out to be a supportive, kind colleague. He begins to appreciate women's gossip: "Men surely could not express themselves so concisely, though they were, in general, more logical and did not cling to facts as women did." By presenting the whole background of a short conversation between two women workers, the author makes readers understand the logic and meaning of the exchange, so that they now perceive the world of women as complete and as having social meaning and coherence. They learn that women's cues make just as much sense as men's, the only difference being that they are specific to *their* world. Even more important is the message that women's thoughts make sense if one is willing to acknowledge them within their full social context instead of dismissing them as "just talk." The story also reveals the fact that socialization patterns and expectations create different worlds for women and men. In the end, the hero of the "Turnip Festival" remains alone with his new insights. He must learn that the world is not (yet?) ready to listen to an account of women's experiences and conceptualizations. Transformed back into his male body, still shaken up by his travels to the world of women, he contacts the newspapers. They are not interested: insights into the women's world are not of general interest.

Probably the most important publication on women under socialism is Maxie Wander's *Protokolle*. This is not a book of fiction but a collection of responses selected from interviews that she carried out in the 1970s. This text serves as a document of women's quest for self-actualization in a socialist society. It also mirrors reactions to the publicly defined "new woman" who is portrayed in the weekly *FÜR DICH*. Wander interviewed women of different ages (16 to 74 years) and occupational backgrounds. While the book has its frustrating aspects—we do not know how much editing was done, nor have we the questions asked by Wander—it must be regarded as the most important source for the understanding of the new socialist female self in print today.

As they become visible in Wander's collection, GDR women have begun to look at *themselves* as *selves,* and to perceive the *man* as an*other* person, outside themselves, separate from them, which implies that these women no longer accept the role of being men's creation. They are aware that men still have not given up this view of women, but they express less and less willingness to play the parts that men have written for them. As noted East German author Christa Wolf comments in the preface, "Men will be ill at ease to note how women rid themselves of their 'feminine' mold, how they size up the man, how they can do without him, how they consider bidding him goodbye. . . . It is too late [for men] to say now that 'we did not intend.' " Indeed, these records are not easy reading for people who are fully committed to traditional gender divisions. A GDR woman in her late sixties said after reading the book: "This should be required reading for all men, so they will know what they will have to face." The women in Maxie Wander's pages have begun a process, which, in the opinion of Western feminists, constitutes the first step toward liberation; that is, they have begun to define themselves and their situation. When reading their views, the question asked in the "Turnip Festival" reemerges: Is the world ready and willing to listen to the insights gained from female experience? In what follows, Wander's subjects will speak for themselves on various issues: their changing understanding of themselves as sexual beings; the role of work in their lives; the tension created by their multiple burdens; their relationships with and feeling for other women; and their relationships with and views of men.

Some of these women speak more openly about their sexuality than the prudish veneer of socialist culture lets us assume. Here, as in other contexts, it becomes quite clear that women have been thinking about themselves rather than fitting their lives uncritically into the lives of others.

> I do not belong to those women who think they can be happy with only *one* man. I meet continuously men to whom I feel attracted and who feel attracted to me. If indeed only two people were meant for each other among the zig-millions in the world, how would those two find each other? . . . Actually, I go occasionally with another man to bed or to hop in a green meadow. Strange, that I am admitting this to you. It is strange, because a man would admit this without hesitating, it would even increase his prestige. But I hide this part of my life from other people because I know how women like me are judged and how badly my husband would fare. . . . After all, sex is for me not only fun but occasionally something 'Absolute.' Through sex I express my whole personality much more directly than in other areas, right? I am not a sex-machine, I am a woman. And everything goes beautifully as soon as a man understands that. (Secretary, 34 years, married.)

Work, of course, emerges as a significant part of women's lives. Some even state explicitly that they feel confident and that they feel as selves due to the fact that they work also outside the home.

> Some think that it is good to completely turn off after work hours. But this is not possible. I have read that work is the metabolism between people and nature. This is the way I feel about it. (Commercial artist, 23 years, single.)

> I would like very much to be accepted into an advanced graduate program of Education so that I could become a principal one day. I do not want to be an elementary school teacher all my life. I wish to test my limits. . . . After all, the most important thing in my life is my profession, and after that, my role as mother. (Elementary school teacher, 30 years, married.)

> It was not during my stay at the health spa [where she met another man], but at my workplace that I got my self-confidence back. I thought to myself: Well, Karoline, you are somebody, but *who* are you actually? (Social worker, 47 years, married.)

The new and multiple responsibilities, however, create tension and at times a longing to let go and relinquish responsibilities, to be protected and pampered. There is also a remarkable absence of guilt over combining the multiple roles of worker, mother, and wife. It becomes clear that these women feel justified in concentrating on themselves. They do not see the double day as a self-imposed situation due to too much personal ambition. They see the problem as structural and existential in their culture.

It is not the job that does one in, it is the responsibility which one must carry alone. (Secretary, 34 years, when discussing her and her husband's roles in marriage.)

At times the wish to let go is great. . . . This beautiful feeling of letting go, which nature forces upon us so that we can renew ourselves is one I only had during my pregnancies. I slept; the child was growing. I trusted. I did not need to count its cells, nor to model its face. I trusted. I was released from the torment of responsibility. (Professor of Art Academy, 43 years, married.)

Some women speak about their feelings for other women. Christa Wolf states in her introduction to the *Protokolle:* "Though this is very difficult, they also discover that women can love each other and be tender with each other."

As a student I met Karin. Karin is actually the first human being—well, how is this, she is my first real friend. Each of us has respect for the other. Still, each wants to be someone, not just a part of the other. We tell each other only that which is good, which is genuine. Therefore, it is a truly noble relationship. We are also affectionate with each other. (Commercial artist, 23 years, single.)

After voicing critical views about other women, one woman said:

That a friendship with another woman is at all possible I found out when I met Anja. Add to this that I found her physically very pleasant. She said something about my bosom and my beautiful arms. This was new for me and moved me deeply. With her, I can be myself. We are equal, loving partners. (Professor of Art Academy, 43 years, married.)

I like to be in direct contact with people whom I like, also with women. Women's hair and women's skin are something fantastic. I am sure that many women feel this way, but they just do not admit it to themselves. (Secretary, 34 years, married.)

The remarks by women about women indicate their willingness to develop their interest in other women and to see themselves as points of reference. This important change in women's self-understanding is also confirmed by their views of female/male relationships. These women do not accept uncritically the role of "other" in men's lives. Their remarks speak of bitterness and pain, but at the same time reveal a sense of strength, a feeling that they are "somebody":

You know what I think? It is harder on Richard [her husband] than on me. He must cope with the new situation. In the long run he will feel better than in the past. After all, I also oppressed him as long as I was oppressed. Now he has the opportunity to live honestly, together with me, and not next to me or against me. (Social worker, 47 years, married.)

The worst for me was that he claimed that I could not follow him any more intellectually. By then he had met a woman with a university degree who could open new horizons for him. Each human being opens new horizons, because he brings with him a new life, true? What is a man, anyway? A man needs someone to whom he can tell his stories anew. He is not so much interested in what the other brings to the relationship, he needs a new mirror. (Assistant director, 41 years, divorced.)

Another woman, recalling her divorce trial, also uses this picture of the woman as mirror:

Marc's sad speech was that he could not be reflected by me anymore. The jurors looked at him as if he were not of this world. . . .

and, referring to her present companion, she continues,

His work is the most important issue in his life. Therefore I never have the feeling that he would fall apart if I left him. That is reassuring. I am not responsible for him as I was for Marc. He is my equal since I can also live without him. (Physician, 34 years, divorced.)

As Christa Wolf pointed out, the woman here has turned the traditional chain of dependency—woman on man—around. Some women now seek themselves in the mirror.

I do not blame men, I am beyond this. They are all so different, but all are interested in me because I am still a nothing. They can see anything and everything in me, and I respond to them. That is the crazy thing about it. I have always made plans with my male friends, but never my plans, always theirs. Only now do I ask myself: "Where am I in all these stories? What actually is mine?" I do not have the faintest idea. I got to know so many lives; it is only my own that I do not know. I want to find myself and not somebody else. (Waitress, 22 years, single.)

The sum of all changes in the social, economic, and ideological spheres has led to what I like to call the "new philosophy of the female self." This can best be explained in terms of dialectics. The second law of dialectics states that a continuous increase in quantity will eventually lead to a new qualitative state. This event is known as the dialectic leap. In a particular social situation, this leap results from a movement that spans considerable time and space. With respect to women's self-development in the GDR, this dialectical process is in progress right now due to changes in two areas. Women in socialist societies live a double and multiple day; they have added nontraditional activities and skills to their traditional roles as mothers and homemakers. While this is becoming increasingly the case for a majority of women in the United States and in Western Europe, the socialist situation is different in that these systems expect women to work outside the home and support them when they do so. While GDR women are without any doubt overburdened, public praise creates a different ideology of the double day than in the West. Women's radius of activities has expanded with public approval.

Women's space has also expanded. Women live and work in two worlds, the public and the private. Due to traditional views that are still part of socialist everyday life, women have a better understanding of the private sphere than men. At the same time they have gained skills and knowledge in and about the public sphere. Considering women's styles of work and social interaction, they have brought values of the private sphere into the public sphere. They are at home in traditionally different worlds and now seem to begin making them one world. With their new sense of self, they are beginning to transform the gender-dichotomized spheres of human existence into one world of humanity.

Note: This chapter is based on the following sources: *FÜR DICH. Illustrierte Wochenzeitung für die Frau (For You. Illustrated Weekly for Women),* selected issues, 1979; Maxie Wander, *Guten Morgen, Du Schöne. Frauen in der DDR. Protokolle [Good Morning, Beautiful. Women in the GDR. Protocols],* Darmstadt, 1978, 5th edition, interviews with GDR women; and Edith Anderson, ed., *Blitz aus heiterm Himmel [A Bolt out of the Blue].* Rostock, 1975. Translations by the author.

SUGGESTIONS FOR FURTHER READING

Hsu, Francis L. "Psychosocial Homeostasis and Jen. Conceptual Tools for Advancing Psychological Anthropology." *American Anthropologist* 73 (1971): 23–44.

Kuhrig, Herta and Wulfram Speigner, eds., *Zur gesellschaftlichen Stellung der Frau in der DDR [The Position of Women in GDR Society].* Leipzig, 1978.

Mead, Margaret and Rhoda Metraux. *The Study of Culture at a Distance.* Chicago, 1953.

Morgner, Irmtraud. *Leben und Abenteuer der Trobadora Beatriz nach Zeugnissen ihrer Spielfrau Laura [Life and Adventures of Trobadora Beatriz as Chronicled By Her Minstrel Laura].* Berlin, 1974. Chapter twelve of this novel has been translated into English and published in *New German Critique* 15 (1978): 121–148.

————*Amanda. Ein Hexenroman* [Amanda. A Witch Novel]. Berlin, 1983. Excerpt in English entitled "Witch Vilmma's Invention of Speech-Swallowing" in Robin Morgan, ed., *Sisterhood is Global: The International Women's Movement Anthology* (Garden City, 1984), pp. 242–244.

Scott, Hilda. *Does Socialism Liberate Women?* Boston, 1974.

Shaffer, Harry G. *Women in the Two Germanies. A Comparative Study of a Socialist and a Non-Socialist Society.* New York, 1981.

Wolf, Christa. *Cassandra: A Novel and Four Essays.* New York, 1984.

Index